Reading
Wang
Wenxing

critical

essays

editors

SHU-NING SCIBAN | IHOR PIDHAINY

East Asia Program
Cornell University
Ithaca, New York 14853

The Cornell East Asia Series is published by the Cornell University East Asia Program (distinct from Cornell University Press). We publish books on a variety of scholarly topics relating to East Asia as a service to the academic community and the general public. Address submission inquiries to CEAS Editorial Board, East Asia Program, Cornell University, 140 Uris Hall, Ithaca, New York 14853-7601.

Cover Image: *Qi Baishi, "Damo." Reproduced with permission.*
© The Collection of National Palace Museum, Taipei, Taiwan.

Number 178 in the Cornell East Asia Series
Copyright © 2015 Cornell East Asia Program. All rights reserved.
ISSN: 1050-2955
ISBN: 978-1-939161-58-1 hardcover
ISBN: 978-1-939161-78-9 paperback
ISBN: 978-1-942242-78-9 e-book
Library of Congress Control Number: 2015945075

contents

I　ESSAYS

SOCIAL AND CULTURAL CRITIQUE

QUESTIONS OF STYLE

REFLECTIONS ON TRANSLATION

REFLECTIONS ON WANG WENXING'S LIFE

II   APPENDICES

A   OUTLINES OF THE NOVELS

B   BIBLIOGRAPHIES

Author's Preface

READING AND WRITING

Wang Wenxing
National Taiwan University

Reading and writing, it ought to be said, can never be separated. First, you need to be able to read before you know how to write. In general, you need to be able to read slowly (*mandu* 慢讀), reading every character carefully, before you truly read and truly know the core meaning of the words and sentences. After having accepted the need to read slowly, how does one read the quality of writing? Once one reads slowly, one can learn that the style of "a calm energy and a leisurely spirit, its form flowing in a slow and natural manner" is beauty, and its opposite is inferior. In this preface I cite several examples to explain and offer as proof of these statements, respectively detailing and discussing what slow reading is and the style of "a calm energy and a leisurely spirit, its form flowing in a slow and natural manner." As space is limited, for the convenience of explanation I draw my examples exclusively from classical Chinese poems. This preface was originally a talk at a workshop, at which due to time limitations I only read the first half. Here I've added the second half for publication to provide the complete picture of that talk.

LOOKING BACK, I'VE always felt that it is better to say that I am a reader rather than to say that I am a writer. This is not only because, considering things over time, I have spent much more time reading than I did writing (it is like that now, but it has been even more

so over the course of my life)—but also because reading basically cannot
be separated from writing. Reading, indeed, is the source of writing.
Even more so, before one can judge what kind of writer an author is, one
must first examine what kind of reader he is. Thus, to say that I am a
writer is not as good as saying that I am a reader.

I go so far as to recognize that I came extremely late to becoming a
reader. It was not until I was in the first year of university that one day
I had an awakening, and only then did I become a true reader. Before
this, I had already become determined to study literature, but what I
read was done hastily, like swallowing a date without chewing; was
done cursorily, like glancing at flowers while riding a horse—when I was
interested, I would stop and read a lot but, uninterested, I would view
the flowers while riding the horse, surveying ten lines of writing in a
glance. I had to wait until I was in the first year of university when one
day I had my awakening. I recall that day very clearly. I was sitting beneath a coconut tree on the campus of Taiwan University, reading a
book, an English translation of Maupassant. Reading near the end of the
first paragraph of one chapter, I suddenly thought, as if out of nowhere:
for the famous writers of the past, a piece of writing required so many
sentences; a sentence required so many words. One cannot read them as
if they lacked any flavor, as I had previously been reading them. Each
word of this piece of literary writing certainly had a deep meaning, and
each word had its unique purpose. To read and feel only that it was fla-
vorless, the fault ought to lie with me and not the writer. So I reread this
short passage in a way that I read one sentence and stopped to think
about this sentence. Although I did not feel this passage was more color-
ful in my second reading of it, I began to understand that this manner of
reading was not without interest, and indeed could overflow with flavor.
From then on, I read all things in this manner, with the result that I was
able to grasp many more hidden and beautiful meanings than I had before. Naturally, after this I read much more slowly. Prior to this, I would
take just ten days to digest a narrative, but afterward a narrative of some
three hundred pages would often require three months before I completed it. But I felt lucky for having my awakening beneath the tree,
because only in this way was I able to digest the books I read. By this

time, when reading great works, I was truly able to understand what made them essentially beautiful and good (*meishan* 美善). Only then was I able to truly read several volumes—perhaps several dozen volumes—of good books. I had an awakening under the coconut tree, and although it was not like the awakening of the Buddha under the Bodhi tree, which saved humankind and helped all human beings, while my own was small and just saved myself, nevertheless I greatly rejoiced over it.

With this kind of reading, one ought to be able to encompass every aspect of the artistry of the narrative. By slowly reading a work as if it were under a microscope, the characteristics of the main actors, the psychology of what is said and what is done, the description of background scenery and objects, the meaning of symbols, the depth of its philosophical thought, the architecture of the structure, the beauty of the style—all become manifest: there is nothing that cannot be discovered. What I gained most from this was recognition of the beauty of style. To judge whether a style is beautiful depends on whether the rhythm of a sentence is good. Of course one ought to include whether the selection of individual words is elegant, however, word choice is a basic component, and any beginning reader is able to recognize this, whereas the rhythm of a piece is usually not within the reach of a beginning reader. It requires the reader's application of slow reading to discern it. After I had the experience of reading slowly, I got the rough impression that the world could be divided into two types of literary styles: the beautiful and the ugly—the beautiful being characterized by a calm energy and a leisurely spirit (*qidingshenxian* 氣定神閒), its form flowing in a slow and natural manner (*congrongbupo* 從容不迫); the ugly being rushed and harried (*huanghuangzhangzhang* 慌慌張張), its form moving like chickens flying and dogs leaping (*jifei goutiao* 雞飛狗跳). Surprisingly, style does not definitively determine the success of a narrative. Often there are styles that are not sufficiently leisurely, but on the whole one can say the narrative is well written. In general, though, one can say that when the form is good this will guarantee that the success of a narrative is not inconsiderable. So at that time I believed the beauty of the style was the basic passport for a good writer, and I still believe that today. So with this rough two-part law—the leisurely and natural as beautiful, chickens flying and dogs leaping as ugly—which writers did I select as good and beautiful stylists? At that time, in second year and continuing through my third year and then up to my graduation in fourth year, the results of my selections were these: there was Maupassant, Flaubert, Loti, Tolstoy, Conrad, and Hemingway. At that time I adored Dostoevsky and Chekhov, but did not select them among the stylists. Today, some fifty years later, as I look back, I still feel that my choices were quite right. Today I still firmly uphold Flaubert and Conrad. Of course, I am able to add numerous other writers as well. The list of authors I've arranged above are all Western writers—I did not list Chinese authors. When I was in my second, third, and fourth years of university, I knew very few Chinese vernacular writers on account of the banning of books under the government's imposition of martial law. Only with great difficulty was I able to find some old "forbidden books" at the book stalls on Guling Street. I deeply felt that Lu Xun and his younger brother, Zhou Zuoren, could be included. But the very best person was Feng Zikai. Because I recognized few of the vernacular writers after the May Fourth movement, I turned toward ancient poetry and prose in my search and, in spite of everything, I felt that Du Fu should be listed as the top stylist—even surpassing the stylists of the May Fourth era. It was fortunate that I discovered Du Fu, for this was the most important event in my process of reading. I had the greatest esteem for the style of calm energy and leisurely spirit, and a slow and unhurried manner, and though Western authors were numerous, I was still unable to find even one Chinese author with a pure Chinese style to worship fully. But then I read Du Fu. Although Du Fu did not write prose essays (sanwen 散文) (there are a few occasional pieces of parallel prose which are not considered very good), his poetry—poetry that had a calm energy and leisurely spirit and was slow and unhurried—was enough. It was sufficient to serve as my model. Because of this, from then on there was not a day when I did not read Du Fu's poetry. Even today I read him. I've chanted his complete works three times, and when I randomly select one of his poems, I chant it joyfully without becoming tired of it. I place Du Fu's poetry at the top of the list of Chinese literary forms. But it is poetry, not prose. Now as for prose, I mentioned Feng Zikai and Zhou Zuoren (and I can also add Yu Dafu), but who among the classical Chinese stylists are to be selected? Classical Chinese also ought to have calm energy and leisurely spirit and flow in a slow and natural manner. As for classical Chinese of the Yuan, Ming, and Qing periods, I later discovered that there were many who might be selected, but to promote one as an outstanding hero who could match up with Du Fu, I put forth Su Che. Definitely after old Du it is the younger Su—Su Che. The poetry of Su Dongpo (Su Che's elder and more famous brother) is good, his lyrics are good, and his prose also is free, bold, and unrestrained, but in general I feel his *yang* spirit is too rich (*yangqi taisheng* 陽氣太盛). As for the question of calm energy and lei-surely spirit in a slow and natural manner—look to his younger brother, Su Che. Although I have not read his complete works three times, I have read through them carefully once. Therefore, in summary, I can say that my ideal ancient Chinese stylists, whom I have continually worshipped and followed, are Du Fu and Su Che. As for May Fourth and beyond, it is Feng Zikai. There is always Feng Zikai. Both Ye Shaojun and Xia Mian-zun are close to him, but it is always Feng Zikai.

Having said all this, it is essential for me to add that writing and reading cannot be separated; however, reading is even more important than writing. As for how to read, once more one must read every char-acter and read slowly before it is true reading. It is not like swallowing dates without chewing; reading superficially deceives oneself and others (I'm sorry if this is too bluntly put). I think I also ought to explain how one reads slowly. I probably ought to select a narrative and demonstrate it, but any narrative would be too long, and I would not be able to man-age it in this limited space, so I will select a couple of ancient poems and use them to explain clearly—this being far more appropriate. The poems I've selected are unfamiliar, and so will be easier to interpret precisely because they are unfamiliar and everyone's impression will be fresh and pure, and the feeling will be relatively deep and clear. However, as for literary style, particularly that of "calm energy and a leisurely spirit, with form flowing in a slow and natural manner," they do not necessarily do it justice. Nevertheless, to understand the meaning of their language, a slow reading ought to be able to bring out the poems' fullness. This is

slow reading's most important objective. I use two Han poems as examples—both are short. The first is "Kuyu guo he qi" 枯魚過河泣 (A
dried-up fish departs from the river, wailing).

These four lines go:

枯魚過河泣　Kūyú guò hé qì，
何時悔復及　héshí huǐ fù jí。
作書與魴鱮　Zuòshū yǔ fángxù，
相教慎出入　xiāngjiāo shèn chūrù (could be read as *chūyì*)。

A dried-up fish departs from the river, wailing,
When will his regret reach its end?
He writes a letter to the bream and silver carp,
Teaching them to be cautious in their comings and goings.

This is a fable poem, or it might even be called a fairy tale (*tonghua*
童話). This kind of fairy tale poem or fairy tale story always has a moral
lesson as its purpose, and this poem is the same. Its meaning is to exhort
one to be discreet in all matters, giving appropriate consideration to the
present and the future to avoid a sudden disaster there will be no opportunity to regret. Poetry critics through the ages have all agreed that
this is a poem about regret.

We can make a careful slow reading of this poem, word by word.
First, the title of the poem—most ancient poems did not have a title, so
later on people took the first line and used it to name the poem, thereby
creating the title.

The dried-up fish (*kuyu*) is not a regular fish dried in the sun. It refers
to a fish that is in a net and out of the water—a fish caught by men.
Crossing (*guo*) the river does not mean going across the river, rather, it
means departing from the river: crossing (*guo*) means going (*qu* 去) and
leaving (*li* 離). The meaning of the first line is a fish, caught by a man, is
departing from the river, crying on the bank of the river. What is he
crying over? He is crying about not being able to regret past mistakes. "When will his regret reach its end?" is equivalent to "when will
he realize his full regret?" The question is, when will this regret ever be

matched? In other words, he recognizes that his regret will not be matched again. So in the following sentence he surprisingly writes a letter to his boon friends—his boon friends being a bream and a silver carp—warning them that when they swim to and fro, they need to be careful about their ingresses and egresses, so as not to swallow a fishhook and end up like he is now. This poem is fantastical and belongs to fantasy literature. Moreover, fantasy that is unbelievable, for the fish not only is able to cry, repent, and realize his mistake but is also able to wield a brush and write a letter—indulging in fantasy so as to cause one to burst out laughing; that is to say, this fantasy reaches the domain of comic representation. This level of fantasy is quite distant from reality. Its purpose is to produce a new reading for one's eyes, to avoid listening to and sighing over the hackneyed and overwrought phrases of a moral lesson, but instead make the moral interesting and exciting. This is indeed the intrinsic purpose of this poem's use of fantasy in its style of writing. This poem uses its wonderful imagination to bring life to its preaching.

Let's look at the second poem, "Shangliutian xing" 上留田行. *Shangliutian* should be read as a place name; *Shangliutian xing* is thus "Song of Shangliutian":

里中有啼兒　Lǐ zhōng yǒu tíér (could be read as *tíyi*)，
似類親父子　sìlèi qīn fùzǐ (could be read as *fùjǐ*)。
回車問啼兒　Huí chē wèn tíér (could be read as *tíyi*)，
慷慨不可止　kāngkài bùkě zhǐ (could be read as *jǐ*)。

In the district a boy is crying,
They appear like father and son.
I turned my cart and questioned the crying boy,
Worked up he goes on, unable to stop.

First, we need to pay attention to reading the characters' pronunciation. There are some line endings that require a change in pronunciation. The character for boy (*er*) should be read *yi*. The characters *zi* and *zhi* can either be changed or left the same. If changed, then *zi* should be read *ji*.

The reason is because ancient pronunciation was not the same as it is today; ancient pronunciation had more dialectal sounds. For those who do not read ancient pronunciations, several of the rhymed words will not rhyme. Of course, we cannot be certain exactly how ancient pronunciations were read, but from the characters' rhyming sound we can infer how some characters need to be changed when read.

With this in mind, I amend the earlier poem, "A Dried-up Fish Departs from the River, Wailing." There is a character that needs its reading to be changed. That is the very last character, the *ru* character of *churu*, which ought to be read *yi*. Reading it as *yi* allows it to rhyme with the earlier characters *qi* and *ji*.

Now let's take a look at "Song of Shangliutian."

The line "In the district a boy is crying" denotes that in a certain district in Shangliutian there is to be seen a boy who is crying. The second line says that beside him there is an adult who appears to be his father; the two should be father and son. Seeing the son crying in such a heart-rending manner, I thus stop my cart and ask the boy why he is crying in such a heart-breaking manner: this is the third line. Afterward I learn why: the crying boy tells in stops and starts that he is mistreated by his stepfather, crying bitterly in a continuous and unstoppable flow of tears. This is the fourth line.

In this poem one must pay the most attention to the second line. In one reading, "They appear like father and son" indicates that the adult is the child's elder brother; the parents are both dead and the elder brother does not love his younger brother but mistreats him. In another reading, the adult is his father, and only the wife is dead, so the father does not love his son. Neither of these two interpretations is in accord with reason, so we prefer to choose the interpretation of the stepfather. As for the fourth line—"worked up he goes on, unable to stop"—some have said it refers to the man in the cart turning back, who after hearing this, sighs without end. But if it refers to the crying child, it is even more coherent—the whole poem focuses on the bitterness of the child alone: the poem's structure is seamless. The one returning in his carriage doesn't say a word, and the pity is even more subtle, for it avoids the extremes of emotion and, on the contrary, fits the principle that less is more when expressing feelings.

The slow reading of these two Han poems clearly explains the idea of slow reading that I always advocate. It can help one discover the source of my writing, and is also helpful in understanding my writings.

How to go from a reading to an understanding of literary style and realize the excellence of "calm energy and a leisurely spirit, with its form flowing in a slow and natural manner" and use examples to explain this— this is perhaps rather difficult. As for using a narrative, on account of its great length being an obstacle, this is not possible. If one were to take a poem as an example, or take two or three poems from Du Fu as examples (although in reality the explication of literary style is still very difficult), literary style could be said to be like an antelope hanging by its horns (in a tree), leaving no trace to be found.[1] But I still think that I would just like to babble on for a while and give it a try, open up Du Fu's poetry by selecting the poem "Chengdu fu" 成都府 (Chengdu prefecture) to discuss the ins and outs of Du Fu's literary style. "Chengdu Prefecture" is not one of Du Fu's famous poems that are often heard and recited, and because it is not a famous piece we will not become bored when we read it exhaustively, nor become indifferent. Just like the two earlier Han era poems we discussed, this is clearly not a familiar work, so our reading and impression will be fresh, our perception precise, and so for this reason I have selected "Chengdu Prefecture."[2]

翳翳桑榆日　　Yìyì sāngyú rì，
照我征衣裳　　zhào wǒ zhēng yīshang。
我行山川異　　Wǒ xíng shānchuān yì，
忽在天一方　　hū zài tiān yīfāng。

---

1. Translator's note: This is a Chan Buddhist image that refers to great literary art that betrays no trace of the writer's effort.

2. Translator's note: For another translation into English, see William Hung, *Tu Fu, China's Greatest Poet* (New York: Russell & Russell, 1969), 1:159.

但逢新人民　Dàn féng xīn rénmín，
未卜見故鄉　wèi pǔ jiàn gùxiāng。
大江東流去　Dàjiāng dōng liúqù，
遊子去日長　yóuzi qù rì cháng。

曾城填華屋　Céng chéng tián huáwū，
季冬樹木蒼　jìdōng shùmù cāng。
喧然名都會　Xuānrán míng dūhuì，
吹簫間笙簧　chuī xiāo jiān shēng huáng。

信美無與適　Xìn měi wú yǔ shì，
側身望川梁　cèshēn wàng chuān liáng。
鳥雀夜各歸　Niǎo què yè gè guī，
中原杳茫茫　zhōngyuán yǎo mángmáng。

初月出不高　Chūyuè chū bù gāo，
眾星尚爭光　zhòng xīng shàng zhēngguāng。
自古有羈旅　Zìgǔ yǒu jī lǚ，
我何苦哀傷　wǒ hékǔ āishāng。

As day darkens, the sun sets upon mulberry and elm,[3]
It shines upon my traveler's clothing.
I've traveled across strange reaches of mountains and streams,
When suddenly I find myself along a distant stretch of the sky.

But now I only meet brand new people,
And cannot predict when I'll see those from my hometown.
The great river eastward flows,
While I have traveled for a long time.

The city walls are filled with beautiful mansions,
In the winter season the trees are green.
Loud is this famous grand metropolis,
Gourds and reeds mix among the flutes.

---

3. Translator's note: Mulberry and elm are a common reference to evening.

Although truly beautiful, I have nowhere to go,
So I lean forward and gaze at the bridge over the stream.
Birds at night each return home,
But the Central Plains are distant and boundless.

The new moon has not yet reached a great height,
The many stars still strive for honor.
From ancient times, others have lived far from home,
Why should I bitterly grieve?

This poem is from Du Shaoling's poetry,[4] and though it is not a representative work, nevertheless it is a good composition; among his emotionally restrained poetry, it can be considered a beautiful and flawless composition. The impression one gets upon reading this poem is that of "gentle intonation" (*yudiao rouhe* 語調柔和). Among the twenty lines, the two which least accord with the overall tone are "The city walls are filled with beautiful mansions" and "Gourds and reeds mix among the flutes." These lines depart from the colloquial nature of the poem and, moreover, they radiate upon the colloquial tone something that feels slightly closer to classical language (*wenyan* 文言), being more concentrated (*nongsuo* 濃縮) and somewhat more compact (*jincou* 緊湊). Strictly speaking, perhaps the first line, "As day darkens, the sun sets upon mulberry and elm," is similar in being concentrated and a little compact, but the hazy warm glow of the setting sun neutralizes the compactness and concentration, for the line still has an overall effect of gentleness of tone; this line: "As day darkens, the sun sets upon mulberry and elm," still matches and agrees closely with the overall poem. The first impression I mentioned—the gentle tone—serves as one aspect of the above-mentioned "moving with a calm energy and a leisurely spirit, with form flowing in a slow and natural manner." I am not saying that "moving with a calm energy and a leisurely spirit, with form flowing in a slow and natural manner" is equivalent to a gentle tone; what I am saying is that "moving with a calm energy and a leisurely spirit, with

---

4. Translator's note: Du Fu's alternate name was Shaoling.

form flowing in a slow and natural manner" can have a variety of dissimilar aspects, such as "stomping feet full of burning passion" (*fenli daofa* 奮力蹈發), "a sustained bitter lament" (*aitong yuheng* 哀慟逾恆), and any other form that does not become "rushed and harried, with a form like chickens flying and dogs leaping." Today I especially selected "Chengdu Prefecture" to illustrate "moving with a calm energy and a leisurely spirit, with form flowing in a slow and natural manner" only because a gentle tone is easiest to represent it. Below we'll also discuss the other strengths of "Chengdu Prefecture." During this discussion we'll be able to approach other aspects that assist and complete "moving with a calm energy and a leisurely spirit, with form flowing in a slow and natural manner." Indeed, all aspects of "moving with a calm energy and a leisurely spirit, with form flowing in a slow and natural manner" can be sufficiently represented by selecting three or four examples. To determine the distinguishing characteristics of the lines, we need to examine them one by one from the top. We've already discussed the opening line, "As day darkens, the sun sets upon mulberry and elm," while the second line, "It shines upon my traveler's clothing," states that this late sun shines upon my traveler's clothing. The lines "I've traveled across strange reaches of mountains and streams, / When suddenly I find myself along a distant stretch of the sky" say: I've traveled a distant road to come here, experiencing countless unique scenes of mountains and streams, while now, suddenly, not knowing how, I find myself in a remote region. The next lines, "But now I only meet brand new people, / And cannot predict when I'll see those from my hometown," mean that I took one road and came to this place, but the new people I meet speak a different dialect and have different customs. Indeed, everything is different from the people of my hometown, and I do not know when I'll be able to return to my hometown. "The great river eastward flows, / While I have traveled for a long time." The great river refers to the Min River—the Min River rushes eastward day and night, while I as a traveler float along this day, which is unfortunately as long-lasting as the rushing flow of this river's water. From "I've traveled across strange reaches of mountains and streams" to "While I have traveled for a long time" consists of three couplets, comprising six lines, and all are written in a gentle tone,

tranquil and indirect (*pingjing weiwan* 平靜委婉). This strength has
been discussed already, but these three couplets have an additional good
quality: that is, each couplet is a matching couplet (*duiju* 對句). These
couplets may not be perfectly matching character by character; however, the meaning of the first line of each couplet and that of the second
line match well. The reader perceives only that these lines are lucid and
natural, not that they are matching couplets. This is the strength of being
completely natural (*hunran tiancheng* 渾然天成). These three couplets
are both gentle in tone and display no trace of the workmanship
involved,[5] making each a perfectly flawless matching couplet. On account of this, each is worthy of our admiration and appreciation. Next
comes, "The city walls are filled with beautiful mansions, / In the winter
season the trees are green." "The city walls are filled with beautiful mansions" states that looking out from Du Fu's perspective, gorgeous mansions are packed within the city walls. One explanation for *cengcheng* is
"high mountain," another is "temple" and yet another is "outer city wall."
I have selected outer city wall. "In the winter season the trees are green"
means that Chengdu is in the south and even when entering it in deep
winter the trees are still green. "Loud is this famous grand metropolis, /
Gourds and reeds mix among the flutes" says that I am now here in
Chengdu, a famous capital city, taking part in a lively banquet. At the
banquet there are flutes and reeds. The four lines from "The city walls
are filled with beautiful mansions" to "Gourds and reeds mix among the
flutes" solely describe Chengdu. These four lines contain the main theme
of the poem, and so the poem is titled "Chengdu Prefecture" and its
inner section naturally focuses on Chengdu Prefecture. The focal point
is the ninth, tenth, eleventh, and twelfth lines—the exact center of the
twenty lines of this piece—and is the heart of this poem. In this, one can
see how Du Fu emphasized his structure.

The structure is very even (*tingyun* 亭匀), with a smooth symmetry.
This also explains how in moving the narrative forward, Du Fu arrived
at the aspect of "moving with a calm energy and a leisurely spirit, with
form flowing in a slow and natural manner." Let's look at the second half

---

5. Translator's note: Literally, "one does not see the ax handle."

of this poem. The thirteenth and fourteenth lines go: "Although truly beautiful, I have nowhere to go, / So I lean forward and gaze at the bridge over the stream." That is to say, the scenery is beautiful. Chengdu's natural scenery and culture are equally good. This being the case, I came to this place as an outsider, and now gaze at the rivers and bridges of the distant road that lead to my hometown. The stream refers to the Min River, for if he returns home, in the north, he must first leave Sichuan, following the Min River, and then the Yangtze, for he must go along the Yangtze River once again going north. Next, "Birds at night each return home, / But the Central Plains are dark and boundless." That is, the sun is setting in the west and the birds have returned to their evening nests. I alone have no home to return to, and gaze northward at the Central Plains, but only see their boundlessness in the distance. The next lines are: "The new moon has not yet reached a great height, / The many stars still strive for honor." That is, it is just when the western sun has set; just before this, the color of the sky darkened a little and the new moon has just risen but it is not high in the sky. At the same time, when you look carefully in the part of the sky distant from the moon, faint starlight can be seen, so it still has not reached the time when the moon is full and the stars are extinguished by moonlight. Then follows: "From ancient times, others have lived far from home, / Why should I bitterly grieve?": I truly believe in my heart that since the distant past, all throughout time, travelers have been forced to wander because of the chaos of war or because of work, so I am not particularly special in this, so why should I consider suffering on account of it? Of the poem's twenty lines, I believe the best ones are: "The new moon has not yet reached a great height" and the three lines that follow. All the lines of the poem except "The city walls are filled with beautiful mansions" and the following three lines, are good, because they all have the effect of a gentle tone, but "The new moon has not yet reached a great height" and its following three lines, in addition to having the excellence of a gentle tone, have other points of excellence as well. Let's first talk about the couplet that begins "The new moon has not yet reached a great height." What is best about these two lines is the tightly wrought (*jinjin kouzhu* 緊緊扣住) description of time in the poem, not only describing the scenery to be seen in every direction—the moon and stars—but closely following the passing of the time of dusk, writing with strict realism of the passing seconds. We said that the first line, "As day darkens, the sun sets upon mulberry and elm," described the time when the sun set in the West. Through the first sixteen lines of singing and chanting, I believe there were pauses when he thought, looked about, sighed, and so on, and I suppose there had to be delays and prolongations until the sun had set, the evening sky was dark, and the half-moon had risen. So the two lines beginning "The new moon has not yet reached a great height" represent a moment of unawareness that, having narrated the passing away of the sun in the West, implicitly described the gradual coming of dusk. This narration is masterly. Not only does it hide in its gentle tone, but the lines "The new moon has not yet reached a great height, / The many stars still strive for honor" have yet another outstanding feature: these two lines also have a meaning to their symbolism that goes beyond the surface level. The meaning of the imagery of these two lines is conveyed obliquely and not developed in a direct manner, so that one can choose to take these images into consideration or not. The meaning of the images is political. The new moon roughly indicates the coming to the throne of an emperor, Suzong (r. 756–762), replacing Xuanzong (r. 712–756). The meaning is that the position of Suzong, on first establishing his rule, is still not very high or firm, hence the line: "The new moon has not yet reached a great height." The many stars are either an image of the power of his enemies An Lushan (703–757) and Shi Siming (d. 761) or the various generals in the palace who did not listen to orders. In summary, these two lines appear to have an implied meaning. This explanation does not at all obstruct the earlier hidden meaning of the passing of time, nor does it block the primary effect of the gentle tone, so long as all of the meanings do not hinder each other. Nor does it tarnish any explanations. On the contrary, many more explanations would only increase the richness of the poetry, and this would allow one to derive even more enjoyment from it. This is connected with the two lines, "The new moon has not yet reached a great height, / The many stars still strive for honor," which go beyond gentle tone to become a probing discussion between the two merits of an oblique depiction of time and flourishing political imagery. Below, we read two more lines from "Chengdu Prefecture" worthy of exploratory reading—those being the last two lines of the poem: "From ancient times, others have lived far from home, / Why should I bitterly grieve?" These two lines do not depict scenery, nor do they narrate events. They are not symbolic in meaning, nor are they philosophic. Instead, they are a kind of absolute nonsubstance (*duan fei shiti* 斷非實體) speaking to something completely empty and nonexistent (*chunwei xumang de suoyun* 春偉虛茫的所云); that is to say, what they depict are feelings, and these feelings are depicted densely and purely. Moreover, there is the effect of a continuous, never-ending reverberation (*yuyin raoliang* 餘音繞樑). So this couplet has a high level of aesthetic sensibility. This aesthetic sensibility of continuous, never-ending reverberation clearly has two sources. First, it has its source in these two lines of graceful music—these two lines of music have the effect of a continuous, never-ending reverberation; second, it is the position these two lines occupy, the last two of the poem's twenty lines, and on account of this these two lines bring the poem to a close but cause you to feel there is still something more. This is the long-lasting effect of a continuous, never-ending reverberation. "From ancient times, others have lived far from home, / Why should I bitterly grieve?"—the continuous, never-ending reverberation of these two lines is clearly a feature of gentle tone. Moreover, one can even say that it is continuous with its meaning not yet exhausted, being many times more gentle in tone than the normal aspect of gentle in tone.

Having discussed the gentle tone of Du Fu's poetry, with the example of "Chengdu Prefecture" used to map out an explanation of the style of "calm energy and a leisurely spirit, with its form flowing in a slow and natural manner," I intend to select another poem by Du Fu—examining a tone that differs from gentle to explain the style of "calm energy and a leisurely spirit, with its form flowing in a slow and natural manner."

This is Du Fu's poem "Bo Xueshi maowu" 柏學士茅屋 (Scholar Bo's cottage).

碧山學士焚銀魚　Bì shān xuéshì fén yínyú，
白馬却走身岩居　Báimǎ què zǒu shēn yán jū。

古人已用三冬足   Gǔ rén yǐ yòng sān dōng zú，
年少今開萬卷餘   Nián shào jīn kāi wàn juàn yú。

晴雲滿戶團傾蓋   Qíng yún mǎn hù tuán qīnggài，
秋水浮階溜決渠   Qiūshuǐ fú jiē liū jué qú。
富貴必從勤苦得   Fùguì bì cóng qínkǔ dé，
男兒須讀五車書   Nán'er xū dú wǔ chē shū (could be read as xū)。

The scholar of blue-jade mountain burned his silverfish insignia,
And fled on a white horse to live in solitude atop this cliff.

The ancients were ready for service after three winters,[6]
Though young, by now he's read more than ten thousand volumes.

White clouds in a clear sky fill his door, like the meeting of friends,[7]
Autumn water flows over steps, like a flood from the canal.

Riches and honors must be obtained through hard work,
Boys ought to read five carts of books.

This is a poem of regulated verse. Its basic meaning is that scholar
Bo, who lives on a green mountain, has renounced his fifth-grade position as an official and does not cherish the idea of government service.
Indeed, he now prefers not to seek officialdom, but to ride a white horse
and retire to this mountain to live a long time. These are the first two

---

6. Translator's note: This is a reference to Dongfang Shuo of the Western
Han dynasty, who wrote Emperor Wu a letter that stated: "At thirteen (twelve)
years I began to study; after three winters my letters and history were sufficient
to be used (by the emperor at court)." See *Hanshu*, "Biography of Dongfang
Shuo."

7. Translator's note: Literally, "White clouds in a clear sky fill his door, unit-
ing like wagon covers touching." Wagon covers were umbrellas that officials
suspended over their carriages to protect them from the elements. When they
encountered another official (friend), their covers would touch and this became
a metaphor for the meeting of friends.

lines: "The scholar of blue-jade mountain burned his silverfish insignia, / And fled on a white horse to live in solitude atop this cliff." The next two lines are: "The ancients were ready for service after three winters, / Though young, by now he's read more than ten thousand volumes." This is to say that when the ancients read books, they read for three years before they were ready to serve and work as an official. Our amazing young Scholar Bo, however, has already read to the full more than 10,000 volumes. "White clouds in a clear sky fill his door, like the meeting of friends. / Autumn water flows over steps, like a flood from the canal." This is a way of describing the living conditions at Scholar Bo's retreat: one large group of white clouds after another gathers at his gate, filling up his entrance. "Wagon covers" convey the meaning of meeting by chance. By autumn—that is, now—on account of the flooding rain, the water of the mountain overflows its channels until it drowns his stairs. "Riches and honors must be obtained through hard work, / Boys ought to read five carts of books." That is to say, there is no shortcut to be found for success and honor in one's life; it is one part plowing and weeding (i.e., hard work) and one part harvesting (i.e., success). An ambitious man must intensively read five carts of books; only then can he become outstanding and render service to the Son of Heaven (emperor) one day. The meaning is that Scholar Bo is studying hard, and eventually the day will come when his talents are recognized and he will enter the court and take up an important position. The character *shu* (book) from this sentence ought to be pronounced—as the previous word was read—*xu*. Ah, to make rhymes like these—the sound and rhythm of the two lines and one couplet are sweet and beautiful.

The best feature of the poem "Scholar Bo's Cottage" is the modulation of intonation (*shengdiao yiyang gaodi* 聲調抑揚高低) and the clarity of the rhythm—it is very mellifluous. The remarkable feature of the modulation in this poem is that it has an infectiousness that allows the reader to experience the great delight and buoyancy of Du Fu's spirit at the time he wrote this poem. Moreover, this poem's mood of elation and feeling of ecstasy (*shencai feiyang* 神采飛揚) equally emerge from the style of "calm energy and a leisurely spirit, with its form flowing in a slow and natural manner." Perhaps it is appropriate to amend this slightly: changing one word from "calm energy and a leisurely spirit, with its form flowing in a slow and natural manner"—replacing "calm energy and a leisurely spirit" with "calm energy and a sufficient spirit (*shenzu* 神足)" to achieve a more accurate description of this poem. At root, though, there is not a great difference between "calm energy and a leisurely spirit, with its form flowing in a slow and natural manner" and "calm energy and a sufficient spirit, with its form flowing in a slow and natural manner." Yes, "Scholar Bo's Cottage" is a poem of "calm energy and a sufficient spirit, with its form flowing in a slow and natural manner." On the whole, one may say there is a little in this poem that goes against "calm energy and a sufficient spirit, with its form flowing in a slow and natural manner" and that is lines five and six: "White clouds in a clear sky fill his door, like the meeting of friends. / Autumn water flows over steps, like a flood from the canal." These two lines are a little close to human artifice, exhibiting a certain ornateness, which harms the spirit of the writing, not reaching what all the other lines reached: "a mood of elation and feeling of ecstasy." The reason the other lines are able to succeed in putting forth "a mood of elation and feeling of ecstasy" is entirely because they are written with the clarity of conversation (*yibai ruhua* 一白如話) and innate effortlessness (*huncheng tianran* 混成天然). This kind of "clarity of conversation and innate effortlessness" is, naturally, the other side of "calm energy and sufficient spirit, with its form flowing in a slow and natural manner," exchanging one sort of explanation for another. The second and third lines: "The ancients were ready for service after three winters, / Though young, by now he's read more than ten thousand volumes," not only have the clarity of conversation, spoken naturally, but also form a beautiful couplet, with not one incorrect character or one poor pairing. This being the case, since it strictly adheres to the rules of prosody concerning antithesis, and has the clarity of conversation, spoken naturally, who would say it is not by way of "a calm energy and a *sufficient* spirit, with its form flowing in a slow and natural manner" that it achieves this, and not because "a calm energy and a *leisurely* spirit, with its form flowing in a slow and natural manner"? Additionally, we can also discuss the last two lines, "Riches and honors must be obtained through hard work, / Boys ought to read five carts of books." These two lines are already in the style of maxims, teaching and guiding tirelessly, urging those who come after to read more poetry and essays, and have been used throughout history as proverbs to exhort students. These two lines take an immortal place not only because the reason (*li* 理) of what is being said is good but also because their sentiments (*qing* 情) are good—the sentiment of the poem's kind-hearted words of advice is good. That in which the sentiments are good and that in which the reason is good allow both aspects to be seen uniquely in relation to the style of "calm energy and a leisurely spirit, with an easy and natural manner." They also make us, the readers, realize that even in a "mood of elation and feeling of ecstasy" the poet can still achieve the style of "calm energy and a leisurely spirit, with an easy and natural manner."

Let me attach a couple of superfluous lines. Regardless of how "Scholar Bo's Cottage" came to possess "a mood of elation and feeling of ecstasy," seemingly for no special reason, within the poem itself I cannot determine why Old Du was roused in this manner of energetic expression. It might mean only that his circumstance and mood were good, and fittingly he wrote this poem, for his "mood of elation" was like this, and it was not Scholar Bo who caused Du Fu to be like this. Now, if Old Du wrote another poem at the same time, and assuming his "mood of elation and feeling of ecstasy" were the same, then we could say it was spoken just like this person, the poetry was like this person, came out of his natural disposition, came out of the sounds of nature—this would be proof.

Du Fu's poetry has various appearances, those of "stately serenity," "suffering unto a desire for death," "loyal to the emperor and patriotic to the country," "zany interest," etc., none of which can be separated from his intrinsically constant style. I hope that the two poems selected here summarize clearly the essentials of his immortal style.

Translated by Ihor Pidhainy

Editors' Preface

READING WANG WENXING: *Critical Essays* is the first book in English that focuses on the writings of Wang Wenxing, one of the greatest language artists in the history of Chinese literature. The current volume consists of fourteen essays, three novel outlines, and three bibliographies. With the goal of presenting a comprehensive picture of contemporary scholarship on Wang Wenxing's works, the authors of these essays have approached Wang's writing from different angles with various methodologies. They are experts in Wang Wenxing studies, sinology, or Chinese linguistics, and several have worked on Wang's writing for decades. Most of the essays, outlines, and bibliographies are being published formally for the first time; the very few reprints that have been included were selected because of their indispensable importance and previous lack of availability. Many of the drafts of the essays, including Wang's "Author's Preface: Reading and Writing," were presented at the conference "Art of Chinese Narrative Language: International Workshop on Wang Wenxing's Life and Works" held at the University of Calgary in 2009.

While this volume was first conceived as an independent book to introduce Wang's writing to the world, it can be read together with *Endless War: Fiction and Essays by Wang Wen-hsing* (also published by the Cornell East Asia Program, Cornell University) which provides a detailed introduction to Wang's life and the development of his writing career, a chronology of his life and a bibliography of his works, in addition to translations of all his short fiction and five essays revealing his views on writing. In addition, Susan Dolling's translation of Wang's first novel, *Family Catastrophe* (University of Hawai'i Press) and Edward Gunn's translation of Wang's second novel, *Backed Against the Sea*, vol.

1 (Cornell East Asia Program, Cornell University) are also available to English readers.

We have adopted the pinyin system to spell Chinese names and other Chinese proper nouns. However, when other spellings of a person or a proper noun are already well known in the English-speaking world, that spelling is used, with pinyin spelling following in brackets the first time the name appears in a piece of writing. For the purpose of introducing research done by Chinese scholars who may sometimes publish in English, the scholars' Chinese names may be presented in pinyin and then followed by the other spellings of their names in brackets. We have decided to use pinyin for Wang Wenxing's name with the earlier transliteration of "Wang Wen-hsing" inserted in brackets following the pinyin spelling when his name appears for the first time in a written text.

Acknowledgments

THE PUBLICATION PROJECT of *Reading Wang Wenxing: Critical Essays* was conceived when the editors prepared for the international workshop on Wang Wenxing at the University of Calgary in 2009. Many years have passed since then, and the editors are pleased to see it reach fruition at last. On the eve of publication, the editors feel grateful to many people for their support and selfless assistance. First of all, we would like to express deep appreciation to Wang Wenxing and Chu-yun Chen for their long-term support of this project, in addition to their contributions in writing and assistance with the cover design. During these years, Wang and Chen have been busy traveling all over the world, attending conferences, doing interviews, and being present at award ceremonies; nevertheless, they were always ready to answer the editors' questions and offer all sorts of needed support. Without them, the completion of this project truly would have been impossible.

Second, the editors wish to thank the contributors—our dear colleagues and friends—who shared the same interests with us all these years, working hard on revisions and waiting patiently and trustingly for any progress in our preparation of the final version. Their moral support is much appreciated. Among them, the editors especially thank Te-hsing Shan for granting us permission to republish "The Stream-of-consciousness Technique in Wang Wenxing's Fiction" and "Wang Wenxing on Wang Wenxing." We also want to thank Anita Lin, Emily Wen, and Roma Ilnyckyj for their assistance in compiling the bibliographies.

As the publication is closely related to the "Art of Chinese Narrative Language: International Workshop on Wang Wenxing's Life and Works" held at the University of Calgary on February 19–20, 2009, the editors thank the Social Sciences and Humanities Research Council of Canada; the Taiwan Ministry of Education; the University of Calgary; the Taipei Economic and Cultural Office in Ottawa; the Taipei Economic and Cultural Office in Vancouver; the late Dr. Leslie Kawamura, founder and Head of East Asian Studies at the University of Calgary; and friends in the Taiwan and Chinese communities in Calgary for their generous financial support of the conference and the publication of this book. We want also to express our sincere gratitude to the advices and all sorts of support from the colleagues at the University of Calgary including Drs. Nick Žekulin, Susan Bennett, Herminia Joldersma, Xiao-Jie Yang, and Wei Cai, Professor Yu-kun Yang, and Mr. Xianming Zhao.

Throughout these years, Mai Shaikhanuar-Cota, the managing editor of the Cornell East Asia Series, has provided us with invaluable advice on the preparation of the manuscript; her support and assistance behind the scenes are much appreciated. The editors also feel grateful to the anonymous reviewers for their comments and suggestions, which we took to heart in preparing the final version of the book.

The editors want to express our sincere gratitude to Ms. Shu-hui Chang and Ms. Chian-hua Liu at the Department of Codification of Cultural Creativity and Marketing, National Palace Museum, Taipei, Taiwan, for their assistance in securing permission for the use of Qi Baishi's painting titled "Damo" in the cover design of the book.

Finally, the editors wish to express our sincere gratitude to our dear and longtime friend Fred Edwards for reading the final draft and selflessly assisting us with the proofreading, and to our families for their love and never-failing support over the years while we were working on this project.

Introduction

Shu-ning Sciban

"Writers should treat language like a goldfish bowl,
wiping away any oily stains to make it crystal clear
in order to see the living fish within."

—Wang Wenxing

READING WANG WENXING: *Critical Essays* examines the
fiction of the internationally renowned language artist Wang Wenxing
(also known as Wang Wen-hsing) 王文興 (b. 1939), the most celebrated
modernist writer living in Taiwan today. Wang published his first short
story in 1958 and continues to be active as a writer. For much of his writing career, his language art was not fully appreciated, but half a century
after the publication of his first story, his achievement and devotion to
language finally began to receive the recognition and respect that it deserves, nationally and internationally. His first novel *Jia bian* 家變 (Family catastrophe) has been listed as one of the best one hundred Chinese
literary works by *Yazhou zhoukan* (Chinese newsweekly) in Hong Kong
and one of the best thirty contemporary Taiwanese literary works by the
Council of Cultural Affairs in Taiwan. Wang has also received three
prestigious awards for his writing: Taiwan's National Award for Arts
(Literature Category) in 2009, the Chevalier de L'Ordre des Arts et des
Lettres from the French government in 2010, and the Huazong Interna-

tional Literature Award, presented to Chinese-language writers, by the *Sin Chew Daily* in Kuala Lumpur in 2011.

Known for the great care he takes in writing his fictional works, Wang has published twenty-three short stories, one novella, one play, and two novels during his career. (He has recently completed a third novel that will be published in 2015.) His low output is directly related to his method of writing, a painstaking process that involves translating the images and sounds in his mind into words or characters that can be reproduced on paper. The entire process, from the moment an idea first appears to the final version submitted to a publisher, is extremely slow. Wang described it during an interview with Te-hsing Shan in 1983, ruefully noting that as a young man he "didn't expect my writing to be so slow." In fact, according to his wife, Jeannette Chu-yun Chen, he writes only thirty characters a day.

Wang's greatness as a writer, however, is not about the slowness of the writing process but the artistic product that comes out of it. The ultimate governing principle of Wang's writing, in my opinion, is "precision" (*jingsheng* 精省). "Our writers," Wang suggests, "have so many things to study—precision is just one, albeit the most important."[1] He goes on to explain: "Words have to be like mathematical symbols, each one having its own function. One word too few, and the piece fall apart. One word too many, and the piece buckles under its own weight."[2] "Words," in his mind, include punctuation marks and every possible typographic device available for a printed text. Wang has dedicated himself to this concept of writing since he was twenty, and it is for this goal of achieving precision that he writes at such a slow speed—those famous thirty characters a day, including punctuation marks.

In the introduction to *Endless War: Fiction and Essays by Wang Wen-hsing* (Cornell East Asia Series 158, 2011), an English-language anthol-

---

1. Wang Wenxing, "*Xin ke de shixiang* xu"《新刻的石像》序 (Preface to *New stone statue*), *Xiandai wenxue* 現代文學 (Modern literature) 35 (1968): 218. The translation is by Martin Sulev in *Endless War: Fiction and Essays by Wang Wen-hsing*, eds. Shu-ning Sciban and Fred Edwards (Ithaca, NY: Cornell East Asia Program, Cornell University, 2011), 370.

2. Ibid.

ogy of Wang's short works, I provided a detailed account of Wang's life and writing career, so there is no need to repeat how he developed his style. Instead, aiming at revealing the art of Wang's language as well as the thought expressed through his words—after all, he says, "words control tone, atmosphere and viewpoint"[3]— this volume focuses on critiques of his writing. We briefly describe the reception of Wang's fictional works.

Wang Wenxing's formal career as a writer was launched with the publication of his first short story in 1958, when he was a first-year student at National Taiwan University. His early stories, with the exception of "Long tian lou" 龍天樓 (Dragon inn) in 1965, did not receive much attention from readers. The publication of his first novel, *Family Catastrophe*, in 1972 changed that completely. Despite an initially negative reception from the reading public, academic scholars and critics have since shown great enthusiasm for Wang's unique language and style. The "classical" scholarship of "Wangxue" 王學 (a term that has become popular in recent years as shorthand for "Wang Wenxing studies") was established in the period from the mid-1970s to the 1980s, and included essays by Yan Yuanshu 顏元叔, Ouyang Zi 歐陽子, Hengsyung Jeng (Zheng Hengxiong) 鄭恆雄, Zhang Hanliang 張漢良, Joseph Lau (Liu Shaoming) 劉紹銘, Wai-lim Yip (Ye Weilian) 葉維廉, Leo Lee (Li Oufan) 李歐梵, Sung-sheng Yvonne Chang (Zhang Songsheng) 張誦聖, Ye Shan 葉珊 (also known as Yang Mu 楊牧 or Wang Jingxian 王靖獻), Wu Dayun 吳達芸, Te-hsing Shan (Shan Dexing) 單德興, and Kang Laixin 康來新. The scholarship in this period, which focused mainly on examining Wang's linguistic strategies, particularly in *Family Catastrophe*, and asserted the importance of his fiction from the perspective of Western modernism, established a solid foundation for further study of his writing.

In November 2001, *Zhongwai wenxue* 中外文學 (Chungwai literary monthly) published a special issue on Wang Wenxing that focused on his second novel, *Bei hai de ren* 背海的人 (Backed against the sea), which came out in two volumes in 1981 and 1999. Edited by Lin Xiuling

---

3. Ibid.

林秀玲 and comprised the most important works in Wang studies from the mid-1990s to the turn of the twenty-first century, this special issue bore witness to the expansion of research interests among scholars. Topics included investigations of story settings and Wang's writing process, discussions of the politics of modernism and modes of modernity, comparisons with Western writers and literature, translators' reflections on their translations of Wang's fiction and translation theory, and Wang's views on classical poetry and architecture. Judged by the tone of the essays, the expansion in research verified a broader acceptance of Wang's writing among academics: the canonization of Wang's works was taking off.

In the West, special interest in Wang's writing emerged in the 1980s. James Shu, Edward Gunn, and Sung-sheng Yvonne Chang are among the pioneer scholars who studied Wang's iconoclasm toward the traditional concept of filial piety, unconventional use of language, innovative prose style, and narratological inventions.[4] Later, Chang made an extraordinary contribution to the establishment of Wang studies in the West with two monographs, *Modernism and the Nativist Resistance: Contemporary Chinese Fiction* (Duke University Press, 1993) and *Literary Culture in Taiwan: Martial Law to Market Law* (Columbia University Press, 2004). In these publications, Chang addresses not only the literary significance of

---

4. The pioneering essays on Wang's writing that I refer to here are as follows: James C.T. Shu, "Iconoclasm in Wang Wen-hsing's *Chia-pien*," in *Chinese Fiction from Taiwan*, edited by Jeannette L. Faurot (Bloomington: Indiana University Press, 1980), 179–93; Yvonne Sung-sheng Chang, "Language, Narrator, and Stream-of-consciousness: The Two Novels of Wang Wen-hsing," *Modern Chinese Literature* 1.1 (1984): 43–55; Edward Gunn, "The Process of Wang Wen-hsing's Art," *Modern Chinese Literature* 1.1 (1984): 29–41. It is worth mentioning that the editor of *Modern Chinese Literature* at the time was Howard Goldblatt, whose contribution to the study of Wang Wenxing can also be seen in his support for the publication of English translations of Wang's three works: *Family Catastrophe*, "Yige gongwuyuan de jiehun" 一個公務員的結婚 (The marriage of a civil servant), and "Da feng" 大風 (Strong wind), the latter two of which are included in *Endless War: Fiction and Essays by Wang Wen-hsing*, edited by Shu-ning Sciban and Fred Edwards (Ithaca, NY: Cornell East Asia Program, Cornell University, 2013), 15–25, 153–63.

Wang's fiction, language, and themes, his connection with Western literary modernism, and his influence on other writers, but also the cultural environment in which Wang was raised and continues to work. In addition, since 1990, younger scholars such as Steven Riep, Christopher Lupke, Sandrine Marchand, and myself have conducted research on a wide range of topics, including thematic interpretations, historical and cultural analyses, typographic theory, genetic criticism, and stylistic and rhetoric analyses.

There have also been several large research projects in the field of Wang studies, beginning with two international conferences. The first was the "Art of Chinese Narrative Language: International Workshop on Wang Wenxing's Life and Works," which I organized at the University of Calgary in Canada in 2009; the second, "Enacting Modernism: Wang Wenxing's Works in Performance and Translation," was organized by Kang Laixin and held at National Central University in Taiwan in 2010. They were followed by three major publications: *Wang Wenxing shougao ji: Jia bian, Bei hai de ren* 王文興手稿集：《家變》，《背海的人》 (Wang Wenxing's manuscripts: *Family Catastrophe, Backed against the Sea*, Xingren, 2010), compiled by Yi Peng, a devoted Wang scholar who emerged in the 1990s in Taiwan; *Endless War: Fiction and Essays by Wang Wen-hsing*, edited by Shu-ning Sciban and Fred Edwards (Cornell East Asia Program, Cornell University, 2011), an English translation anthology that contains all of Wang's short fiction and selected essays in which he discusses his thoughts on writing and literary language; and *Mandu Wang Wenxing congshu* 慢讀王文興套書 (Slow reading Wang Wenxing) (seven volumes), edited by Huang Shuning (Shu-ning Sciban), Kang Laixin, and San-hui Hung (Hong Shanhui) (National Taiwan University Press, 2013). These publications resulted from the lengthy effort to provide manuscripts, English translations, and Chinese-language references to students and researchers.

With the goal of continuing to build the scholarship on Wang's writing, *Reading Wang Wenxing: Critical Essays* was first proposed in the fall of 2007 during initial preparations for the University of Calgary conference in 2009. Originally conceived as a volume of conference proceedings, it grew to include not only papers by the participants but also from

Wang scholars who had not attended. These essays represent the current critical understanding of Wang Wenxing and his narrative art.

In this first English volume of scholarship on Wang's works, *Reading Wang Wenxing* consists of twenty-one items, including the "Author's Preface: Reading and Writing" by Wang Wenxing himself. The rest are grouped into two parts: Part I comprises fourteen scholarly essays; Part II provides appendices to Wang's work, including outlines of his novels and bibliographies of his writings, works of Wang scholarship, and translations of his works.

In his author's preface, an expanded version of his keynote speech at the Calgary conference, Wang provides an explanation of his approach to writing through a demonstration of "mandu" (慢讀 slow reading). He emphasizes literary realism as a fundamental principle and demonstrates his sensitivity to the tone and rhythm of a text. The essay also attests to the development of Wang's strong interest in classical poetry, particularly his appreciation of Du Fu's 杜甫 works. If reading and writing can never be separated, as Wang says, this article ought to provide the reader with clues about the nature of his literary world.

The essays in Part I are grouped under four headings: Social and Cultural Critique, Questions of Style, Reflections on Translation, and Reflections on Wang Wenxing's Life.

Social and Cultural Critique consists of four essays. In "Wang Wenxing and Lu Xun: High-Culture Quest, Enlightenment Rationality, and the Modernist Duality," Sung-sheng Yvonne Chang explores Wang's life-long practice of modernist aesthetics from a sociopolitical perspective, comparing him with another Chinese literary giant, Lu Xun 魯迅. Chang finds that both writers, though living in different historical eras, share the same spirit in their pursuit of high culture, as reflected in their anti-tradition, pro-Enlightenment stance. Switching from the usual focus on innovation in the linguistic features of Wang's writing, Chang's analysis sheds light on the constitution and formation of Wang's modernist aesthetics and the modernity of his work in which Enlightenment rationality serves as the foundation for the writer's "modernist duality"—the literary configurations of his writing. In the earlier monographs, Chang studied and elucidated the influence of Western modernism on Taiwanese literature, which included the relationship between Wang's writing and modernism. While clarifying the similarities in the cultural dispositions and literary configurations shared by Wang and Lu Xun, this essay situates Wang within the context of Chinese and East Asian modernization in the twentieth century.

Like Chang, Ihor Pidhainy in "Archetypes in Wang Wenxing's Early Fiction: Insecure Intellectuals and Dangerous Women" also deals with a larger issue in Wang's writing: character typology and gender. Probing Wang's early short stories, Pidhainy specifically examines the images of two common character types—young boys and mature women—and their relationship with each other. He finds that the former usually take on the characteristics of either weak intellectuals or bullying antagonists, whereas the latter are destructive and domineering. As he delineates the individual character of each type, Pidhainy also offers deep readings of each story. The broad picture of the character archetypes drawn in the essay helps clarify Wang's views and concerns about human nature and relationships, not only in his early but also in his later works.

Whereas Pidhainy studies women in general, Darryl Sterk, in "Screwed by Fate? The Prostitute and the Critique of Liberalism in *Backed Against the Sea*," studies the role of prostitutes and the thematic significance of prostitution in *Backed Against the Sea* from sociopolitical and socioeconomic perspectives, as well investigating Wang's liberalism, foregrounding his criticism of capitalism. This is a topic that has not been explored much in Wang studies, despite the fact that Wang's social criticism has been evident from the very beginning of his writing, in stories such as "Yitiao chuiside gou" 一條垂死的狗 (A dying dog, 1958), his second published story, written at the age of just nineteen. Sterk's essay indeed offers a fresh outlook on Wang's writing.

Jane Parish Yang's "Leaving Home: Foreshadowing, Echo, and Sideshadowing in Wang Wenxing's *Jia bian*" is a close examination of the plot design of *Family Catastrophe*, with particular focus on the use of the techniques of foreshadowing and sideshadowing in the revelation of the perplexing and tangled father–son relationship in the novel. In her intriguing and detailed analysis, the complicated relations between whole and part and between theme and plot become clear, revealing the meticulous design of the novel.

The second section of Part I, "Questions of Style," consists of five essays, focusing on Wang's literary technique. This section begins with Wai-lim Yip's "Wang Wenxing: Novelist as Lyric Sculptor." Though Wang is not famous for writing poetry, he does stress poetized prose in modern literature when he says that "the language of modern fiction, without exception, meticulously follows the language of poetry."[5] Investigating Wang's lyricism, as defined by Edgar Allan Poe, Yip puts Wang's writing in line with Western modernist literature and argues that the essence of Wang's fiction is the poetic lyricism of high modernism. He uses "Xiawu" 下午 (Afternoon, 1959), "Muqin" 母親 (Mother, 1960), and "Da feng" 大風 (Strong wind, 1961) to demonstrate the three methods Wang uses to "arrest" the reader's attention at key poetic moments in his stories.

Placing Wang Wenxing within the history of Chinese literature, my essay "*Family Catastrophe* and Its Connection with Traditional Chinese Literature" probes several configurations of *Family Catastrophe*, illustrating Wang's use of two common structural features in traditional Chinese literature—the fourfold structure (exposition-development-transition-conclusion) and the introductory function of the beginning section. This essay challenges the previous view of Wang Wenxing as an artist of *quanpan xihua* 全盤西化 (wholesale Westernization) and encourages a reconsideration of the influence of Chinese literature on Wang's writing, particularly as his prose published over the past decade reveals his study and appreciation of classical Chinese literature.

5. Wang Wenxing, "*Xiandai wenxue lun* xu"《現代文學論》序 (Preface to *Criticism of modern literature*), *Xiandai wenxue lun—Lianfu sanshi nian wenxue daxi pinglun juan*, vol. 3《現代文學論—聯副三十年文學大系評論卷 3》(*Criticism of modern literature—anthology of literary criticism selected from the Literary Supplement of Lianhe Daily News in the past thirty years*) (Taipei: Lianhe bao, 1980), 33–40. This essay was reprinted as "Qianlun xiandai wenxue" 淺論現代文學 (A brief discussion on modern literature) in *Shu he ying* 書合影 (Books and films) (Taipei: Lianhe wenxue chubanshe, 1988), 187–93. The quotation is on p. 189. The English translation is by Christopher Lupke in *Endless War: Fiction and Essays by Wang Wen-hsing*, p. 374.

Inspired by the complexity of the linguistic structure of Wang's novels, Wei Cai's "The Use of *Liheci* in *Family Catastrophe*" studies the employment of *liheci* 離合詞—words consisting of two morphemes that can be used with or without other constituents inserted in between—with a special focus on their morphological structure and the patterns of their function in Wang's first novel. This essay, the first investigation of Wang's language employing linguistic methodology with quantified data and referential materials, represents a breakthrough in research approach.

Like Wai-lim Yip and Sung-sheng Chang, Hengsyung Jeng has studied Wang's writing for a long time. His first investigation of *Backed Against the Sea*, vol. 1, was published in 1986. In "Harmony, Counterpoint, and Variation in *Backed Against the Sea*," a continuation of that initial study of the musicality of Wang's second novel, Jeng analyzes the musical structure of both volumes of *Backed Against the Sea* by employing classical musical theory, particularly that pertaining to vocal music and the composition of variations, demonstrating Wang's acoustic design in his writing. As Wang is extremely keen on the musical quality of written language, Jeng gives his full analytical attention to it, brilliantly illuminating the musicality of the novel.

Although Wang's fame rests on his two novels, his early short fiction, though less discussed, is also remarkable, and has been examined by scholars such as Ye Shan, Wu Dayun, and Steven L. Riep.[6] Te-hsing Shan was among this group when he wrote "The Stream-of-Consciousness Technique in Wang Wenxing's Fiction," in which he made a thorough

---

6. These scholars have spoken highly of Wang's mastery of writing fiction. Their critiques include Ye Shan 葉珊, "Tansuo Wang Wenxing xiaoshuo li de beiju qingdiao" 探索王文興小說裡的悲劇情調 (Exploring the tragic sentiment in Wang Wenxing's fiction), *Xiandai wenxue* 現代文學 (Modern literature) 32 (1967): 60–67; Wu Dayun 吳達芸, "Wang Wenxing xiaoshuo zhong de zhuangshi jiqiao" 王文興小說中的裝飾情調 (The craftsmanship of embellishment in Wang Wenxing's fiction), *Xin chao* 新潮 (New tide) 19 (1969): 20–28; Steven L. Riep, "A Case of Successful Failure: 'Dragon Inn' and Wang Wen-hsing's Critique of Official History and Anticommunist Literature," *Selected Papers in Asian Studies*, New Series no. 67 (2001): 1–34.

examination of the use of stream-of-consciousness starting with the early works and continuing through the novels. Shan's close readings reveal not only that Wang was able to use this technique in a mature manner at the age of twenty but also that it was essential in the composition of the first volume of *Backed Against the Sea*. Shan's essay was first published in 1985, but due to its importance in emphasizing the Wang's development of this technique from an early stage right through to his maturity, as well as the essay's lack of availability to contemporary scholars, the editors decided to republish it in this volume.

The next section, "Reflections on Translation," contains articles by three translators of Wang Wenxing's fiction in which they discuss their translation theories as well as the pragmatic solutions and strategies they used in dealing with the challenges of translating Wang's works. Sandrine Marchand, translator of *Processus familial* (the French translation of *Family Catastrophe*, published by ACTES SUD in 1999) and many of Wang's stories into French, offers an interpretation of Wang's writing process based on how his consideration of a word's visual and aural aspects influences his placement of text on a page. In "The Poetics of Rhythm in Wang Wenxing's Novels," Marchand sheds light on the writer's use of blank space, an outstanding rhetorical trope Wang is famous for employing, and reflects on her translation of *Backed Against the Sea*. In "Translating and Editing Wang Wenxing," Fred Edwards, a writer, translator, and coeditor of *Endless War: Fiction and Essays by Wang Wenhsing*, writes of his personal experience in translating and editing Wang's stories, delineating the multilayered editing of a translation as well as highlighting the multifaceted challenges faced by a Chinese–English translator. In "Reflections on Translating *Jia bian*," originally a speech given at the international conference on Wang Wenxing at National Central University in Taiwan in 2010, Susan Dolling, translator of *Family Catastrophe* (University of Hawai'i Press, 1995), provides her translation philosophy and recounts some of the challenges she faced during the course of translating the novel.[7]

---

7. For an even better understanding of translating Wang Wenxing, these essays should be read along with Edward Gunn's "Bei hai de ren yiji fanyi

The section "Reflections on Wang Wenxing's Life" offers descriptions of this author from two different angles—biographical and autobiographical, giving us a comprehensive understanding of Wang and the private domain of his life. The first article, "A Quiet and Simple Life" by Jeannette Chu-yun Chen—Wang's wife—reveals for the first time her "close observation" of Wang as a husband, scholar, writer, and individual. Chen and Wang were colleagues at the Department of Foreign Languages and Literatures in National Taiwan University; they retired at the same time in January 2005, after teaching for forty years. Their marriage of more than forty years provides rich source material for this valuable and refreshing biographical reference about the writer; readers will also find a detailed description of Wang's daily writing routine and lifestyle. The second article, "Wang Wenxing on Wang Wenxing," is a reprint of Te-hsing Shan's 1983 interview with the writer. Their discussion about Western literature and its relation with Wang's works provides extremely valuable information about the design of Wang's stories and reveals the strong Western literary influences on his writing. Shan is a scholar whose expertise includes interviews with intellectuals, both Chinese and Western. He has published five interviews with Wang Wenxing,[8]

---

zhunze"《背海的人》以及翻譯準則 (*Backed Against the Sea* and translation principles) in the special issue on Wang Wenxing of *Chungwai Literary Monthly* (30.6): 115–34. Gunn is the translator of *Backed Against the Sea*, vol. 1, published by the Cornell East Asia Program, Cornell University, in 1993.

8. The five interviews are: Shan Dexing 單德興, "Wang Wenxing tan Wang Wenxing" 王文興談王文興 (Wang Wenxing on Wang Wenxing), *Lianhe wenxue* (Unitas) 3.8 (1987): 166–95; reprinted as "Chuilian wenzi de ren" 錘煉文字的人 (The wordsmith) in *Duihua yu jiaoliu* 對話與研究 (Dialogues and interchanges) (Taipei: Maitian chuban, 2001), 39–83; "Ou kan tianyan qu hongchen—zai fang Wang Wenxing" 偶看天眼覷紅塵—再訪王文興 (Heavenly glance at the mundane world—the second interview with Wang Wenxing), *Zhongwai wenxue* 中外文學 (Chungwai literary monthly) 28.12 (2000): 182–99, reprinted in *Duihua yu jiaoliu* 對話與研究 (Dialogues and interchanges) (Taipei: Maitian chuban, 2001), 80–104; "Wenxue yu zongjiao: Shan Dexing zhuanfang Wang Wenxing" 文學與宗教：單德興專訪王文興 (Literature and religion: Shan Dexing's interview of Wang Wenxing), *Yinke* (Ink) 7.6 (2011.2): 120–43; Shan Dexing and Lin Jingjie 林靖傑, "Zongjiao yu wenxue: Wang Wenxing fangtanlu" 宗教與文學：王文興訪

but this is the only one available in English. In it, Wang acknowledges the Western influence on his work, describes the composition process and style development of his novels, and explains the design of his characters and themes.

Part II of the volume consists of appendices that we provide for the research interests of scholars and teachers of Chinese literature. Section A includes the outlines of the plots of *Family Catastrophe* and both volumes of *Backed Against the Sea*. These outlines have proven useful in teaching as well research on Wang's novels, serving as indexes for the quick location of plot details. Section B offers bibliographies of Wang Wenxing biographical references, critiques of Wang's writing, and translations of his works.

Reading Wang Wenxing presents a rich sample of the current international scholarship on Wang's life and works from a wide range of methodologies. It is also the first book in English that concentrates solely on Wang and his writing. The editors hope this volume will fulfill its function as what the Chinese call *pao zhun yin yu* 抛磚引玉 (to cast a brick to attract jade), encouraging further research into the writing of this magnificent and devoted Chinese language artist in the future.

談錄 (Religion and literature: Interview of Wang Wenxing), *Sixiang* 思想 (Reflexion) 19 (2011.9): 203–31; "Xiaoshuo beihou de zuozhe shijie: Wang Wenxing dingtanlu" 小說背後的作者世界：王文興鼎談錄 (The private world of the fiction author: The Three-person interview of Wang Wenxing), *Quegu suolai jing: dangdai mingjia fangtanlu* 卻顧所來徑: 當代名家訪談錄 (Reflection: Interviews of contemporary prominent writers and scholars) (Taipei: Yunchen wenhua, 2014), 95–128.

I Essays

SOCIAL AND CULTURAL CRITIQUE

1 Wang Wenxing and Lu Xun: High-Culture Quest, Enlightenment Rationality, and the Modernist Duality

Sung-sheng Yvonne Chang
The University of Texas at Austin

THIS CHAPTER REVISITS some specific aspects of the literary project of Wang Wenxing 王文興 (b. 1939) with extensive references to the life and work of Lu Xun 魯迅 (1881–1936). The undertaking is predicated on the assumption that a common set of intellectual forces underpinned the writings of a particular class of modern East Asian writers active in different parts of the twentieth century and in different locales. Their fruitful comparability, if convincingly demonstrated, has the potential to advance literary studies of the region beyond conventional boundaries. Although Lu Xun and Wang Wenxing enjoy equally prominent status in the literary establishments of China and Taiwan, respectively, they are usually situated within different genealogies, and few have attempted to draw a direct lineage between them. The enthralling voices coming from their works resonate with each other in several ways, luring us to seek some possible common ground in their intellectual orientation. It is easily demonstrable that in the early stages of their careers, both authors earnestly espoused an anti-traditionalist and pro-Enlightenment agenda, patently a product of the "high culture quest," a prevalent form of resistance-through-emulation in modern East Asia.

Did this shared epochal imperative play any significant role in shaping these authors' literary pursuits?

To better tackle the thorny issues surrounding the relationship between aesthetic features and historical contexts, I resort to insights provided by such distinguished sociologists as Pierre Bourdieu and Peter Bürger. In particular, the former's concepts of the *field* and *habitus*—including such related notions as the coexisting, mutually defined *positions* within the same cultural field and the socially constructed *dispositions* (habitus) of individual writers—form an important basis for my analytical scheme:

> To understand the practices of writers and artists, and not least their products, entails understanding that they are the result of the meeting of two histories: the history of the *positions* (in the cultural field) they occupy and the history of their *dispositions.* Although position helps to shape *dispositions*, the latter, in so far as they are the product of independent conditions, have an existence and efficacy of their own and can help to shape *positions.*[1] (emphasis added)

This essay begins with a delineation of the history of the particular position that Wang Wenxing assumed in the early years of Taiwan's post-1949 era. In particular, it argues that Wang's intellectual and literary dispositions were significantly shaped during this period's nostalgic—and heavily politically inflected—reincarnation of the May Fourth Enlightenment project. The second part of the essay is devoted to analysis of the literary configurations of a particular set of Enlightenment dispositions that Wang shares with Lu Xun. Special emphasis is placed on the symbolic articulation of these authors' persistent preoccupation with the unfathomable and that which goes beyond the experiential realm, reflecting simultaneously a subscription to the rational mode of reasoning and the uncanny desire to tamper with the inherent liminal quality of rationality.

---

1. Pierre Bourdieu, *The Field of Cultural Production: Essays on Art and Literature* (New York: Columbia University Press, 1993), 61.

Emulation of Western High Culture: An Epochal Imperative

A few words of justification are in order regarding my decision to juxta-pose Wang Wenxing with Lu Xun, the towering cultural figure from China's Republican era (1911–1949), whose status as a trailblazer of modern Chinese literature is well established. No doubt there is a great disparity between these writers in terms of their ideological outlook, literary practice, and above all the nature and scope of their consecra-tion. Whereas Wang, a living author in Taiwan, is revered by critics and scholars for his exceptional achievements as a literary modernist, Lu Xun is widely venerated as "the conscience of China" for his unflinching critical spirit. What is more, during the eight decades since he passed away, Lu Xun has been transformed by extraordinary political forces into a larger-than-life figure and remains a national icon in the People's Republic of China. Despite these differences, however, there are interest-ing parallels in the career trajectories of these two writers that merit close attention. Both made their debuts as cultural iconoclasts bolstered by Enlightenment ideals. Subsequently, they seriously engaged in re-examining the literary aspects of traditional China. Both harbored bitter resentment against the harsh surveillance they received from an author-itarian government. Both became embroiled mid-career in internecine political strife in the literary field, leading to a new self-positioning that significantly affected the way they approached literature and politics in the more mature stages of their careers.

These similarities in the writers' literary trajectories form the base on which I explore questions of greater magnitude: as creative writers who are at the same time uncompromising independent thinkers, how do Lu Xun and Wang Wenxing negotiate with the dominant intellectual influences coming from the West? Given that the political eras they re-spectively represent—the Republican era (1911–1949) and post-1949 Taiwan—are adjacent to each other, with significant continuities in terms of cultural institutions, which the Nationalists brought with them during the 1949 retreat, I present a selective comparison of how these two writers relate to contemporary literary institutions, the artistic and ideological paradigms available for them to choose from, and the mo-tives and consequences of their personal choices. This promises to shed light on the "epochal functional determinants," to borrow from Peter Bürger, of the broadly conceived modern Chinese literary institution.[2] The fact that Wang Wenxing's aesthetic choices depart from Lu Xun's in such a polarized manner makes this comparison immediately relevant to a set of thorny questions in East Asian literary history revolving around the left-versus-right contention, questions that remain unresolved.

The term *qimeng* (啓蒙), the Chinese translation of "Enlightenment," has not been a popular word in the intellectual discourse of post-1949 Taiwan, either due to historical accident or deliberate manipulation. As the conventional wisdom goes, the Nationalist government blamed the radical turn of the May Fourth movement for the rise of the communist revolution, so the Nationalists' reception of that tradition in post-1949 Taiwan was patently selective. Notions and attitudes generally associated with the term have largely been dissolved into *xiandaihua* (現代化, modernization) and taken for granted by the intellectual class. Wang Wenxing's adherence to the Enlightenment ethos, however, is more specific, deep-rooted, and thoroughgoing than that of most of his contemporaries. It was first on display in his iconoclastic critique of traditional family ethics in his novel *Jia bian* 家變 (Family catastrophe; 1972), and then in his forthright defense of the pro-Westernization stance during the *xiangtu wenxue* (鄉土文學, nativist literature) movement. In both, Wang exhibited a radicalism that is often associated with a "wholesale Westernization" (*quanpan xihua* 全盤西化) position.[3]

That this position corresponds to an epochal drive in East Asia's long twentieth century, one that prescribes pro-Westernization, anti-

---

2. In Bürger's words, the institution of art refers "to the productive and distributive apparatus and also to the ideas about art that prevail at a time and that determine the reception of works" and consists of "the epochal functional determinants of art within the bounds of society." Peter Bürger, *Theory of the Avant-garde* (Minneapolis: University of Minnesota Press, 1984), 22, and 4–5.

3. This epochal drive is frequently a focus of controversy everywhere and has assumed an additional layer of complexity in China's socialist period, not only because communist ideology assigned different contents and values to the categories "radical," "liberal," and "conservative" but also because the pro-Westernization stance itself was heavily stigmatized and denounced by ultraleftist regimes.

traditionalism, and a resolute faith in the emulation of Western high culture as an effective means for self-rejuvenation, is evidenced by episodes of a popular documentary put out by Chinese Central Television in 2006, *Da guo jueqi* 大國崛起 (The rise of great nations). The first episode is about Russia's Peter the Great (1672–1725), who disguised himself as a commoner while sojourning in Europe to acquire knowledge of advanced technologies. Upon returning, the young tsar adopted radical means to modernize Russia, but his unconventional behavior met with deadly resistance, which he brutally suppressed. Another episode concerns Meiji Japan, which launched all-out Westernization programs not long after its traumatic encounter with the West on the arrival of Admiral Matthew Perry's "Black Ships." The narrator of the documentary employs dramatic phrases, saying the Japanese were "first shocked, then infatuated, and finally became obsessed" (*shi jing, ci zui, zhong kuang* 始驚，次醉，終狂), to accentuate Meiji Japan's passionate reception of Western civilization's accomplishments. Both examples convey the unmistakable message that radical measures taken to emulate Western high culture are ultimately justified, as eighteenth-century Russia, Meiji Japan, and contemporary China all aggressively assimilated modern Western institutions, including capitalist ones, and achieved stellar growth in national strength.

To be sure, as a thinly veiled declaration of China's ambition to become a global superpower, the next "great nation," *The Rise of Great Nations* contains officially sanctioned political messages, such as the critical role played by strong leadership in choosing the right path for the nation. The film's romanticized vision of this "right path" is by no means shared by Chinese intellectuals. The ongoing vehement contention between the so-called New Left and the Liberals testifies to this variation of opinion. Nevertheless, for our purposes, the explicit reference to radical pro-Westernization as a legitimate paradigm speaks to its potency as an epochal determinant of the institution of literature, or "the set of basic assumptions and norms in a given historical context that validate particular literature practices and denigrate others,"[4] which I believe

---

4. Russell A. Berman, "Introduction," in Peter Bürger, *The Institutions of Art* (Lincoln: University of Nebraska Press, 1992), xiv.

both Lu Xun and writers of the early phase of post-1949 Taiwan shared to a certain extent. This would be their shared position in the cultural field: the position of enthusiastic modernists.

The resurfacing of the radical pro-Westernization stance in contemporary China may be traced back to the 1980s (Liu Xiaobo was one of the spokesmen) and the reevocation of the May Fourth heritage in the "humanity-spirit debate" of the early 1990s, which was accompanied by a notable resurgence of Lu Xun studies. But the lineage connecting Wang Wenxing and Lu Xun, or even the May Fourth movement, cannot be uncritically assumed. While the posthumous canonization of Lu Xun by the Chinese Communist Party has made him a symbol of the revolutionary ethos, in post-1949 Taiwan the "author function" (à la Michel Foucault) of Lu Xun's name was quite different: as leader of the recalcitrant leftist intellectuals he was an "archenemy"; anyone accused of having "read Lu Xun" could have been arrested and incarcerated. This took place along with many other forms of reinscription, suppression, and reinvention of key terms and visions associated with May Fourth, including that of *qimeng*, or Enlightenment. Therefore, despite the closeness in time, the heritage of May Fourth was transmitted to post-1949 Taiwan largely in oblique, convoluted ways, as a "selective tradition."

According to Wang Wenxing, though they were officially banned, May Fourth literary works were still available in underground circulation, and humanities students like him typically sought them out to read. Nonetheless, Lu Xun's work never exerted such a crucial influence on Wang Wenxing as it did on Chen Yingzhen 陳映真, in either a literary or ideological sense.[5] Rather, as Wang has asserted, the main source of his literary orientation was the rich collection of Western literature in the library of the Department of Foreign Languages and Literatures at National Taiwan University, where he was a student. It is therefore more reasonable to consider Lu Xun and Wang Wenxing as more or less independently reacting to the same overarching epochal drive of high culture quest. Their connection consists of having been stimulated by their

---

5. Chen was the leading figure of the leftist faction of the nativist literary movement.

exposure to Western culture and then pledging to emulate Western high culture as a way to rejuvenate a corrupt and obsolete indigenous cultural tradition.[6]

It is important to note that Wang's radical pro-Westernization stance did not evolve in a vacuum but had a great deal to do with the nascent liberal public sphere that emerged in 1960s Taiwan. The sapling, of course, was nipped in the bud with the government crackdown on two liberal magazines, *Ziyou Zhongguo* 自由中國 (Free China review) and *Wenxing* 文星 (Literary star). Yet the idealism it imparted to its earnest participants, including Wang Wenxing, may be credited with having nurtured some of Taiwan's best-known public intellectuals.[7]

John King Fairbank, the eminent U.S. historian of China, once remarked that thanks to the Korean War, history gave the Nationalists a second chance. The "Sino-liberal" reformers of the Republican era, who favored a gradualist model of nation-building but lost the opportunity to implement it as a result of the success of the communist revolution, could do so in Taiwan after 1949. Their impressive accomplishments, however, were mostly achieved in the economic and social/educational realms, with limited freedom of speech in the public sphere. By and large, the intellectual class of post-1949 Taiwan adopted a version of "Cold War liberalism" as they immediately strived for liberal democracy and subscribed to anticommunist ideology. This was understandable given that they were mainly mainlander émigrés of gentry-class background whose left-behind family members were direct victims of the communist land reform. Because anticommunism was closely tied to national security, it became the most effective pretext for cultural control and tight surveillance of intellectuals. Around 1956, however, there was a visible shift from hard-core, coercive cultural control to a soft-core hegemonic one. The shift may be explained by a number of factors, in-

6. Except for an early article by James Shu, this aspect has rarely been discussed in studies of Wang's work. See James C.T. Shu, "Iconoclasm in Wang Wen-hsing's *Chia-pien* [*Jia bian*]," in *Chinese Fiction from Taiwan*, ed. Jeannette L. Faurot (Bloomington: Indiana University Press, 1980), 179–93.

7. Nanfang Shuo 南方朔 comes to mind, for example.

cluding a reluctant acceptance of the Cold War deadlock after the sign-
ing of the Sino-American Mutual Defense Treaty in 1954 following the
end of the Korean War. The relative relaxation of state surveillance
quickly resulted in greater freedom of expression and emboldened liberal intellectuals to make concrete demands for political reform, although the arrest of Lei Zhen 雷震 for advocating in the *Free China
Review* the founding of an opposition party and the aborted attempt by
Peng Mingmin 彭明敏 and Wei Tingchao 魏廷朝 to issue a democracy
manifesto in 1964 made it abundantly clear that steps of this kind would
not be tolerated by the authoritarian government.[8]

The most notable cultural event embodying this critical spirit was
"Zhongxi wenhua lunzhan" 中西文化論戰 (Debate on the relative merits of Chinese and Western civilizations) in 1962, which was launched on
the pages of *Literary Star* magazine, with Li Ao 李敖, then a twenty-
seven-year-old graduate student in history at National Taiwan University, its charismatic champion. A self-proclaimed protégé of Hu Shi
胡適, Li Ao invoked the May Fourth "wholesale Westernization" discourse and anti-traditionalist iconoclasm in his book *Chuantong xia de
dubai* 傳統下的獨白 (A monologue under the tradition; 1963), which pit-
ted Western liberal ideas against the conservative, neotraditionalist culture endorsed by the Nationalist government. Li was incarcerated soon
after the debate, which was both political punishment and a warning to
others.

Wang Wenxing started writing *Family Catastrophe*, with its echoes of
the May Fourth attacks on Confucian family ethics, within a few years of
the debate, which seems to be an indication that the novel was conceived
within the same intellectual climate. There were two significant implications. First, as a vibrant revocation of May Fourth pro-Westernization,
antitraditionalist iconoclasm was an important part of the backdrop of
Wang's literary development. The May Fourth legacy was reincarnated
in post-1949 Taiwan at a moment when a fledgling liberal public sphere
vied with the authoritarian ruling regime, which may very well account
for Wang's radical, rebellious inner drive that found expression in *Family*

---

8. Lei Zhen was a longtime senior Nationalist Party member and editor-in-
chief of the *Free China Review*. He was arrested in 1960.

Catastrophe's ethical criticism and continued to undergird his later career developments in different ways. Second, Wang's ideological makeup is an interesting mix of radical intellectual disposition and subscription to liberal sociopolitical views. To the extent that the forum of the debate, *Literary Star*, was also the chief organ for early works by the modernists, including stories by Wang, it is evident that Euro-American modernist aesthetics, Cold War liberalism, and criticism of the dominant conservative culture may all be subsumed under the same intellectual mix that bore the imprint of postwar U.S. hegemony.[9] Writers and artists who avidly subjected themselves to the modernist influence included some military personnel who had been enlisted in the turbulent years of the civil war on the mainland, as well as the generation—mainlanders and Taiwanese alike—who had been educated under the Nationalists. This explains the seemingly contradictory fact that despite his gut-level resentment of the government's unfair social practices and its surveillance and suppression of intellectual freedom, Wang—like his peers in the latter cohort—did not oppose the conservative government's sociopolitical ideology, including its Cold War anticommunist agenda.

Having commented on the combination of radical intellectual disposition and liberal ideological stance evidenced in Wang Wenxing, which marks a major difference from Lu Xun, we may proceed to explore whether these writers' shared position in the cultural field, that is, their shared epochal drive and (some) shared sources of intellectual influence, lead to meaningfully comparable features in their ostensibly different literary practices.

Literary Configurations of the Enlightenment Discourse

Enlightenment rationality was undoubtedly an important factor that enabled progressive East Asian intellectuals to desacralize premodern in-

---

9. In the first ten to fifteen years of the post-1949 era, as older Taiwanese writers and artists whose formative years had fallen in the Japanese period were handicapped by abrupt, politically induced changes, the cultural field in Taiwan was dominated by mainland émigrés.

digenous belief systems in the early stages of modernization. The main argument I put forth here is that under the same epochal imperative to emulate Western high culture, Lu Xun and Wang Wenxing both developed a specific *rationalist* disposition, which not only bolstered their iconoclastic attacks on traditional values but also underpinned their literary enterprises. This is first evidenced in a signature rhetorical device used in their prose writings. Then I proceed to discuss certain characteristically modernist features of their literary works that at once point to the influence of Enlightenment and post-Enlightenment Western thought and promise to illuminate aspects of the evolution of the modern Chinese literary institution from the Republican period to Taiwan's post-1949 era.

Exemplary use of an ideologically functional rhetorical strategy may be found in two essays by Wang Wenxing and Lu Xun. In an editorial note titled "*Xiandai wenxue* yi nian" 現代文學一年 (Anniversary of *Modern Literature*), Wang Wenxing semi-jokingly criticizes the imagined opponents of the magazine's central activity—literary creation modeled on the West—by comparing them to a tyrannical father who forbids his son "to play ball, sing songs, ride bicycles, and listen to the radio," simply because these activities are all "Western."[10] Here he employs a rhetorical strategy that challenges an unexamined assumption—that one can make an effective distinction between the indigenous and the imported—by implicitly asserting the superiority of modern Western civilization, as evidenced by its omniscient presence in modern life. The rhetorical effect depends on readers' shocking discovery of their own faulty assumptions, overpowered by the ostensibly rational reasoning with which the radical message is conveyed. This is a rhetorical style that Wang Wenxing and Lu Xun employ with great frequency in their prose.

Even a first impression alerts the reader to striking resonances between this passage and Lu Xun's 1918 article "Women zenyang zuo

---

10. Wang Wenxing 王文興, "*Xiandai wenxue* yi nian"《現代文學》一年 (Anniversary of *Modern literature*), *Xiandai wenxue* 現代文學 (Modern literature) 7 (1961.3): 4–6.

fuqin" 我們怎樣做父親 (What should we do as fathers), not to mention that many of the highly rationalist propositions that Lu Xun makes in this famous article aptly describe the core thematic agenda of Wang Wenxing's *Family Catastrophe,* published half a century later. The similarities are unmistakable: both authors attack the seat of cultural authority in Chinese society; they argue that the real motive for the conservative fathers' safeguarding a stagnant, outdated, and harmful tradition is self-interest. Their propositions are essentially the same: to regenerate the community, one must foster environments conducive to the son's personal growth, and the parent–child relationship in the West serves as a model.

Of course it is true that during the interval between their comments, the Chinese family and socioeconomic environment changed a great deal. The two authors' objectives also differ in their magnitude: Lu Xun was calling for revolutionary changes that would take the Chinese people over the threshold of modernity; Wang Wenxing was merely attempting to justify his journal's adoption of Western models. What actually interests us is the revealing resemblance in their style of argumentation. Lu Xun begins his essay with a trenchant criticism of the father's absolute power and authority over the son in Chinese society by exposing the fallacious logic by which the arrangement had normally been rationalized. The parent–child hierarchy is based on the assumption that life-giving entails ownership, or a favor to be repaid, but that is practically wrong because:

但祖父子孫，本來各各都只是生命的橋梁的一級，決不是固
定不易的。現在的子，便是將來的父，也便是將來的祖。我
知道我輩和讀者，若不是現任之父，也一定是候補之父，而
且也都有做祖宗的希望，所差只在一個時間。

In reality, grandfather, father, son, and grandson are simply different stages of the bridge-path of life, and they by no means are fixed, unalterable positions; one who is at the present time a son will become a father later, and a grandfather in the future. I know for a fact that I myself, as well as my readers, if not currently a

father, then must be a father-to-be, with the likely prospect of
becoming an ancestor; the difference lies only in *time*.[11]

Regardless of their targeted audiences, these authors resort to logical
reasoning in communicating a provocative message. Their radicalism
lies not just in the progressive content of the messages but in the very
rhetorical strategy they employ, which asserts reason as the source of
authority and legitimacy and rationality as a vehicle for reaching hith-
erto unrecognized truth. In fact, the inversion of prevalent—indeed,
dominant—ways of legitimating truth in Chinese culture is a salient feature of the prose work of Lu Xun and Wang Wenxing. Both frequently
engage in the task of exposing as problematic the foundations on which
authoritative opinions—whether cultural, political, or aesthetic—are
grounded. Perhaps to avoid pandering unwittingly to authority holders
through reinforcement of their rhetorical methods, the writers are prone
to use mundane details of everyday life in presenting their arguments
(playing ball, listening to the radio, or parenthood as property ownership). Realizing, as they do, the immense difficulty of effecting attitudinal change in their readers, which is always the real objective of their
persuasive rhetoric, they often propose extremely pragmatic solutions,
even expedient measures. There is abundant evidence attesting to their
conscious intention to beseech attitudinal changes in their readers so
that they might better adapt themselves to the modern age, in accordance with the core animating spirit of Enlightenment. Wang Wenxing's
editorial note explicitly pleads for greater open-mindedness from the
conservative father, whereas Lu Xun famously implores the readers of
"Kuangren riji" 狂人日記 (Madman's diary) to exercise the faculty of
reason by emphatically repeating the statement "凡事總須研究，才會
明白" (Everything needs to be investigated in order to be truly understood).[12] As a work of fiction, this message is even more forcefully ac-

11. Lu Xun 魯迅, "Women zenyang zuo fuqin" 我們怎樣做父親 (What
should we do as fathers), *Xin qingnian* 新青年 (New youth) 6.6 (1919.10): 3.
    12. Quoted from the beginning of chapter 3 in Lu Xun 魯迅, "Kuangren riji"
狂人日記 (Madman's diary), *Xin qingnian* 新青年 (New youth) 4.5 (1918.5).

centuated by the deliberate juxtaposition of the pseudologic of the madman's skewed reasoning and the latent paradoxical truth that awaits recovery—a more demanding task for those capable of independent rational thinking.

It would be useful to compile a list of examples (which I plan to do eventually) of how such rhetorical devices are plentifully employed by Lu Xun and Wang Wenxing in the *zawen* (雜文, miscellaneous essays) of the former and the *shouji* (手記, journals) of the latter and discuss the finer distinctions of their usage. Limited by time and space, for now it suffices to say that such devices function to fortify Lu Xun's trenchant cultural and political criticisms—which earned him the dubious reputation of being a *Shaoxing shiye* (紹興師爺, an attorney from his hometown of Shaoxing, a group known for their sharply legalistic writing style), whereas for Wang Wenxing, a loyal disciple of Formalist aesthetic principles, they are a powerful tool to achieve the effects of "defamiliarization" or "deautonomization" and to uncover hidden aesthetic qualities of things that elude the reader as a result of habituation. The ostensibly differing theme-contents of Lu Xun's *zawen* and Wang Wenxing's *shouji* should not obscure the fact that in an epistemological sense they both place strong faith in original observation, and the strategies they employ to communicate also accentuate rationality. For our purposes, this stylistic penchant serves as an index to the degree to which they both had internalized Enlightenment rationality, an integral part of the modernist mindset.

The role Enlightenment rationality plays in the habitus (as Bourdieu defines it) of these literary masters is unquestionably much more complex.[13] In what follows, I explore, with specific examples, whether and how the modernist propensity of these authors inclines them to take a skeptical position toward the positivistic promise of rationality, as well

---

13. Randal Johnson gives a useful summary in his introduction to Bourdieu's *The Field of Cultural Production*, in which "habitus" is said to be "a set of dispositions which generates practices and perceptions" and "the result of a long process of inculcation, beginning in early childhood, which becomes a 'second sense' or a second nature" (p. 5).

as its efficacy in answering difficult questions about life, questions that modernist writers are predisposed to ask in their literature.

If the special type of rhetorical strategy described in the foregoing discussion points to the internalization of Enlightenment rationality by Lu Xun and Wang Wenxing, who put it to good use in their prose writings, then a heightened awareness of the limits of reason or even the deliberate intention to expose the liminal qualities of rationality—either of its potential to slip into its opposite, irrationality, or its inability to cope with the "ultimate concerns" of life—may be seen to have contributed to the defining "modernist" feature in their more elaborate literary works. Both writers show such a proclivity for registering in the thematic and formal structures of their fictional works recognition of the coexistence of irreconcilable, inherently contradictory elements in human affairs that it may be attributed to a characteristically "modernist" epistemological trait that orients them to the particular mode of perception that foregrounds "duality." In my view, this distinctive literary habitus, more than the artistic accomplishments of their literature in a more concrete sense, is what ranks both writers among the most sophisticated East Asian modernist artists.

One finds abundant unresolved tension in their fictional works that speaks to the acknowledgment of the inherently dualistic quality of the subjects under representation. The dualistic tension strewn all through Lu Xun's work has been perceptively grasped by some of his most discerning contemporary critics. The title of a path-breaking study of Lu Xun from the post–Cultural Revolution era, Wang Hui's dissertation, "Fankang juewang" 反抗絕望 (Resisting/countering despair; 1988), captures this underlying cognitive dualism, which also is a constitutive element of the specific "mental structure" of Lu Xun identified in the study. In her introductory essay for a new translation of the Japanese scholar/activist Takeuchi Yoshimi's (1910–1977) "Lu Xun lun" 魯迅論 (On Lu Xun), written in 1942, scholar Sun Ge insightfully elaborates Takeuchi's core argument on the "perpetually self-denying" dialectical quality of Lu Xun, situated within the frame of revolutionary ethos. By positing "modernist duality" within different interpretive frames, these scholars provide forceful corroborative evidence of its central role in Lu Xun's habitus as an intellectual and as a writer.

As for examples of the actual literary configuration of "modernist duality," one does not have to look beyond their most celebrated representative works. Lu Xun's "Madman's Diary" features multiple layers of dualism—insanity/insight, reason/pseudo-logic, predator/victim, and so on—and further embeds them in a highly elaborate structural design. It also functions as a key structural principle in Wang Wenxing's *Family Catastrophe*,[14] and accounts for the large dose of tension contained in its concluding scene: although the father is still missing in spite of the guilt-ridden and dutiful son's long and diligent search, mother and son are said to be leading a more harmonious, healthier life, with the mother aging peacefully while the son's physical shape gradually assumes that of a grown man. Wang Wenxing himself admits that the frequently posed question as to whether Fan Ye 范曄 is a filial, pious son is a moot point. In view of the author's emphatically modernist habitus, the dualistic quality in this matter is a given.

It may not be too difficult to delineate, in broad strokes, the intellectual influences that helped shape this modernist habitus in Lu Xun and Wang Wenxing. In the epoch of earnest high culture quest, East Asian writers were not just inspired by a set of Enlightenment values to engage in antitraditionalist struggles, they also were fully cognizant of

---

14. The story tells how a senile father, unable to take the daily abuse of his ultra-sensitive, would-be-artist son, disappears from home one windy afternoon. As the agonized, guilt-ridden son goes on a painful journey in search of his runaway father, the story slowly reveals the traditional Chinese family system, along with the cornerstone Confucian ethic of filial piety, as an archenemy of the healthy constitution of modern man, individualism in particular. Yet unlike the essays of Lu Xun on the conservative father, the novel represents and problematizes the messages simultaneously. Its structure highlights the formal-ideological correspondence valued so much by the New Critics who privilege literary modernism in exercising pragmatic criticism. The form imposes a layer of unity over the schizophrenic nature of the son's relationship with his father while accentuating the tension that results from its inherent dualism, culminating at the end.

more recent critiques of the Enlightenment ethos, critiques that posed
questions supposedly more pertinent to the "modern condition of mankind." That Friedrich Nietzsche, as well as an army of twentieth-century
existentialist writers including Franz Kafka, Jean-Paul Sartre, and Albert
Camus, were so widely popular among first- and second-generation
modern East Asian writers speaks loudly to this fact. In contrast to such
thinkers as Leibniz, who engaged in philosophical interrogation of the
Christian faith and its doctrines, intellectuals like Nietzsche held greater
appeal because of their poetic energy and dualistic mode of thinking.
Both Lu Xun and Wang Wenxing paid homage to Nietzsche in their
works: the former's *Yecao* 野草 (Wild grass; 1927) contains flamboyant
allusions to the Nietzschean Superman; one of the four books the protagonist in *Bei hai de ren* 背海的人 (Backed against the sea) took with
him in his exile from Taipei is *Thus Spoke Zarathustra*. How did the
shocking wave of repercussions from Nietzsche's proclamation "God is
dead" hit the presumably secular Chinese writers?

In 1960s Taiwan, literary treatment of existentialist angst enjoyed
prominence as well as status. Three early short stories by Wang Wenxing, "Rili" 日曆 (Calendar; 1960), "Zui kuaile de shi" 最快樂的事 (The
happiest thing; 1960), and "Mingyun de jixian" 命運的迹線 (Line of fate;
1963), were undoubtedly conceived within such a climate. All three feature the main character's shocking encounter with the "ultimate concern" of life and ensuing struggles in the dark abyss. Drawing a calendar
to kill time, the teenage protagonist in "Calendar" is entirely unprepared
when the years and months of the calendar take him to his old age and
the inevitable end of his life. Overwhelmed by his sudden realization of
the limited span of human life, a message reinforced with mathematical
certitude, he sheds tears, apparently feeling betrayed by the deceptive
signs of life—his youthful age and boundless energy. In "Line of Fate,"
one of the most celebrated stories from the period, a boy uses a razor to
cut his palm to extend his lifeline in an attempt to negotiate with Fate.
The young man who commits suicide after his initiation to sex, said to be
the "happiest thing in the world," while succumbing to the nihilistic acceptance of the ultimate meaninglessness of human existence, asserts
his own capacity to choose with the same defiant gesture. These are

unquestionably the classical topoi of existentialist/modernist literature. What strikes one as interesting is the persistent recurrence of them in Wang Wenxing's lifelong quest for the "ultimate meaning of life."

The fact that Wang Wenxing continues to be preoccupied with the same type of existentialist questions as those haunting his early literary works ultimately may be attributed to a specific aspect of his personal habitus that inclines him to act with astonishing persistence. Jeannette Chen [Chu-yun Chen or Chen Zhuyun], Wang's wife, noted in her speech at a University of Calgary conference on Wang's life and works that he has had "a strong sense of purpose" as long as she has known him.[15] Arguably, this sense of purpose is sustained by his radical engagement with Enlightenment rationality, which functions as a tool for seeking answers to difficult, existentialist questions—albeit in a somewhat unreliable (insufficient) form—and as a means to achieve utmost control, including control over the artistic media (powerful evidence for this is found in his recent lectures on *Backed Against the Sea,* which disclose meticulously reasoned compositional details).

Metaphysical incertitude also seems to be lurking behind dark moments in Lu Xun's literary texts, but the anxiety it elicits seems to be more diffused, latent, and embedded in various mundane concerns. Wang Wenxing, on the other hand, brings it into sharp relief when he deploys rationality to portray his fictional characters' metaphysical quest. For instance, when the protagonist of *Backed Against the Sea,* echoing the boy in "Line of Fate," is tantalized by an uncanny desire to poke into the mystery of the unknown while performing make-do fortune-telling, the intensity of the metaphysical incertitude is effectively magnified. Even more intriguing is the way rationality functions as a means to achieve control. The notion of control is liminal, as it at once implies the opposite of control—excess. Logical excess constantly appears to cast a shadow over the main characters of Wang's fiction, whose occasional

---

15. Professor Chen's speech, titled "A Quiet and Simple Life," was given at the international conference on Wang Wenxing's life and works held at the University of Calgary in 2009. The full text of the speech is included in this book; see Chapter 13.

lapses into unrestrained reasoning inclines them to extremist behavior: suicidal or murderous, like the characters in "The Happiest Thing," "Wanju shouqiang" 玩具手槍 (Toy revolver), and "Line of Fate"; fanaticism or self-delusion in *Family Catastrophe* and *Backed Against the Sea.* For example, during sleepless nights Fan Ye sometimes indulges himself in pedantically rationalistic critiques of the Chinese family system and filial piety or in random musings on his parents' unseemly behavior. The logic of his reasoning, however, often takes on a life of its own and leads him away from the realm of common sense.

Two short pieces by Lu Xun, "Tu he mao" 兔和貓 (Rabbits and cat; 1922) and "Ya de xiju" 鴨的喜劇 (Comedy of the ducks; 1922), also written somewhat early in his career, bear a limited yet highly instructive resemblance to the three stories by Wang Wenxing just discussed. By witnessing the killing of small creatures by animals higher up the food chain—newborn baby rabbits devoured by a black cat, pet tadpoles eaten by ducks that were also raised as pets—the speaker/narrator is confronted with the stark reality of life, taking him out of the comfortable zone of daily normality. There certainly is anger and sadness, but for the most part the narrator's reaction could more appropriately be described as "cosmic melancholy" rather than the existentialist angst experienced by Wang Wenxing's characters. In a contemplative mood, he laments the cosmic tragedy; in a gesture of genuine irritation, the narrator of "Rabbit" hints at possibly using poison to avenge the deaths of the innocent baby rabbits. The way Lu Xun seizes on the occasion to draw out broader implications about life—the eerie feeling that the traces of death are immediately erased—is undoubtedly in the same vein as Wang Wenxing's existentialist theme, only at a lower level of emotional disturbance. A sharp contrast, however, is found in Lu Xun's (or his narrator-persona's) eloquent narrative depicting either the victimization of human subjects by predatory interpersonal relationships and defunct social institutions. Such examples are the fictional characters Xianglin's Wife 祥林嫂 in "Zhufu" 祝福 (New year sacrifice) and Kong Yiji 孔乙己 (in the story of the same title); tragic deaths caused by circumstances unique to a historical era, be it the political martyrdom of Liu Hezhen 劉和珍 and Rou Shi 柔石; or the self-destruction of such lost members of the declining gentry as Fan Ainong 范愛濃 in "Fan Ainong" and Wei Lianshu 魏連殳 in "Guduzhe" 孤獨者 (The loner). Undoubtedly, the qualities of embittered indignation and profound empathy in his writing are what have earned Lu Xun the highest respect for his powerful sociocultural commentary.

In the following passage, I tried to suggest a comparative frame for further discussions of how Chinese and Western writers might have initially experienced the onslaught of modernity:

> In his essay "Modernity—an Incomplete Project," Jürgen Habermas says that Max Weber "characterized cultural modernity as the separation of the substantive reason expressed in religion and metaphysics into three autonomous spheres," namely, science, morality, and art. The differentiation of these three distinct spheres, he continues, was a result of the disintegration of the unified worldviews of religion and metaphysics. Given the indisputable differences between Chinese and Western varieties of metaphysics, one may nonetheless argue that in the course of industrialization and modernization in Chinese society, a process similar to that of the collapse of religion in the West has occurred, which may be summed up, in an oversimplified manner, as the disintegration of neo-Confucianist moralism and the terms of interpersonal relationships stipulated according to the model of family hierarchy.[16]

Initiation to the existentialist question of the "meaning of human existence"—a prominently legitimate literary motif found in East Asian writings from early phases of the modern epoch—may serve as an appropriate point of departure for exploring the following question: would the distinctively secular ethical views of traditional China leave significant imprints on modern Chinese writers' encounter with the grave existentialist question? A positive answer is conceivable, as the nature of

---

16. Sung-sheng Yvonne Chang, *Modernism and the Nativist Resistance: Contemporary Chinese Fiction from Taiwan* (Durham, NC: Duke University Press, 1993), 13.

this encounter is necessarily conditioned by the nature of the faith vacuum these writers were thrown into in the first place. At the same time, it is reasonable to expect an incremental change across the generations in these writers' conception and treatment of this difficult question. This is the basis on which the following examinations on Lu Xun and Wang Wenxing and their historical eras are conducted. In any case, whether seeking to reform a religious or a secular traditional authoritative system, one of the primary bastions of conservatism was the patriarchy, which both Lu Xun and Wang Wenxing confronted as part of their enlightenment project.

We should not spend time belaboring the point that Lu Xun and Wang Wenxing were influenced by different sets of Western ideas (social Darwinism and Hegelian historical philosophy for the former and Jungian myth theory, Freudian psychology, and certain Christian doctrines for the latter), as they were obviously part of the prevalent intellectual discourse at the time, accessible to these authors in either concrete or diffused forms. What requires more careful scrutiny is how the presuppositions underlying these ideas interact with competing meaning systems in the authors' own repertoire, and how they are processed through the mediation of the authors' personal habitus. A possible focal point may be the ways Lu Xun and Wang Wenxing conceive the relationship between humanity and the implications of evolutionary theory for ethical ancestor–descendant relations.

The two sets of writings only resonate with each other to a certain degree; one key difference lies in that the psychological disturbance of Wang Wenxing's characters is caused by a sudden awareness of the inevitability of human mortality, whereas the wistful mood of Lu Xun's narrators is occasioned by his inadvertent witnessing of a biological phenomenon in which the animal predator feeds on its prey. True, predation in the animal world is often used to hint at human relationships, as in Lu Xun's figurative deployment of the wolf image in several of his short stories: "New Year Sacrifice," "Ah Q zhengzhuan" 阿Q正傳 (The story of Ah Q), and "Yao" 藥 (Medicine). At the same time, however, Lu Xun specifically conceptualizes humans and animals as occupying different positions in the evolutionary hierarchy. Although numerous scholars have expounded on how social Darwinism and the Hegelian teleological view of history shaped Lu Xun's conception of evolution, I find that the following passage from "What Should We Do as Fathers" well serves the purposes of our discussion:

生命何以必需繼續呢？就是因爲要發展，要進化。個體既然免不了死亡，進化又毫無止境，所以只能沿續着，在這進化的路上走。走這路須有一種內的努力，有如單細胞動物有內的努力，積久才會繁複，無脊椎動物有內的努力，積久才會發生脊椎。所以後起的生命，總比以前的更有意義，更近完全，因此也更有價值，更可寶貴；前者的生命，應該犧牲於他。

Why should life be carried on? It is because of the needs of development, of evolution. While death inevitably occurs in the life of individuals, and while evolution has absolutely no end, therefore (life) has no choice but to continue, to march forward on the path of evolution. This marching forward requires an inner drive/effort. For example, only because the single-cell creatures possess such inner drive/effort, they become multiple-cell creatures over a long period of time; invertebrates possess such inner drive/effort, they acquire spines over a long period of time. As a result, lives that come later are always more meaningful, closer to perfection than lives that come before; they possess greater value, and deserve to be cherished more. Lives that come before should make sacrifices for (lives that come later).[17]

This passage not only makes evident Lu Xun's hierarchical view of different types of life on Earth; more important it reveals how he places human and animal life on the same chain of evolution, as different phases of the same process, and thus envisions an all-encompassing collective life. Naturally focusing his attention on the most highly evolved, that is, human beings, positioned at the top of the hierarchy, he inadver-

17. Lu Xun, "What Should We Do as Fathers."

tently applies ethical criteria derived from the human world to all creatures in the biological world. Revealingly and with a touch of humor, in
"Rabbits and Cat" the narrator's mother is said to be quite upset about
the lack of motherly instinct on the part of the female parent rabbit.
While manually forcing her to nurse her babies, the narrator's mother
further insists that she give all the babies equal access to her breasts, the
weak ones as well as the strong. We find interesting echoes of certain
strands of European thought derived from evolutionary theory on which
racial discrimination is based, but here it is more relevant to point out
that it also provides Lu Xun with a logical basis for his rationalization:
fathers should make sacrifices to ensure the well-being of their offspring
because the latter possess greater value from the standpoint of the collective life. It may not be too far-fetched to argue that the moral urgency
with which Lu Xun makes his plea has its roots in Confucian ethics or
more culturally specific Chinese meaning systems. The fact that Lu
Xun's favorite childhood reading was a pictorial edition of the mytho-
logical *Shanhai jing* 山海經 (Classic of the mountains and seas)—he later
transformed a mythical figure in the book, Xing Tian 刑天, into a heroic
archrebel, possibly modeled on the Nietzschean Superman—may suggest
that the quasi-anthropomorphic cosmic view of premodern China was
lurking behind his newly conceived evolutionary hierarchy.

It is not surprising that the horizon of cosmic imagination for Wang
Wenxing, born fifty-eight years after Lu Xun, was shaped by traditional
Chinese texts to a much lesser extent. Wang appears to situate man
within the universe along with other fellow creatures—all God's creations?—who are equally subject to the laws of nature. While Lu Xun,
having transposed human ethical order to the biological world, ascribes
moral instincts to all members of the collective life, Wang Wenxing
seems to perceive things from the reverse angle: he sees the internal
dynamics of natural law as impinging on human ethical relations, exert-
ing nonnegotiable constraints. This clearly constitutes a central theme of
Family Catastrophe. Even though he touchingly observes the blood sellers' actions as indicative of fatherly love as well as the drive to preserve
the human race, Fan Ye submits to the economic laws that reign supreme

in human relationships, even within the family, and is caught in the mercilessly self-motivating, self-determining cycle of cosmic life. Clearly, his mistreatment of his senile father becomes aggravated after he becomes the family breadwinner. The final scene of the novel can be plausibly interpreted as conveying the message that life prospers after ritualistic symbolic patricide. Rather than relying on the goodwill of its members—as Lu Xun seems to suggest—the collective life demands the replacement of the father by the son for its rejuvenation and preservation. Remarkably, these same overpowering constraints of natural law cause the excruciating existentialist agony in the characters of Wang's three early stories already discussed.

Keen awareness of the liminal quality of rationality seems to underpin Wang Wenxing's journey in pursuing religious faith. Wang converted to Catholicism in the mid-1980s. Around the same time, he delivered a captivatingly eloquent keynote speech, "Shi wei zhijizhe si" 士為知己者死 (A gentleman dies for those who recognize his value) at the 1986 conference "Religion and Literature," which also featured two other Christian writers, Graham Greene (who was too ill to attend, so a recorded speech was given) and Endo Shusaku 遠藤周作 (1923–1997).[18] In "A Gentleman Dies," Wang identifies a peculiar, much-celebrated type of self-sacrifice in traditional China: a gentleman of honor who magnanimously pays with his life for favors received from an aristocratic patron or other deserving acquaintances. In Wang's view, it is a quintessentially unique cultural phenomenon, categorically different from other modes of voluntary life-taking for lofty causes, including Christian martyrdom. The very incomprehensibility of the justifying motive to someone of a modern mindset is left at that, without further explanation—emphatically so, without the euphemistic (read: hypocritical) praise modern commentators habitually bestow on a bygone era's gentry-class code of honor. Wang's stoic abstention from value judgments underscores a rationalistic recognition of relativism in culturally specific human belief systems. At the same time, the act of suspension, although squarely an-

---

18. The conference was held at Fu Jen Catholic University in Taipei.

chored in rationality, generates a tension that is at once intellectually
provocative and aesthetically appealing.

This essay deserves special attention in that it routes us back to an
area of fruitful comparability between Wang Wenxing and Lu Xun. In
the latter's writings, we often encounter a similar, rationally braced,
tension-ridden suspension. "Nü diao" 女吊 (Female ghost incarnations;
1936), an enchanting piece of folk theater in which a blissful, matter-of-
course indiscrimination between the worlds of the living and the dead is
betrayed by the performer's costume details, serves as a good example.
Both writers are fully cognizant of the solid yet unexplainable faith of
people who inhabit the "nonmodern" world. The chasm between different life-worlds and meaning systems is thus at once made evident and,
in a certain sense, bridged.

This chasm features centrally in some of Wang Wenxing's and Lu
Xun's works that allude to traditional China, albeit for different purposes. In "A Gentleman Dies," Wang Wenxing projects a characteristically modernist question—one conceived within the frame of the modern
mind-set—onto the life-world of premodern China without preposter-
ously intruding into it. In a collection of stories published shortly before
his death, *Gushi xinbian* 故事新編 (Old stories retold; 1936), Lu Xun also
grafts a sociopolitical conundrum unique to his own time onto an imaginary world set in China's ancient past. His purposeful highlighting of
the chasm, however, is clearly meant to burst open the fiction of authoritative—though no less fabricated—historical representations and
the moralist messages they carry. Perhaps the most aesthetically capti-
vating pieces of this category are Wang Wenxing's "Mingyue ye" 明月
夜 (Nights of the shining moon; 2006) and Lu Xun's "Zhu jian" 鑄劍
(Forging sword; 1926). Despite the predictable differences in the apparent morals of these stories, both works feature, in a palimpsest style,
plots written over the erased traces of a traditional story of the *chuanqi*
傳奇 (records of the strange and miraculous) subgenre in an uncanny
manner. The effect goes beyond that of intertextual allusions, as the stories tamper with the unknown and unfathomable, predestination and
the enigmatic existence of a pre-inscribed blueprint—of the universe as
well as individual fate.

Conclusion

There is a broad consensus in Taiwan today that the works of Wang Wenxing have attained the status of contemporary classics, and Wang himself is a widely recognized master in the realm of literary art. The reception of his work has traveled a long way from the days when his first novel, *Family Catastrophe*, was blacklisted (in some form) by the government, and the first of the two volumes of *Backed Against the Sea* (vol. 1, 1981, and vol. 2, 1997) was decried as vulgar and offensive by readers of the *Zhongguo shibao* 中國時報 (China times) literary supplement, which serialized it. In 2009, Wang received Taiwan's prestigious National Award in the Arts, which was preceded in 2007 by an honorary doctorate from National Taiwan University, where he studied and taught for about four decades. Particularly noteworthy is the attention given to the artistic workings of Wang's two novels: a grant from the National Sciences Council supported the recording of Wang's reading of the texts in a soundproof laboratory, a project that took a whole year to complete; this was followed by an elegantly produced volume of the handwritten manuscripts of these novels in 2010. Admittedly, the nation's eager celebration of "world-class" artistic accomplishments by its citizens—with Wang referred to as a "national treasure"—can be interpreted in light of global soft-power competition. At the same time, the seemingly anachronistic legitimation of such classic modernist visions of art as the *les mots justes* principle; the conception of fiction as a self-sustaining, verbally re-created microcosm; the insistence on an allegorical interpretation of the meaning of life; and so on through showcasing Wang's lifelong dedication to putting them into practice invites serious deliberation on some thorny issues pertaining to the history of modern literature in Taiwan.

Typical of contemporary capitalist societies, modernist aesthetics perform various functions in Taiwan in the new millennium. Obviously, broad-based readership for Wang's fiction—especially his second novel, *Backed Against the Sea*, which demands cultivated high-brow taste—is practically inconceivable. Yet thanks to the media, Wang's awe-inspiring, quasi-religious devotion to perfecting the language of his fiction for nearly half a century appears to have assumed legendary status. The plot lines of his novels are usually conceived within a month, we are told, but since he can manage to write only thirty to seventy words a day, an entire novel takes decades to complete. At the same time, one can readily identify a number of artists whose vocational visions and creative practices in the past two decades embody a quintessentially modernist spirit one way or another, despite the visible decline of the modernist critical discourse in the same period. The following works of fiction undoubtedly belong to this category: Li Yongping's 李永平 *Haidongqing* 海東青 (Eagle from east of the sea, 1992), Guo Songfen's 郭松棻 *Jinye xingguang canlan* 今夜星光燦爛 (The stars are splendid tonight, 2002), Wu He's 舞鶴 *Luanmi* 亂迷 (Bewilderment, 2006), and Zhu Tianwen's 朱天文 *Wuyan* 巫言 (Witch talk; 2008). Insofar as three writers of this group have explicitly acknowledged influence or inspiration from Wang Wenxing, it is fair to suggest that Wang represents the prototype of a particular paradigm of literary modernism in contemporary Taiwan. Through a less direct lineage, modernist aesthetics are also the guiding principle for such internationally renowned auteur directors from Taiwan as Hou Hsiao-hsien (Hou Xiaoxian), Edward Yang, and in particular, Tsai Ming-liang (Cai Mingliang).[19]

What are the implications of the sustained potency of aesthetic modernism in the literary production of a non-Western society like Taiwan during a period when modernism is undergoing a sharp decline in its place of origin? How does this phenomenon speak to existing narratives

---

19. See my discussion in "Twentieth-Century Chinese Modernism, the Globalizing Modernity, and Three Auteur Directors of Taiwan New Cinema," in *Geo-Modernisms: Race, Modernism, Modernity*, edited by Laura Doyle and Laura Winkiel (Bloomington: Indiana University Press, 2005), 133–50. Distinctively modernistic traits were also dominant in other art forms, notably painting and sculpture and the Little Theatre movement, and the like, that served as the aesthetic foundation of their more recent evolution. However, this essay focuses on literature, albeit a redefined category with expanded boundaries, as the more appropriate form for tracing the authors' adoption of Enlightenment ideals and values.

about the histories of modern and modernist literature in different societies of East Asia?

That Lu Xun and Wang Wenxing have seldom been mentioned in the same category may be largely explained by the fact that the two adjacent historical periods in which they were active—Republican China and post-1949 Taiwan—were separated by a flagrant rupture, namely, the retreat of the government of the Republic of China from the mainland to Taiwan in 1949. This study's attempt to draw a genealogy across the dividing line of the mid-twentieth-century era transition, therefore, may be seen as an effort toward remapping the field of modern Chinese literary studies. Focusing my analysis on literary traits betraying an Enlightenment ethos, on the other hand, extends the category of modernism to encompass the region-wide cultural enterprise of a bygone era. I hope that, taken together, these approaches may help transcend the boundaries that have traditionally demarcated the terrain of East Asian literary studies.

2 Archetypes in Wang Wenxing's Early Fiction: Insecure Intellectuals and Dangerous Women

Ihor Pidhainy
University of West Georgia

WANG WENXING'S FAME as a writer is based to a great extent on his novels *Jia bian* 家變 (Family catastrophe) and *Bei hai de ren* 背海的人 (Backed against the sea), both of which are outstanding examples of modernism in Chinese literature.[1] However, his earlier

1. I use modernity in this essay as defined in the experimental literature of twentieth-century figures such as James Joyce, Virginia Woolf, William Faulkner, and other Western writers who established a new form of writing that eschewed traditional methods of narration and yielded a severe critique of contemporary society, seeing a falseness in the conventions and norms of that society, whether in economic, political, or sexual terms. Wang Wenxing is a self-described modernist. Chi Pang-Yuan (Qi Bangyuan) noted that this modernity is rooted in the "Chinese" experience, citing Wang's early comments that his stories "describe Chinese characters, move in a Chinese setting, develop Chinese themes. No man is named John, no woman Mary. They eat rice with chopsticks." From Wang's preface to *Modern Short Stories, An Anthology of Contemporary Chinese Literature: Taiwan, 1949–1974*, vol. 2, edited by Chi Pang-Yuan (Taipei: National Institute for Compilation and Translation, 1975), 3. For later discussion of *Backed Against the Sea* as a modernist work, see Sung-sheng Yvonne Chang, "Wang Wenxing's *Backed Against the Sea*, Parts I and II: The Meaning of Modernism in Taiwan's Contemporary Literature," *Writing Taiwan: A New Literary History*,

writings, although more traditional in narrative and sensibility, still make up an important part of his overall oeuvre.[2] Beginning to write fiction as a high school student, Wang published his first short story, "Shou ye" 守夜 (The lingering night), in 1958; it's about a young man who stays awake all night striving to produce a story and yet fails to write more than a couple of lines.[3] Wang continued to write short fiction through his days in college, his two-year stint in military service, and into his time in the creative writing program in the United States at Iowa in 1963–1965. These works span a mere seven years and show a writer developing his literary talents and creating a number of memorable stories that focus on the troubles of generally young, intelligent men beset by the questions of creativity, sexuality, and the meaning of existence. Wang's short stories have received critical but limited attention. Much of this has been analysis of themes in the stories and characters presented.[4] Less attention has been paid to the gender relations of the stories. However, the binary of strong, powerful female figures who dominate and (sometimes) destroy their wooers and the weak male protagonists of

eds. David Der-wei Wang and Carlos Rojas (Durham: Duke University Press, 2007) 156–80.

2. For a brief introduction to the collection *Shiwu pian xiaoshuo* 十五篇小說 (Fifteen stories), see Wang Jinmin 王晋民, *Taiwan Dangdai wenxue* 台湾当代文学 (Modern literature of Taiwan) (Nanning, 1986), 176–80. Also see Zheng Yayun 鄭雅云, "Tan Wang Wenxing zaoqi de *Shiwu pian xiaoshuo*" 談王文興早期的十五篇小說 (A discussion of Wang Wenxing's early collection *Fifteen Stories*), *Wentan* 文壇 (Literary world) 249 (1981): 61–69. Also see articles in volumes 1 and 2 of Huang Shu-ning 黃恕寧 and Kang Laixin 康來新, eds., *Wu xiuzhi de zhanzheng—Wang Wenxing zuopin zonglun* 無休止的戰爭—王文興作品綜論 (Endless war: general essays on Wang Wenxing) (Taipei: National Taiwan University Press, 2013).

3. Translations, unless otherwise stated, are drawn from Shu-ning Sciban and Fred Edwards, eds., *Endless War: Fiction and Essays by Wang Wen-hsing* (Ithaca, NY: Cornell East Asia Series, Cornell University, 2011).

4. Li Wenbin 李文彬 has borrowed E.M. Forster's notion of flat characters in discussing Wang's early stories. See his "'Longtian lou' zhong de xiangzheng jiqiao" 〈龍天樓〉中的象徵技巧 (The techniques of symbols in "Dragon inn"), *Zhonghua wenyi* 中華文藝 (Chinese literature and arts) 12.5 (1977): 88.

Wang's stories has generally gone unremarked.[5] The author himself,
though, has commented about the masculine nature of some of his early
stories.[6] The series of awkward males who usually occupy the protagonist position of the stories tend to set their sights (when they can) on
distant and generally unattainable women. The protagonists almost always fail in their attempts to achieve the experience that beckons and
find only bitterness and disappointment as their reward. The repressed
male intellectuals and the sexually vibrant but inaccessible women they
seek are tropes central to the author's understanding of the new, modern
world about him. With a few exceptions, the female characters in the
early stories are limited in their development—indeed, they are almost
exclusively represented in the male characters' words and observations.

The backdrop to Wang's fiction was a rigidly hierarchical world that
sat atop a complex mix of "traditional" and "modern" norms and values.
The state was governed by a one-party system where the KMT (*Guomin-
dang*), with its head, Chiang Kai-shek, ruled with a great deal of authority.[7] Many of the families in Taipei (where the stories are mostly
set) had come over from the mainland along with the KMT armies, as
had Wang's family, so the characters are generally from this group.

---

5. However, see Fred Edwards's comments in "Wang Wenxing in Translation" in this volume (Chapter 11).

6. In particular Wang referred to "Longtian lou" 龍天樓 (Dragon inn),
where he used *Shuihu zhuan* 水滸傳 (Water margin) as the basis of his charac-
terization in the story. Chen Wenfen 陳文芬, "Wang Wenxing: Kanjian Zhongguo nanxing de liliang" 王文興：看見中國男性的力量 (Wang Wenxing: Seeing
the strength of Chinese men), *Chengpin haodu* 誠品好讀 (Eslite Reader) 24
(2002.8): 6. For a careful analysis of this story, see Steven Riep, "A Case of Successful Failure: 'Dragon Inn' and Wang Wen-hsing's Critique of Official History
and Anticommunist Literature," *Selected Papers in Asian Studies*, New Series 67
(2001): 1–34.

7. The early stories generally do not directly address political matters. The
later novella "Dragon Inn," written in 1966, however, dealt with KMT officers
going into exile. More typical of the short stories was the satirical portrait of a
feeble government clerk who married his maid in "Yige gongwuyuan de jiehun"
一個公務員的結婚 (The marriage of a civil servant) or the social conflicts suggested in "Liang furen" 兩婦人 (Two women).

However, Taiwan had a native population and also an indigenous population.[8] Both native and indigenous characters appear in Wang's stories, but the various differences among the peoples are never overtly described. Protection of the state was paramount, and so control of the state from internal enemies and a strong military to protect against potential attack from communist China were maintained. This meant compulsory military service for all men.

The U.S. military was present in Taiwan throughout the years of these stories (and did not withdraw until 1979), and its presence was both protective and disruptive.[9] Lifestyles of the American military personnel had an influence on the population of Taipei.[10] This aspect can be noted in various social gatherings in Wang's fiction where the popular culture of music and mixed-sex dancing was prevalent. However, the men of Wang's generation were influenced by traditional Chinese values concerning courtship and relationships. This "Confucian" value system was more rigid and austere than the U.S. system, and this formed one of the social and cultural underpinnings for many Chinese. Indeed, modern Western and Japanese fiction served as a counterweight to traditional Chinese writing and thought. This tension is present but unstated in the stories.

The intellectually overwrought young male in Wang's fiction is often

---

8. "Native" here refers to Chinese who had come over to Taiwan before 1945, some as far back as the seventeenth century. "Indigenous" refers to the non-Chinese populations that are currently protected and encouraged to maintain their identity. They had been subject to various forms of discrimination from the earliest contact with the Chinese. See Emma Teng, *Taiwan's Imagined Geography: Chinese Colonial Travel Writings and Pictures, 1683–1895* (Cambridge, MA: Harvard University Asia Center, 2004), 101–48.

9. In addition to providing security against potential invasions from the mainland, the U.S. government provided aid and markets to Taiwan, with total aid coming to some $1.5 billion between 1951 and 1964. Jan Taylor, *The Generalissimo: Chiang Kai-shek and the Struggle for Modern China* (Cambridge, MA: Belknap Press, 2009), 484.

10. There were more than 10,000 U.S. soldiers on Taiwan by 1957, and along with them came "hospitals, PXs, moviehouses, bowling alleys, baseball fields." Taylor, *The Generalissimo*, 490.

a creative artist who is sensitive to the world around him and is tortured by questions of the heart. His desire to work on his art is a constant that keeps him aloof or distant from his peers, classmates, and social acquaintances. The art is almost always conceived of as fiction, though poetry and even academic work are occasionally alluded to. Love, particularly physical love, is the standard question that arises in several of the stories. Sometimes the protagonist desires a particular woman and is rebuffed in his attempt; sometimes there is a vague longing in a lonely world. However, this physical love is leavened by the desire for a true romantic love—the physical act itself is an ambiguous problem in the fiction. It is a reward for the stylish and trendy young bucks, easily bestowed by women who love them whole-heartedly. Wang's protagonists are almost always bookish, though, and often do not appeal to the female sex. Those who do experience some form of physical contact with women, however, are disgusted or disturbed by the experience. The protagonist is rarely consoled in this by family or friends. When families appear in the stories, there is a true disconnect and a generation gap. The relationship between son and father is distant, and that between mother and son verges on oedipal at times.[11] The protagonist in these stories is an individual who lurks solitarily in the world around him.

The female figures that are drawn in the fiction are those of the male's imagination and desire. These are not fully constructed characters by any means; rather, they serve as muses whom poets hunger after. Not being fully drawn, they tend to be distant from the protagonist and the narrator. Sometimes they appear in the stories, but frequently they remain off-stage, and we do not actually meet them. Female sexuality is constant in the stories but is usually a reflection of male desire. This reflected desire is almost always problematic because the protagonists are not the proper vehicles of its reception; rather, they watch at a distance.

---

11. Margaret Hillenbrand's discussion of the story "Mother" highlights the incest theme, where the mother and another woman, both *d'un certain age*, compete for the affection of the young boy. See *Literature, Modernity, and the Practice of Resistance: Japanese and Taiwanese Fiction, 1960–1990* (Leiden: Brill, 2007), 193–99, especially 194.

The women encompass a range of positions and ages: they are students, mothers, goddesses, and prostitutes, among others.

The other characters in these stories tend to be used to flesh out the narrative or give a somewhat different perspective of the events in question. These characters are used to confirm or test the problems the protagonist has, sometimes serving as antagonists. In some of the more complexly constructed stories, Wang alters this paradigm by redistributing parts of the prototype to a variety of characters. This makes for a much more complex set of characters.

The story "Xiawu" 下午 (Afternoon), written in 1959 when Wang was nineteen, is a remarkable study of domestic violence and gender power dynamics. That Wang plotted this through a ten-year-old female babysitter and her very young male charge underscores the hidden or obscured aspect of this dynamic. (Wang uses this technique later in "Heiyi" 黑衣 [The black gown], discussed below.) The story revolves around Ah Yin, the babysitter, and her frightening watch over Little Mao, her ward, who spends most of the story crying. One of the first incidents of violence is when she scolds the child for wetting himself: "You're going to die, you nasty little brat. Put on your clothes and stop crying!" (p. 63).[12] She refers to him as "a hateful little child." A little later, she is described dancing for the child:

> When she first looks at herself in the mirror, she's startled, but then an enchanted, intoxicated smile comes to her face and she whirls around in front of the mirror with one hand on her waist and the other raised above her head. ... Then she loses the gentle rhythm completely and shakes her arms wildly toward the sky, shouting madly at the top of her lungs, as if a miraculous light had appeared in the heavens. Now she throws her arms up at an angle and raises one foot like she wants to fly to heaven. She has forgotten the dance she learned in school and just dances and

---

12. All the quotations of Wang Wenxing's short stories are from *Endless War: Fiction and Essays by Wang Wen-hsing*, edited by Shu-ning Sciban and Fred Edwards (Ithaca, NY: Cornell East Asia Program, Cornell University, 2011).

sings the way she wants. She doesn't stop until she is exhausted and out of breath. When she stops, she spits on her palm and wipes some of the dust from a section of the mirror. This allows her to see her own face clearly. She is shocked. The hair that used to fall neatly down her back now is a big mess covering her face, and her pale white face is really scary. She can't stop herself form flinching back behind the dusty part. ... She turns around and calls Little Mao: "Woooo—here comes a ghost!"

(p. 67)

The reader must reconcile a ten-year-old child being described as moving in a trance like an ecstatic in a religious ceremony. Her transformation into a spirit is completed with her identification as a ghost. This startles Little Mao, and Ah Yin first tries comforting him and then, out of frustration, pushes him to the ground. Her relationship to him is then weighed in economic terms, where she offers to sell him first to the owl on the wall, then to the image of Jesus. Ah Yin plays hide and seek with Little Mao and proceeds to go into another transformation: "She laughs and speaks in a strange voice ... . 'Boo!' She suddenly appears in front of Little Mao with a loud shout, giving him a hell of a fright. She laughs uproariously. 'I scared you to death, ha ha ha ha. Let's do it again!'" (p. 71). The games become even more dangerous for the child until finally Ah Yin wraps Little Mao in a tiny blanket and suffocates him to death.

What surprises is not that the story ends in death, but that it is about a fearsome female agent who dominates a weak boy and destroys him (literally), and this resonates throughout Wang's early fiction. The later story "Haibin shengmu jie" 海濱聖母節 (The day of the sea goddess) features a distended version of Ah Yin as the Goddess Mazu and Little Mao as Sa Keluo, an indigenous, good-for-nothing layabout, who has made a promise to Mazu to perform the lion dance. The sexually charged aspect of the day is suggested through the prostitutes who come to pick up their catch and the dance that Sa Keluo performs, in some ways mimicking the dance of Ah Yin. The performance literally kills him, as he collapses and dies before the festival ends that day. In "Jian yue" 踐約 (Contract fulfilled), the Lin family consists of three children: the eldest son, who is in America; a middle son who lives in fear of the young girls his younger sister brings over; and the younger sister herself, who is a high school student. The younger sister reads *Lolita* and sneaks off with a girlfriend to a dance where they do the jitterbug, becoming entranced by the dance. The middle son is perhaps twenty-two and ends his days of frustration with a three-day binge, during which he gets a crew cut, spends a wad of cash, and returns home with an empty box of condoms; there is a strong indication that the money went to prostitutes. Females as the helpless sex is not a major theme in the stories. An exception is "Dafeng" 大風 (Strong wind), in which a thirteen-year-old prostitute is portrayed sympathetically (and prevented from committing suicide) by a pedicab driver and a policeman. Elsewhere, there is sympathy for the girl in "The Black Gown," which is discussed later.

Little Mao was a helpless little boy. Similarly in "Muqin" 母親 (Mother), a young teenager is seduced by an older woman. Part of the seduction involves a belittling of the young fellow:

> "Mao'er, Mao'er, Mao'er," [the older woman] suddenly begins to laugh, clear and melodious.   "Oh, why did your Mama name you Mao'er?   Do your ears really look like a cat's?"
>   His little ears redden.   His eyes look like an angry little tiger's.   He hates his mother. (p. 105)

Part of her seduction involves baring herself to him, dominating him with a vision of her nakedness. After the doffing and donning of clothing, "Miss Wu opens a box of chocolate candies and offers them to him" (p. 105). The narrator clearly indicates that the boy is dominated by an older mother figure who controls every movement to which he succumbs. In "Hanliu" 寒流 (Cold front), a boy, Huang Guohua, not yet thirteen, is dominated by drawings he makes of naked women. As a form of escape from lust (he is driven to concepts of purity involving abstention), he sleeps naked in cold weather, and as a result, "he coughed

violently. It felt as though a fire was burning in his throat and his whole
body was engulfed in flames. … Because of the cold, the crowing [of the
morning rooster] was especially intense" (p. 242).[13]

However, the helpless male trapped or destroyed by the stronger
woman is not limited by age. In an early story, "Yige gongwuyuan de
jiehun"一個公務員的結婚 (The marriage of a civil servant), a government official, Mr. Liu, has begun a relationship with a maid and at one
point is reduced to the state of being a child through a simile: "Mr. Liu
burst into tears, like a little boy" (p. 23). In "Canju" 殘菊 (Withered chrysanthemums), the unhappily married teacher, Guo Muxian, wishes on
the approach of his wife, "he could shrink so small that he could escape
her attention" (p. 32). Finally, in "Liang furen" 兩婦人 (Two women),
what initially appears to be the story of a loutish, lazy mainlander taking
advantage of his Taiwanese wife turns out to be her means to ensure
that she keeps her husband rather than his bringing the first wife (and
their children) over from Hong Kong. The narrator reports, "There even
[was] a rumor that it was [the wife] who intentionally engineered [her
husband's] corruption, that it was she who purposefully induced him
not to work" (p. 144). Thus it is suggested that she is the dominant figure
in the power dynamic. The infantilization of the male is a theme that
runs throughout these stories. Whether these men are self-deluded is
another question.

It might also be argued, before going on to the longer readings, that
these female characters are somewhat mysterious because they are
underdrawn and underrepresented in Wang's early fiction. The women
are distant because the narrators tend to be distant from interacting and
understanding "women." Women are a mystery because they are *not*
present in these stories. In "Bi" 痹 (Paralysis), an early story (1959) that
focuses on a dance that university students have arranged, Wang shows

---

13. Chen Yizhi 陳義芝 reads this within context of Sigmund Freud (sex as a
basic instinct) and Arthur Schopenhauer (as the will to live). See his "Jie xiangzheng de fangshi Wang Wenxing duan pian xiaoshuo renwu fenxi" 借象徵的方
式－王文興短篇小說人物分析 (The use of symbols—an analysis of characters in
Wang Wenxing's short stories) in Huang and Kang, eds., *Wu xiuzhi de zhanzhen*,
2:129.

insight into the young men and their "depraved" thoughts but little indication of the girls' thinking. In both "Wanju shouqiang" 玩具手槍 (The
toy revolver) and "Jieshu" 結束 (Conclusion), the girls who have rejected
the protagonists are not actually present. Mazu, too, is not present in
"The Day of the Sea Goddess," though she is, properly speaking, a deity.
Prostitutes (or sexually active women) are relegated to the shadows: in
"Zui kuaile de shi" 最快樂的事 (The happiest thing), the woman is not
seen or described; in "Dadi zhi ge" 大地之歌 (Song of the earth), the girl
is seen at a distance in the embrace of another young man; in "Contract
Fulfilled," the prostitute (?) who introduced the protagonist to sex is only
alluded to. Indeed, the temptress in "Cold Front" is merely an artistic
representation of a nude woman, an actual object to fetishize over. (The
young protagonist indeed creates a book of erotic drawings where he
repeats this fetishization.) Finally, in "Caoyuan di sheng xia" 草原底盛
夏 (Midsummer on the prairie), in a story that uses the author's experiences during his period of military service, there are no female characters at all, but a female presence is inserted through the imagery:

> The rain arrives. ... The rain, like a young girl, walks on lithe,
> delicate feet. The rain, he can see, wears gauzy white robes. From
> the west side of the prairie, she rushes forward like a lover. ...
> Now, he thinks, I shall give myself up to a newly arrived mistress.
> (p. 128)

> The trees on the hills look dense, damp and green in the purity of
> their grace, just like wise women. The trees are all the same
> height, arranged neatly without any distinction, full of a solemn,
> holy beauty. (pp. 128–29)

> The dark prairie is like a vast, soft bed. At the same time, it is also
> like a warm woman, her chest quietly rising and falling when she
> breathes. ...
>   Warm earth, loving earth, she is eternal. Without exception,
> whether beautiful or ugly, her bosom accepts all, embraces all. (p.
> 131)

Nature is feminine or female and speaks of a larger mystery that goes beyond the social elements displayed in many of the stories. These images conjure both the tradition of feminizing the landscape as well as female creativity in Daoism: "Nameless, it is the origin of the myriad things; named, it is the mother of the myriad things."[14] This, however, shows that the feminine can be disassociated from embodied characters, and allows the female to represent an abstract aspect of desire and male self-realization. Next I examine several stories to follow up on these themes.

"The Toy Revolver," written in 1960, tells of a young man, Hu Zhaosheng, who has been invited to his classmate Ma Rulin's birthday. At this party, which he attends out of commitment to social form, he has an encounter with a very popular classmate by the name of Zhong Xueyuan, who proceeds to play a game of Russian roulette with him until Hu embarrasses himself by admitting to a failed attempt at romance with Yang Yumei, a girl who rejected him soundly. Hu feels roundly humiliated by this trial before everyone's eyes, so he chooses his own moment to attempt to humiliate Zhong. Hu does so by making Zhong confess his own romantic history. However, it turns out that Zhong's romantic history involved success with none other than Yang Yumei, Hu's failed paramour. Hu, feeling absolutely shamed, leaves the party and returns home.

The young protagonist Hu fits the prototype suggested above. He is an academic who spends a good deal of his free time in reading and writing.[15] Physically, he is mocked for being short and not very manly (indeed, almost feminine).[16] Throughout the story, he repeatedly thinks

---

14. From the first part of the *Daodejing*, as translated in Richard John Lynn, *The Classic of the Way and Virtue: A New Translation of the Tao-te ching of Laozi as Interpreted by Wang Bi* (New York: Columbia University Press, 1999), 51.

15. Ye Ruxin 葉如新 reads this as a critique of intellectuals, *Taiwan zuojia xuanlun* 臺灣作家選論 (A discussion of selected Taiwan writers) (Hong Kong: Zhongliu chubanshe, 1981), 61.

16. Chen Yizhi notes that when Zhong Xueyuan greets Hu, he asks him why he looks so *qingxiu* 清秀 (which might be rendered "delicate and pretty"), a term almost exclusively used for girls, Huang and Kang, eds., *Wu xiuzhi de zhanzhen*, 4:129.

of returning home to read a newly received anthology of T.S. Eliot's poetry and how much time he will have lost because of this social adventure. His name can also playfully be read as one who recklessly seeks trouble and courts disaster.[17] The name of Hu's antagonist can also be read as one who esteems scholarship.[18] This is obviously the reverse of each character's personality. Nevertheless, Hu's attitude toward others at the party is for the most part condescending—they are of the great, unwashed masses who possess little understanding of the arts. They are easily amused, whether it be in a game of cards or playing with the toy revolver that belongs to Ma Rulin's young brother. Indeed, they are most amused by the show trial that Zhong Xueyuan conducts in regard to Hu's love life.

Hu's love life is fairly straightforward. He fell in love with a classmate and wrote a long letter expressing his love for her. She rejected it, forcing him to take it back, and, in no uncertain terms, made clear her displeasure and disgust toward him. This story is brought forth through the show trial and, once out, Hu broods over it. As an aside, the choice of T.S. Eliot as the author Hu desires to return to read is most appropriate. Eliot was the consummate poet of frustrated and aestheticized male intellectual love. His poem "The Love Song of J. Alfred Prufrock" is a similar tale of a young man in love with a woman who is not interested in him. Eliot intones:

> In the room the women come and go,
> talking of Michelangelo ...

> If one, settling a pillow by her head,
>   Should say: "That is not what I meant at all.
> That is not it, at all."[19]

---

17. That is, the name "Hu Zhaosheng" 胡昭生 reads as *huluan zhao huo sheng shi* 胡亂招禍生事 (recklessly seek trouble and court disaster).

18. Here we read *Zhong Xueyuan* 鍾學源 to mean *zhong ai xue shu yanjiu* or *yuanquan*, 鍾愛學術研究 or 源泉 ("to esteem learning" or "its source").

19. T.S. Eliot, "The Love Song of J. Alfred Prufrock," in *Selected Poems* (London: Faber and Faber, 1965), 11, 14.

The idea of love and aesthetics rushing through Prufrock's head is similar to that of Hu's desires, whereas the elder woman that Prufrock courts shares with Yang Yumei a disinterest in the poet's love. Yang is difficult to capture in this text—we get her through the two male characters, and the best that we can surmise is that she is a young woman who is attracted to the popular Zhong while running away from the bookish, awkward Hu. Of course, her name, which is quite common and translates as Jade Plum, also can be translated as "propagating ignorance."[20] This suits Hu's final view of her. Nevertheless, the story is not about her. She merely serves to connect the world of the intellectual aesthete and that of the popular Zhong.

The conversations that Hu overhears at the party are linked to sexuality. The miss-and-kiss aspect of the love triangle is only the surface aspect of this theme. The setting of the story conveys a strong sexual atmosphere. Situated in the coldest period of the year, the protagonist enters the warm hearth of his friend's parents' home. The color red is prominent in the house (the color of happiness, weddings, and love). The music that pounds in the background is rock and roll—in this case most likely referring to American rock of the late 1950s, such as Elvis Presley, Chuck Berry, and Jerry Lee Lewis. The sexuality of this music is hinted at in the way Hu's entrance and exit are framed within the sound of this music. Indeed, when Hu is being interrogated by Zhong, the raw sexuality of the audience is noted by the narrator:

They were laughing and shouting, shoving and pushing around him like a tribe of Africans performing some ritual dance for the gods. ... These savages had already killed their sacrificial offering and were going to eat him raw. They were ranting and raving so ecstatically. (p. 87)

This occurs about halfway through the story and links with the raucous music of the opening and closing. Hu, however, is explicitly shown to be

---

20. We take Yang Yumei 楊玉梅 as *Yang yumei* 揚愚昧 (propagating ignorance). This word play nicely corresponds to the bitterness that the intellectual protagonists show toward their unattainable muses.

outside this world. One example reveals just how asexual he is: while listening to a fairly excited conversation, Hu can't figure out what *kouzi* (口子) means. Although an expert in language (he is, after all, a writer), he remains baffled until it dawns on him: "broad" is slang for a woman. The author's coup de grâce is having Hu use this same term during his vengeful interrogation of Zhong. The result is not to Hu's liking!

Finally, the centerpiece of the story is the toy revolver. The phallic connotation of this object does not need belaboring. The use of a toy revolver belonging to a prepubescent boy connect it to undeveloped sexuality. It is also the innocent toy that both adults use in their forced interrogation. The more experienced and popular Zhong actually fires it off several times and forces an admission from Hu through his continued threatening use of this "toy." Hu, on the other hand, is unable to use this toy successfully. Having forced a confession from Zhong about kissing Yang Yumei (the broad), Hu throws down the gun and rushes out of this house of experience. For him, the revolver serves as a reminder of his lack of sexual experience and his humiliation at the hands of the alpha male Zhong. In a description reminiscent of "Afternoon," the narrator notes, "Hu Zhaosheng was submissively curled in Zhong Xueyuan's cm brace, like a child who tried to act cute by snuggling up to his mother" (p. 90). This underscores the childlike nature of the man and helps connect Hu to other typical protagonists.

Hu's failure, though, hides some other aspects of his character that are utterly lacking in charm. On being bested in the first show trial, Hu sulks. During this sulk, he reasons that Yang was the source of the gossip that reached Zhong, that everyone around him must be laughing at him, and that women are detestable. Hu's revenge is also revealing. His first attempt at vengeance involves mocking and tearing apart Zhong's specious comments about a popular film—it is a useless bit of vengeance that does not succeed. Hu's second try is in aping the more popular show-trial format that Zhong had earlier succeeded in using on him. His failure here, too, leaves him a very bitter and lonely man, so he runs off for the cold comfort of Eliot.

"Qianque" 欠缺 (Flaw) also deals with frustrated love, though in this case it is the story of "innocent" first love—puppy love. An eleven-year-old boy, who goes nameless, describes his first love for an older, married seamstress and businesswoman of about thirty-five (*d'un certain age*), who also goes nameless, his distant longing, and the eventual disappointment that he feels about her when she skips town with her family, having robbed numerous locals through a confidence game.[21]

There is a double game going on here: the narrator recollects his own love as a precocious child, while his intrusive commentary guides us in reading a story of lost innocence. The boy is a miniature version of the frustrated artist encountered earlier: different from other boys, he is acutely aware of his own fears of sexuality. The narrator stresses that the boy has "an instinctive fear of glamorous and sophisticated women" (p. 245). He adds that this has continued to the present day. The woman who is idealized is the natural, kind type: she is described as not wearing any sort of makeup and as having a kind, gentle face. The protagonist accepts his fate to love the woman deeply and without recompense.

The young boy is also a solitary figure. This is a state conveyed more through artistic manipulation than actual fact, for the narrator does mention his many friends and sports participation a number of times in the text. However, we never actually see or hear about any of the other boys—they are part of vague groups who are not described individually at all. References are made to two boys, one a neighborhood boy and the other the son of the amah, a part-time helper at the narrator's home. Neither of these boys are actually present when mentioned. Furthermore, the father is absent from the narrative. The only men who appear are the husband, son, and a possible suitor of the seamstress—and they have only very brief cameos.

Female characters actually are more richly represented in "Flaw" than are males. Here again the author manipulates the audience with the presentation of flat characters rather than fleshed-out ones. The seamstress appears a couple of times but is actually trumpeted throughout the narrative by the young boy in his recollection of his love—she is the great object—to be kept in mind but not seen or heard. Indeed, what we

---

21. The theme of lost innocence is explored by Zhuang Mingxuan 庄明萱 in Liu Denghan et al., eds., *Taiwan wenxue shi* 台湾文学史 (History of Taiwan literature) (Fuzhou: Haixia wenyi chubanshe, 1991–93), 2:218.

learn of her negative activities comes through the mouths of several women who describe how she duped the locals: she absconded one night with her pile of loot, leaving behind an angry group of cheated workers and customers.

The other two women in the story are the boy's mother, who appears at a number of points to either warn the boy of his shortcomings or complain about how the world is becoming more corrupt, and the amah, who serves as a counterpart to the seamstress. She is described as "that kind old woman ... [whose face was] the perfect blending of simple goodness and unpretentious love" (pp. 248–49). She is constantly praising the "young Master," as the narrator is known to her. The amah is a local native (she speaks Taiwanese, not Mandarin) who goes about barefoot year-round. The simplicity of this portrait points to questions of class and the division between those Chinese who had lived on Taiwan for a long time and the more recently arrived Chinese from the mainland. The amah shares with the seamstress certain traits: both are kind, good women, plain in their attire and outlook. However, whereas the seamstress only seems the part, the amah is the real deal. One notes, though, that both disappear from his life: the seamstress immediately absconds with his heart, while outside the immediate narrative, yet earlier in time than when the narrator speaks, the amah is also lost to him: society has become new, complex, and modern.[22]

Sexuality and rejection are important elements in this story. Although it is about puppy love and there is no danger of sex occurring as part of the actual plot, sexual imagery and suggestions of sex lurk within the story's confines. At first, the pastoral setting blinds the reader to this: the author makes clear this is a world far removed from modernity. It is his family's first home on Tong'an Street, two homes removed from the boy's later days and a place surrounded by the natural world—there is a riverbank, an empty meandering path, and an absence of cars. Yet the author immediately notes that spring, the season of love, is upon this world. Cats are sketched strolling lazily about, while flowers and plants

---

22. The issues of class and race play parts in Wang's writings. His sympathy toward those outside the mainstream is quietly noted.

are busily blooming. The boy realizes his love for the woman during spring vacation, which he notes was "right after the soft spring showers, in the blossom-filled month of April" (p. 245). Although he does not understand what love means—the narrator spells this out in his lack of clarity on the relationship of the seamstress and her husband—the imagery again points to sexual awakening: the boy describes his furious attempts to teach himself how to swim in the river, despite fears of drowning. He fails in this struggle (he stops trying to swim), but the connotations of this imagery are clearly sexual.

The rejection is also presented in this manner: the boy brings a piece of clothing to the seamstress's shop to have a button sewed on. The woman gives his clothing to one of her workers to deal with. However, we note: the shop is exclusively for women's clothing and by entering the shop the boy is trespassing into the world of women. The seamstress's rejection of the boy is displaced onto one of the girls who work there: a young girl is more appropriate for him as a lover than the much older woman. Finally, after retrieving the clothing, the boy flees just as his amah enters the shop, avoiding a confrontation of the two kind women in his life.

The story presents the boy's awakening to the corruption hidden within a flawless face. The older woman is physically perfect—yet she holds within her the flaw of not being who she seems to be. This last point complicates the author's earlier description of kind women versus sophisticated women. The young boy, no doubt, is on the path to discover the danger of not only this woman but that of all women and the difficulties of love.

The short story "Song of the Earth" provides the reader with another variant of the awkward male. The plot of this story is very simple: a young man is in a café reading a book when he spies a couple who, believing themselves to be hidden from sight in the corner of the café, are making out. The young man watches them surreptitiously until they conclude their activities and leave. Shortly thereafter, the young man exits.

The narration of the story is third-person omniscient, and it is at a great remove from the activity that occurs in the story. The opening places the Classical Music Teahouse discreetly off of Hengyang Road. The narrator notes that it is almost exclusively home to college kids, then he places the action of the story on a Thursday afternoon in October, when the place is virtually empty.

The recognizable frustrated male in this story is a nameless college student. He is reading a foreign novel when we encounter him. He is described as being an outsider, but he differs somewhat from the earlier models. He is described as strong and powerful with broad shoulders. He wears poor clothing, and he is from the countryside.[23] We learn that he has lost money playing cards and is writing his mother for additional money.

The two members of the couple bring together the distant female and the man with whom the protagonist cannot compete. Both are city-bred and so distinct and beyond the voyeur. The young man is stylish with a "ducktail" haircut that screams the easy modishness so typical of this sort of male. He is clearly confident in his dealings with the woman, receiving her full attention and adoration in return.

The woman is the most sexually enticing of the characters so far encountered. She is described as wearing a tight sweater from which her firm breasts press up and outward. She and her boyfriend embrace and kiss. He fondles her breasts, and though she slaps at his hand, they draw closer together until she appears on the verge of complete surrender. At this point, the two of them leave the teahouse.

The narration returns to the young man, who lingers in the café for a penultimate paragraph, but then heads out into the humid Taipei night in the ultimate paragraph. Feeling "a ferocious animal hunger," he goes in search of food, the story concluding with a mélange of yellow and red street lights (disguised as floating fruits). This ending picks up on the subtle play of color imagery throughout the story. The use of yellows and reds began as separate indicators of individuals: the young man twice was noted for his yellow khaki pants, and repeated references are made to the girl's red sweater. Her lover, though, was excluded from any

---

23. Here again Wang explores class issues. This young man could have stepped out of the amah's family in "Flaw."

bright colors—indeed, the symbolism here suggests a sexual linkage between the lonely man and the unattainable girl.[24] The imagery is master-
ful in suggesting a wished-for sexual encounter on the part of the man,
yet the distance between them is stressed in how they wear their clothing. The young man's "tight-fitting khaki pants" actually translates the
word to describe a child being tightly swaddled (*beng* 綳), whereas the
unattainable woman's sweater is merely close-fitting (*jin* 緊). This picks
up on the theme of the infantilized male—likewise, the young man's impotence in other areas is noted in brief at the start of the story: he is reli-
ant on his widowed mother for his pocket money, and he cannot manage
even that, once in his possession.

This story varies the formula by enhancing the bookish, frustrated
male with a tinge of class. He is divided from the promise of love and sex
because of poverty as much as his own aesthetic quality. However, the
question of sexuality is much more upfront in this story—this is no longer just a kiss but foreplay verging on the final frontier—or "the happiest
thing," as another story has it titled. Female sexuality does not frighten
the poor student, but his own connection to women is to his mother, an
intentional image of the child not yet cleaved from his mother. The emphasis on the manipulation of the woman's breasts by her boyfriend
would be paralleled by the student's connection to his mother's milk.
This is sublimated in the flow of money she provides for him instead.
This connection is not developed but can be suggested by the parallel-
isms the author enjoys employing between the pairings.

In "The Happiest Thing," Wang examines characters obliquely. This is
a story of a young man's extreme unhappiness and disappointment with
his first sexual experience: in his case, he commits suicide. The male
character is again an awkward intellectual male: he appears brooding
and bookish and expostulates on the horridness of sex in English. This is
again the world of J. Alfred Prufrock and discomfort with the world of
the body. The young man clearly sees this as an existential problem, for

---

24. The use of red is subtly brought in elsewhere in the story. The male protagonist is flushed in the café, while the girl also wears nail polish (which might
be red in color).

reflecting on the loathsomeness of sex and contrasting it with its supposedly being "the happiest joy," the narrator proves to himself the lack of any need to continue to exist and commits suicide.[25]

The woman is completely submerged in the sexual act. We learn nothing about who she is, what she looks like, or any other detail. Is she a prostitute with whom he is disgusted? Is she a young woman who has given herself to the man? The young man's rejection of the sexual act also is a complete rejection of the woman, as she is equated with sexuality. The misogyny that lurks within the minds of not a few of Wang's protagonists is present here as well. This misogyny finds its strongest expression in "The Black Gown."[26]

"The Black Gown" tells the story of a very handsome thirty-year-old man, Mr. Jin, who, wearing a traditional black costume, goes to a party and scares a young girl, Qiuqiu, half to death. The story has Mr. Jin arrive at a social event where he is seated with a host of people, including a woman and her little ward. Qiuqiu takes a dislike to Mr. Jin, who attempts to ingratiate himself into her good graces. She refuses to have anything to do with him. Mr. Jin becomes angry, drinks excessively, sulks, and then makes a most terrifying ugly face—demonlike, in fact—which scares the girl out of her wits. Qiuqiu screams her head off and is led off to bed. Mr. Jin excuses himself from the group and finishes the night by being most sociable with others at the party.

"The Black Gown" deals with the protagonist and narrator in a different manner than the earlier stories. Here a third party narrates the story, giving us a somewhat objective view of Mr. Jin and Qiuqiu. This stands us in good stead when we consider the earlier misogyny that was not quite at the surface.

---

25. Xu Junya 許俊雅 notes this is one of several contemporary Taiwan stories fixated with death and suicide. See *Taiwan wenxue lun—cong xiandai dao dangdai* 臺灣文學論—從現代到當代 (A discussion of Taiwan literature from modernity to contemporary) (Taipei: Nantian shuju, 1997), 229.

26. As early as 1969, Wu Dayun 吳達芸 had written about the macabre element to this story, see her "Wang Wenxing xiaoshuo zhong de zhuangshi jiqiao" 王文興小說中的裝飾技巧 (Wang Wenxing's techniques of depiction) in Huang and Kang, eds., *Wu xiuzhi de zhanzhen*, 2:101–2.

By the account of the narrator, Mr. Jin is quite a successful young man. He holds a good position at the university, publishes regularly on foreign topics, and is about to set off abroad. This is carefully contextualized by our narrator. His good position at the university is owed to his ability to flatter his superiors and gain promotion by working the system. His publications, which are many and well considered, are the work of basic plagiarism—Mr. Jin takes ideas and articles wholesale from Western sources and translates them into Chinese as his own. Interestingly, his expertise includes T.S. Eliot! The narrator's awareness of this situation speaks of truly informed views, in contrast to those held by society in general. The trip abroad is similarly a product of such hard work and cultivating the right person.

In addition to the phoniness of Mr. Jin's cultivation and knowledge, the narrator gives us insight into the man himself. He is outstandingly vain. He is quite the guest when he is patronized by those around him, but when the child does not do as her elders do, he immediately forms a plan of revenge.

Is Mr. Jin the same sort of hyper-intellectual as those we met in previous stories Wang wrote earlier? Or is he a variation of the good-looking, stylish man who gets what he wants because of his personality and not on account of any particular gifts? The answer to this is not clear-cut. Mr. Jin does share with earlier villainous types a certain self-love and ease of transport among his elders and superiors. He is also a notorious fake—he steals others' ideas and passes them off as his own. Yet he shares with the earlier protagonists a similar frustration at the hand of women (even if she is only a child) and possesses misogynistic leanings. He is also well enough educated to be able to read and steal material from other languages. In that, he is a variant on the protagonists of the earlier stories. One of the complications here is the narrator. He speaks with a quiet, objective authority on the matters involved. From the little we learn, we may surmise that the narrator is older than Mr. Jin, better informed about many of the matters he writes about, and a shrewd judge of his character. With this in mind, I suggest that the overaestheticized protagonist also finds a home in the narrator. The narrator's remove from the social world (he attends because of family connections) and his quiet, unobtrusive behavior recalls that of the Hu Zhaosheng in "The Toy Revolver." His knowledge is similar to the earlier protagonists, who were far removed from the limited concerns of society in general. However, he appears more mature and comfortable in his own skin. The question of sexuality is not important to the narrator—or there is no reason to believe it to be so.

The archetypal female that we have seen in earlier stories is present in the main female character, Qiuqiu. She is a mere child, though, and thus belongs to the world of innocence seen in other stories. Nevertheless, Qiuqiu shares with the earlier women an unattainable quality. She is an extremely good-looking child, and she disdains to show proper courtesy to Mr. Jin. Qiuqiu also cannot be wooed or won by Mr. Jin through gifts, such as a pen or a wristwatch. Indeed, this would be all very humorous, but Mr. Jin takes offense, drinks heavily while eating little, and finally exacts vengeance. This brings Hu Zhaosheng's earlier situation to mind. Mr. Jin, though, is exceedingly successful—Qiuqiu is reduced to howls and tears and needs to be taken off to bed by a maid.

The story has come full circle. Qiuqiu—the aloof female who rejects the poor male—is now defeated by that male through his talent (even if it is somewhat perverse). Mr. Jin's demonic transformation (and his symbolic black gown) speaks of the distance the character has to travel to exact vengeance against the aloof, unattainable woman.[27]

Wang Wenxing's early stories provide readers with a window on the question of the relationship between men and women in his fiction. The male characters are given the dominant role in the stories—it is their perspective, their outlook, their world-view that the reader is immersed in. The female characters are gazed on and viewed from a distance—indeed, sometimes they do not even exist beyond a name or a set of squig-

---

27. Critics have noted the struggle between good and evil as an important theme in this story. Wang Jinmin points out that Wang Wenxing himself suggested that Mr. Jin serves as an exemplar of evil whereas Qiuqiu is representative of good. See Wang Jinmin, *Taiwan Dangdai wenxue*, 179, referring to Wang Wenxing's preface to *Shiwu pian xiaoshuo*, 3.

gles in a notebook, but they conversely hold the power that determines life and death for several of the protagonists. The characters feed into archetypes: the pining lover, the athletic antagonist, the adored muse, the detested whore, and so on. Yet these archetypes are laced with psychological layers: the men are still boys, the women destroyers. The principal males are often of a type: overwrought intellectuals concerned with artistic and academic pursuits, desirous of a deep mysterious love that cannot be answered, and sometimes on the verge of a truly venomous loathing of the *hoi polloi*. However, they also are individualized, so that Hu Zhaosheng, Mr. Jin, and the boy of "Flaw" come alive, even without a name attached to the character. The women are less individualized. They are often flat characters. They are rarely portrayed in any great depth, yet they bring out a death wish among the men. Indeed, the lack of a woman's presence in a story does not mean that at some level the woman, as either destroyer or comforter, is not there. In "Cold Front" the doctor interprets the misguided boy's try at lengthening the lifeline on his hand as a suicide attempt over a failed love affair. Even when the story is not about the destructive element a woman wields, the author manages to slip in the misunderstanding that male love is part of a gender dynamic in which the woman holds all the power. Wang Wenxing makes use of these archetypal characters and often negotiates between them, undercutting the dominant perspective and suggesting alternative readings to the meaning of the stories. Whether the early fiction ought to be read as humanistic and spiritual or as a demonstration of the hideous and repulsive, it is important to recognize the dynamic of gender structures undergirding these perspectives.

3 Screwed by Fate? The Prostitute and the Critique of Liberalism in Backed Against the Sea

Darryl Sterk
University of Alberta

WANG WENXING'S *BEI hai de ren* 背海的人 (Backed against the sea[1]) deals with the personal and social danger of undisciplined desire in the context of a country undergoing capitalist modernization (both industrialization and urbanization). It deals with desire in terms of Buddhism and liberalism. This chapter argues that the novel represents liberalism as a more capacious container for desire than Buddhism, and it offers a not entirely negative sketch of the bourgeois family. Wang Wenxing critiqued the traditional Chinese family, and the family in general, in his first novel, *Jia bian* 家變 (Family catastrophe).[2] *Backed Against the Sea* shows the reader what fate might have in store for a vulnerable, dissolute person who is so worried about getting tied down (Wang 261) that he never forms a family on Taiwan.

---

1. The English translation of the novel was by Edward Gunn for the Cornell East Asia Series in 1993. In this article, I cite Gunn's translation of the first volume and Wang Wenxing's original, for instance, "Damn!" (Gunn 1; Wang 1). For the second volume, I supply my own translation. The page numbers for Wang Wenxing's original novel *Bei hai de ren* (Taipei: Hongfan shudian, 2013) are split between two volumes: vol. 1 (originally published in 1981) covers pp. 1–182 and vol. 2 (originally published in 1999) covers pp. 185–371.

2. This novel was translated by Susan Wan Dooling for University of Hawai'i Press in 1995. Wang's original novel *Jia bian* was published in 1973.

The main character Ye, or "Daddy," is a slave to his desire. When the novel opens, Daddy has fled a gambling debt in Taipei to a little fishing village called Deep Pit Harbor and set up a fortune-telling stand; whenever he has any money, he blows his wad at the brothels. The figure of the prostitute represents the dangerous object of desire Daddy finds impossible to resist. The first volume of *Backed Against the Sea* ends with four encounters with prostitutes (five counting a girl he remembers visiting in Taipei): a repulsive girl who repeatedly says "yuck," a girl who looks like the bodhisattva Guanyin, a teahouse girl who turns out to be in mourning, and a healthy, happy hooker. Yet the narrative order is different from the story (i.e., temporal) order.[3] Daddy uses his earnings from the fortune-telling stand on his fourth day in Deep Pit Harbor to visit the yuck girl and the teahouse girl on the fourth and fifth days, before a fellow named Zhang Fawu signs him up for a meal ticket at a government bureau called BOCDO (Gunn 71).[4] Daddy abstains from paid sexual services for two days, then visits the healthy, happy hooker and finally the girl who looks like Guanyin but turns out to be a dominatrix. The significance of the discrepancy between narrative order and story order is that Daddy's indulgence of his desire has left him unable to think straight.

If the first volume is the story of Daddy's satisfaction of his sexual desire, the second volume is about his inability to satisfy his longing for love. He falls hopelessly in love with an indifferent old whore named Red Hair. Rejected by her, Daddy remembers a girl in Taipei named Cai Suzhen, who fell hopelessly in love with him and even broke with her family to be with him. In return, Daddy tried to prostitute her to a gam-

---

3. See the tables compiled by Hengsyung Jeng and checked by Wang Wenxing, Chapter 8 in this volume.

4. BOCDO is an acronym for Bureau of Compilation, Research, Investigation, Editing, Filing, Classification, and Management of Materials on Regional Speech and Popular Local Customs During the Past Century, Deep Pit Harbor Branch Office. It is charged with researching local customs and dialects, but is "in fact a sanatorium" (Gunn 90; Wang 127), a place where the government sends mentally or physically ill personnel.

bling buddy. He wonders whether she ended up slipping into prostitution after he rejected her (Wang 268).

The second half of volume 2 details the desperation of a man who
cannot satisfy even the basic desire for food. Daddy manages to borrow
money from a Canadian Catholic missionary but gets passed over for an
official position at BOCDO. He spends an evening with a successful capitalist, Dong Yutang, who has disciplined his own desire and the desire of
everyone (both producers and consumers) in his rice ball empire, but
Daddy does not receive any assistance from him in return. In the end,
Daddy lets himself go completely: he tries to mug people and buy visits
to the brothel on credit, declaring that he wants to live like "an emperor"
(Wang 361), someone who can fulfill his every desire. Unsurprisingly
given the absence of police in the village, the locals exact vigilante justice: they break into the bathroom Daddy is living in, beat him to death,
and throw him into the ocean. This is the last thing he wanted to happen.

Almost three-tenths of the novel is taken up with Daddy's serial
whoring (Wang 153–82 and again on 361) and his attempt to love a
whore and pimp a girl who is in love with him (Wang 185–269). What
does it mean?

In a word, Daddy's problem is screwing—*cao* 操, the very first word
of the novel—for screwing is the principal form his desire takes. Through
wordplay, Wang links Daddy's screwing to his demise.[5] Daddy imagines

---

5. The term *cao* has several syntactic functions. It is an expletive, like "fuck!"
In this sense it is the first word in the novel. Gunn translates it as "Damn" (Gunn
1; Wang 1). It can be used intransitively, as in "I fuck" (Wang 1), which is weird
in English, hence Gunn's idiomatic translation "Fuck it" (Gunn 1). It can take an
object, as in "Fuck your mother!" (Wang 1), "Fuck your mother's cunt!" (Wang
1), or: "Fuck this endless fuckin' rain … . Oh, fuck the hills, the gray ocean, the
sky; fuck the sunless days of plopping rain, and pitch-black nights, and this
whole place, this whole earth, the entire human race and every society in it,
every culture, system, economic structure, and money—right, fuck the money,
and every one of those rich people, and everyone in the past, everyone in the
future, fuck all my ancestors and all my descendants, and, oh, fuck me!" (Gunn
1–2; Wang 1–2). "Fuck … all my descendants" turns out to be ironic because
Daddy never has children. Semantically, Gunn's "damn" is a religious impreca-

it may be possible to "screw fate," while in the end he seems to get screwed by fate.[6] A more critical reader perceives that it is only because Daddy tries to screw everyone like a punter screws a prostitute that he ends up screwed mostly (though not of course entirely) by himself.

Ending in the death of the protagonist, which is foreshadowed from the beginning, the novel seems a typical tragedy, affirming the power of fate over human life.[7] But of course, it is only Daddy's tragedy, not the reader's. The reader's fate, after all, is undecided. In the character of Daddy, Wang Wenxing offers the reader an object lesson in the dangers of desire, showing how damaging desire can be, and not just to Daddy. The desire of men like Daddy has drawn women from around the island of Taiwan into prostitution. But the novel does not stop at showing how damaging desire is for both self and society, it also hints at provisional

---

tion, whereas *cao* is explicitly sexual. *Cao* implies manipulation, similar to the English "screw." At a public talk Wang Wenxing gave on *Backed Against the Sea*, he asked a young woman to read a passage containing the phrase "screw your mother." The young woman, consciously or not, just skipped over: the word *cao* remains viscerally powerful in Mandarin today. Wang's use of the word in his novel is realistic, because veterans of the Chinese civil war used to "drop the c-bomb." It also allows Wang to immediately establish Daddy's attitude toward the world.

6. Christopher Lupke has drawn attention to the phrase "screw fate" (Gunn 53) in his "Divi-Nation: Modern Literary Representations of the Chinese Imagined Community," in *The Magnitude of Ming* (University of Hawai'i Press, 2005), 311, in reference to Wang 74.

7. Wang Wenxing foreshadows Daddy's tragic fate with leitmotifs such as dog-killing, drowning, and circling birds of prey. As Yvonne Chang puts it, Daddy is "a prey of fate" ("The Meaning of Modernism," in *Writing Taiwan: A New Literary History*, edited by David Der-Wei Wang and Carlos Rojas [Durham, NC: Duke University Press, 2007], 174). Seeing that "tragedy" is etymologically "goat song" (*tragos* "goat" + *oide* "song"), we might call *Backed Against the Sea* a "dog song." In one interpretation of tragedy, a bearer of sins, a scapegoat, is ousted from the community to assert the integrity of community identity (see Adrian Poole, *Tragedy: A Very Short Introduction* [Oxford: Oxford University Press, 2005], 51–55). Daddy is a scapedog. Yvonne Chang interprets his tragic end in terms of ethnic politics: Daddy, a mainlander, is murdered by local people, in whose homeland he is an interloper ("The Meaning of Modernism," 174).

solutions to the problem of desire, ways to bring it under control and channel it. The novel offers two philosophical contexts for desire: Buddhism and liberalism.[8] The central claim in this article is that a Buddhist interpretation of the novel is contained within a liberal one. I argue that the family is a liberal institution, and in *Backed Against the Sea* the variable that decides survival for veterans of the Chinese civil war like Daddy is not whether they have mastered Buddhist philosophy but whether they have managed to rein in desire by forming a family in Taiwan. I consider an objection to the argument that the novel represents the family in a positive light, namely, that Wang Wenxing parodies the literary forms that typically serve as vehicles for the virtue of liberal sympathy, particularly the love story and the sob story. In response, I note that Daddy participates in the parody, and for a fallible narrator such as Daddy to parody a literary form does not undermine its central value. In other words, a parody of a love story is not in itself a denial of love, though it certainly problematizes "love." Finally, I argue that the character Fu Shaokang embodies the bourgeois ideal in the novel.

Daddy as Buddhist

Daddy attempts a Buddhist solution to the problem of desire. After he visits the first prostitute, he takes a vow of abstinence. Six days later, he "[breaks] the vow of abstinence" (Gunn 115; Wang 163). Literally, he "breaks sexual discipline." "Discipline" here is the Buddhist term *jie* 戒.[9]

---

8. In this chapter, artistic creation as a solution to the problem of desire receives short shrift. The obvious theory to invoke would be Sigmund Freud's sublimation, where desire is sublimated into art (in some sense in the way that a solid sublimates into a gas). Freud is mentioned in Daddy's monologue (Gunn 114; Wang 162); perhaps Daddy has even heard of the theory of sublimation. Daddy's own theory is that composing poetry is like "sexual desire" (Gunn 68; Wang 98). He also says that love should be a work of art (Wang 269). In any form of art—be it the art of poetry, sex, or love—one exercises freedom while imposing restraint. A truly free work of art would not be a work of art at all: it would be formless.

9. In a kind of cultural translation, Daddy generalizes the Buddhist term by

In breaking discipline, Daddy returns to the brothels and spends all of
his money. The need for discipline comes up again in the second volume—in the context of smoking this time—(Wang 289)—by which time it
is too late: the vigilantes are already waiting outside the bathroom door.
After visiting the first prostitute (in the first volume), Daddy says he is
filled with "this overwhelming sense of regret" (Gunn 114; Wang 162)
about spending so much money on an activity that brings him no lasting
satisfaction. Yet when it comes to desire, Daddy has no self-discipline.
Desire, of course, is a key term in Buddhist philosophy: according to the
Buddha, desire is the cause of suffering. As Daddy puts it, the "**pursuit
of pleasure**" is actually a "search for suffering" (Gunn 115; Wang 163).
He also realizes that desire is, as the Buddhists say, empty: it is not that
one has a certain amount of sexual desire that is depleted with satisfaction, but that satisfying desire increases desire.[10] Insofar as *Backed
Against the Sea* offers a Buddhist treatment of desire, it resembles traditional Chinese "cautionary tales of overconsumption and lack of self-
control"[11] like the *Jin Ping Mei* 金瓶梅 (The golden lotus), in which sexual desire is deadly.

There is another, deeper level of Buddhist philosophy in *Backed
Against the Sea*. Daddy quotes the *Platform Sutra*:

Bodhi originally has no tree
The mirror also has no stand
From the beginning not a thing is
Where is there room for dust? (Gunn 65)

In other words, all "things" are illusory. We only desire certain things
because we do not realize we are not separate from them, that there is
ultimately no distinction between self and other, between subject and
object of desire. To use the idealist imagery of the *Platform Sutra*, there

applying it to the Catholic priest who, Daddy is shocked to learn, has taken a
vow abstaining from the pleasures of female flesh (Wang 321–22).
    10. Daddy's formula for this insight is 1 − 1 = 2 (Gunn 119; Wang 169).
    11. Martin Huang, *Desire and Fictional Narration in Late Imperial China*
(Cambridge, MA: Harvard University Press, 2001), 110.

is ultimately no distinction between mind as mirror of the world and the world itself. The mind perceives things in the world, not realizing they are all in the mind. This is part of the significance of the parable Daddy cites to explain his own whoring. In the parable, an ignorant fellow sees the moon in a pool of smelly water and jumps into it in the hope of becoming one with the moon. He does this over and over again, knowing full well it is not the real moon (Gunn 114; Wang 162). In Buddhist terms, he is wrong not because he jumps at a reflection of the moon instead of the real thing but because he jumps at all.

A Buddhist interpretation of the novel finds extratextual support. After a talk in July 2014, Wang Wenxing described Daddy as a "crazy monk," explaining that Daddy is modeled on the crazy monks of Chinese tradition. One thinks of the crazy monks in *The Dream of the Red Chamber*, and of Jia Baoyu leaving the human realm to join them at the end of the novel. Daddy ends up backed against the sea instead of deliberately turning his back on the social order: in the end, he fails as a crazy monk in that he is unable to truly let himself go in the Buddhist sense (i.e., he never manages to let his self go).

There is a place for Buddhist discipline and philosophy in an interpretation of *Backed Against the Sea*. Daddy's insights into the nature of desire might inform a theory of consumer psychology: he suffers from a serious case of buyer's remorse after repeatedly handing over money for a service he does not really need. However, I argue that a Buddhist interpretation of the problem of desire has to be embedded within a liberal interpretation, and in Fu Shaokang the novel represents a transcendence (or sublimation) of desire in the liberal institution of the bourgeois family.

Daddy as Liberal

Classical liberalism is a commitment to the greatest possible individual freedom in the personal, social, political, and economic spheres.[12] Eco-

---

12. For this four-part analysis of society, see Jean Bethke Elshtain, *Public Man, Private Woman*, 2nd ed. (Princeton, NJ: Princeton University Press, 1993).

nomic liberalism declares the greed of small producers to be good. We expect our dinner "not from the benevolence of the butcher, the brewer, or the baker ... but from their regard to their own interest."[13] According to Adam Smith, rational self-interest was socially beneficial. However, Smith, like the Buddha, realized that desire is a strange thing, for some desires are unlimited: "The desire of food is limited in every man by the narrow capacity of the human stomach; but the desire of the conveniencies [sic] and ornaments of building, dress, equipage, and household furniture, seems to have no limit or certain boundary."[14] This is a problem because our means are limited. The liberal solution is that the satisfaction of the desire for conveniences via the market is a means, not an end. One possible end of life from a liberal perspective is a convenient—that is, comfortable—family life. Seventeen years before publishing *The Wealth of Nations*, Smith published *The Theory of Moral Sentiments* about the virtue that animates family life: sympathy. Smith writes of the "pleasure" of a visit to a family "where freedom and fondness, mutual raillery and mutual kindness, show that no opposition of interest divides" the family members.[15] "Kindness" in this passage is a synonym for sympathy; sympathy, not self-interest, was the logic of the family. The family was theoretically separate from the market, as a place of consumption rather than production or exchange.[16] Moreover, the virtue of sympathy, cultivated at home, in theory would humanize the market, based on the Enlightenment-era idea that human beings should not be bought and

13. Adam Smith, *The Wealth of Nations: Books I–III* (1776; rpt. New York: Penguin Classics, 1982), 41.

14. Ibid., 269. Economists discuss the nature of desire in terms of the elasticity of demand. The demand for food is highly inelastic, because although we can't eat an infinite amount of food, we do need to eat and would pay any price if we were starving; the demand for sex and conveniences is by contrast relatively elastic because we don't really need them.

15. *The Theory of Moral Sentiments* (1759; rpt. New York: Penguin Classics, 2010), 35.

16. See, for instance, Jürgen Habermas, *The Structural Transformation of the Public Sphere: An Inquiry into a Category of Bourgeois Society* (Cambridge, MA: MIT Press, 1991), 43–50.

sold like commodities, as they still were in Taiwan in 1962, the year in which *Backed Against the Sea* is set. The persistence of human trafficking, which requires a total abnegation of sympathy for strangers, is a reminder of the practical problems of liberalism. The persistence of gross flaws—from a liberal perspective—in individuals requires social institutions like the family and the state, charged with such functions as justice and education. The acceptance of the need for such institutions distinguishes liberalism from individualism, libertarianism, or anarchism. Social institutions, of course, are themselves flawed, deserving of critique—which is where a writer like Wang Wenxing comes in—but amenable to improvement.

In *Modernism and the Nativist Resistance*, Yvonne Chang describes liberalism as the basic intellectual stance of Taiwan's modernist writers. She notes the irony of the fact that while many European modernists were antirationalists, nationalists, even fascists, or, at the opposite extreme, radical leftists, Taiwan's modernists were liberals. European modernist writers criticized modernity; Taiwan's modernists embraced it (p. 23 *et passim*). Taiwan's modernists subscribed to Matthew Arnold's "positivist vision" of culture as the Good Thing that would save society from anarchy.[17] In the early 1960s, Taiwan's liberal modernist writers were college students eager to assert artistic autonomy under martial law. Their artistic autonomy had a political edge. They "preceded the socialistically inclined Nativists in challenging the ideological constraints of the hegemonic culture in Taiwan's post-1949 era."[18] But in the 1970s, after the rise of literary nativism, the liberal modernists were more supportive of the Chinese Nationalist regime's project of modernization. Chang notes that in a speech in 1978, at the height of the nativist literary debate, while Wang Wenxing was in the midst of writing the first volume of *Backed Against the Sea*, Wang even defended capitalism.[19]

17. Yvonne Chang, *Modernism and the Nativist Resistance* (Durham, NC: Duke University Press, 1993), 9.

18. Ibid., 185.

19. Ibid., 20. Wang still affirms "economic liberalism" today, or at least he said so when I asked him in July 2014.

Still, to judge from his fiction, Wang is hardly starry-eyed about the liberal project. His liberalism is pessimistic, in the style of Lionel Trilling, for whom liberalism was "a political position which affirmed the value of individual existence in all its variousness, complexity, and difficulty."[20]

Backed Against the Sea has not been discussed in terms of Wang's liberalism. Chang describes Wang as a liberal but does not invoke liberalism in any of her discussions of *Backed Against the Sea*. She has instead approached the novel in terms of Wang's humanism, his rationalism, and his modernism.[21] To be sure, she is dealing with similar issues, as liberals are humanists, rationalists, and sometimes even literary modernists.[22] These terms do occur in *Backed Against the Sea*, making them "emic" terms, text-internal terms, and thus easily justifiable approaches.[23] First, Daddy claims to be a "humanitarian" (Gunn 122; Wang 173) by screwing tea girls properly so that they get something out of the experience. Second, he claims his decision to take a half-day holiday has to do with the "modern employment system" (Wang 331). Third, Daddy realizes that in ascribing significance to the lifeline on his palm, he runs "contrary to reason" (Gunn 36; Wang 50).[24] By contrast, the term *ziyou* appears *et passim*.

Ziyou 自由, the liberal part of liberalism *ziyou zhuyi* 自由主義, is a key word in *Backed Against the Sea*. In traditional Chinese, *ziyou* was a reflexive pronoun *zi* 自 and a verb *you* 由, to self-follow. In modern Chinese, *ziyou* is a compound word used to translate either liberty or freedom. It actually translates as either free-dom or free, because *ziyou* is

---

20. Lionel Trilling, *The Liberal Imagination: Essays on Literature and Society* (New York: Scribner's, 1976), viii.

21. "The Meaning of Modernism," 175.

22. There were liberal modernists, namely, E.M. Forster, who became for Trilling the prototypical liberal.

23. In anthropological research, an emic term is a culture-internal term, whereas an etic term is a concept the anthropologist brings to a culture he or she is studying.

24. Clearly, Daddy references these newfangled Western notions facetiously, but the reader can use them to think about Daddy's situation and the kind of society he lives in.

both a noun and an adjective. One might simply interpret *ziyou* in terms of freedom and fate. One of Daddy's questions for the Canadian Catholic priest is whether individuals are really free: "We people, is everything about us, in the end, **Heaven's Dispensation** , or , is there, individual , **free dom** ?" (Wang 319). The context is religious; there is no need to invoke liberalism.[25] As a reader of the Chinese original, I could not help associating *ziyou* and *ziyou zhuyi*, freedom and liberalism, especially since there are also copious references to the personal, social, political, and economic philosophy of liberalism, which the ideal of freedom has inspired.

Clearly interested in key liberal tenets, Daddy wrangles with them in the classic liberal manner, in which the individual reflects on the practical complexities of his or her ideals. He mentions the "freedom of speech" (Gunn 30; Wang 41), the freedom of occupation (he refers to his fortune-telling as a "**free occupation**" [Gunn 37; Wang 51]), religious freedom (in Daddy's words, "'spiritual' freedom" [Gunn 30]), and the "**freedom** of the **individual**" (Gunn 70). Daddy asserts that food and sex, the basic needs of life according to the traditional formula *yinshi nannü*, are basic rights in terms of Western-style liberal democracy: "Food and sex are the most genuine and straightforward pursuits of happiness in terms of democratic principles of '**People's Civil Rights**'" (Gunn 14; Wang 18).[26] Here Edward Gunn has overtranslated *minzhu* (democracy) into "demo-

25. The relationship between Christianity and liberalism is complex but has to be alluded to because of Wang Wenxing's conversion to Catholicism in 1986, while he was still writing the second volume of *Backed Against the Sea*. Liberalism inherits the notion of freedom from "free will"; in liberalism, the individual is free to act in his or her own self-interest, whereas in Christianity he or she is free to sin, for otherwise nobody could be held accountable. Liberalism seems to turn the Christian doctrine of freedom on its head, except that, as I have emphasized, liberalism also inherits the Christian virtue of sympathetic love, which is supposed to humanize the market. There are many examples of Christian liberals, such as Matthew Arnold.

26. The challenging style of *Backed Against the Sea*, which tests the limits of the writer's freedom and the reader's tolerance, has been discussed by Edward Gunn in "The Process of Wang Wen-hsing's Art," *Modern Chinese Literature* 1.1 (1984): 29–41.

cratic principles of 'People's Civil Rights,'" and even added the pursuit
of happiness from the U.S. Declaration of Independence. This is not to
say Gunn has gone against the spirit of the original, for in this same section Wang Wenxing is reminding the reader of U.S. hegemony. Daddy
goes on to tell us what U.S. liberalism means in practice. The main freedom is the freedom to consume: it is, Daddy says, "as if they live their
entire lives solely just to get these [modern conveniences]" (Gunn 23;
Wang 30), not because conveniences make life more convenient, but as
a form of "status-seeking" (Gunn 31; Wang 41). Daddy initially claims
that he transcends U.S.-style consumerism, but then realizes he wants
the same thing as the North Americans. He finds a "contradiction"
(Gunn 23; Wang 31) in himself between infinite desire (for Adam Smith's
conveniences) and finite resources. He describes his insight as follows:
"freedom actually amounts to an even greater 'bondage'" (Gunn 31;
Wang 41). A liberal would add: freedom is bondage only if one is unable
to properly use one's freedom.

This is not to say that Daddy has anything like a coherent philosophy, let alone that his philosophy is liberalism. He contemplates Buddhism, as explained already, and conservatism (Wang 214), and the
Nietszchean will to power. He even brings *Thus Spoke Zarathustra* with
him to Deep Pit Harbor (Gunn 22; Wang 29). As a philosopher, he is intellectually catholic. He invokes liberal concepts facetiously. For instance, he disparages the freedom of speech which Wang Wenxing is
implicitly exercising or asserting in publishing *Backed Against the Sea*.
Daddy has no deep understanding of liberal concepts. He has little structural understanding of society. For instance, he sees no need for the police. One of the reasons he is so happy to have his freedom in Deep Pit
Harbor is because there aren't any "cops" there (Gunn 12; Wang 16).
Police are clearly necessary because of people like Daddy, who disrespect the freedom of others: He says, "I can do *whatever* I feel like doing,"
including swindling and even mugging people (Gunn 30; Wang 40–41).
Daddy completely misses the idea in liberalism of responsibilities that
balance rights. He does not state a central claim of economic liberalism,
namely, that self-interest in the economic sphere will lift all boats, so to
speak. He has no sense of participation in an organic economy, where he

provides services to others and receives services in return, to everyone's benefit. His brief stint as a fortune-teller aside, Daddy is lumpenproletariat, without capital and outside of production. As such, he has not succeeded in harnessing his desire for any personal or social purpose. Instead, he indulges his desire, which in *Backed Against the Sea* is symbolized by the figure of the prostitute.

Daddy as Punter

Since the nineteenth century, there have been broadly speaking two ideological representations of prostitution: Marxist and liberal. In Marxist literature, the prostitute is a figure of exploited labor under capitalism. Under capitalism, prostitution becomes "industrialized," with standardization of service and fee.[27] The pimp would be the capitalist or industrialist, the prostitute the means of production. A major liberal prostitution narrative was the story about the hooker with the heart of gold and her paramour. Such stories dealt with the liberal separation between market and family. Men fell in love with courtesans, and either followed through on their true emotions, turning the whore into a wife by bringing her into the home, or turned their backs on love, choosing bourgeois respectability instead.[28]

Backed Against the Sea draws on both narratives to investigate the two sides of the coin of the problem of desire—the social and the individual. As Taiwan modernizes and urbanizes, young women from around the country are sold into fleshly bondage in big cities like Taipei. Daddy notes, "Women with any sex appeal at all are packed up and shipped off to Taipei, the whole lot of them sold off to Taipei" (Gunn 12; Wang 15).

---

27. Khalid Kishtainy, *The Prostitute in Progressive Literature* (London: Allison and Busby, 1982), 61.

28. Pierre L. Horn and Mary Beth Pringle accuse male writers who write about prostitutes of instilling their stories with "patriarchal values." (*The Image of the Prostitute in Modern Literature* [New York: Fredrick Ungar, 1984], 2). This accusation is unfair if leveled at critical writers. Wang Wenxing has not instilled *Backed Against the Sea* with patriarchal values, even if Daddy is a male sexist pig.

Chang quotes this passage and writes of the "blood" of the countryside "being sucked by the unremitting process of urban expansion."[29] Daddy is indifferent to the process or his part in it, but we can assume an ironic distance between what he says and what the author or the text means. At any rate, Daddy hints at a macroeconomic perspective on desire, the perspective of a political economist. A related perspective on the desire targeted by prostitution is governmental. Foxy the Vamp, a prostitute who visits BOCDO, brings out this response more clearly than anyone in the novel. Tang Lin, one of the officials at BOCDO, is "like some well-to-do pillar of the community about to leap upon her" (Gunn 79; Wang 112). The director worries in this regard that "**public   morality is   declining   daily**" (Gunn 82; Wang 116). Prostitution is a threat to the community. Prostitution in the novel is also an issue of public space. Daddy remarks on the names of the teahouses and the brothels: "House of Spring Fragrance, Garden of Spring Delights, Little Miss Peach, ... Rainbows" (Gunn 14; Wang 18). These advertisements are designed to pique and profit from desire by false representation, meaning that prostitution is also a personal issue.

Prostitution is a problem for the individual in *Backed Against the Sea*. Daddy himself is concerned about diseases spread by prostitutes and takes notice of ads placed in the newspapers by quacks promising to cure such maladies (Gunn 113; Wang 161).[30] But the thought of a visit to the brothel proves irresistible, because it is an easy way to exercise what Daddy calls the "**freedom of pleasure**" (Gunn 30; Wang 40), consisting of "casual sex, wild, crazy sex, sex, sex, sex" (Gunn 30; Wang 40), enjoyed by "human boomerangs[31] beyond the force of gravity up in outer space,[32]

---

29. "The Meaning of Modernism," 163.

30. Prostitution is also a public health issue, but the novel does not take the perspective of a public health official.

31. Gunn's image of the boomerang goes against the idea of transcendence of gravity, because a boomerang returns to where it is thrown. There is no boomerang in the original.

32. Chang argues that the year in which the novel was set, 1962, is significant because it was at the beginning of Taiwan's economic modernization ("The Meaning of Modernism," 163), but it may also be significant because of the be-

with nothing to hold them back or tell them which way is up or down, enjoying a freedom that truly deserves to be called 'freedom'" (Gunn 30; Wang 40). Daddy knows this is impossible, however attractive the idea of infinite decadence might seem. He knows that a person's freedom of pleasure must sometimes be restricted for his own good. Should someone with consumption ever be allowed to gamble and go whoring? "Absolutely not! He shouldn't!" (Gunn 93; Wang 132), answers Daddy, obviously not considering himself to belong to the category of people with consumption, that is, people whose personal freedom ought to be restricted.

Daddy does not restrict his own freedom, with calamitous effects. As noted already, his vow of Buddhist discipline fails him, as does his aesthetic revulsion from what he is doing—which he tries to cultivate in himself with the parable of the guy who keeps jumping in a pool of smelly water—and he ends up visiting the brothels and teahouses a second time. Daddy's series of visits to brothels and teahouses illustrates the danger of the industrialization of desire for the undisciplined individual. There is a mass-produced seriality to these episodes, reflected in the form of the novel, one erotic experience after another. From the capitalist's point of view, this seriality is the ideal form of consumer behavior: capitalists want consumers to keep consuming, over and over again, in a compulsively regular or even regulated fashion. Daddy has a certain number of minutes to spend with the girl. He can only come once. He tries to bargain with her for a second time for 40 percent off (Gunn 113; Wang 160), but the market price is already fixed, supposedly by the market mechanism (but in practice partly by consensus).[33] Each experience he has in the brothel is different, but to Daddy it seems he is purchasing a single commodity: "I know perfectly well that every broad is actually

ginning of manned space flight, which supplies Daddy with his imagery in the passage above. The day of Daddy's death, February 20, 1962, was the first day a human being orbited the Earth in space.

33. An example of a consensus that interferes with the supposedly free operation of the market mechanism is that no prostitute will kiss Daddy (Gunn 110; Wang 156). Ideally you could bargain for this or there would be a specific price for the service. In reality, some practices are not "marketed."

alike, just the same" (Gunn 114; Wang 162). Power enters into what is supposed to be an economic exchange. The Guanyin prostitute is a dominatrix, and Daddy forces the girl in mourning to satisfy him by using her hand on him. Daddy is also abusive toward the girl in the teahouse in Taipei: "I viciously drove home my assault on her" (Gunn 121; Wang 171), he says. One prostitute sells Daddy the experience of abjection, another illusion of power.

At the same time, in these episodes there is seemingly a yearning for something more than the satisfaction of crude sexual desire or the will to power. Daddy longs for the Guanyin dominatrix because "she [has] a face on her remarkably gentle and benevolent, the kind that's 'pure and saintly' that kind, the kind of young woman, the newlywed, the young wifely sort that prays to Kuan Yin [Guanyin] for a son" (Gunn 41; Wang 58). What Daddy longs for is a wife to love and sympathize with in the separate space of the home. One prostitute in the novel sells the "girlfriend experience," the illusion of love and sympathy. The tea girl in Taipei asks Daddy if he has a "girlfriend" (Gunn 120; Wang 170) and goes on to tell him a sob story about her construction worker father, to which Daddy responds: "I'd never been so moved ... Why does a girl like her have to suffer like this? ... When faced with another's pain, what can you **do**?" What he does is pay her twice as much as he owes her, having "sympathized" with her (Gunn 121–22; Wang 172–73). He also promises her a free gift of money, $30,000, no strings attached. He assures her, "You don't have to   marry me" (Gunn 122; Wang 174). Daddy never delivers the gift, but the episode demonstrates his desire for something more than sex. He does not even have sex with the healthy, happy hooker. With her, Daddy experiences a kind of vapid companionship. They laugh and cry and sing for sheer joy (Gunn 127; Wang 181). It is companionship Daddy wants, and he has to pay a 71 percent premium for it whenever he visits a teahouse instead of a brothel (Gunn 115; Wang 163). What he wants most of all from Red Hair is communication. Red Hair is willing to have sex with Daddy in exchange for a fee but not talk to him (Wang 199). Daddy writes her letters expressing his feelings and trying to arrange a rendezvous, but it turns out Red Hair is illiterate (Wang 202).

Daddy as Lover

In the second volume, Daddy theorizes his longings in terms of "love."
He has a lot of pretty ideas about love. That love should not be possession but rather mutual enjoyment (Wang 212). As noted in note 8, that
love should be a work of art (Wang 269). To be sure, he also disparages
sympathetic love. He says he favors traditional polygamy (Wang 214),
having described love in Buddhist terms as beginning "in ignorance" and
resembling a vat of smelly water (Wang 189). It seems to me that Daddy
protests too much, and what he really wants is a life of monogamous
bourgeois bliss based on a bond of sympathetic love.

The logic of sympathetic love in the novel is gift exchange. Once the
only form of exchange in tribal society, gift exchange was in the liberal
order largely (though not entirely, given the phenomenon of modern
charity) confined to the intimate sphere of family and friends.[34] Daddy
mentions an ancient formula of gift exchange in reference to Dong Yutang's visit: one gives a peach, and the other reciprocates with a plum
(Wang 187). Similarly, Dong Yutang gives Daddy his business card, and
Daddy describes giving water to Dong and lighting a candle for him as
acts of great goodness (Wang 345). But Daddy also tries to apply the
same principle in his dealings with women. He offered a gift to Mei-chu
in Taipei then fails to give it (Wang 172–73). He gives Red Hair what she
does not want. He will freely give his time (Wang 190). Daddy pawns his
watch and wastes the money on an expensive gift, a bag, for Red Hair,
which she stomps on (Wang 221). These efforts to start what could be
called a gift economy—that is, a systematic series of reciprocal gift ex-
changes—fail; Red Hair does not want anything from Daddy besides his
money. In a perversion of the gift economy, at least from a liberal perspective (in which gift exchange is between two spouses who have freely

---

34. For the anthropological tradition and modern philosophical uses of the
idea of gift exchange, see the essays in *The Logic of the Gift: Toward an Ethic of
Generosity*, edited by Alan Schrift (London: Routledge, 1997). Communication
can also be theorized in terms of gift exchange.

chosen each other), Daddy tries to give Cai Suzhen to a gambling buddy
to reinforce their fraternal relationship (Wang 243).

There is an obvious objection to the notion that bourgeois existence,
specifically sentimental love in a nuclear family, is presented in a positive light in *Backed Against the Sea*. As scholars have argued, Wang
Wenxing is sending up literary clichés, particularly the love story but
also the sob story. Chang argues that Daddy's failure to deliver a gift of
money to Mei-chu parodies stories about nice guys saving prostitutes
with hearts of gold who have been forced into the business by economic
necessity, stories like Chen Yingzhen's "A Race of Generals."[35] To Chang,
the healthy, happy hooker is a "positive, but no less caricaturized character."[36] Since the healthy happy hooker does not reappear in the second
volume, in retrospect she seems a parody of the Earth Mother prostitute
in Huang Chunming's classic nativist story "Days of Watching the Sea,"
set in Nanfang'ao, where Wang Wenxing did four months of military
service and on which Deep Pit Harbor (Shenkeng'ao) is based. Liao
Ping-hui asserts that the love story about Daddy and Red Hair is a grotesque parody of the traditional talented scholar: lovely lady stories and
the mandarin ducks and butterflies stories of the early twentieth century. By reading a love story with grotesque characters, the reader loses
his or her appetite for romance.[37] For Liao Binghui (also known as Liao
Ping-hui), the Red Hair romance is an example of Wang Wenxing's modernist aesthetics—in other words, his unsentimental realism.[38] Finally,
the episode that follows Daddy's failure with Red Hair, the Cai Suzhen

---

35. *Modernism and the Nativist Resistance*, 136.

36. Yvonne Chang, "Language, Narrator, and Stream-of-Consciousness: The
Two Novels of Wang Wenxing," *Modern Chinese Literature* 1.1 (1984): 54.

37. Liao Binghui 廖炳惠, "Wang Wenxing yu tade piaobo shidai—Ye de huo-
ban" 王文興與他的漂泊世代—爺的夥伴 (Wang Wenxing and his diasporic
generation—Ye's companions) in *Xuanxiao yu fennu: Bei hai de ren zhuanlun* 喧
囂與憤怒：《背海的人》專論 (Sound and fury: critical essays on *Backed
Against the Sea*), edited by Kang Laixin 康來新 and Huang Shuning 黃恕寧 (Taipei: National Taiwan University Press, 2013), 141–51.

38. Ibid., 142–44.

story, begins with a bicycle collision, another cliché of romance fiction.[39] Wang Wenxing destroys the sentimental effect by setting the wrong tone aesthetically in noting the carnage of the incident: Cai Suzhen's hand is all bloodied (Wang 249). (Though perhaps Daddy's mention of blood makes the scene all the more romantic, in that their respective injuries allow an "**exchange** of **blood**" [Wang 249]).

Certainly if a literary genre is a shallow misrepresentation of reality, Wang Wenxing is right to parody it, as he does when he has Daddy declare, "But **I love her!**" (Wang 227). In this way, "love" becomes ridiculous. But the object of parody here is fake sentimentality, a superficial discourse of love that might be exploited for mercenary purposes. It is important to note that Daddy participates in the parody, that he himself is a sophisticated reader of love stories. He self-consciously retells his story in terms of the romantic formula of love in sentimental fiction: A loves B, B loves C, C loves A (Wang 234). Daddy notes that Cai Suzhen is so taken with him because she has been reading too many sentimental novels, that her existence has been "popular fiction alized" (Wang 248). By simply noting the presence of parody and seeing through the tropes of sentimental fiction, the reader has only made the same move as Daddy. To be a better reader than Daddy, the reader of *Backed Against the Sea* must perceive the impulse of sympathy that the love story is about in a superficial way.

One perceives this impulse very occasionally in *Backed Against the Sea*. Daddy falls in love with Red Hair because she reminds him of his long-lost elder sister on the mainland (Wang 216). This detail is ambiguous, because he mentions the resemblance between Red Hair and his sister to Little Flower Face, his go-between during his attempted love affair with Red Hair, perhaps to elicit sympathy. He could be making it up as he goes along. But there seems to be something authentic in it, even to a reader on guard against sentimentality. When Daddy's heart is moved to pity by the daughter of the Cao family, a lame girl, his sentiment is paternal. His assurance that the little girl has a bright future is

---

39. Chang, "The Meaning of Modernism," 171.

poignant (Wang 363).[40] Even Daddy's name, which connotes arrogance (as in "who's your daddy?"), also reminds the reader of how alone he is, with only fictive family members to keep him company: his nicknames for his various ailments are the terms for children in a Chinese family (Gunn 9; Wang 12). The reader must not be so sophisticated as to repress the impulse of sympathy in him- or herself.

These examples are all familial, and in the introduction I mentioned that the key to survival or success for the middle-aged mainlander men in the novel seems to be not mastery of Buddhist philosophy but success in forming a family. There are no renunciates in the novel to compare Daddy with (besides the Catholic missionary), although there are a number of married men. This assertion has to be qualified. One middle-aged married mainlander's fate has been spectacularly bad: Yu Shiliang, who had the bad luck to choose a mentally ill wife. Yet it is hard to sympathize with him because he is so spineless that he takes up an offer to waste time and money on a game of mahjong when he should be taking care of his wife and family.[41] Still, Yu Shiliang's fate is infinitely better than Daddy's. Then there is Dong Yutang, the most conventionally successful of anyone in *Backed Against the Sea*. Dong Yutang married a much younger woman after he got rich (Wang 349). He now has a young daughter. Yet Dong Yutang is a horrible person, an indictment of capitalism in his rule over his rice ball empire. He tells Daddy about a grandmother who produced substandard rice balls and was kicked out of the production team. She dragged her two grandchildren to see Dong Yutang, knelt down before him, and told him a sob story. Dong Yutang asks Daddy a rhetorical question: "How could I ... be moved by her?" (Wang 354). Dong Yutang illustrates a failure of familial sympathy to humanize the market. He also illustrates the failure of the state to regulate the market. He is in Deep Pit Harbor with official cooperation: he has bor-

---

40. Daddy narrates his meeting with the Cao family, a family of settlers, at the end of volume 2, right before he is murdered by vigilantes.

41. As Chang notes, Yu Shiliang likely purchased his bride, even if the marriage was conceptualized as a gift exchange of a woman in exchange for a betrothal gift (*Modernism and the Nativist Resistance*, 135).

rowed a car from a local police station. Instead of ameliorating social contradictions, the state is abetting exploitation.[42] There is at least one character who does seem to embody the bourgeois ideal—the ideal family man, not the ideal consumer—who has not been discussed in the critical literature in English despite being the most decent character in the book: Fu Shaokang.

Fu Shaokang is the secretary at BOCDO. Fu Shaokang is first introduced as being impressed with the sign Daddy has written to be hung over the bathroom: "Close Door When Entering or Leaving" (Gunn 89; Wang 126). Daddy comments that "the way Fu Shao-k'ang [Fu Shaokang] acted when he saw [the characters of the sign] was something like this, I believe, he stood right in front of the door to the bathroom, he had his pants pulled down still, he'd forgotten to pull them back up, and simply stood there in place with his mouth open hollering on and on you know about how great they looked" (Gunn 89; Wang 126). Caught with his pants down, Fu Shaokang seems to be an unlikely ideal. Daddy mocks him mercilessly. However, he turns out to be Daddy's best friend in Deep Pit Harbor. He listens to Daddy's completely fabricated sob story: Daddy claims he was in the export business in Taipei with a partner and did the honorable thing when his partner went bankrupt by forgiving his partner's debt. Fu Shaokang responds in the right way, from a liberal perspective, "out of a sympathy," Daddy says, "he felt for what my life had been like and the situation I'm in" (Gunn 89; Wang 126).[43] Is Fu Shaokang stupid to believe the story? Perhaps we can imagine him seeing through Daddy's yarn but feeling sympathetic anyway, because as a fellow mainlander and fellow human being, Daddy deserves sympathy. Fu Shaokang would turn out to be an ideal reader, responding

---

42. If Wang Wenxing is actually an economic liberal, a proponent of the free market, he might endorse men like Dong Yutang, who bring down the cost of food production and distribution. If Dong Yutang had succeeded in selling his rice balls in Deep Pit Harbor earlier, Daddy might have had affordable food to eat.

43. Sympathy and the Chinese term *tongqing* 同情 are similar morphologically and semantically. Sympathy means "same feeling" (usually a negative feeling), and *tongqing* 同情 is "same sentiment" or "same situation."

with sympathy to people like Daddy, who seem unworthy of sympathy. The reader, of course, is free to turn away from Daddy and the other flawed characters in Deep Pit Harbor and from the unsympathetic people in their own lives, but doing so would be an illiberal failure to sympathize universally.[44]

Fu Shaokang also acts on his sympathy. In the first volume, he mentions to Daddy the possibility of a position at BOCDO and, in the second volume, helps him make arrangements, loaning him money for fabric for a suit, a gift for the director. When the director assigns the position to someone else, Daddy makes a scene and loses his meal ticket. It is unclear whether Daddy might have received some assistance from Fu Shaokang if he had held his tongue. Fu Shaokang might have forgiven him his debt, the way Daddy forgave his fictitious partner's debt.

At any rate, it turns out that Fu Shaokang is married, and in his own small way embodies the bourgeois ideal, cultivating sympathy at home and spreading it beyond. He lives in a new "heaven and earth" behind BOCDO, a staff dormitory, a place for eating and happiness (Wang 332). When he sees Daddy there, he invites him into his home for a visit, and introduces his wife and children, two middle school–aged sons and a daughter. The Fus live a life of petty bourgeois bliss; *Backed Against the Sea* would have been a much less interesting novel had it been about Fu Shaokang. Perhaps in reading about Daddy, the reader can indulge in his or her desire to be decadent. But the other thing reading about Daddy brings home to the reader is that one cannot live like Daddy.

---

44. The entirety of *Backed Against the Sea* can be read as a gigantic sob story, an attempt to keep the reader's attention and elicit sympathy. *Backed Against the Sea*–as–sob story is ground for a comparison with Fyodor Dostoyevsky's *Notes from Underground*, one of the books Daddy brings with him to Deep Pit Harbor (Gunn 22; Wang 29). Both novels contain prostitutes with hearts of gold telling sob stories to vicious customers who become a little less vicious when the stories move them to pity. In both novels, a fallible narrator sees through the love story and the sob story while using them to keep the reader's attention. Both novels thereby force the reader into a self-consciousness of the narrative forms through which we understand the world and the values they transmit. The novels cultivate and question cynicism in the reader.

Conclusion

This chapter has argued that *Backed Against the Sea* deals with the social and personal aspects of the problem of desire, considers two solutions—Buddhist and liberal—and privileges the latter: the Buddhist solution has to be considered part of the liberal one. A modern consumer
can clearly benefit from a Buddhist perspective on desire, but the effects of desire in the world—both the real world and the world of
Backed Against the Sea—are too complex to understand without the
structural concept of society invented by men like Adam Smith, the
perspective of political economy. Karl Marx inherited this perspective,
but *Backed Against the Sea* can still be read as a liberal work that offers
a liberal solution to the problem of desire: regulation by individuals,
social institutions like marriage, and the state, combined with sympathy in the human realm that reduces market conflicts. *Backed Against
the Sea* is clearly a critique of the logic of state-abetted capitalism, as
represented by Dong Yutang, but obviously the reader can imagine a
society in which freedom reigns in a more rational way. The novel also
critiques capitalism from the perspective of the individual. Daddy's
personal story illustrates the central contradiction of economic liberalism: that it is in the interests of sellers for customers to buy what they
don't need beyond their means, often at great personal cost. Of course,
we can blame Daddy for being the author of his own fate, which would
be paradoxically more liberal than to say that his fate was externally
decided; it would be even more liberal to notice that in a sense Daddy
is typical. As behavioral economists have been arguing for several decades, people are not very good at judging their own interests and
managing their own desires. No human being is a *Homo economicus*,
the rational consumer of economic theory.[45] People are flawed. Readers
familiar with Wang Wenxing's fiction will recognize the importance of
flaws, personal and institutional, in *Backed Against the Sea*. The novel

---

45. See, for instance, Daniel L. McFadden, "The New Science of Pleasure,"
National Bureau of Economic Research Working Paper 18687, available at http://
www.nber.org/papers/w18687.pdf.

offers the naive reader an education in how people and institutions operate in the real world. But one plank in the liberal program is, I have argued, positively represented here: the institution of the bourgeois family and the value of sympathy on which the family is founded, whereby individual desire is transcended or sublimated into bourgeois bliss. The figure of the prostitute was useful to Wang Wenxing in his cutting critique of capitalism and his modest defense of the family for three reasons: because she is an instance of the danger of the unfettered liberal market, she is a dangerous temptation for the dissolute individual, and she betrays Daddy's blurring of the separation between the private sphere of the market and the intimate sphere of the home.

Now that most people in Taiwan have entered the middle class, it is possible for almost anyone to maintain the boundary between the private sector (the market) and private life (the home). Poor Taiwanese parents do not sell their children anymore, a practice that erased the boundary between home and market. The women who are forced into prostitution tend to be from poorer countries. But desire is, to put it crudely, still a problem. Today the problem is of a surplus economy, outsourced production, and ceaseless attempts to promote consumption, which is presented as the only way to maintain economic growth (which in turn is an unquestioned desideratum). In 1962, the advertising of objects of desire was limited to the titillating names of the brothels in Deep Pit Harbor. Today the attempt to produce desire by marketing fills the space of everyday life. Though Taiwan may now be a democracy, willpower in private and public to face such problems as environmental degradation remains lacking, partly because people are too busy satisfying the desire to consume.[46] The counsel in *Backed Against the Sea* against

---

46. Like some developing countries today, Taiwan was drowning in trash in 1962. (Sometimes it still seems to be now.) Writing from the mid-1970s to the 1990s, Wang invests *Backed Against the Sea* with an environmental consciousness. He writes, "The closer you get to the ocean here, the more trash you find—I was at some seaside places once along the shore north of Taipei—Chin Shan, Pa-li, Fu-lung and the like—to take in the grand sights of nature. Well, was I in

indulgence is as relevant today as it was then, and Wang Wenxing's sadder and wiser liberal project continues.

---

for a jolt, whew! Everywhere I looked the entire seashore was buried in a mindless orgy of trash, trash, and more trash" (Gunn 14; Wang 19). This is not so much antiromantic—Daddy is not saying nature is not as beautiful as we think—as it is brutally honest about the way modern people trash nature.

4 Leaving Home: Foreshadowing, Echo, and Sideshadowing in Wang Wenxing's Jia bian

Jane Parish Yang
Lawrence University

IF, AS MARK Currie states, humans are "narrative animals, as *homo fabulans*—the tellers and interpreters of narrative,"[1] then our first task of analysis is to interpret how the telling of Wang Wenxing's *Jia bian* 家變 (Family catastrophe) creates meaning. That is, how do its narrative parts interact to create an overall meaning? How does the counterpoise of foreshadowing and echo between and among sections affect or alter meaning? In other words, how do earlier small events presage later larger events, and earlier larger events find an echo in later small events? How, for example, would the narrative meaning differ if plotted solely chronologically as the young son's maturation (sections 1, 2, 3, etc.) up to the father's disappearance, rather than beginning with the father's disappearance and the family's search for him (sections A, B, C, etc.), and then later inserting earlier childhood scenes? To answer some of these questions, I have borrowed the term *counterpoise* from Angelina Yee, which she defines as a "coupling procedure ... applied to the novel's overall design ... in the dual sense of opposition and balance."[2] In this deliberately disjointed narrative, events that chronologically fore-

---

1. Mark Currie, *Postmodern Narrative Theory* (New York: Palgrave, 1998), 4.

2. Angelina C. Yee, "Counterpoise in *Honglou meng*," *Harvard Journal of Asiatic Studies* 50:2 (1990.12): 614.

shadow later events are instead counterpoised as echoes. Inverting chronology and interweaving the present with the past reinforce theme by placing similar events adjacent to one another.

This type of thematic emphasis is most striking in the opening sections. The narrative in section A opens with a description of the father leaving the house. Within two lines the word *li* 籬 (bamboo fence) is used three times in such combinations of *limen* 籬門 (bamboo fence gate), *lihou* 籬後 (behind the bamboo fence), and *liwei* 籬圍 (bamboo fencing). Sandwiched in between is the explicit word *li* 離 (to leave or go away) (*Jia bian* 7; *Family Catastrophe* 5). The repetition of the sound *li* is deliberate and precise—it seems to shout "Leave, leave, leave!" (Of course, this aural signal *li* is lost in English translation). The narrative view pans over the leave-taking through the bamboo fence to focus on the decaying, dilapidated Japanese-style frame house from which the father departs.

Separation from the family is further emphasized in section B with the son's reaction to the news from his mother that the father has disappeared:

"Who cares where he's gone to? *Who* has seen him? I am I and he is he; it's not as if we have anything whatsoever to do with each other, you know." (*Family Catastrophe* 6)

"誰看到他沒有？我是我，他是他，根本拉不上關係。"
(*Jia bian* 8)

When the narrative changes from the present time of sections A through C to the flashback of the son's childhood memory in section 1, the family's dysfunctional relationships have been well established. It is therefore a shock to be abruptly drawn into the loving relationship of the son's childhood.

There seems to be no relation between the flashback in section 1 and the father's leave-taking in section A. The narrative that opened with the father's final break with the family as the first event in the text then presents the reader with the first flashback of a scene depicting the close, warm relationship between father and son. Indeed, the flashback almost seems to have been placed there in deliberate contrast to section A. As section 1 unfolds, the young father is teaching his preschool child to recognize simple Chinese characters while they stroll along the street. He points out such ideographs as *da* 大 (big or great), *men* 門 (door or gate), and *ren* 人 (man or human being):

一個年輕相貌的父親，牽携一個小孩的手，沿街漫步。
"大，大，門，人，人，"孩子指着街旁的店招認呼。
"人人商店，厦門大茶行，那個字呢？毛毛。"
"公。還有門字，爸！爸！你看，好多門，爸。"
"哎，是，很多，厦門公司，厦門百貨行，厦門飲冰店。"
父親温敦煦融的笑着，他的小手舒憩適恬的卧在父親煖和的
大手之中。(*Jia bian* 23–24)

A youngish looking father and a small child were walking slowly down the street, hand in hand.

"*Great, great, door, man, man*," the child called out, pointing to the words he recognized on the storefronts along the way.

"*Man*, Every-*man* Department Store. Hsia-*men*. *Great* Tea Company? And what about that word, Sonny?"

"*Grand*. And there's the word for *door* again, Pa! Pa, look! Many *doors*, Pa."

"Yes, indeed, many. The *doors* or *men* in Hsia-*men* Company *Grand* Opening, and Hsia-*men* Department Store, and Hsia-*men* Ice Drinks."

Father gently explained to him in his kindly, loving voice. His little hand rested comfortably in Father's large, warm hand. (*Family Catastrophe* 22, with minor changes from the editors)

If this scene had been placed first in a story plotted as the young son's maturation, it would not necessarily be remarkable, except to illustrate the father's kindness and patience and the son's sense of safety in his presence. Placed as the first flashback of the son's childhood after the father's disappearance, the son's growing unease with the father's absence, and finally his trip south to search for him (sections A, B, and C), the scene resonates with more symbolic meaning.

The choice of Chinese characters *da*, *men*, and *ren*, which with a slight rearrangement turns the separate characters into the more meaningful terms of *daren* and *men* (big person or adult and door or gate), now serves as an echo of section A in which the father, *the adult, leaves* and goes out of the bamboo *gate*. A chronological plotting would have made section 1 foreshadow the father's final leave-taking, whereas the disjointed narrative of present time/flashback employs it as an echo of section A. Thus the small event in section 1 echoes the large event of section A and gives greater play to the seemingly random selection of characters which the father and son read and comment on. *The adult goes out the gate—the adult leaves*—is the implied message, despite the depiction of the loving adult presence with the young child.

Similarly, the father's leave-taking that opens section A is echoed in section 51 when he leaves the family to go on a business trip (*Jia bian* 61–64; *Family Catastrophe* 62–66) and mother and son vicariously track his movements and anticipate the reward of his return: presents and extra income. The happiness derived from the short trip foreshadows the last section of the novel, section O, in which both mother and son find happiness, or at least contentment, in great contrast to the period when the father was a part of the household. The narrator informs the reader that it had been almost two years to the day that the father had been absent:

然而在范曄的現在的家庭裏邊他和他之媽媽兩個人簡單的共
相住在一起生活似乎是要比他們從前的生活較比起來髣髴還
要更加愉快些。(*Jia bian* 200)

For Fan Ye, however, life at home, living with his mother, simply, from day to day, just the two of them, was much happier, much easier than it had ever been before. (*Family Catastrophe* 248)

Despite the wife's and son's initial anguish, the father's permanent absence from the family in the end leads to their happiness and prosperity, something already hinted at in the narrative structure with the mini-leaving taking in section 51.

Echoes of the son's search for his father in sections A, B, and C are found in the father's search for his son in section 83 when Fan Ye is late returning home one winter evening. The father's initial search is unsuccessful and he goes out again, only to get lost himself on the second attempt to make his way to his son's elementary school. While the father's search is a structural echo of the son's search in sections A, B, and C that open the text, section 83, of course, chronologically foreshadows the grown-up son's search for the elderly father (*Jia bian* 92; *Family Catastrophe* 98–99).

The disjointed narrative that skips between present time and past remembrances adds a further complication by offering the reader what Gary Saul Morson calls sideshadowing or "the possibility of possibility,"[3] which he explains as

> a middle realm of real possibilities that could have happened even if they did not. Things could have been different from the way they were, there were real alternatives to the present we know, and the future admits of various paths.[4]

In other words, there is not a direct and obvious path from point A to point B, as foreshadowing would have one believe. Instead, the text introduces contingencies into the plot. The story could in fact branch to one side or the other. A small event may not necessarily directly foreshadow a later event. It may be a dead end or a false possibility—it may develop no further, or may function as a reminder that events did not have to turn out the way they did.

It is Morson's belief that sideshadowing allows for a certain freedom in the plot. He states: "In contrast to foreshadowing, which projects onto

---

3. Gary Saul Morson, *Narrative and Freedom: The Shadow of Time* (New Haven, CT: Yale University Press, 1994), 119.

4. Ibid., 6.

the present a shadow from the future, sideshadowing projects—from the
'side'—the shadow of an alternative present."[5] Sideshadowing introduces
into the narrative what he calls "the ghostly presence of might-have-
been or might-bes."[6] For *Jia bian*, the sections present a kind of alternative scenario to the father's presence or absence and revolve around the
state of the family finances and the son's hope that the father would finally be able to bring home a decent wage.

These sections are often lyrical, with description of the surroundings
mirroring the calm contentment of the impressionable young son, and
contrast strongly with the cruelty and quarreling in sections depicting
the family's poverty. For example, a lyrical episode heralding a new possibility directly follows section 118, in which the father runs into difficulty at work and is about to be transferred but is saved by a mental
breakdown and the new director's reluctance to punish him, and section
J, in which the family's search for the father slackens as their financial
position improves with one less mouth to feed. The lyrical description of
the son's time on the river, where he has gone to rent a boat, seems to be
leading the narrative in a different direction:

> 這時是春天剛起的時節，天色淺灰，寒風猶峭。水面上傳來
> 一股子輕腥嗅覺。。。就只有他一個人划槳。。。他乃蕩槳
> 划向上游，行過一處艸色葱葱的河邊防岸，。。。水色是明
> 澄的鉛黑色。這裏擺槳的聲音越來越清楚了。行過一座看來
> 荒冷的小沙島，島上延滋的青草因爲峭寒所以凍成死綠色
> 澤。。。天候好時金陽射在斯島上，沙和草的地上黃花萌
> 放，一座島看起來宛若是一顆彩蛋一樣。。。他現在把艇槳
> 擱淺。。。眼下所見的山景是淡墨迹的山脈，還有後前薄濃
> 的層片。(*Jia bian* 143)

It was the start of spring. The sky was a pale gray, and the wind
was still sharp. A faint smell of fish rose up to greet him as he
approached the water's edge ... He was the only oarsman on the

---

5. Ibid., 11.
6. Ibid., 118.

water. Heading upstream, he passed a grassy bank, green like the
shoots of spring onions ... the water was a deep, clear gray, the
color of lead. The further he went, the clearer the sound of his
oars, dipping and paddling in the water. He drew abreast of a
small sandbank, a deserted-looking place. The green here was
just as thick and abundant but it was a dead green, withered by
the blasts that cut across the island ... Then the golden arrows of
the sun aimed straight at this island, quickening the yellow blossoms among the sand and grass, transfiguring the sandy mound
into a fantastic, huge, multicolored egg nestling in the water ...
He stopped rowing ... A mountain scene from a black and white
ink scroll painting appeared before him, in darkening layers,
from far to near. (*Family Catastrophe* 170–71)

The description of spring ends with an explicit statement of hope as he
catches sight of a star in the sky at dusk. After a dark period of crisis and
poverty in section 118, the family situation seemed a bit more stable.
Chronologically, this possibility is ironically not realized until section J,
in which the family burden of having one less mouth to feed results in a
happier time for the mother and son. The result is a possibility that
things might work out now, and the next two sections from the son's
childhood, 119 and 120, echo that new hope with a lyrical description of
the environment and the coming of spring.

The text as structured has opened up the possibility of change and
redemption for the family at the expense of the father's presence in the
household. That is, dogging the possibility of better times for the father
and the family, raised in the numbered childhood section 118, is section
J, which shows the actuality of better times after the father disappeared.
Thus the placement of section J right before the lyrical sections 119 and
120, which celebrate possibilities for the family after the father's loss of
his job was averted, in actuality mocks the very possibility that the family will now prosper, as real positive change is shown to have occurred
only after the father went away.

Closely following these sections is section 122, which again seems to
present the new beginning for which the son is wishing. The father
brings home news of a business opportunity with an old colleague from

his life in China. The family reacts happily. The son and mother are "overjoyed." The son looked around him at the shabby furnishings "and envisioned a complete makeover, ... He could hardly *contain* his exuberance." The mother even offers dinner "in high spirits," and the family members seem to treat each other quite differently than before, when they constantly quarreled. The description continues with the statement that the family was "in raptures"; the father wore an "inebriated grin on his face"; Fan Ye "would be the happiest person on earth" (*Family Catastrophe* 174, 176). It is difficult to recall a time when the family had been so happy together.

Of course nothing had actually changed, yet they were treating each other decently, even with kindness. When before had the mother graciously offered to make dinner? When had the father been respected and the son truly happy? It was all because of the promise of a little wealth and economic security. This depiction of the alternate reality, the sideshadow or temporary respite from the actual trajectory of events, teases the reader with the possibility that they might have been able to avoid the family catastrophe with a little more luck and a little more money. The promise of the business deal collapses in the end, yet the son realizes a truth: "We've been given ten months of *pure happiness*" (*Family Catastrophe* 183). The family members had behaved well toward each other based on a falsehood. What if it had been based on reality—would that have averted the family catastrophe? It is tantalizing to project the state of affairs if the promising trajectory had continued and the tragedy so explicitly revealed in the opening scene had been avoided.

Much as the bamboo gate and fence (*limen* 籬門 or *liwei* 籬圍) became the signifier of the father's departure and continuing absence in section A at the opening of part 1, part 2's opening section I repeats a detailed description of the bamboo fence, variously described as *liba* 籬笆, *liqiang* 籬牆, *lizhu* 籬竹, or *zhuba men* 竹笆門 (*Jia bian* 119). The bamboo fence thus becomes an important line separating life within and without the family, as the son returns home from his unsuccessful trip south in search of the father. This short section of the son's return to within the confines of the bamboo fence is echoed immediately by section 111 of the childhood narrative in which the son, now sixteen years

old, dashes outside on hearing the roar of a twin-engine prop plane
overhead:

而今在他的家約早前二年蓋起的籬竹後頭佇了一會，看一看
籬牆外的世界，（天，和綠樹梢）. (*Jia bian* 121)

At the moment, he was standing behind the bamboo fence that
had been erected around his house about two years ago; he was
looking out at the world beyond the bamboo, at sky and green
branches. (*Family Catastrophe* 139)

Demarcation of "the world beyond the bamboo" 籬牆外的世界 (*li qiang-
waide shijie*) (*Jia bian* 121) and the world within the bamboo becomes
more and more problematic as the teenager slips into his own fantasy
world of the "simple, leisurely life" of the Russian countryside of the
nineteenth-century Russian novels he devours, reading and rereading
Turgenev, Chekhov, and Gogol as he lies around inside the house (*Family Catastrophe* 139).

Just as his world within the bamboo barrier was interrupted by the
sound of the airplane invading the airspace above his house, his own
private space is invaded first by his mother, then by both parents: "Into
this world that his reading had created the shrill voice of his mother
came crashing through" (*Family Catastrophe* 139). The mother's voice
was soon joined by the father's voice, yelling at the neighbor kids who
gathered on the other side of the bamboo fence to gawk at his mother's
berating another neighbor for leaning a pole of wet clothes against their
fence. Suddenly it does not seem clear where he belongs. His identification with his mother and father is strained as he watches incredulously
their selfish, petty display of protecting their small space

搖搖歪歪的，恍似從洪荒時代越出的兩個「原始人」。   (*Jia
bian* 123)

acting like two "aborigines," swaggering and strutting about as
if they had recently emerged victorious from out of the Flood.
(*Family Catastrophe* 142)

This is one of the rare occasions in which both parents seem to incur his wrath. In subsequent instances, his father alone bears the brunt of his anger. Invasion of the son's private world and private space is later echoed in part 3, section 124, in which a plane's noisy overhead roar again interrupts his reading. This time the continued hovering presence of his father in the house and at times in his own room leads to an angry shouting match (*Family Catastrophe* 190–95).

As detailed already, in part 2 of the narrative in which the search falters and flashbacks show an ever-increasing frustration at home, one can still find sections echoing each other, building on the hope and promise of a new life with the turn of the seasons and the beginning of spring. Even in part 3, the tug between hope and despair continues, as in section 133 when the son goes to his father's office to find the father occupying the director's office in the director's absence. The son is astonished yet overjoyed:

他〔范曄〕不禁覺得超乎意料所臻的高興，他衷心足慰地感到他的父親到底猶然還有他的尊重啟敬的一犄面。 (*Jia bian* 170–71)

Fan Ye was in raptures; it was like a benediction; he was profoundly comforted, immensely grateful for this glimpse into the possibility for commanding respect that seemed to have been hiding somewhere in the wings of his father's personality. (*Family Catastrophe* 210)

Although the English version is perhaps overtranslated in this description, it does point to the sideshadowing that is occurring here: this brief encounter in the office allows the son a "glimpse into the possibility" that the child's fantasies of having a father worthy of respect could somehow be realized.

Even this late in the game, so to speak, the narrative holds out a tantalizing glimpse of how relationships could have evolved if the father had been able to accomplish more in his career and hold the family above the abject poverty such as that depicted in section 47, for example, in which

他復再又感到一片陰影籠罩上家里了，從前那感受過的難以
忘懷底貧窮底雲影。(*Jia bian* 56)

he felt the dark shadow cast over their household, the same
shadow of poverty that had left its indelible impression on him
once before. (*Family Catastrophe* 57)

This shadow of poverty drives him to wish emphatically for a different
kind of life than the one he had been living. Section 51, in which the
father leaves on the business trip, serves as a counterbalance to the dark
thoughts of this section.

Similarly, in section 117, the decaying house and repulsive public
toilet lead the narrator to declare: "He felt nothing but revulsion for this
poverty-stricken environment" (*Family Catastrophe* 159). Of course, as
detailed already, soon afterward, in section 122, the father's and the family's hopes rise again with the promise of the business deal with an old
colleague. Family life takes another turn, albeit temporarily, for the better (*Family Catastrophe* 173–83). The alternate trajectory of his life, the
sideshadowing episodes that could have become his life but in the end
did not, remain only a tantalizing distraction as Fan Ye is pulled first in
one direction, then in another. Fan Ye's life improves once the father
disappears, so in the end, ironically, by his action of leaving, the father
appears to give his family one last gift: a modicum of success.[7]

---

7. I do not completely agree with Christopher Lupke when he characterizes
the novel this way: "The development of the novel along two strains, wherein
these narrative modes vie with each other, the first telling of the dutiful son's
search, the second depicting his loathing for the father and the ritual of filiality
that serves to symbolically imprison Fan Ye within the family unit, raises the
issue of closure." See his "Wang Wenxing and the 'Loss' of China," *Modern Chinese Literary and Cultural Studies in the Age of Theory: Reimagining a Field*, edited
by Rey Chow (Durham, NC: Duke University Press, 2000), 134. As I have demonstrated, even toward the end of the text the son is still wishing that the father
might live up to the dreams and hopes of the son. See also Sung-sheng Yvonne
Chang, *Modernism and the Nativist Resistance: Contemporary Chinese Fiction
from Taiwan* (Durham, NC: Duke University Press, 1993), 111–18.

QUESTIONS OF STYLE

5 Wang Wenxing: Novelist as Lyric Sculptor

Wai-lim Yip
University of California, San Diego

ADMITTEDLY, THE TITLE of this chapter is a rewrite of Donald Davie's book on Ezra Pound, *Poet as Sculptor.*[1] To call Wang Wenxing novelist as sculptor would not puzzle any reader of his works. Not only is he a dedicated practitioner of the carving of language in the long tradition of classical Chinese poetry, in which the act of *lianzi* (cudgel one's brains for the exact word 煉字) and *lianju* (alchemy of sentence, 煉句), leading to the architecture of an art product of words, has been a highly regarded staple, following the spirit of Du Fu's "I would risk death groping without rest until I find this startlingly eye-opening word." He is also squarely in the tradition of Flaubert/Pound's "*le mot juste,*" "style is absolute," "language calling attention to itself," as well as Baudelaire's (as quoted by Edgar Allan Poe) "no one point in its composition is referable either to accident or intuition—that the work proceeded, step by step, to its completion with the precision and rigid consequence of a mathematical problem."[2]

---

1. All the quotations of Wang Wenxing's short stories are from *Endless War: Fiction and Essays by Wang Wen-Hsing*, a book of translations (Cornell East Asia Program, Cornell University, 2011) edited by Shu-ning Sciban and Fred Edwards, some of which, for the sake of discussion, I have taken the liberty of modifying to reflect the stylistic features in the original. My modifications are indicated at the end of every quotation.

2. Edgar Allan Poe, "The Philosophy of Composition," *Selected Writings Edgar Allan Poe*, ed. Edward H. Davidson (Boston: Houghton Mifflin, 1956), 454.

This last gives rise to Pound's "Poetry is a sort of inspired mathematics, which gives us equations ... for human emotions,"[3] which Eliot reformulates as "objective correlatives," "a set of objects, a situation, a chain of events which will be the formula of that *particular* emotion; such that when the external facts, which must terminate in sensory experience, are given, the emotion is immediately evoked."[4] The best testimony, however, comes directly from Wang Wenxing himself. It is already a legend that for years, presumably practiced still, he writes only three hundred characters a day (that was what he told me then) and later reduced this to only thirty characters![5] Weighing every word before writing it down is a daily ritual. Witness his DVD, "How I Write Fiction."[6] He spent 100 minutes to anatomize just the first two pages of his novel *Family Catastrophe*; his explication reads like the notes of a film director about the making of every shot, taking into consideration the deployment of space, direction of viewing, atmospheric condition of the moment, backgrounding, backlighting, foregrounding, frontlighting, effect of distance, period style of objects, objects evoking personality of owner/protagonist, and so on. In fact, he constantly reminds the audience of the perceiving direction of *his* camera. Nothing is left to chance; everything is planned for maximum attention. Like one of his favorite poets, William Carlos Williams, Wang writes every turn of phrase as a maneuver to make his readers *attentive* to the cuts and turns of the events, visual or psychological, at every step. Yes, Wang Wenxing is a *conscious* artist, *par excellence*. In at least two interviews, he recounts how he prepared a detailed outline for his novels, writing down numerous cards of the content, selecting, arranging, categorizing, and numbering them, so as to ensure the proper order as planned. "Every day, I take pains

---

3. Ezra Pound, *The Spirit of Romance* (Norfolk: New Directions, 1953), 5.

4. T.S. Eliot, *Selected Essays 1917–1923* (New York: Harcourt, Brace, 1932), 124–25.

5. Lin Xiuling 林秀玲, "Wang Wenxing zhuan fang: tan *Bei hai de ren* yu Nanfang'ao" 王文興專訪：談《背海的人》與南方澳 (Wang Wenxing exclusive interview: *Backed Against the Sea* and Nanfang'ao), *Zhongwai wenxue* 中外文學 (Chungwai literary monthly) 30.6 (2001): 43.

6. Wang Wenxing, *Wo ruhe xie xiaoshuo* 我如何寫小說 (How I write fiction) (DVD) (Taipei: National Taiwan University Press, 2007).

to complete *only* one to two sentences in my earlier draft. This often takes quite some time to execute. Unlike other writers who might want to leave some interesting details to be completed the next day, to me it is not a matter of interesting or uninteresting. After all, these are [intended] messages that must be bodied forth by writing. When do I stop? When I reach the set number of characters, even if the message is only half-said."[7] When the interviewer commented that in the manner of writing he set for himself there is little or no possibility of acceleration in writing, including the sudden quickening of flow that one sometimes finds in the creative process, he answered that he dreads the moment when the pen drives the author along, ending in unexpected terrains. "The author must direct the pen, not the pen direct the author."[8] Everything he said and did fulfills the recipe of Poe/Baudelaire: "The work proceeded, step by step, to its completion with the precision and rigid consequence of a mathematical problem." Nothing he does is shy of the label of a high modernist.

Why *lyric* for a novelist in the title of this chapter? In both perception and expression, structure and texture, Wang Wenxing has embraced a sizable amount of what would be characterized as *lyrical* as understood and practiced in symbolist and modernist writings, in spite of the narrative nature and impulses inherent in the novel form. Here, we need to rehearse the development of this word, *lyric*, from a genre designation to a special mode of poetry with certain working dynamics cut out and heightened as an organizing, constituting aesthetic core. The first poet to make this cut is Poe, whom both Baudelaire and Mallarmé translated and called "Master" or "Teacher."

Poe argues that for the reader to maintain sustained attention in reading, a poem must be brief. All narrative poems, especially epic poems, are nothing but a series of "poetic moments" linked by prose, and only those moments that can arrest the reader's full attention or even raise his consciousness to a trance dimension can be called poetry. The gist of this theory is found in his two essays, "The Poetic Principle" and "The Philosophy of Composition." In these essays, he is of the opinion that one aim of

---

7. Lin Xiuling, "Wang Wenxing zhuan fang," 43.
8. Ibid.

good poetry is to create a vivid effect "wrought by incident or tone, whether by ordinary incidents or peculiar tone, or the converse, or by peculiarity both of incident and tone."[9] And this effect must be achieved not by accident or intuition, but by letting the work proceed "step by step, to its completion with the precision and rigid consequence of a mathematical problem." For readers to arrive at a unity of impression, they must finish reading the poem "at one sitting," because "if two sittings be required, the affairs of the world interfere, and everything like totality is at once destroyed."[10] He thinks that the so-called long poem does not exist; at least "one half of the *Paradise Lost* is essentially prose—a succession of poetical excitements interspersed, *inevitably*, with corresponding depressions—the whole being deprived, through the extremeness of its length, of the vastly important element, or unity, of effect ... that pleasure which is at once the most intense, the most elevating, and the most pure, is ... found in the contemplation of the beautiful. When, indeed, men speak of Beauty, they mean, precisely, not a quality, as is supposed, but an effect ... that intense and pure elevation of soul, not of intellect nor of heart."[11] He further explains that the contemplation of Truth (intellect, reason) and that of Passion (the excitement of the heart) must be distinguished from that of Beauty, which alone guarantees the elevation of the soul. "I would define, in brief, the Poetry of words as *The Rhythmical Creation of Beauty*."[12] In this case, Poe is against not only the epic but also the heresy of the didactic and endorses what later becomes the motto of symbolism and modernism, namely, "the poem per se" and "art for art's sake": "under the sun there neither exists nor *can* exist any work more thoroughly dignified—more supremely noble than this very poem, this poem *per se*—this poem which is a poem and nothing more—this poem written solely for the poem's sake." It is "*through* the poem, or *through* the music, we attain to but brief

---

9. Poe, "The Philosophy of Composition," 453.
10. Ibid., 454.
11. Ibid., 456.
12. Edgar Allan Poe, "The Poetic Principle," *Selected Writings Edgar Allan Poe*, ed. Edward H. Davidson (Boston: Houghton Mifflin, 1956), 470.

and indeterminate glimpses. ... It is in Music, perhaps, that the soul most nearly attains the great end for which, when inspired by poetic sentiment, it struggles—the creation of supernal Beauty."[13]

To prove his point, Poe goes on to demonstrate how he constructs his "Raven": the choice of images and atmosphere of darkness; the raven's mysterious arrival, tapping and rapping, bordering ghostliness; dark night; somber rhythm (the rhyming with "lore," "evermore," "nevermore," all of which leave nothing accidental.[14] As I said, Baudelaire's and Mallarmé's endorsement led to Pound, Eliot and most, if not all, modernist poets. It is not an accident that the appeals to *effect, Beauty, Music, the intense Moment,* and *antidiscursiveness* all stay at the core of the aesthetics of the symbolists and the modernists: Baudelaire, Mallarmé, Pater, Pound, Eliot, and Williams, to name a few.

What are the structure and operative dynamics of this *lyric*? One essential fact about the lyric, even in its melic stage and the later subjective variety, is that it does not emphasize sequential time. Often in a lyric, the poet promotes the stimulus of an emotion or an experience of a scene at a certain heightened pitch. The motivation of action and the contour of a linear development, often found in a narrative poem, are ambiguous and not fully accounted for in a lyric (even in a story lyric such as "Edward, Edward") or submerged in the background (as in Rilke's Orpheus Sonnets). A lyric is the texture of the emotional stimulus pushed to the front. Quite often, it is a moment of time arrested at its most pregnant instant—pregnant in the sense of suggesting the multiple lines of development that precede this instant and the possible lines of development that might follow. It is an instant, a point, not a period of time, in which temporal sequence does not play an important role. The linguistic sequence in the lyric is the spatial expansion of the interior of an instant. It is as if we reach out from the center to the circumference, and move back and forth between them. In a lot of cases, the reader finds himself placed in the center of an instant radiating out toward various spaces and times. Even in its melic

---

13. Ibid.
14. Poe, "The Philosophy of Composition," 460–63.

stage and structure, a simple outburst of emotion or statement of emotion is built up into an impact by incremental repetitions and variations through musical emphases and interplay.

Because it is an intensely exciting or moving experience raised to a certain heightened pitch, a lyric often begins with a profound contact or consort with some essential reality: the sudden awareness of the primitive one-world vision; witnessing the great silent making of Nature; some mystical, religious communion with the supernatural; or the attack of some private ecstasy. In this kind of consort, there is a certain remove from the ordinary consciousness; we are thrown into a trancelike and even dreamlike condition where images and symbols visible in unusual light and space play themselves out in a manner unrestricted by sequential time as they are now cut off or hidden away from temporal logic, opening a terrain waiting for the readers to move in, meet these objects as if for the first time and reflect on them. The progression of the lyric often follows the incremental repetitions and variations of the musical structure, moving back and forth and in a circuitous manner. Its rhythm is associative, meditative, irregular, discontinuous, unpredictable, beyond the threshold of consciousness, relying on sound links, ambiguous sense links, or memory links. Readers are often arrested by certain intense images or events without, at that instant, fully grasping their morphology, development and levels of meaning. Led by a strong feeling, they must enter and roam about in it before patterns of doubling, tripling voices and meanings emerge.

Many of Wang Wenxing's short stories, or at least large paragraphs from them, echo well this description, particularly the last three sentences. Here we are not identifying all his output as *lyrical* or *lyricist novels*, although on many levels, he can definitely be so labeled along with Virginia Woolf, Marcel Proust, and James Joyce, or the Kerouac of *The Subterraneans*, all word sculptors and masters of *rhythmical creation of beauty*, with attention-sustaining musical drive or the drift of stream-of-consciousness as intense vortices to cohere rather than merely lead readers through some goal-directed, get-there story lines. Like a director/composer, Wang Wenxing's art of *sustaining effect* must be a *spontaneity arranged*. Or as Stein would say: "Composition [as in Cézanne and as in

Beethoven] as Explanation."[15] Words, like colors and forms in painting, like notes in music, she argued, are not limited to being a vehicle for meanings or ideas. They should perform exactly like colors, forms, and tones to form a composition. Just as colors (in painting) and sounds (in music) are given equal value, words should be allowed to fully express themselves. From Cézanne, Stein took the idea that in composition one thing is as important as another thing. We are saying, then, that novelists of a *modernist* persuasion, like most modernist poets, are *architectonic* in their construction of a work of art, which demands their readers to deconstruct their works with equal (if not fuller) attention to their *architectonic* dynamics.

This is one of the ways Wang Wenxing achieves the effect of sustaining the reader's attention, as, for example, in his short story "Mother." His "Mother" consists of four panels of visual and auditory activities in making up a diptych. It departs from linear progression so as to engender multiple inner correspondences of *motifs* and *leitmotifs* echoing or playing against each other in spatial counterpoint. A work like this is not abridgeable, because every word counts. To facilitate closer examination of these inter-pointing activities in some of the paragraphs, we first lay out, reluctantly, in abbreviated manner, the major "events" in the four panels, labeled below as ABCD, and the following *leitmotifs* as lowercase abcd. The subtext of the interplay between Nature (N) and City/Technological culture (T) will be represented as N > < T.

(A) Noon. Sun, like the continuous hum of silent (a) music (b/B), shines on the suburban fields. Across the river, a stone-crushing plant's motor monotonously makes a plop-plop sound (b *reverses* a) like the beat of a feeble heart (*to be echoed by* B/b).

(B) Disjointed monologue of a pale, neurotic or even schizophrenic Mother which has three features: monotonous rhythm (b1), monotonous because of emptiness and deathlike silence (b2), and the con-

---

15. "A Transatlantic Interview, 1946," *Primer for Gradual Understanding of Gertrude Stein,* ed. Robert Bartlett Hass (Santa Barbara: Black Sparrow Press, 1976), 15–35.

dition of her life changing from wax to wane (b3) (*echo A/a*), calling for her son Mao'er (Cat's ear, *intimate address*) wondering where is he and what might have happened to him … dubious obsessive /possessive tone (*suggestive of petting gesture*) toward her son who is not there … drifting into the thought of the new neighbor, divorced Miss Wu, whom she distrusts and despises.

(C) Boy under a big banyan tree, posture mimicking that of a proud grown-up (*reverse B*) … the leaves on the treetop sway with a rustling sound (*with the sound of the stone-crushing machine in the background*) (N > < T) waiting for a person.

(D) A pink parasol appears. Boy follows (*identity of neither was revealed until later, Boy being Mao'er and person holding the parasol being Miss Wu*). Miss Wu invites Mao'er to her apartment to have a cup of cold water. The electric fan blows open the curtain across the bedroom doorway. Miss Wu is in the bedroom … her whole body is exposed (d), voluptuous, flawless, perfect, dazzlingly white …. She changes clothes, comes out and offers chocolate candies to Mao'er (*contrasts B*).[16]

Even in its skeleton form, one can detect concordant and discordant tropes of *leitmotifs* and themes. If we highlight many of these *leitmotifs* and themes in the whole narrative, say, with various colors, we immediately see how one theme/*leitmotif* is repeated with various imagings, variations, extensions, joined with counterthemes/counter*leitmotifs*, interwoven into a dense texture like music, including nuances of light and dark, and atmospheric build-up, prepared, latent, or hidden in the supposedly external description of the ambience in the first two paragraphs, which are carefully spaced out as phases of perception:

The July sun, like the continuous hum of silent (a) music (b/B), sings from morning until evening (*sound in silence+monotony, anticipating* b/ B). After mid-day, the suburb's rice fields, dense clusters of new-built bungalows (*agricultural countryside culture*/N

---

16. Italics within parenthesis are comments by Yip.

side by side with rising city culture/T), eucalyptus trees and sand beach all lie prostrate (b/B), quiet (a), patient (C), wrapped in a thin gray fog (*echoes* B, *contrasts* D), waiting for still distant dusk to fall. In a blue sky filled with white smoke (*from Nature, perhaps mixed with that from the plant*/N+T), a mass of white cloud lolls about, fearlessly stretching its fat body (*pointing to* D) like a pregnant mother (B+D, *Mother superimposed on Miss Wu, reversing Mother sick in bed, at the same time suggesting voluptuous Miss Wu*) lying on a bed, resting (B). The water in the river has already dried up (b3/B *wax to wane*), a black sand beach emerging in the middle of the riverbed (b3/B). In the shallow water of a hollow in the sand, naked boys roll around, slapping the water and shouting (d, *variation and contrast with* b/B).

On the opposite bank of the river is a stone-crushing plant (T *and pointing to* B). In the morning, workmen push boats toward the middle of the river with poles and half fill them with gravel. When the boats reach the shore, the men's wives and children gather and shovel the gravel onto trolleys. The women and children push the trolleys along rails that creep toward the plant. (T > < N) Now there is no one on the beach, and the trolleys are pushed together to one side; some boats are gathered on the bank, the poles stuck in the water. The workmen have to wait until dusk to resume their work. (T > < N) The plant's motor makes a throbbing sound (b/B, *reemerge in C with contrasting atmosphere and mood*) like the beat of a feeble heart (*anticipating* B/b).[17]

This is visual music, so to speak, or at least the piece is designed like music or painting where spatial deployment of motifs or colors is para-

---

17. Translated by Michael Cody, in Shu-ning Sciban and Fred Edwards, eds., *Endless War: Fiction and Essays by Wang Wen-hsing* (Ithaca, NY: Cornell East Asia Program, Cornell University, 2011), 101–6, with Yip's modifications. Modified space breaks by Yip according to original; italics within parentheses are comments by Yip.

mount. Like the workings of a poem, inner correspondences are the stitches that complete the emotional fabric therein. Like the lyric, too, the motivation of action and the contour of a linear development, often found in a narrative, are ambiguous and not fully accounted for and are submerged in the background. We are not given clues for the cause of Mother's neurotic condition, nor the exact cause of Mao'er "hating" his mother. He has given us some highly suggestive hints to capture the slight tremblings of a possibly dubious relationship radiating from a complex that borders psychic pulses and impulses of a sexual nature in the subconscious. Wang Wenxing keeps us at the edge, tremulous with meanings. The piece demands close reading, being attentive not just to possible word meanings but to the spatial deployment, the visual rhythm, the counterpointing relationship, and so on. Although not everything Wang Wenxing writes always has this design, everything he writes demands this rigorous attention in our reading.

The second way of sustaining the reader's attention is the pulsation, the incremental speed (tempo) with which a certain physical or psychical flow that his language imitates. This is comparable to Charles Olson's theory of projective verse, where the energy construct has to be an energy discharge reflected in the phasing and phrasing of language units showing the cuts and turns of the morphology of the feeling at hand. Olson's explanation contains the configuration of pulsating energy and urgency at work:

ONE PERCEPTION MUST IMMEDIATELY AND DIRECTLY LEAD TO A FURTHER PERCEPTION. It means exactly what it says, is a matter of, at *all* points ... get on with it, keep moving, keep in, speed, the nerves, their speed, the perception, theirs, the acts, the split second acts, the whole business, keep it moving as fast as you can, citizen. And if you also set up as a poet, USE USE USE the process at all points, in any given poem always, always, one perception must must must MOVE, INSTANTER, ON ANOTHER.[18]

18. Charles Olson, *Selected Writings*, ed. Robert Creeley (New York: New Directions, 1971), 17.

Or witness this example of spontaneous prose from Jack Kerouac's *On the Road*:

> The most fantastic parking-lot attendant in the world, he can back a car forty miles an hour into a tight squeeze and stop at the wall, jump out, race among fenders, leap into another car, circle it fifty miles an hour in a narrow space, back swiftly into a tight spot, *hump*, snap the car with the emergency so that you see it bounce as he flies out; then clear to the ticket shack, sprinting like a track star, hand a ticket, leap into a newly arrived car before the owner's half out, leap literally under him as he steps out, start the car with the door flapping, and roar off to the next available spot, arc, pop in, brake, out, run.[19]

Similar uses of incremental tempi in which the readers are driven along with felt mindscapes or events moving in quick shifts leaving no break for them to think or analyze the now, the immediate, melt-in sentient experiences abound in Wang Wenxing. We see it in his "Afternoon," in the scene in which Ah Yin, alone in the room, is suddenly seized with fear by the sneaky descent of some mysterious being ("It") of her imagination, which drives her increasingly crazy to the degree of finally screaming explosively:

> ... Perhaps just now when she wasn't paying attention that thing had sneaked in. Perhaps it has been lurking where nobody could find it for a long time now. "Its" form is very indistinct. It seems like its mouth is open and its tense eyes wide open. "It" squats as it walks along with its hands touching the floor. But its hands and feet don't make the slightest noise. Just now, when it was walking, it seemed like it was getting closer to her. Now it knows she is paying attention, so it stops all of a sudden. Where is it? It seems to be in the hallway, just behind the door with its ear

---

19. Jack Kerouac, *On the Road*, ed. Scott Donaldson (New York: Viking Penguin, 1979), 9.

pressed to the paper, listening to her movements. Her hands freeze and she doesn't dare move. Listen! "Creak!" The sound of the floor straining under "its" weight! Her only chance is to risk running over and closing those two doors. She struggles with herself then eventually summons up her courage. Slowly, she stands up and narrows her eyes. Without blinking even once, she almost flies over to the living room door. With her head down she slams it shut, without ever daring to look through it. Then she rushes over to the other door and slams it shut. But just at that moment a huge, heart-rending metallic crash suddenly explodes in the frozen atmosphere. She covers her head with her hands and screams ...[20]

The passage is full of *mis-en-scène* qualities; readers have to hold their breath, so to speak, and with continually tightening emotion, get caught in the author's language strategies in emulating the morphology of feeling, rising and falling with Ah Yin's pulsating fear. We see similar pulsating and tightening of tension in his "Strong Wind," the killer typhoon, coming at the pedicab driver in accelerating vehemence:

A monster typhoon, a real howler, is on its way. It must be midnight by now. Hey! What's that? So fast? It's coming, it's coming, the big blow's on its way! Here's the rain! Boy, it sure is coming down, like a waterfall. Let me stop and put on my rain slicker, mister. That rain's washing my face. It's warm, like Shaoxing wine. There's the bridge up ahead.

Wow, the river's really swollen! It's not a river anymore, it's an ocean! Not a soul on the bridge, the wind must be fierce up there. Hear that sound, like peals of thunder. Shit! Charge! ... I can hardly breathe ... the bridge looks like it's swaying, it's made of sturdy concrete ... I don't imagine it'll ... last year a pedicab

20. Translated by Terrence Russell, in Shu-ning Sciban and Fred Edwards, eds., *Endless War: Fiction and Essays by Wang Wen-hsing* (Ithaca, NY: Cornell East Asia Program, Cornell University, 2011), 61, with Yip's modifcations.

crossing this bridge during a typhoon was swept into the river ...
said it can't be crossed, but we're halfway there ... halfway makes
me as happy as if we were already on the other side, with the first
half behind us, the rest of the way should be easy ... the first half,
now the second half ... we made it, mister!...............
    Whoosh. This wind's a real shrew. She grabs me by the hair
and shakes my head, she turns me cross-eyed. The next gust's
going to be even stronger. Listen to this sound ... it's My God,
knocked me over ... ow—ow—you fucking ... ow ... let me catch
my breath, sit here on the ground and catch my breath ... I
thought it was going to pick me right up off the ground just then,
I damn near took off flying, all that stopped me was the concrete
curb. Cut my face, I'm bleeding, must be deep. Hurts like hell,
like a knife gouging my face. How come I can't steady myself?
The wind must be stronger than I thought. I'm gasping for air,
like a bellows. My lungs feel like they're about to leap into my
throat.[21]

The cohesive power in these examples comes from a tensional distribution of energy reflecting the activities of the perceiving moment engen-
dering an attentiveness in the readers, in the words of Olson, "*at all
points*," the readers being now pulled into *immediate presencing* of the
energy in action, into the core of action *now* unfolding, *at once* viewing
and receiving/participating in what is happening before their eyes with
cinematic directness. Wang Wenxing is a master of controlled speed. I
have elaborated elsewhere on the use of rhythmic control to slow down
the progression in his "Mid-Summer on the Prairie" and "The Day of the
Sea Goddess," which leads to very different types of lyric condition.[22]
    The third way of sustaining readers' attention, with equal immediate

---

21. Translated by Howard Goldblatt in Shu-ning Sciban and Fred Edwards,
eds., *Endless War: Fiction and Essays by Wang Wen-hsing* (Ithaca: Cornell East
Asia Program, Cornell University, 2011) 159, 160, with Yip's modifications.
    22. Wai-lim Yip 葉維廉, *Zhongguo xiandai xiaoshuode fengmao* 中國現代小
說的風貌 (The style of modern Chinese novels) (Taipei: Chengzhong, 1970).

presencing, is the use of the monologue as a centripetal and centrifugal vortex of energy, at once sucking in and radiating out experiences/feelings that the writer/speaker is, *at this moment*, riding on. Monologue or soliloquy begins from an unusual moment of intensive crux of psychic disturbances or dislocation, a moment triggered by a heightened sense of a crisis. A monologue is actually a semi-monologue, addressing at once the speaker himself/herself and an intended audience that is absent. The speaker often projects him- or herself as the listener, expecting, in tone and attitude, some response from him or her. The response is actually furnished by the speaker, as it is reflected in the nuance of the monologue. Because a monologue arises from a moment of experience that is removed from the ordinary consciousness, unique and like no other, with all the events *synchronically* coming from one concentrated undivided instant that defies temporal-linear streamlining of ordinary logic, its progression, like the lyric, often moves "back and forth and in a circuitous manner. Its rhythm is associative, meditative, irregular, discontinuous, unpredictable, beyond the threshold of consciousness, relying on sound-links, ambiguous sense-links, or memory-links."[23] The speaker is caught into the indeterminable drift of disruptive events. This is why the erratic monologue in "Mother" takes on the flavor of a lyric:

Mao'er, come—....

He sneaked out while I was sleeping. Outside the sun severe. What if he gets heatstroke? Always make Mama worry. I don't know where he went. I don't have a clue where he went. Could it be—the ten-wheeled truck, so dark, oh, no not permitted—cannot—not possible. Calm down, calm down. The doctor said you have to stay calm. Think about something else when agitated. Sometimes I can't help worrying. Gufang tells me not to. The boy so big now. He says the doctor was right: I am the nervous-type. Alone in the afternoon sudden worry about him. Like seeing his classmates bully him, beat him up. I

---

23. This sentence is adapted from Northrop Frye, *Anatomy of Criticism: Four Essays* (Princeton, NJ: Princeton University Press, 1957), 254.

dash right to the school. Nearing school my heart was pounding, as if   leaping out of my throat. Now my heart is pounding fiercely. I didn't dare go in to see. Oh, thank heavens he is
sitting in the classroom fine. My heart is beating fiercely. Calm
down, calm down. They tell me not to let my imagination run
wild.

But I'm not well. If they want to cure me they have to tell
Mao'er not to leave me. Mao'er always must be at my side,
every single moment. Always at my side. Now I will follow the
doctor's orders. I will follow his orders and be an obedient
child. I can be a very obedient child. Doctor, am I your obedient child? Oh, no no no no. That's ridiculous. He looks young
enough to be a schoolboy....Mao'er. Mao'er, come find Mama,
come.... He was as tall as my shoulder. ......?......He is completely
different from when younger. Oh, you are Mama's again and
again little darling, your pouting little mouth when angry really
makes you cute, let Mama kiss you kiss you kiss you.... Mama
can't guess what is in your mind. You have built up a wall keeping Mama out.... You are hurting Mama's feelings. Oh, how
dumb how dumb. How can I lying so comfortably in bed let my
tears flow like this? Really a nervous wreck. Truly a laughing
stock. Little fool, little fool. Tears, tears won't make you a nice
child. You will not be the doctor's nice child. Doctor, am I your
nice child?[24]

The off-and-on, fragmentary, disjointed character of the speech, a Laca-
nian schizophrenic condition where the signifying chain is broken, reflects not only the psychic condition of Mother but also the interiority of
experience (itself as a contrast of the exteriority of the events in the
other three panels as well as subjective echoes to the visual rhythm of
the objective world) in which the language is nebulous at best, often
half-formed or at the edge of being formed. All monologues that we *read*

---

24. Whole passage modified, including syntax, from Michael Cody's translation by Yip to reflect disjointedness in the monologue.

are not *real* monologues; they have been *arbitrated* by organized and organizing language. What is offered is the *semblance* of a monologic condition by decreasing as much as possible the traces of the author's *interference* from which Wang Wenxing, a conscious language sculptor, is not always freed. This raises the question of *voices* in writing.

Eliot once talked about the three voices of poetry: "The first is the voice of the poet talking to himself—or to nobody. The second is the voice of the poet addressing an audience, whether large or small. The third is the voice of the poet when he attempts to create a dramatic character speaking in verse; when he is saying, not what he would say in his own person, but only what he can say within the limits of one imaginary character addressing another imaginary character."[25] The result of the third voice has become the genre of *dramatic monologue*. A dramatic monologue, by definition, is always a *conscious* representation or re-creation. Although these distinctions are very useful for the sake of discussion, the voice or voices that operate in a poem are often mixed and not so clear-cut. A case in point is the doubling and tripling voices in Eliot's *The Waste Land*.

The use of the *dramatic monologue* as the cohesive core in Wang Wenxing's masterpiece, *Bei hai de ren* 背海的人 (Backed against the sea) is ambiguously complex. I am not about to embark on a text of epic proportion by talking about it as if it were a monumental *Lyric*, which, in a sense, it can be. But I raise some questions for consideration here. In an interview, Lin Xiuling asked Wang Wenxing whether he also uses third-person perspective (or Eliot's second voice) in his narration in *Backed Against the Sea*. Wang answered: "*All* from the first-person perspective. Did I ever use third-person perspective?" This dead-serious affirmation is manifesto-loud. His use of the monologue form is intended to have the readers reside, *at all times*, with the psychic core of Ye's experience-feeling-complex. If they have any judgments, conclusions, or reactions to this narrated complex, he wants them to project these, with partial and hopefully total *sympathy and identification* with the speaker, within

---

25. T.S. Eliot, *The Three Voices of Poetry* (New York: Cambridge University Press, 1954), 6–7.

the contours set up in the monologic condition. Before I raise other questions to elaborate the complexities therein, let me bring up Wang's answer to Lin's question about the relationship with or possible continuity from his *Jia bian* 家變 (Family catastrophe). Wang said:

> Backed Against the Sea is different from *Family Catastrophe*, totally different. This is a conscious choice ... in that I want to write a *free* novel, *free, carefree*. I want it to be *borderless*, and *unrestrained*, like Whitman's *Leaves of Grass*. ... Family Catastrophe is purely an *introvert* novel. *Backed Against the Sea* is an *extrovert* novel; it does not have too many elaborations of "introvert life," even if there are some such passages, they are lodged in the surface phenomena of life. ... [*Backed Against the Sea*] hopes to embrace the myriad phenomena. It presents and represents not only the life of Ye, but the life of all mankind, like, say, the millions of truths/dharmas/methods in the Buddhist saying "All truths are void," this is to say, to embrace all faces of the world.[26]

He wants an all inclusive *miscellany*, or an *encyclopedic* spread of events and ideas, personal, historical, sociopolitical, brimming with tragic tangents, dark humors, irony, including all the forces that have gone into the making of the four modes of modernity discussed by Liao Ping-hui (Liao Binghui): alternative modernity, singular modernity, multiple modernities, and repressive modernity.[27] As such, it calls for a more or less objective representation of things and events (planned agenda) that happened in a *period* of time, complete with temporal sequencing and linear progression. It is clear that on the one hand, Wang uses the monologue form to move freely in and out of the *borderless* and *unrestrained* psychic terrain, an intense sustaining cohesive moment at once sucking in and

---

26. Lin Xiuling, "Wang Wenxing zhuan fang," 38.

27. Liao Binghui 廖炳惠, "Taiwan wenxue zhong de sizhong xiandaixing: yi *Bei hai de ren* xia ji weili" 台灣文學中的四種現代性：以《背海的人》下集為 例 (Four modern characteristics of Taiwan literature: taking *Backed Against the Sea* as an example," *Zhongwai wenxue* 中外文學 30.6 (2001.11): 75–92.

radiating out to multiple evocative images and ideas, and demands that readers reside inside this same complex as they read/sense their way through the ups and downs, cuts and turns of this outward odyssey; on the other hand, he wants to relate to readers his all-inclusive miscellany visions that he bodies forth from his notecard plot agenda. The conflict and tension therein is obvious. The second voice is threatening to break the cohesive core of the monologic condition. Only by letting the two impulses merge and operate in a nebulous relationship can the intended effect be preserved to allow the myriad events to flow out freely, as it were, from *one* voice, *one* mind-heart consciousness. Wang made his point clear: the protagonist is a composite persona who has some resemblances to a military officer he met in Nanfang'ao (a fishing harbor) where Wang once served part of his required military training before his graduation from university: "I only borrowed features of his looks, some of his living habits, his sick condition due to overdrinking perhaps ..."[28] This is why we are hearing both voices at work, keeping close sometimes to Ye, and sometimes to Wang or, shall we say, the alter-persona of Wang, when the speech is supposed to be delivered by Ye. The long paragraph of description of the surroundings of Shenkeng'ao is a good example. It reads like a page from a travel writing or diary, probably written down as such by Wang some time before he wrote this novel. Voice changes are frequent, from swearing Ye to erudite and diction-conscious Ye, who wells up every now and then with pockets of unmatched knowledge, ranging from literary history and aesthetics to philosophical discussions on the human condition or on power dynamics in politics. With this ambivalent voice that rides through the novel, we find Wang continues to work on atmosphere, nuances of light and dark, musical progression, and so on, typical of lyric writing. Take the description of Shenkeng'ao. Like Poe using images and atmosphere of darkness in "The Raven," the bird's mysterious arrival, tapping and rapping, bordering ghostliness, dark night, somber rhythm, the rhyming with "lore," "evermore," "nevermore"; like Baudelaire's inter-reinforcing images of "weighty lid of rain-clouds," "prison-bars," "spider-webs working into the depth of

---

28. Lin Xiuling, "Wang Wenxing zhuan fang," 33.

the brain" in his "Spleen"; or Mallarmé's incandescent sunlight, white swan caught in cutting white glacier, Wang weaves out of his oppressive prison-like harbor village with bleak shabby mountain ranges, endless miserable rains, darkening light, gray sea, all-edge-dissolved black night, favus-affected-like mountaintops, arid desert terrain.

Pound's 800-page *Cantos* has been called "a long poem that contains history." If Poe's dictum that all long poems are "poetic moments" linked together by prose is correct, we may wonder how Pound achieves poetry in his epic-oriented *Cantos*. The answer is that he builds an epic with highly *lyricized* fragments that demand intensive close reading. We don't know if the much preferred sustained attentiveness achieved in works of pregnant instants as evidenced in modernist lyrics can still be achieved in an infinitely extended monologue such as that in *Backed Against the Sea*. But one thing is clear: the invitation to pay attention, *at all times*, to the carving of words in Wang Wenxing's language art in *Backed Against the Sea* is an invitation to an odyssey intended to awaken all the sensing antennae of our (w)holistic sentient being, which has been eclipsed for a long time by the reductive regimentation of the lifeworld in modern times.

6 Family Catastrophe *and Its Connection with Traditional Chinese Literature*

Shu-ning Sciban
University of Calgary

CHINESE LITERATURE SINCE the May Fourth era has been heavily influenced by the West. Scholars have devoted great effort to depicting this influence by employing methodologies including comparative literature, influence studies, and translation theory. At the same time, it is not uncommon for modern and contemporary Chinese writers themselves to openly acknowledge the foreign influences in their works. Since Western influence in Chinese literature has been widely recognized and admitted, it is important to understand not only what this foreign influence is but also how it works in the process of producing Chinese literary works. Considering that the medium of Chinese literature is the Chinese language, it is unavoidable that the conventions of the Chinese literary tradition are applied and therefore cannot be neglected in trying to understand the process of writing Chinese literary works. In other words, a comprehensive understanding of modern Chinese literature requires an awareness of the "formula" for combining the foreignness of Western literary influence and the native aspect of Chinese literature. To verify this theory, I analyze the use of Chinese literary conventions by a "Westernized" Chinese writer, Wang Wenxing 王文興, in his famous novel *Jia bian* 家變 (Family catastrophe).

Wang Wenxing (b. 1939) is a prominent Taiwan writer whose reputation is based on his unique style and use of language. He is considered a Westernized writer for a variety of reasons. First, there is his educational background. He received his bachelor's degree from the Department of Foreign Languages and Literatures at National Taiwan University in 1961 and an MFA from the creative writing program at the University of Iowa in 1965. He was a university professor of English literature for forty years until his retirement in 2005. Both his post-secondary education and his career have been in the field of English literature. Second, Wang has openly admitted his admiration of Western writers and literary works. For instance, he has said he seldom reads Chinese books; he prefers Western fiction. His reason for this is that he regards the form and narrative techniques of Western fiction to be more highly developed than those of the Chinese, while all the merits of Chinese fiction could be found in its Western counterpart.[1] Many interviews with him have documented the influence of Western literary techniques on his writing. The two most detailed were conducted by Shan Dexing (also known as Te-hsing Shan).[2] In speaking with Shan, Wang pointed out that he often employed the Western narrative technique of "interior monologue," and liked montage—a modern film editing technique. He further admitted

---

1. Xia Zuli 夏祖麗, "Mingyun de jixian—Wang Wenxing fangwenji" 命運的 迹線—王文興訪問記 (The line of fate—an interview with Wang Wenxing), *Wobi de ren* 握筆的人 (Holders of the pen) (Taipei: Chunwenxue zazhishe, 1978), 29–30.

2. Shan Dexing [Te-hsing Shan] 單德興, "Wang Wenxing tan Wang Wen-xing" 王文興談王文興 (Wang Wenxing on Wang Wenxing), *Lianhe wenxue* 聯合文學 (Unitas) 3.8 (1987): 166–95. Reprinted as "Chuilian wenzi de ren" 錘煉文字的人 (The wordsmith) in *Duihua yu jiaoliu* 對話與交流 (Dialogues and interchanges) (Taipei: Maitian chuban, 2001), 39–83. The English translation of this interview is also included in this anthology, but it first appeared in *Modern Chinese Literature* 1.1 (1984): 57–65. Shan Dexing, "Ou kai tianyan qu hongchen—zai fang Wang Wenxing" 偶開天眼覷紅塵—再訪王文興 (Heavenly glance at the mundane world—the second interview with Wang Wenxing), *Zhongwai wenxue* 中外文學 (Chungwai literary monthly) 28.12 (2000): 182–99. Reprinted in *Duihua yu jiaoliu* 對話與交流 (Dialogues and interchanges) (Taipei: Maitian chuban, 2001), 80–104.

how Western writers, such as Maupassant, Tolstoy, Chekhov, Dostoevsky, Hemingway, Mann, Beckett, Huxley, Ring Lardner, and others,
had influenced him.[3]

Even so, since 1974, Wang has written several critical essays on Pu
Songling's 蒲松齡 *Liao zhai zhi yi* 聊齋志異 (Strange tales from make-
do studio), a collection of classical short stories published in 1680.[4] More
surprising was his 1993 publication of "Huai Zhongyuan" 懷仲園 (Zhongyuan: an appreciation). This revealed that the person who had most influenced his writing was a childhood friend named Zhongyuan, who had
introduced him the magnificence of both Chinese and Western art and
literature.[5] Zhongyuan turned out to be Min Zongshu 閔宗述, a professor of classical Chinese poetry at National Zhengzhi University in Taiwan. Furthermore, Wang's nonfiction publications during the past ten
years have increasingly been composed with linguistic features of *wenyan* 文言, the classical Chinese written language. As for subject matter,
these publications have often been about his reading of classical Chinese
poetry. This about-face is relevant to the question raised at the beginning of this essay: How does this phenomenon affect our understanding
of Wang Wenxing's writing? How are we to understand the relationship
between Wang Wenxing's writing and traditional Chinese literature?
How do Western and Chinese influences interact in Wang's writing?

Family Catastrophe, Wang's first and most famous novel, was published in 1972. It attracted much attention and sparked enthusiastic discussion among critics immediately after its publication. The discussions
focused mainly on two issues: the novel's portrayal of conflict between
a father and son, and the author's unconventional writing style. In keep-

---

3. Te-hsing Shan [Shan Dexing], "Wang Wen-hsing [Wang Wenxing] on
Wang Wen-hsing [Wang Wenxing]," *Modern Chinese Literature* 1.1 (1984.9): 57–
65.

4. Wang's first publication on *Strange Tales from Make-Do Studio* is: "*Liao
zhai* zhong de Dai'aonixi'an xiaoshuo 'Hu meng'" 聊齋中的戴奧尼西安小說
「狐夢」 ("Dreaming of fox," a story of Dionysian style in *Strange tales from
make-do studio*), *Youshi wenyi* 幼獅文藝 (Youshi literary arts) 39.4 (1974): 106–21.

5. Wang Wenxing, "Huai Zhongyuan" 懷仲園 (Zhongyuan: an appreciation), *Zhongguo shibao* 中國時報 (China times daily), August 22, 1993.

ing with Wang's educational background and the information he revealed in interviews, many scholars have associated *Family Catastrophe*
with Western modernist literature.[6] It was easy to assume there would
be no significant traces of techniques unique to Chinese literature in
Wang Wenxing's writing.

Zhang Hanliang, however, looked into the native Chinese character
of Wang's writing and claimed that his unique employment of Chinese
characters in fact "rejuvenates" the Chinese written language.[7] Zhang's
theory directly inspired my earlier discoveries of the other functions
(i.e., audio, visual, and semantic) of Chinese characters as used by Wang.[8]
Reading *Family Catastrophe* closely, I have found further characteristics
that are unique to Chinese classical literature, one of them being traditional plot structure. The structure of the plot resembles Chinese traditional literature in two aspects. First, the deepest structure of the plot, or
the structure of content, is similar to the general structure of classical
poetry, with four parts: *qi* 啓 or exposition; *cheng* 承 or development of
the theme; *zhuan* 轉 or transition; and *he* 合 or conclusion. Second, the
function of a story's introduction is to allude to its major themes and
foreshadow the development of the plot; these two functions of the introduction are also seen in classical Chinese novels. I demonstrate the
existence of these two aspects in *Family Catastrophe* to prove that despite what we may conclude from Wang Wenxing's earlier statements,
his literary style derives in part from traditional Chinese fiction.

---

6. Just to mention two examples of this kind of opinion: Li Oufan 李歐梵,
"Zai Taiwan faxian Kafuka: yiduan geren de huiyi" 在臺灣發現卡夫卡：一段個
人的回憶 (Discovering Kafka in Taiwan: one individual's recollection), trans.
Lin Xiuling, *Zhongwai wenxue* 中外文學 (Chungwai literary monthly) 30.6
(2001): 175–86. Li Youcheng 李有成, "Wang Wenxing yu xifang wenlei" 王文興
與西方文類 (Wang Wenxing and Western literary genres), *Zhongwai wenxue* 中
外文學 (Chungwai literary monthly) 10.11 (1982): 176–93.

7. Zhang Hanliang 張漢良, "Qian tan *Jia bian* de wenzi" 淺談「家變」的
文字 (A brief discussion of the language of *Family catastrophe*), *Zhongwai
wenxue* 中外文學 (Chungwai literary monthly) 1.12 (1973): 122–39.

8. Shu-ning Sciban, "Wang Wenxing's Poetic Language," dissertation, University of Toronto, 1995.

Family Catastrophe's Plot

In the composition of Chinese classical poetry, several rules and forms must be followed: in *jueju* 絕句 and *lüshi* 律詩 poetry, *qi, cheng, zhuan,* and *he* form the basic structure of a poem's content. *Qi* occurs when the beginning of a poem (one line for *jueju*, one couplet for *lüshi*) gives rise to a thought; *cheng* occurs in the second part to continue the thought of the first part; *zhuan* is the transition; and *he* concludes the thought and the narrative. For example, let us look at Du Fu's 杜甫 (712–770) "Jiang-nan feng Li Guinian" 江南逢李龜年 (On meeting Li Guinian in Jiang-nan):

> I often saw you in Prince Qi's house,
> And heard you a number of times in the hall of Cui Di.
> At this time, the scenery in Jiangnan is very beautiful.
> And here, in the season of fallen blossoms, I meet you once again.[9]

This is a seven-syllable *jueju* poem. In line one, the poet recalls his past meetings with the musician Li Guinian in a prince's residence. The location of their meetings suggests that Li was famous and popular at that time and also hints that his situation may be quite different now. Line one begins the story of Li Guinian; therefore, it is called the *qi* of the poem. In line two, the poet continues the theme, describing his past experiences of hearing Li perform in an influential official's hall. This is called the *cheng* line of the poem. In line three, Du Fu changes his subject, giving a general comment on the present scenery of Jiangnan and bringing us to the present time. This is the *zhuan* line. In line four, we read that the poet meets Li again, and this time they meet in a season of "fallen blossoms," which suggests that the famous musician, like the fallen blossoms, is also in the autumn of his life. The last line presents a stark contrast between Li's past and present, conveying in this contrast

---

9. This translation is based on one by David Hawkes with some of my own alterations. David Hawkes, *A Little Primer of Tu Fu* (Oxford: Clarendon Press, 1967), 212.

the poet's sentimental feelings. This line accords with the requirement of the *he* line of a poem.

With this demonstration of the basic structure of a Chinese classical poem, we should be ready to examine Wang Wenxing's *Family Catastrophe* to see if it follows the same arrangement. *Family Catastrophe* is subtly designed; looking carefully, one finds two levels of organization—narrative and temporal sequences are both enclosed in its plot.

Family Catastrophe is a symbolic novel about the transformation of Chinese traditional culture.[10] The fate of the *jia* 家 (family or home) and, more importantly, the father–son relationship symbolize the fate of the culture.[11] I use the development of the relationship between the father and son to demonstrate the plot structure of the novel.

First, the structure of the narrative sequence reflects the structure of classical Chinese poetry. Beginning with the disappearance of the father, *Family Catastrophe* actually develops two plot lines, one in the present and one in the past. The former is the son's search for his father; it is divided into fifteen sections marked sequentially with the letters of the English alphabet. The plot in the past follows the father–son relationship from the son's preschool days to the time of his father's disappearance. This plot line is divided into 157 sections marked with Arabic numerals and distributed among the 15 sections of the present-time plot line. The author also divides the whole story into three parts, "Diyi bu" (part one), "Di'er bu" (part two), and "Disan bu" (part three). The following scheme depicts the intermingling of the two plot lines:

<hr/>

10. In a conversation with Endo Shusaku, a famous Japanese writer, Wang Wenxing said: "The father in *Family Catastrophe* is symbolic. He is both the father of the Fans and the tradition of a culture." Wang's explanation helps affirm our understanding of the novel's theme. This conversation is recorded in "Cong Chenmo dao Jia bian—Yuanteng Zhouzuo yu Wang Wenxing de wenxue duihua" 從《沉默》到《家變》—遠藤周作與王文興的文學對話 (From *Silence* to *Family Catastrophe*—the literary dialogues between Endo Shusaku and Wang Wenxing), *Shu he ying* 書和影 (Books and films) (Taipei: Lianhe wenxue chubanshe, 1988), 320.

11. A discussion of the theme of this novel, particularly an analysis of Wang Wenxing's technique of naming, can be found in the third part of this chapter.

SCHEME 1

Diyi bu: A B C, 1–18, D, 19–25, E, 26–44, F, 45–51, G, 52–87, H, 88–110.

Di'er bu: I, 111–118, J, 119–123.

Disan bu: K, 124–127, L, 128–151, M, 152–155, N, 156–157, O.

This scheme, with its alphabetic and Arabic and Chinese numerals all signifying different divisions, shows the complexity of the narrative structure. However, according to some critics, although the structure of *Family Catastrophe* appears complicated, it is in fact very simple.[12] These critics hold that the novel is arranged according to its temporal sequence, and thus the structure of the novel is easy to understand. In other words, texts marked with Arabic numerals should be moved to the front and the texts marked by the letters of the alphabet to the back:

SCHEME 2

1–157, A–O.

Scheme 2 is much simpler than scheme 1. However, there is one thing in scheme 1 that is missing in scheme 2: the markers "part I, part II, part III."

In "Introduction to the Structural Analysis of Narratives," Roland Barthes asserts, "Art is a system which is pure, no unit ever goes wasted."[13] Wang, in his preface to *Xinke de shixiang* 新刻的石像 (New stone statue), expresses an almost identical concept: "Literary language must be like the signs of a mathematic formula; every word is useful. There cannot be one word more, neither one word less."[14] Considering the fact

---

12. Ouyang Zi 歐陽子, "Lun *Jia bian* zhi xingshi jiegou yu wenzi jufa" 論「家變」之形式結構與句法 (On the structure and syntax of *Jia bian*), *Zhongwai wenxue* 中外文學 (Chungwai literary monthly) 1.12 (1973): 51; Zhang Hanliang, "A Brief Discussion of the Language of *Family Catastrophe*," 122.

13. Roland Barthes, "Introduction to the Structural Analysis of Narratives," in *A Barthes Reader*, ed. Susan Sontag (New York: Hill & Wang, 1982), 261.

14. Wang Wenxing, "*Xin ke de shixiang* xu"《新刻的石像》序 (Preface to *New stone statue*), *Xiandai wenxue* 現代文學 (Modern literature) 35 (1968): 218. The translation is by Martin Sulev in *Endless War: Fiction and Essays by Wang*

that this 196-page novel took Wang Wenxing seven years to complete and his emphasis on the concept of "no wasted word," I assume that all of the markers in *Family Catastrophe* are there for a reason. Moreover, if every single word is important, the narrative sequence cannot be without semantic significance. What do these markers—the letters of the English alphabet and Arabic and Chinese numerals—tell us?

My answer to this question is that *Family Catastrophe*'s plot reflects the basic structure of Chinese classical poetry: the four stages of *qi*, *cheng*, *zhuan*, and *he*; and all the markers, including "Diyi bu," "Di'er bu," and "Disan bu"; the letters of the English alphabet; and Arabic numerals indicate this structure. The following scheme gives us a better idea of the structure:

SCHEME 3

Qi	*Cheng*	*Zhuan*	*He*
A B C	D–H	I–J	K–O
	1–110	111–123	124–157
(Diyi bu)		(Di'er bu)	(Disan bu)

The introduction of *Family Catastrophe* includes sections A, B, C. In section A, we see the father walking out of the home, the result of many family conflicts, especially the deterioration of his relationship with his son, Fan Ye, and thus the beginning of the terrible situation the Fan family faces throughout the novel. In sections B and C, the author touches slightly on every aspect of the family's crisis related directly or indirectly to the father's disappearance, such as the relationships between the father and the protagonist, the mother and the protagonist, the mother and the second older brother, the second older brother and the father, and so on. These aspects fully unfold in the latter parts of the novel; therefore, these three sections give a good introduction to the novel as a whole and are called the *qi* or the expository part.

Wen-hsing, eds. Shu-ning Sciban and Fred Edwards (Ithaca, NY: Cornell East Asia Program, Cornell University, 2011), 370.

The other sections of "Diyi bu" or part I, from D to H and from 1 to
110, are the *cheng* part of *Family Catastrophe*. Superficially, only the sections from D to H seem to continue sections A, B, and C because they all
describe the present time. However, two plot lines are actually developed out of the exposition: one in the present (sections D–H) and one in
the past (sections 1–110). Although these lines differ in time, they are
parallel in theme, that is, they are the descriptions of the father–son relationship in two generally harmonious periods.

In the expository part, we read that the father leaves home because
his relationship with his son has deteriorated. However, as revealed in a
dream of the protagonist, this relationship was rather harmonious in the
protagonist's childhood, at the beginning of their relationship. Sections
1–110 are depictions of this period. In section 4, five-year-old Fan Ye
expresses his preference for his father over his mother (p. 20). In section
16, we find that he feels very comfortable and safe sleeping beside his
father because his father is like a great wall that can block the invasion
of any danger (p. 27). In the bath scene of section 40, he is surprised by
the beauty of his father's body; he compares its whiteness to the color of
a lily, a symbol of holiness. Although their relationship does not deterio-
rate suddenly, there are some omens of that change in sections 1–110,
such as sections 28–29, in which Fan Ye is irritated by the fact that he
has to suspend his schooling for a short time because his father loses his
job and is not able to pay his tuition fees (pp. 40–42). In section 109, Fan
Ye is angry because his father does not intervene when his mother
makes accusations against innocent people (p. 108). Nevertheless, the
description of the conflicts between father and son in these sections is by
no means comparable, in quality and quantity, to that of the harmonious
aspect of their relationship. Because the author in sections 1–110 gives a
realistic portrayal of the early period of the father–son relationship,
which has already been pointed out as the central problem of the family
crisis, these sections can be regarded as a continuation of the introductory sections, although they deal with a different time period.

Sections D–H are descriptions of Fan Ye's first long trip to the south
to look for his father. This trip is planned at the end of section C and is
obviously a continuation of the introduction. However, the importance

of these sections is not that they occur at the same time described in the introductory sections but that they are descriptions of the second harmonious period of the father–son relationship reflected by Fan Ye's ardent search for his father.[15] No doubt the relationship at this time is far different from what we see in sections 1–110, and the fact the father has disappeared reveals that the relationship is actually very bad. Nevertheless, considering Fan Ye's feeling of unease when he discovers his father is gone, we must say that he has not entirely lost his affection for his father. For this reason, we may consider the relationship described in sections D–H to be comparatively harmonious.

Given the harmony with which the father–son relationship is depicted, we see that sections D–H and sections 1–110 are actually parallel in theme. Because these sections describe two beginning phases of different stages of this relationship, they should be considered the development of the theme that arises out of the exposition: they are the *cheng* part of the novel.

The transitional part of the novel, or *zhuan*, is "Di'er bu" or part II, including sections 11–123 and I–J. Here, the two plot lines from the previous parts continue to develop but involve major changes in the father–son relationship. The past plot line stresses the unhappy experience Fan Ye goes through; his experiences cause him to detest his father more and more. Sections 111 to 123 are full of incidents through which he sees his father's shortcomings. In section 111, his father rudely scares away the poor neighbors' children (p. 116); in section 112, he is shown as being incapable of supporting the family economically and complains that his colleagues mistreat him (pp. 117–19); in section 116, he is shown as being incompetent in dealing with women and does not have any self-respect (pp. 125–29); in section 122, the Chen Boqi incident makes Fan

---

15. The enthusiasm is shown in several sections in this part. In section F, for instance, Fan Ye, while searching for his father, particularly likes being close to old people who are the same age as his father (p. 49). In section H, walking outside of a Catholic church that he thought might be a place where his father would go, he feels helpless and is in a state of emotional turmoil because it is the end of his trip and he still has not found his father. He prays to God not to shatter his last hope—that his father will have returned by the time he returns home.

Ye realize that his father is utterly incapable of improving the family's financial situation (pp. 139–45). In this period, Fan Ye gradually loses his respect for his father, and clearly the Chen Boqi incident marks a sea change in the father–son relationship.

In sections I to J, the author describes the change in the son's attitude toward his father's disappearance. On the one hand, disappointed by fruitless searching, Fan Ye becomes skeptical about his father's disappearance; he suspects that his father is in a battle with him—hiding somewhere to see if his son is sincere in wanting him to return (p. 136). On the other hand, he tends to believe that his father will never come home again, so he moves the father's desk and throws away his father's shoes (pp. 136–37).

From what is described in sections 111–23 and sections I and J, we can tell that Fan Ye of the past and Fan Ye of the present are both in transitional stages in terms of the relationship with his father. The former changes from loving his father to detesting him; the latter goes from wanting his father to come home to preferring him to stay away for good. These changes of attitude confirm that these sections form the transitional part of the novel.

"Disan bu" or part III, including sections 124–57 and sections K to O, is the last part of the structure of the content, the conclusion of the novel. Here the author concentrates on the depiction of the destruction of the relationship between father and son.

In sections 124–57, Fan Ye, now an adult, regards his father as a weakling, associating him with cats (pp. 150, 194), fragile girls (p. 151), or a young child (pp. 173, 175). His attitude toward his father becomes more and more distant; in sections 124 and 125, he contradicts his father openly (pp. 152, 153–54); in section 126, he laughs at his father's habits (p. 154), looks down on his father's knowledge (pp. 154, 155) and, surprising even to himself, he finds that he does not care whether his father lives or dies (p. 156). In section 156, he does not allow his father to eat with him, the father has to eat after the son finishes his meal; often he does not allow his father to eat at all and once even locks him in the bedroom for three days (pp. 189–93). At this point, we can see that the son reverses family roles with his father and treats the old man inhumanely.

During the destruction of the relationship, Fan Ye is not completely ignorant of his role as a son; he also has a sense of guilt but is determined not to deal with it and eventually forces his father to leave home. Section 153 tells us that Fan Ye often strongly regrets this behavior and wants to change (pp. 184–85). However, in section 156, the most severe conflicts occur. On his father's birthday, Fan Ye orders him to leave the dining table before he has finished his dinner (pp. 191–92); on another occasion, he locks his father up because he discovers his father has written a letter to a relative in the United States asking for money (p. 193). We see that Fan Ye's sense of regret is insincere, serving only to soothe his conscience.

This attitude is explicitly reflected in the other plot line in the conclusive part. From sections K to O, the description of Fan Ye's second search for his father, we find that he no longer cares whether he finds his father, but he goes through the motions of traveling simply to soothe his uneasy conscience. In section K, at the beginning of his second trip to the south, the narrator tells us that it has been a long time since Fan Ye looked for his father. He only resumes the search because an institution for the poor in a southern city asks him to take a look at an old man they have recently found to see if he is Fan Ye's father. He decides to take this opportunity to visit other places to look for his father. He does not hold out much hope for success, but by going to look, he can ease his conscience (p. 148).

In section O, the very last section of the novel, we see that during the two years since his father's disappearance, Fan Ye and his mother seem to be much happier (p. 194). From sections K to O, Fan Ye simply wants to prove to himself that there is no use looking for his father, so he takes a second trip to the south. He believes his conscience will no longer bother him if, after such an effort, he stops searching. Therefore, we can conclude that the father–son relationship has vanished; the marker of this section, O, the same sign as zero, can be understood as implying the emptiness or non-existence of the relationship.[16]

16. I am grateful to Milena Doleželová-Velingerová, who first observed this and mentioned it to me during a course titled "Contemporary Chinese Fiction" I took with her in 1989.

Sections 124–57 and sections K–O portray the deterioration of the father–son relationship until it disappears completely; they mark the resolution of the central problem of the story and the end of the novel. Therefore, this part is called the *he* of the novel.

In short, from the foregoing analysis, we can see that *Family Catastrophe*'s structure of content reflects the basic structure of Chinese classical poetry; it has all four parts of poetic structure: *qi, cheng, zhuan*, and *he*. "Diyi bu" contains the *qi* and *cheng*, "Di'er bu" contains the *zhuan*, and "Disan bu" is the *he*.

The Exposition of *Family Catastrophe*

The introductory part of *Family Catastrophe* is contained in the first three sections of the novel. Judging from the two functions of this part—revealing the themes of the novel and foreshadowing the plot—we can say that it resembles the prologue of a Chinese classical novel.

What is the function of the prologue in a Chinese classical novel? Zhang Zhupo 張竹坡, a seventeenth-century literary critic, described the role of "chapter one" in a classical novel:

> Chapter one in a one-hundred chapter narrative could be likened to a myriad of individual hairs tied together by a single thread [and spread over the back of the body] or to the sprinkler of a watering can which, when lifted, simultaneously releases individual thread-like streams.[17]

In other words, the beginning chapter of a novel should be a "miniature model" for the whole novel that is spread out in later chapters.[18]

---

17. Zhang Zhupo, *Gaohetang piping diyi qi shu* Jin ping mei 皋鶴堂批評第一奇書金瓶梅 (Gaohetang's commentary on the first masterpiece, *Jin ping mei*), 1b–2a. The translation is Doleželová-Velingerová's from "Seventeenth-Century Chinese Theory of Narrative: A Reconstruction of Its System and Concepts," in *Poetics East and West*, ed. Milena Doleželová-Velingerová, Toronto Semiotics Circle Monograph Series, no. 4 (Toronto: Toronto Semiotics Circle, 1988–1989), 146.

18. Doleželová-Velingerová, "Seventeenth-Century Chinese Theory of Narrative: A Reconstruction of Its System and Concepts," 146.

Chapter 1 of *Honglou meng* 紅樓夢 (Dream of the red chamber) well exemplifies this theory. In this chapter, the relationship between Shenying Shizhe 神瑛侍者 (Divine Luminescent Stone-in-Waiting) and Jiangzhu Cao 絳珠草 (Crimson Pearl Flower) foretells the relationship between Jia Baoyu and Lin Daiyu in the novel and foreshadows the plot development. On the other hand, the names of the location where the stone—Jia Baoyu's identity in the heavens—is found by the Daoist priest and the Buddhist monk, Dahuang Shan 大荒山 (Great Fable Mountain), Wuji Yai 無稽崖 (Incredible Crags), and Qinggeng Feng 青埂峰 (Greensickness Peak), imply the two themes of the novel: love and the absurdity of the real world.[19] Therefore, chapter 1 is a mirror of the whole novel, and a full understanding of it is definitely helpful in understanding the novel.

As in chapter 1 of *Dream of the Red Chamber*, *Family Catastrophe*'s first three sections are a miniature version of the whole novel because they are, in Zhang Zhupo's term, the "sprinkler head" from which issue individual plots and themes. Let us look at the plot aspect first. As I mentioned earlier, this novel, beginning from the *cheng* part, including sections D–H and sections 1–110, develops two plot lines; one is present time and the other is past time. In the present, it describes the protagonist's process of searching for his father; in the past, it is the description of the Fan family relationship, focusing on that between the father and son. This relationship is at first harmonious, then deteriorates, and eventually vanishes. In the introductory sections, this type of development is implied in both plot lines.

In sections B and C, when Fan Ye realizes that his father is really gone, his reaction prefigures his methods of seeking his father in the later parts of the novel: his intensive reading of the newspapers; searching the neighborhood; phoning his second oldest brother; planning to take a trip down south to check churches, temples, and institutions for the poor all foreshadow his placing an advertisement in the newspaper— included at the beginning of each later section marked by a letter of the

---

19. For an explanation of how chapter 1 of *Dream of the Red Chamber* pre-announces the novel, including the clues I mention here, see Lucien Miller, *Masks of Fiction in Dream of the Red Chamber* (Tuscon: The University of Arizona Press, 1975).

alphabet—his two trips to the south, his visiting of churches (sections E, H), temples (section H), police stations (section K), institutions for the poor (section K), and his brother's home (section N).[20]

His two dreams in this part pre-announce how the father–son relationship develops from beginning to end. In the first dream, Fan Ye sees his father returning home. In this dream, his father is only in his thirties, and Fan Ye is glad to see him; these are allusions to the early harmonious relationship between them (pp. 6–7). In the later dream—more correctly, a daydream—Fan Ye imagines the situation when his father comes home, but this time he is disgusted by the father's old game of withholding information that people are eager to know (p. 13). This feeling of detestation is also an omen for the destruction of their relationship.

In addition to the two lines of development in the plot, there are many problems, such as Fan Ye's relationship with his mother, the mother's conflicts with the second oldest brother, and the mystery of the eldest son of the Fan family, which are also brought up at the beginning and then fully elaborated in latter sections.

As for the themes of the novel, Wang Wenxing uses the same method that the author of *Dream of the Red Chamber*, Cao Xueqin 曹雪芹, employs to disclose the themes of his story, which is "naming."

Before we analyze the father's and the protagonist's names as examples, we should first state the main theme of the novel. Chen Dianyi in an article on *Family Catastrophe* points out that it is a novel describing the transformation of Chinese traditional culture in the minds of the Chinese who fled from mainland China to Taiwan after 1949.[21] To give a full explanation of this theory is impossible in this short chapter, but an understanding of the significance of the protagonist's and the father's names will give us some idea of it.

In section B, the names of the father and the protagonist are intro-

---

20. I am grateful to Allen Wu (Wu Guoqiang) who first mentioned to me that all the methods Fan Ye uses to search for his father in the entire story can be found in the expository part of the novel.

21. Chen Dianyi 陳典義, "*Jia bian* de rensheng guanzhao yu chaofeng" 「家變」之人生觀照與嘲諷 (View of life and irony in *Family Catastrophe*), *Zhongwai wenxue* 中外文學 (Chungwai literary monthly) 2.2 (1973.7): 148–49.

duced. The father is called Fan Minxian 范閩賢. The second character—*min*—is a short name for the province of Fujian in China, the province that is closest to Taiwan and the motherland of the majority of Taiwanese. Hence, *min*, from the perspective of a resident of Taiwan, can be a word that means China or the Chinese tradition and traditional culture. The third character—*xian*—means "to be capable" or "to be virtuous." The concept of *xian* was stressed strongly by scholars and the court in ancient times. Combining the meanings of these two characters, we can interpret the symbolic meaning of the father: on the one hand, he represents Chinese traditional culture, which was thought to be splendid; on the other hand, he also personifies the orthodoxy of this culture, such as Confucianism or the government.

In section 126, Fan Ye criticizes some of his father's "laughable" customs, such as putting a hot towel on his face after supper, believing that it helps the circulation, or rinsing his mouth with cold water in the summer, thinking that it is good for releasing summer heat (p. 154). This criticism is directed at the old customs of the culture and the culture in general. In section 152, Fan Ye's attacks on the concept of *xiao* 孝 (filial piety)—the most important obligation one should have in Confucianism—can be seen as the rejection of Confucianism. In section 133, when the father encounters some problems in his office, Fan Ye criticizes him and his way of dealing with them. This is a criticism of the traditional bureaucracy (pp. 164–70). At the end of the same section, the father, having often been made fun of by his colleagues, eventually fights with one of them; the person's name is Huang Chuan'ou 黃傳歐. If we accept the hypothesis that the father symbolizes China, then the name Huang Chuan'ou is also meaningful: it means that the culture of China—represented by the character *huang* (yellow) because it is the color of China—has been defeated by Western culture, hinted at in *Chuan'ou* (*chuan* is "to hand down something from generation to generation"; *ou* is Europe or the West). The fight between the father and Huang Chuan'ou also symbolizes the struggle Chinese culture has experienced with the "invasion" of Western culture in the twentieth century.

From these sections, we know that the father is the embodiment of China, Chinese culture, Confucianism, and the government, and this is implied in the second and third characters of the father's name. What about the son's name? Since he is the son of China and the heir to Chinese culture, we assume that his name will reveal the future of the nation or the fate of the culture. The son's name is Fan Ye. The character for Ye is 曄, the combination of two components "sun" 日 and "China" 華, suggesting a meaning of "sunny China." However, the family name is Fan 范, which can be associated with its homophone *fan* 反 (opposite or against). Therefore, the son's full name can be interpreted this way: although China and Chinese culture seem to be as dominant in the Chinese people's life as usual, they actually are losing their influence without the common people realizing it.[22]

One more thing that should be mentioned is that the name Fan Ye is also the name of the author of an ancient classic, *Houhan shu* 後漢書 (History of the Latter Han). Wang Wenxing's choice of this name for the protagonist of the novel can also be interpreted as that the character bearing this name will write the history of the future China. This implication is found in the title of the book historian Fan Ye wrote: *Houhan shu*; *hou* means "latter, later or future," *han* means "China," *shu* is "history or records." Although the historian Fan Ye wrote *History of the Latter Han*, the present Fan Ye will write the future history of China. No wonder the occupation of our protagonist is that of a teaching assistant in the Department of History at the University of C (C means China, too).

In brief, as discussed, the information revealed in sections A, B, and C covers almost all of the major plot developments and themes of this novel. It proves that the introductory part of *Family Catastrophe* functions the same way "chapter 1" does in a classical novel.

Wang Wenxing, like many writers of the May Fourth Movement, has emphasized the importance of literary techniques learned from writers

---

22. At a dinner on February 22, 2009, Wang Wenxing admitted to some friends and scholars that he mistook the pronunciation of 曄 for *hua* when he was writing *Family Catastrophe*; he chose this character particularly for its pronunciation. Although this reason may be purely acoustic, it does not rule out the possibility of it also being semantic, which is reflected by the pronunciation.

of Western fiction. Nevertheless, in his work we can still find characteristics of Chinese classical literature. *Family Catastrophe* offers good examples. The structure of the plot is identical to that of classical poetry; it
consists of all four parts: *qi, cheng, zhuan,* and *he.* Also, the *qi,* or exposition of *Family Catastrophe,* exemplifies the function of chapter 1 of a
classical novel, projecting the major themes and pre-announcing the
plot's development. Our discovery of the connections between Wang
Wenxing's *Family Catastrophe* and classical literature clarifies one thing,
which is that the vitality of Chinese literary tradition in this century
should not be underestimated. The stylistic about-face in Wang's recent
writing has two possible interpretations. First, it could reflect the change
in Wang's reading agenda. In his speech on "Reading and Writing,"
Wang states:

> Looking back, I've always felt it is better to say that I am a reader
> rather than to say I am a writer. This is not only because, consid-
> ering things over time, I have spent much more time reading
> than writing (it is like that now, but it has even been more so
> over the course of my life)—but also because reading basically
> cannot be separated from writing. Reading, indeed, is the source
> of writing. Even more so, before one can judge what kind of
> writer a writer is, one must first examine what kind of reader he
> is. Thus, to say I am a writer is not as good as saying that I am a
> reader.[23]

Like many writers, Wang understands that he has been influenced by
many great writers before him. In the speech, he went on to say that
during his four years as a university undergraduate he read mainly
Western literature; later, at an unspecified time, he discovered Du Fu.
Since then, he has been reading him daily. His recent publications on

---

23. This speech was given at the international conference "The Art of Narrative Language: Wang Wen-hsing's Life and Works," held at the University of
Calgary, February 19–21, 2009. Wang's comments were translated by Ihor Pidhainy and are included in this anthology.

other classical Chinese works and writers could be understood as the
result of his reading expanding further. The second interpretation is that
the influence of native culture is usually overlooked in studies of literature influenced by a foreign culture. This reminds us of what Wang reveals in his "Zhongyuan: An Appreciation," mentioned earlier . A childhood friend, by exposing him to both traditional Chinese and Western
arts and literature at a young age, influenced his writing throughout his
life. The native influence has been the foundation and has always been
present. In light of that, it would be beneficial to our study of twentieth-
century Chinese fiction—or all literature with a foreign influence—if, in
addition to exploring foreign influences, we could investigate the presence of native traditions as well. Only by doing both can we possibly
move further—discover the "formula" of combining foreign and native
literary traditions in the process of creating a new art of writing. Let me
conclude by quoting an analogy from Wang Wenxing: "The history of
human art is like a long train with each car painted a different color.
When a car is added, there is no need to jettison the previous car: all the
cars may proceed along the same track." [24]

24. Wang Wenxing, "Qiantan xiandai wenxue" 淺談現代文學 (A brief discussion of modern literature), in *Shu he ying* 書和影 (Books and films) (Taipei:
Lianhe wenxue chubanshe, 1988), 188. The translation is by Christopher Lupke,
in Shu-ning Sciban and Fred Edwards, eds., *Endless War: Fiction and Essays by
Wang Wen-hsing* (Ithaca, NY: Cornell East Asia Program, 2011).

7   *The Use of* Liheci *in* Family Catastrophe

Wei Cai
University of Calgary

Introduction to *Liheci*

Liheci are hotly debated phenomena in Chinese language studies. They consist of two morphemes and can be used with or without other constituents inserted in between. An example of a *liheci* is *xi zao* (洗澡, to take a shower). *Xi* and *zao* may be used together as illustrated below in example (1); particles or a measure word may be inserted between the morphemes, as shown in examples (2), (3), and (4).

(1)

他	每天	晚上	洗澡。
Ta	meitian	wanshang	xizao
He	everyday	evening	shower

He takes a shower every evening.

(2)

他	洗	了	澡	就	睡觉	了。
Ta	xi	le	zao	jiu	shuijiao	le
He wash	Pfv	shower		then	sleep	Prc[1]

He went to bed after taking a shower.

---

1. The abbreviations used in this essay are adopted from J.S. Wu: Exp stands for the experiential marker; CL stands for a classifier; DE stands for the possessive/modifier marker (的/得/地), Dur stands for the durative marker; Prc stands

(3)

他	已经	洗	过	澡	了。
Ta	yijing	xi	guo	zao	le
He	already	wash	Exp	shower	Prc

He has already taken a shower.

(4)

他	想	去	洗	个	澡。
Ta	xiang	qu	xi	ge	zao
He	want	go	wash	CL	shower

He wants to take a shower.

The number of *liheci* in Chinese is large. Shi Aibing[2] documents that there are 4,066 *liheci* in the *Contemporary Chinese Liheci Usage Dictionary*[3] and 3,260 disyllabic *liheci* in the *Contemporary Chinese Dictionary*.[4]

The majority of *liheci* have a verb-object or verb-complement construction. For *liheci* with a verb-object construction, the first morpheme indicates an action; the second morpheme indicates the object to which the action is related. What can be inserted between the morphemes includes aspectual particles (e.g., *shuo guo hua* 说过话), pronouns (e.g., *qing tamen ke* 请他们客), classifiers (e.g., *ju ge gong* 鞠个躬), and complex modifiers (e.g., *fuwan le yubeiyi junguan yi* 服完了预备役军官役).

---

for a sentence particle; Pfv stands for the perfective marker. J.S. Wu, "Terminability, Wholeness and Semantics of Experiential *Guo*," *Journal of East Asian Linguistics* 17.1 (2008): 1–32.

2. Shi Aibing 石爱兵, "Jiushi niandai hou liheci yanjiu zongshu" 九十年代后离合词研究综述 (A comprehensive review of the studies of *liheci* after the 1990s), *Hetian shifan zhuanke xuexiao xuebao* 和田师范专科学校学报 26.6 (2006.7): 108–9.

3. Yang Qinghui 杨庆蕙, *Xiandai hanyu liheci yongfa cidian* 现代汉语离合词用法词典 (Contemporary Chinese liheci usage dictionary) (Beijing: Beijing Shifan daxue chubanshe, 1995).

4. *Xiandai hanyu cidian* 现代汉语词典 (Contemporary Chinese dictionary) (Shanghai: Shangwu yinshuguan, 1996).

For *liheci* with a verb-complement structure, the first morpheme indicates an action; the second represents the outcome of the action, such as *kanjian* (看见) or *shuofu* (说服). Wang Sumei reports that in the *Contemporary Chinese Dictionary* (1996) there are 3,184 *liheci* in the verb-object form, making up 97 percent of the total number of *liheci*; the number of verb-complement *liheci* is 80, making up 2.4 percent of the total; the number of other types of *liheci* is very low.[5] This chapter specifically focuses on the verb-object *liheci*.

Controversies exist over whether *liheci* should be categorized as words or phrases and what criteria should be used to delineate *liheci*. Zhou Shangzhi compared and summarized different types of criteria in his book *A Study of Chinese Liheci*.[6] He argued that the criteria used for defining *liheci* are only meaning- and function-based because the Chinese language does not have morphological variations. These criteria are more subjective than the more transparent form-based criteria. Therefore, "such criteria can only be relative, indefinite and indecisive. ... This is decided by the nature of the Chinese language."[7]

Zhao Shuhua and Zhang Baolin have proposed four criteria for judging *liheci*.[8] First, the word should contain a bound morpheme. An example is *daoqian* (道歉), in which the nominal constituent *qian* (歉) is the bound morpheme. Second, the constituents in *liheci* are subject to strict collocation restriction. For example, the verbal constituent *bi* (毕) when used in the word "to graduate" is collocated only with *ye* (业); the nominal constituent *yang* (殃) when used to mean "to suffer" is collocated only with *zao* (遭). Third, a non–verb-object structure is used as

5. Wang Sumei 王素梅, "Lun shuangyinjie liheci de jiegou, kuozhan ji yongfa" 论双音节离合词的结构、扩展及用法 (A discussion on the structure, extension, and usage of disyllabic *liheci*), *Shenyang shifan xueyuan xuebao* 沈阳师范学院学报 23.4 (1999): 62–66.

6. Zhou Shangzhi 周上之, *Hanyu liheci yanjiu* 汉语离合词研究 (A study of Chinese *liheci*) (Shanghai: Shanghai waiyu chubanshe, 2006).

7. Ibid., 66–67.

8. Zhao Shuhua 赵淑华 and Zhang Baolin 张宝林, "Liheci de queding yu liheci de xingzhi" 离合词的确定与离合词的性质 (Definition and nature of *liheci*), *Yuyan jiaoxue yu yanjiu* 语言教学与研究 1 (1996): 40–51.

such. An example is *youyong* (游泳) in which the two morphemes were originally in a coordinate relationship but subsequently *yong* (泳) came to be regarded as the object of *you* (游). Fourth, the word can be extended and used as a noun or adjective. *Zhengqi* (争气) is a qualified candidate of this group of *liheci* in the sense that it is used as an adjective and can be extended by inserting 了 (争了气) or 口 (争口气) in between. Zhao and Zhang argue that a word that satisfies any of the four criteria is a *liheci*. *The Contemporary Chinese Dictionary* includes the symbol // to mark *liheci* and serve as an explicit reference for the study of this type of word.

The Use of *Liheci* in *Family Catastrophe*

This chapter investigates the use of *liheci* in the novel *Jia bian* 家变 (Family catastrophe) written by Wang Wenxing.[9] I use the *Contemporary Chinese Dictionary* (version 5) as the basis for determining a *liheci*.[10] For words that are not collected in this dictionary, I adopted the criteria Zhao and Zhang proposed to decide whether a word belongs to the category of *liheci*.

As the *Contemporary Chinese Dictionary* (version 5) records words used in Putonghua, I also consider regional differences in language use between Taiwan and mainland China and Wang's distinctive style in coining words or using existing words in a creative way. This is for the purpose of truly reflecting the use of *liheci* in his novel. For instance, *tanqi* (叹气) in Putonghua means "to let out one's long breath audibly as from unhappiness" (*Contemporary Chinese Dictionary*, p. 1324). In *Family Catastrophe*, *tanxi* (叹息) is used for this meaning and therefore counted as a *liheci* in this study.

Using these principles, I collected 102 sentences containing *liheci*

---

9. Wang Wenxing 王文兴, *Jia bian* 家变 (Family catastrophe) (Shenyang: Liaoning daxue chubanshe, 1988).

10. *Xiandai hanyu cidian (diwu ban)* 现代汉语词典（第五版）(Contemporary Chinese dictionary, version 5) (Shanghai: Shanwu yinshuguan, 2006).

with constituents inserted between the two morphemes. In the following discussion, the term *liheci* is used specifically to refer to this type of word unless specified otherwise. (*Liheci* without constituents inserted between are not considered here.) Table 7.1 records the usages of *liheci* in the novel.

Table 7.1 reveals the features of the use of *liheci* in *Family Catastrophe*. First, the frequency of the use of *liheci* in this novel is similar to that in other literary works. Wang Chunxia analyzed the *Contemporary Chinese Study Corpus* and found that the average use of *liheci* in novels is 11.71 occurrences per 10,000 characters.[11] The number of occurrences of *liheci* in *Family Catastrophe* is 102 of the total 90,000 characters.

Second, the distribution of the different types of *liheci* in Wang's novel displays differences from that in other literary works. In decreasing order of frequency, the three major types of *liheci* used in *Family Catastrophe* are words containing post-verbal constituents (49.0 percent), words containing both post-verbal constituents and a modifier of the second morpheme (25.5 percent), and words with a modifier of the second morpheme (23.6 percent). Among the specific categories, the most heavily used *liheci* are those containing aspectual markers (29.4 percent) and those including both post-verbal constituents and modifiers of the second morpheme (25.5 percent); the next most frequently used *liheci* contain complements (12.7 percent) and numeral-measure words (11.8 percent). *Liheci* containing an adjective modifying the second morpheme (6.9 percent), repetition of verbs (5.9 percent), and a pronoun modifying the second morpheme (3.9 percent) are also used to some extent in the novel.

Using Laoshe's novel *Sishi tongtang* 四世同堂 (Four generations under one roof) and Lü Xiaoming's drama *Kewang* 渴望 (Longing) as databases (800,000 characters), Wang Haifeng recorded 1,029 sentences

---

11. Shi, "A Comprehensive Review of the Studies of *Liheci* after 1990s." Wang Chunxia 王春霞, "Jiyu yuliaoku de liheci yanjiu" 基于语料库的离合词研究 (The study of *liheci* by using database). MA thesis, Beijing Language and Culture University, 1991.

Table 7.1 The use of *liheci* in *Family Catastrophe*

Forms	Inserted Constituents	Token	Percentage	Example
Postverbal constituents (49.0%)	Aspectual markers *zhe* (着), *le* (了), *guo* (过)	30	29.4	*she le zong* (失了踪) (p. 12) *sheng le qi* (生了气) (p. 109)
	DE (的/地/得)	1	1.0	*tu de xue* (吐的血) (p. 121)
	Complements of verbs	13	12.7	*di xia tou* (低下头) (p. 31) *shen chu shou* (伸出手) (p. 83)
	Repetition of verbs	6	5.9	*tan le yi tan tian* (谈了一谈天) (p. 114)
The second morpheme containing a modifier (23.6%)	Noun	1	1.0	*shuo guan hua* 说官话 (p. 35)
	Adjective	7	6.9	*yan jia xi* 演假戏 (p. 151)
	Pronoun	4	3.9	*qing tamen ke* 请他们客 (p. 139)
	Numeral-measure word	12	11.8	*chu yici chai* 出一次差 (p. 46)
Postverbal constituents + modifiers of the second morpheme		26	25.5	*fu wan yubeijunguan yi* 服完预备军官役 (p. 153) *si le zhe yitiao xin* 死了这一条心 (p. 93)
Others		2	2.0	
Total		102	100	

containing *liheci*.[12] He found that the most heavily used *liheci* are words with the second morpheme modified (40%); percent); this is followed by words containing post-verbal constituents (35 percent). Another finding of this study is that 15.6 percent of *liheci* have a preposed nominal morpheme, which does not occur in Wang's novel. Only 9.6 percent of *liheci* contain both post-verbal constituents and modifiers of the second morpheme.

The statistics presented here reveal that a much larger percentage of *liheci* used in Wang's novel contain both post-verbal constituents and words modifying the second morpheme (25.5 percent). Examples of this kind of *liheci* are cited as follows.

(5)
不 知 那时 才　享　得　上　儿子 养伺　的 福。(p. 21)
Bu zhi nashi cai　xiang de shang erzi yangci de fu
Not know when only enjoy DE up　son tend to DE blessing
I wonder how long it will be before I can sit back and let my son take care of me.[13]

(6)
他 说 他 和这 苏汉轩　谈 了很 一 阵 天。(p. 179)
Ta shuo ta　he zhe Su Hanxuan tan le hen　yi zhen tian
He say　he and this Su Hanxuan talk Pfv very one CL　time
He said he chatted with Hanxuan Su for quite a while.

Third, there is no use of *liheci* with a preposed noun in the novel. Hua Yushan has pointed out that "in some *liheci*, the object can be moved

---

12. Wang Haifeng 王海峰, "Xiandai hanyu liheci lixi dongyin chuyi" 现代汉语离合词离析动因刍议 (A preliminary discussion on the formulation of liheci with constituents inserted in between in modern Chinese), *Yuwen yanjiu* 语文研究 3 (2002): 29–34.

13. The majority of translations of the example sentences are reproduced from *Family Catastrophe*, the English translation of *Jia bian* translated by Susan Wan Dolling; some minor revisions were made by the author. Susan Wan Dolling, trans., *Family Catastrophe* (University of Hawai'i Press, 1995).

before the verb and functions as the subject because the internal elements of *liheci* are highly independent and free."[14] This usage emphasizes the object, as shown in the following example.

(7)

他们	婚	都	结	了，	我们	就	什么	也	别	说	了。
Tamen	hun	dou	jie	le	women	jiu	shenme	ye	bie	shuo	le
They	marriage	all	marry	Prc	we	then	anything	too	not	say	Prc

They have even got married. Let's not say anything.

In *Family Catastrophe*, there is no such usage.

Fourth, the inserted adjective is very complicated, as shown in the following example.

(8)

他	做	许许多多	跳	来	跳	去，
Ta	zuo	xuxuduoduo	tiao	lai	tiao	qu
He	made	many	jump	here	jump	there

变	得	好快	好	快	的	梦。(p. 19)
bian	de	hao kuai	hao	kuai	de	meng
change	DE	very fast	very fast	DE	dream	

He had a lot of fast-moving, prickly, jumpy dreams.

The Pragmatic Usage of *Liheci* in *Family Catastrophe*

Zhao and Zhang have pointed out that "the norm of the use of *liheci* is when the two morphemes are placed together. Separating the two morphemes is a variant of *liheci* which is caused by the flexibility in the use of words."[15] When a *liheci* is used with a constituent inserted between

---

14. Hua Yushan 华玉山, "Guanyu liheci de yuyong wenti" 关于离合词的语用问题 (About the pragmatic function of *liheci*), *Yunnan shifan daxue xuebao* 云南师范大学学报 3.3 (2005.5): 35.

15. Zhao and Zhang, "Definition and Nature of *Liheci*," 44.

the morphemes, it may express a meaning different from the original form when the morphemes are placed together. The semantic emphases of the different types of *liheci* may vary as well. Building on existing studies,[16] I discuss the pragmatic functions of *liheci* in relation to examples used in *Family Catastrophe*. In the following cited examples, V stands for the verb morpheme and O stands for the object morpheme.

1. V+ *zhe* + O: this pattern indicates the progressiveness of an action or the continuation of a state. In the novel, it is mostly used to describe the details of an action.

(9)

一	个	白头	老	公公	走	上来，
Yi	ge	baitou	lao	gonggong	zou	shanglai
One	CL	white-haired	old	grandpa	walk	up here

妈妈	和	他	说	着	话。(p. 24)
mama	he	ta	shuo	zhe	hua
mother	and	he	say	Dur	remarks

An old man with white hair came toward them; Mother spoke to him.

(10)

一	路	的	心	想	着	她、	爱恋 着	她、	叹	着	气、
Yi	lu	de	xin	xiang	zhe	ta	ailian zhe	ta	tan	zhe	qi
All	road	DE	heart	think	Dur	her	love Dur	her	sigh	Dur	breath

一	路	走	离，	二哥	他	也	在	坏	脾气 里。(p. 63)
Yi	lu	zou	li	erge	ta	ye	zai	huai	piqi li
all	way	walk	away	second elder brother	he	too	in	bad	temper inside

She was all he could think about; he was hankering after her, sighing for her, all the way out of the auditorium. His second elder brother, too, was in a bad humor.

---

16. Rao Qin 饶勤, "Liheci de jiegou tedian he yuyong fenxi" 离合词的结构特点和语用分析 (An analysis of structural features and pragmatic functions of *liheci*), *Hanyu xuexi* 汉语学习 97 (1997.2): 32–35; Wang Sumei, "A Discussion on the Structure, Extension and Usage of Disyllabic *Liheci*."

2. V+ *le* + O indicates the occurrence of a past action or the completion of a future action. See the following examples.

(11)

他 还	不能	全然	的	肯定	父亲	真的
Ta hai	buneng	quanran	de	kending	fuqin	zhende
He still	not able	to completely	DE	certain	father	really

已	失	了	踪。(p. 12)
yi	shi	le	zong
already	lose	Pfv	trace

He still couldn't be absolutely certain that Father had truly disappeared.

(12)

过不久	爸爸	有天	偶	失	了	手	将	妈妈
Guobujiu	baba	youtian	ou	shi	le	shou	jiang	mama
Soon	father	one day	accidentally	lose	Pfv	hand	took	mother

那	对	梳妆镜	中	的	一	个	打	破掉。(p. 41)
na	dui	shuzhuangjing	zhong	de	yi	ge	da	podiao
that	CL	dresser mirror	in	DE	one	CL	hit	broken

In no time, one day Papa accidentally smashed one of the pair of Ma's hand mirrors.

   If a special emphasis is placed on the completion of an action, *le* (了) is inserted after the verb morpheme, such as in *shi le zong* (失了踪), *shi le shou* (失了手). *Le* (了) may be inserted in non-*liheci* and performs the same function. For instance,

(13)

爸爸	离	了	走	之后，	但	觉到	早上	的 时间
Baba	li	le	zou	zhihou	dan	juedao	zaoshang	de shijian
Father	leave	Pfv	leave	after	but	feel	morning	DE time

延长	多	了。(p. 46)
yanchang	duo	le
extend	more	Prc

After Papa left, the morning dragged on.

3. "V + *guo* + O" is used to emphasize the experience of performing an action. Examples from this novel are as follows.

(14)

她	去年	过年	时	曾经	到	这里	来
Ta	qunian	guonian	shi	cengjing	dao	zheli	lai
She	last year	spend New Year	time	ever	arrive	here	come

为	你	拜	过	年！(p. 114)
wei	ni	bai	guo	nian
for	you	pay a call	Exp	New Year

Last New Year, she was here to pay a New Year visit.

(15)

你	吃	过	饭	了	没有。(p. 101)
Ni	chi	guo	fan	le	meiyou
You	eat	Exp	meal	Prc	not

Have you eaten?

In *Family Catastrophe*, the author also used "V + *guo le* + O" to indicate the completion and experience of a past action, such as,

(16)

只	在	其一	说	过	了	话	之后
Zhi	zai	qiyi	shuo	guo	le	hua	zhihou
Only at		one of them	say	Exp	Pfv	remarks	after

就	回身	复	进去	了。(p. 176)
jiu	huishen	fu	jinqu	le
then	turn round	again	enter	Prc

After one of them had said what she came in to say, (his brother's wife) disappeared once again behind the curtain.

4. "V + *nide* / *wode* / *tade* + O" is used to refer to the people related to the action.

(17)

就	如是	和尚	背	他的	经	那样。(p. 139)
Jiu	rushi	heshang	bei	tade	jing	nayang
Just	like	monk	recite	his	scripture	like that

Much like the way a monk mouths his liturgies

De may be omitted in this pattern:

(18)

他的	父亲	会同	是	来	请	他们	(的)	客
Tade	fuqin	huitong	shi	lai	qing	tamen	de	ke
His	father	as if	be	come	invite	them	DE	guest

似地	呼引	他们	道：... (p. 139)
side	huyin	tamen	dao
like	call	them	say

His father would call to them, as if inviting guests to a banquet, saying, ...

The occurrences of this type of *liheci* in *Family Catastrophe* are low.

5. "V + *de* + O" is often used to emphasize the components after *de* (的).

(19)

仿佛	每	一	口	新	吐	的	血	均	是
Fangfu	mei	yi	kou	xin	tu	de	xue	jun	shi
As though	every	one	CL	new	throw up	DE	blood	all	be

他	头	一次	首日	的	血。(p. 121)
ta	tou	yici	shouri	de	xue
he	first	time	first day	DE	blood

Each time it was as if he threw up blood for the very first time.

6. "V + *shenme* + O" indicates dissatisfaction, scorn, questioning or denial.

(20)

这样	简单	的	答案，	这样	浅显	的	理由，
Zheyang	jiandande		da'an	zheyang	qianxian	de	liyou
Such	simple	DE	answer	such	shallow	DE	reason

他 莫非 <u>受 什么 蛊</u> 了，到 现在 始 想到。(p. 5)
ta mofei shou shenme gu le dao xianzai shi xiangdao
he could it be suffer what enchantment Prc till today begin think of
What a simple answer. Such obvious reasons. How stupid of him not to
have thought of them sooner!

In this example, *shou shenme gu* (受什么蛊) indicates "dissatisfaction" or
"scorn."

7. "V + *ge* + O" includes a classifier and is often used in colloquial speech.

(21)
我 是 要 等到 样样 证据 都 看 得 切切确确 了
Wo shi yao dengdao yangyang zhengju dou kan de qieqiequeque le
I be want wait all kinds of evidence all see DE precise Prc

始才 正正当当 有凭有据 的 和 你 好好
shicai zhengzhengdangdang youpingyouju de he ni haohao
start rightful fully substantiated DE and you well

算 个 帐。(p. 149)
suan ge zhang
settle CL accounts
I was just waiting for all the evidence to come in, to make sure I have an
airtight case against you, before I formally confronted you with it.

8. "VO + *yi* + VO" reveals casualty and briefness of the action. The extended forms include "V + *yi* + VO," "VO + VO," and so on. The following examples show this usage.

(22)
就 要 这样 让 你 害怕 一 害怕。(p. 114)
Jiu yao zheyang rang ni haipa yi haipa
Then will such let you scare one scare
I just want to scare you like this.

(23)
并且 他 还 要 他的 母亲 不 可 擅断 的
Bingqie ta hai yao tade muqin bu ke shanduan de
In addition he still ask his mother not allow arbitrary DE

每一天	的	暮暗	时	要	开出	个	份	账单
meiyitian	de	muan	shi	yao	kaichu	ge	fen	zhangdan
everyday	DE	dusk	when	will	produce	CL	CL	bill

提出	了	给	他	接来	过	一	过	目 。(p. 166)
tichu	le	gei	ta	jielai	guo	yi	guo	mu
bring	Pfv	give	him	receive	look	one	look	eye

In addition, at the end of the day she must account for each expenditure without fail, filling in a ledger and showing it to him.

(24)

不过	收收	公文,	登记	登记,	保管	一下,
Buguo	shoushou	gongwen	dengji	dengji	baoguan	yixia
But	collect	document	register	register	take care of	a short time

妈妈	也	会 (p. 35)
mama	ye	hui
mother	too	can

Things like filing documents, registering this and that, putting stuff away—these are things Mama can do.

The examples reveal that *liheci* with constituents inserted in between are more expressive than those without in that they express both prototypical and extended meanings. Typically, the completion, progression, or experiential aspects of the actions are marked with the particles *le*, *zhe*, *guo* 了/着/过; other inserted constitutes may express causality, increase the colloquialism of language or convey subtle feelings.

The Use of *Liheci* in Relation to Wang's Writing Style

In spite of the fact that the percentage of *liheci* in a novel is generally not high, the analysis of this type of word reflects a writer's overall language style. The use of *liheci* in *Family Catastrophe* illustrates Wang's colloquial writing style and his creativity in language use.

It is noteworthy that Wang created unusual and fresh effects by using newly coined characters, *zhuyin fuhao*, Latin letters, the combination of classical and vernacular languages, and so on. Some scholars believe that he resorted to these unique usages purposefully to create "unsmoothness" in the reading of his novel to avoid a superficial effect.[17] Wang's use of *liheci* demonstrates this characteristic as well. As discussed in the previous section, he inserts long and complex constituents between the two morphemes of *liheci*. A typical usage is example 8, in which Wang inserted *xuxuduoduo, tiaolaitiaoqu, biandehaokuaihaokuai,* and *de* between the two morphemes of *zuo* and *meng*. The use of the unusual number of modifiers between the two morphemes of *liheci* made his writing more expressive and lively but on the other hand also created a cumbersome effect.

Studies reveal that the frequency of the use of *liheci* is affected by the genre of the text in which they occur. Wang Haifeng analyzed the use of *liheci* in different corpuses, including authentic spoken language, novels, drama, prose, news reports, academic works, and legal documents.[18] His study shows that the occurrences of *liheci* vary with the formality of the texts. For instance, the percentages of *liheci* in authentic spoken language, drama, and novels outnumber their occurrence in news reports, academic works, and legal documents. Wang's study includes an article of the Law of the People's Republic of China on Road Traffic Safety in which no *liheci* with inserted constituents are used, whereas his examples selected from authentic spoken language include *liheci* with inserted constituents, such as *ke ge tou* 磕个头 (to kowtow), *bang ge mang* 帮个忙 (to help).

---

17. Zhang Hanliang 張漢良, "Qiantan *Jiabian* de wenzi" 淺談「家變」的文字 (An analysis of the language of *Jia bian*), *Zhongwai Wenxue* 中外文學, 12.1 (1973.5): 122–41; Zhou Guozheng 周國正, "Ziyou yu zhiyue" 自由與制約 (Flexibility and restrictions), *Xiandai zhongwen wenxue pinglun* 現代中文文學評論 1 (1994.6): 53–77.

18. Wang Haifeng 王海峰, "Xiandai hanyu liheci lixi xianxiang yuti fenbu tezheng kaocha" 现代汉语离合词离析现象语体分布特征考察 (An investigation of the distribution of *liheci* with constituents inserted in between in different texts of modern Chinese), *Yuyan wenzi yingyong* 语言文字应用 (2009.3): 81–89.

In addition to the formality of the texts, subjectivity is a factor affecting the use of *liheci*: a text focusing on the expression of emotions generally has a higher density of *liheci* than a text presenting factual statements. For instance, novel writers who communicate with readers by disclosing the feelings of their characters tend to use a larger number of *liheci* than do producers of legal documents, whose focus is on the presentation of objective statements. Even in the same genre, the use of *liheci* varies with the subjectivity of the text. As Wang cited in his study, in one conversation when the speaker narrates his or her experience with a focus on revealing his or her own personal attitude and feelings, he or she resorts to *liheci* with constituents inserted in between, such as *bang le mang* 帮了忙 (have helped), *fa tade cai* 发他的财 (he became rich), and *shou tade qi* 受他的气 (to be bullied by him). In contrast, in another cited example, when the speaker narrates another person's past experience without self-involvement, he or she uses *liheci* without other inserted constituents, such as *zhaoji* 着急 (worried), *jiehun* 结婚 (to get married), and *shengqi* 生气 (angry). Wang's use of *liheci* is not only consistent with the novel writing style but also contributes to a true and vivid portrait of the main characters. In *Family Catastrophe*, flashback is used to describe Fan Ye's childhood. The casual and light tone created by *liheci* helps provide a vivid description of the mental state of Fan Ye as a boy. Example 5 illustrates this effect: the inserted modifiers of *meng* (*xuxuduoduo, tiaolaitiaoqu, biandehaokuaihaokuai*) reflect Fan Ye's mixed and fast-changing feelings in that scenario: he was sick and his parents took him to the doctor; he was happy with his father's promise of buying bananas for him, but later, having found that the promise was unreal, he was extremely disappointed. The inserted constituents between *zuo* and *meng* well represent the changing feelings the child experienced that day.

The data show that Wang's usage of *liheci* in *Family Catastrophe* is similar to that in other novels. This seems to indicate that the author might not have deliberately employed this type of word to produce a certain effect in his creation of the novel. This is unlike his use of Latin letters, *zhuyin fuhao*, newly coined words (such as onomatopoeic words), which Wang made more conscious use of to achieve fresh and unusual effects.

Conclusion

Using *Family Catastrophe* as the corpus, I analyzed the different forms of *liheci* and discussed their semantic meanings and pragmatic functions. As shown, the different forms of *liheci* may reveal different semantic meanings and perform different pragmatic functions. As Wang's language in this novel has been heatedly debated since its publication, it is hoped that this essay has been able to increase our understanding of the author's language style by viewing it through the lens of *liheci*. However, we should bear in mind that *liheci* do not constitute a high percentage of the words in *Family Catastrophe*. Therefore, we still need to have a comprehensive linguistic analysis of the whole novel to fully appreciate Wang's writing.

8 *Harmony, Counterpoint, and Variation in* Backed Against the Sea

Hengsyung Jeng
Translated by Chu-yun Chen
Department of Foreign Languages and Literatures
National Taiwan University

Prelude

Those readers familiar with Taiwan's literary scene know that Wang Wenxing is a writer who writes exceptionally slowly. In writing *Bei hai de ren* 背海的人 (Backed against the sea), he averaged only about thirty characters a day,[1] which meant that each volume required several years to complete. For example, the first volume took more than five and a half years, from January 6, 1974, to October 19, 1979. The second volume took more than three times longer, from August 17, 1980, to August 7, 1997. The main reason for this painstaking slowness is that Wang treats each Chinese character as a musical note, meticulously hammering out each

---

1. Shan Dexing [Te-hsing Shan] 單德興, "Wang Wenxing tan Wang Wenxing" 王文興談王文興 (Wang Wenxing on Wang Wenxing), *Lianhe wenxue* 聯合文學 (Unitas) 3.8 (1987): 172; Lin Xiuling 林秀玲, "Lin Xiuling zhuan fang Wang Wenxing: tan *Bei hai de ren* yu Nanfang'ao" 林秀玲專訪王文興：談《背海的人》與南方澳 (Wang Wenxing exclusive interview: *Backed Against the Sea* and Nanfang'ao), *Zhongwai wenxue* 中外文學 (Chungwai literary monthly) 30.6 (2001): 43.

character, a task so strenuous that only a limited number can be written each day to ensure the desired musicality. The hammering is literal. He describes the process as being "like a blacksmith pounding on a piece of iron, I use a pencil to hammer out each Chinese character."[2] In the process, "many a piece of furniture has suffered … in his effort to achieve the beauty of the music in the language," according to Liao Binghui.[3]

Since he began writing, Wang has been searching for ways to realize the musicality of language in depicting characters and themes. As he puts it in an interview with Shan Dexing [Te-hsing Shan]: "Chinese characters are like musical notes, arranged in long or short sequences."[4] Speaking at the forum "A Discussion on Creative Writing with Professor Wang Wenxing" held at the National Taiwan University library in 2000, Wang made his intentions even clearer: "Euphony is not the aim. I wish I could achieve euphony. The purpose of the sound of my language is to convey meaning; in other words, each sentence should carry its own unique emotion."[5] As for his grasp of language and musicality, he says: "It only began to improve with the writing of *Jia bian* 家變 (Family catastrophe), but I still felt constrained then. Only when I was writing *Backed Against the Sea* did I begin to feel free."[6] Accordingly, *Family Catastrophe* was the turning point in his musical use of language; in *Backed Against the Sea* he achieved a greater degree of freedom, intricacy, and sophistication in his control of the music of language.

About music, Wang says, "I am a stranger to musicology, musical structure and the history of music. With such a limited knowledge, I cannot match Thomas Mann's feat in basing the structure of an entire novel on musical structure. I can only aim for the cadence of each sen-

2. Shan Dexing, "Wang Wenxing on Wang Wenxing," 171.
3. Lin Xiuling 林秀玲, "Zuotan zhuti: yu Wang Wenxing jiaoshou tan wenxue chuangzuo" 座談主題：與王文興教授談文學創作 (Forum: a discussion on creative writing with Professor Wang Wenxing), *Zhongwai wenxue* 中外文學 (Chungwai literary monthly) 30.6 (2001): 372.
4. Shan Dexing, "Wang Wenxing on Wang Wenxing," 182.
5. Lin Xiuling, "Forum: A Discussion on Creative Writing with Professor Wang Wenxing," 374.
6. Shan Dexing, "Wang Wenxing on Wang Wenxing," 179.

tence, based on my own musical sense."[7] In fact, the structures of music and language share many commonalities because music is also language in its expression of emotion, and the two have a similar basic rhythm. For instance, the cadence he mentions, like that in music, is based on a metrical unit. In Western poetry this unit is known as the foot; in Western music, the bar or measure. There are four common types of feet in Western poetry: the iamb (an unstressed/short syllable followed by a stressed/long one), the trochee (a stressed/long syllable followed by an unstressed/short one), the anapest (two unstressed/short syllables followed by a stressed/long one), and the dactyl (a stressed/long syllable followed by two unstressed/short ones). There are also four common types of musical measures consisting of musical notes and beats with strong or weak accent:[8] the 2/4 meter (one quarter note to a beat, two beats in a measure: a strong beat followed by a weak beat); the 3/4 meter (one quarter note to a beat, three beats in a measure: a strong beat followed by two weak beats); the 4/4 meter (one quarter note to a beat, four beats in a measure: the first beat is the strongest, the second is a weak beat, the third is the next strongest, and the fourth is weak); the 6/8 meter (one eighth note to a beat, six beats in a measure: a strong beat followed by two weak beats and another strong beat followed by two weak beats).[9] In addition to duration[10] and accent, rhythm also involves tempo.[11] In Western poetry, tempo is not governed by any set rules, but is determined by the poet and interpreted by the reader with regard to content and context. In Western music, however, there are Italian terms

---

7. Ibid., 182–83.

8. On the website of Oxford Music Online (http://www.oxfordmusiconline .com), there is an article about meter from *The Oxford Companion to Music* (ed. Alison Latham, 2001), pointing out that Western musical meter was borrowed from poetic meter in the thirteenth century. That is why the four common types of musical measures are similar to those of poetic meter.

9. David D. Boyden, *An Introduction to Music* (New York: Knopf, 1970), 537. Explanations in parentheses are provided by the present author.

10. Duration in music is indicated by the whole note, half note, quarter note, and eighth note.

11. Boyden, *An Introduction to Music*, 26.

to indicate general tempo, such as "adagio," "andante," "moderato," "allegro," and "presto." It can also be indicated by a metronome marking, for example, "M.M. = 120"[12] means that "the quarter notes are played 120 to the minute or two per second."[13] Adagio has approximately a tempo of between 66 and 76 beats per minute; andante between 76 and 108; moderato between 108 and 120; allegro between 120 and 168; and presto between 168 and 200. Therefore, duration, accent, and tempo are essential elements in creating musical rhythm. When an interval[14] is added to a particular rhythm, a melody is generated.[15] In Western poetry, the metrical foot can be used to form larger units, such as the line, couplet, stanza, sonnet, ode, and epic. Likewise, the musical bar can form the motive, phrase, period, movement, and various forms of compositions such as the fugue, sonata, symphony, and concerto.[16]

In comparing the similarities in the structures of units in language and music, David D. Boyden states: "The smallest unit in building a melody, its basic fragment, is the *motive*, consisting of at least one characteristic interval and one characteristic rhythm. Several of these may be combined in a *phrase*; and several phrases, in a *period*. The combination of two periods is called a *double period*. In such fashion complete melodies are constructed, just as sentences in language are composed of phrases and words."[17] Because language and music share many characteristics, it should not be difficult for a writer who appreciates the rhythm of language to handle musical rhythm. Wang's scrupulous attention to the musical qualities of Chinese characters ensures that his language achieves a high degree of musicality. Ye Weilian [Wai-lim Yip]

12. M.M. stands for "Malzel Metronome," invented by Johann Nepomuk Malzel in 1816.

13. Boyden, *An Introduction to Music*, 15.

14. An interval is formed by the distance between the pitches of two adjacent notes.

15. Boyden, *An Introduction to Music*, 22–26.

16. Ibid., 55–83; Qiu Chuitang 邱垂堂, *Yinyue yu xinshang* 音樂與欣賞 (Music and its appreciation) (Taipei: Yueyun chubanshe, 1998), 50–72. The form of concerto is the author's own addition.

17. Boyden, *An Introduction to Music*, 26.

discusses Wang's short story "Mother" by demonstrating that the repetitions, variations, and extensions of the motives and images in this story intermingle with the counter-motives to form a tightly interwoven texture.[18] Ye's concepts of motive and texture in the story are similar to what Boyden says about motive and texture, an indication of the similarities between music and language.

In Western music, in addition to the basic elements of rhythm and melody, there are the more complex factors of harmony and counterpoint. This is due to the development of organum[19] in European church music during the ninth century, in which different voices were counterpointed to form polyphonic chants. Harmony and counterpoint have been used to increase the richness and depth of musical compositions ever since. Oriental music, in contrast, tends to be monophonic and focus on the development of a single melody without harmony and counterpoint.[20] Harmony is usually based on the lowest-sounding root note, combined vertically with one, two, or more notes in a higher voice or voices on the scale to form a chord.[21] Counterpoint parallels the melodies in various voices horizontally, and each of the melodies can be

18. Ye Weilian [Wai-lim Yip] 葉維廉, *Zhongguo xiandai xiaoshuo de fengmao* 中國現代小說的風貌 (The style of modern Chinese fiction) (Taipei: National Taiwan University Press, 2009), 229 (reprint of the 1970 edition with additional essays).

19. Descriptions of organum first appeared in *Musica enchiriadis* at the end of the ninth century.

20. Boyden, *An Introduction to Music*, 42; "The Nature of East Asian Music," *Encyclopaedia Britannica Deluxe Edition CD-ROM* (North Sydney: Encyclopaedia Britannica Australia, 2004). But the Japanese musicologist Kurosawa Takatomo 黑澤隆朝 collected some folk songs of the Austronesian peoples of Taiwan in 1943 and found that many of these folk songs do have the harmony of the triad and counterpoint of different voices. These folk songs were published by him in 1973 and subsequently published as *Zhanshi Taiwan de shengyin* (1943) 戰時台灣的聲音 (1943) (Sounds from Wartime Taiwan 1943) (Taipei: National Taiwan University Press, 2008). The harmonious and contrapuntal qualities of these folk songs provide counter-evidence to the Western view of Oriental music.

21. Boyden, *An Introduction to Music*, 48; *Encyclopaedia Britannica Deluxe Edition CD-ROM*.

played successively or simultaneously to create a contrapuntal effect. Even though musical compositions can be characterized by harmonic or contrapuntal/polyphonic texture, the two structures are closely intertwined.[22] Counterpoint by nature involves harmony, and a series of chords can form a contrapuntal melody. Beethoven's *String Quartet in B Flat Major, Opus 130,* is a classic example, in which two violins, a viola, and a cello carry on a fluent, harmonious dialogue such as that between four old friends.

Another musical technique is variation. In a piece of music, a theme may be presented and then followed by a number of variations. Some composers may write new pieces of music by altering parts of the theme of another composer, such as its melody, rhythm, or harmony, while retaining the general pattern of the original theme.[23] A case in point is Paganini's *24 Caprices for Solo Violin, No. 24.* It is composed with eleven variations on the initial theme. The virtuosity of Paganini's *24 Caprices* is such that several composers have written a number of famous variations, such as Liszt's six *Etudes d'Execution Transcendante d'apres Paganini,* Brahms's *Variations on a Theme of Paganini,* and Rachmaninov's *Rhapsody on a Theme of Paganini,* and so on. This relationship in music between a theme and its variations is similar to the intertexuality that exists within and between literary texts. In fact, intertexuality is found in all musical compositions and literary works, since no work is produced out of nothing. Wang describes his own work as imitation: "I've always been imitating ... even today; perhaps not intentionally, but I myself can see the influences from earlier writers."[24] It can even be said that no great artist can avoid such creative imitation. Unimaginative copying, of course, has no artistic merit at all.

To analyze the complex musicality of language in the volumes of *Backed Against the Sea,* the concepts of harmony, counterpoint, and variation are used together with those of rhythm, melody, motive, theme, movement, form, and the whole gamut of male and female voices. Such

---

22. Boyden, *An Introduction to Music,* 42–44.

23. Ibid., 59.

24. Shan Dexing, "Wang Wenxing on Wang Wenxing," 168.

an examination of the novel's musical effects demonstrates the intricate relationships of its narrative structures, characters, and themes, and the emotions Wang hopes to convey.

In light of the strong emphasis Wang placed on the musicality of language while writing the first volume of *Backed Against the Sea*, I coined the term "mock symphony" to describe the novel's musicality and narrative structure.[25] The monologue of the narrator/protagonist Ye[26] resembles a mock symphony in that the four episodes of the first volume form four musical movements with different tempos: the first, which begins with "Damn! This rat's ass rat's cunt rathole!," is "allegro puro" (dignified) (*Backed* I: 1–10);[27] the second, on the fishermen's misfortunes, is "adagio sereno" (*Backed* I: 10–60); the third, horseplay at the BOCDO[28] office, is "allegro animato" (*Backed* I: 60–107); the fourth, presenting the allure of sex, is "presto passionato" (*Backed* I: 107–28).[29]

---

25. Zheng Hengxiong [Hengsyung Jeng] 鄭恆雄, "Wenti de yuyan de jichu—lun Wang Wenxing de *Bei hai de ren* de" 文體的語言的基礎 – 論王文興的《背海的人》的 (The linguistic foundation of literary style—on Wang Wenxing's *Backed Against the Sea*), *Zhongwai wenxue* 中外文學 (Chungwai literary monthly) 15.1 (1986): 146.

26. "Ye" is the narrator/protagonist's self-reference, which in Chinese literally means "your daddy" or "your lord," a very self-glorifying term revealing the arrogant and haughty personality of the narrator/protagonist. Hereafter, "Ye" is used to refer to the narrator/protagonist.

27. Translator's note: translations from volume 1 of *Bei hai de ren* follow Edward Gunn's *Backed Against the Sea* (Ithaca, NY: Cornell East Asia Program, 1992), referred to as "*Backed* I." Page references are to this translation. Spellings have been converted to the pinyin transliteration. Translations from the second volume are by the translator, referred to as "*Backed* II." Page references are to the original Chinese version.

28. Editior's note: BOCDO is short for "the Bureau of Management of Materials on Regional Speech and Popular Local Customs during the Past Century, Deep Pit Harbor Branch Office."

29. Descriptions of the tempos of the four movements here are intended to have burlesque effects. These descriptions of the tempos generally match those of Wang's own reading of the first volume of *Backed Against the Sea* as recorded on the CD included in Wang's recent publication: Wang Wenxing 王文興; Yi Peng 易鵬, comp., *Wang Wenxing shougao ji: Jia bian, Bei hai de ren* 王文興手稿

In my earlier work mentioned above, I also have pointed out that in the first volume of *Backed Against the Sea* Wang employs no fewer than eleven devices to manipulate rhythm: (1) syntax, (2) tone of voice, (3) punctuation marks (including quotation marks, lines or dots alongside characters, commas, semicolons, colons, juxtaposing marks, periods, ellipses, dashes, exclamation marks, question marks, and insertion marks), (4) boldface type, (5) variant Chinese characters, (6) coined Chinese characters, (7) coined phrases, (8) same words with different Chinese characters, (9) the Mandarin phonetic alphabet, (10) alliterated Chinese characters, and (11) the English alphabet and English phonetic symbols.[30] Wang's own explanation, given at the Wang Wenxing International Conference held at National Central University in Taiwan on June 4, 2010, is that these devices were indeed developed according to musical concepts. The reason for inventing such complex devices is because, as mentioned earlier, poetic tempo, unlike musical tempo, lacks hard-and-fast rules. Since *Backed Against the Sea* is written in prose, without even the benefit of poetic meter, the only way for him to guide readers to perceive the prose rhythm as he intends is to adopt such an approach. Furthermore, Wang contends that just like the audience of classical music following its tempo in an unhurried way, the ideal reader should read a literary work at the speed dictated by the text and refrain from

---

集：《家變》, 《背海的人》 (Collection of Wang Wenxing's manuscripts: *Family Catastrophe, Backed Against the Sea*) (Taipei: National Taiwan University Library, National Taiwan University Press, Xingren wenhua shiyanshi, 2010).

30. Zheng Hengxiong, "The Linguistic Foundation of Literary Style—on Wang Wenxing's *Backed Against the Sea*," 146. Zhang Hanliang points out a twelfth device, the use of the blank space, which is similar to a rest in a piece of music. But according to Wang's own reading in 2010, the device of the blank space is generally similar to the ellipsis mark, the dash, and the insertion marks in indicating a rest. However, the dash may also indicate lengthening of a sound. Zhang Hanliang 張漢良, "Wang Wenxing *Bei hai de ren* de yuyan xinyang" 王文興《背海的人》的語言信仰 (Wang Wenxing's language beliefs expressed through *Backed Against the Sea*), In *Wenxue yu zongjiao—Diyi jie guoji wenxue yu zongjiao huiyi lunwen ji* 文學與宗教—第一屆國際文學與宗教會議論文集 (Literature and religion—collected essays of the first international conference on literature and religion) (Taipei: Shibao wenhua chubanshe, 1987), 443.

speed reading.[31] Since Wang has created a style based on musical compositions and thinks literary works should be appreciated like music, it
is therefore appropriate to analyze the novel in accordance with musical
principles.

This essay applies the above-mentioned musical terms in the interpretation of the musicality and narrative structures of the two volumes
of *Backed Against the Sea*. The concept of harmony will be used chiefly
to explain Ye's monologues superimposed with shorter responses of
other voices. Counterpoint will be used to interpret the longer interactions between Ye's monologues and the locutions of other voices. However, harmony and counterpoint are only relative to each other and there
is often no clear-cut distinction between them, so there may be some
overlap in discussing these concepts. Finally, variation will be used to
show how the rhythms, themes, and narrative structures of volume 2 are
derived from those of volume 1.

Harmony and Counterpoint in the First Volume
of *Backed Against the Sea*

The two volumes of *Backed Against the Sea* present Ye's monologue during a single night. The first volume registers the monologue that takes
place from the evening of January 12 to the dawn of January 13 in 1962,
in which the one-eyed Ye recalls his flight to Deep Pit Harbor during the
previous ten days (January 2–11, 1962). These episodes, in which he
ridicules his own embarrassing moments during his escape, are divided
into four parts or movements, presented in a richly varied rhythm alternating between allegro, adagio, allegro, and presto like the four movements in a symphony (or mock symphony). Due to the fact that the
events are related out of sequence, the monologue seems to be confusing
and perplexing. Table 8.1 sets out, in chronological order, Ye's actions
from January 2, when he escapes to Deep Pit Harbor until he begins his
monologue on the night of January 12.

---

31. Shan Dexing, "Wang Wenxing on Wang Wenxing," 182.

Table 8.1 Chronology of Ye's Ordeals in Deep Pit Harbor (Volume 1)

Date	Incident and Livelihood	Food and Drink	Sexual Encounters
January 2	To escape prosecution over his gambling debts and a money scam, he flees from Taipei to the rainy harbor (pp. 1–9), where it rains every day except this day (p. 11); he is plagued by three ailments: a bleeding ulcer, asthma, and hemorrhoids (p. 9); no cops here, what a "Peach Spring Paradise" (p. 10).		
January 4	Begins telling fortunes in front of the Mazu Temple (pp. 10–11).		First sees a woman resembling the goddess Guanyin (pp. 41–42).
January 5	Four customers appear: (1) a man in white long johns; (2) a young boy in a red windbreaker; (3) a fishing boat captain; (4) a man with heavy stubble (pp. 47–53).		First visit to prostitute Yuck (pp. 108–13); second glimpse of Guanyin look-alike (pp. 42, 108).
January 6	Boat captain puts out to sea; encounters disaster; captain survives; deaths of customers 1, 2, and 4 (pp. 53–55).	First sees Zhang Fawu juggling an empty gasoline drum with one arm on the pier (p. 61).	First visit to teahouse for sex (pp. 119–20, 123–24); recalls similar visit in Taipei (pp. 120–23); sees Guanyin look-alike the third time (p. 42).

(continued)

155

Table 8.1 *Continued*

Date	Incident and Livelihood	Food and Drink	Sexual Encounters
January 7	Sees "vessel of doom"; captain returns to sea (pp. 59–60).	Second encounter with Zhang Fawu on the pier, who is saluting the departing "vessel of doom" (p. 60). Zhang visits Ye at home and suggests he take his meals at BOCDO (p. 70).	
January 8		Ye begins taking his meals at BOCDO (pp. 70–71).	
January 10	Zhang asks Ye to write "Close Door When Entering or Leaving" in Chinese calligraphy to be posted on the door of the toilet, and Fu Shaokang, the secretary, likes his work and wants to find him a job at BOCDO (p. 89).		Second visit to teahouse, meeting a happy hooker (pp. 124–28).

January 11	After lunch, Cui Liqun challenges Tang Lin to a chess game (p. 106).		Sees Guanyin look-alike the fourth time, who turns out to be a prostitute; seeks her favors and is thoroughly humiliated (pp. 115–18).
January 12	Ye begins monologue at night, recalling the past until daybreak (pp. 1–128), including his three ailments (p. 9), his ridicule of various religions (pp. 15, 64–66), a lone dark eagle (pp. 18–19), his "omni-bed" (pp. 19–20), his addiction to cigarettes, alcohol, and tea (pp. 24–26), his own squalid circumstances (pp. 27–30), etc.	Nonstop drinking of alcohol during monologue, sometimes smoking and drinking strong tea (pp. 1–128).	Sees Sheng Qizhi leaving a brothel (or is it the night before? He can't be sure) (p. 107).
January 13	"Daybreak," monologue ends (p. 128).		

The following discussion will deal with the use of harmony and counterpoint as they appear in the four movements in *Backed Against the Sea*, volume 1. The first movement begins with a rapid string of Ye's monophonic swearing "Damn! ... dog shit! shit!" (*Backed* I: 1) in the tempo of allegro puro. With his deep bass forming the root note, his ranting verbalizes the two themes: his bitter cynicism about society and his flight to Deep Pit Harbor. Other voices subsequently enter his low-pitched monologue, creating harmony and counterpoint. The first part of this volume therefore corresponds to the first allegro movement of a symphony and provides the exposition of this volume's two major themes.

Whenever Ye mentions Wanli Emporium and Blackface Tiger, his sentences become short, the tone breathless, and the tempo rapid, all of which establish the bass melody for later contrapuntal effects. The younger baritone voice of the gambler Wu Xiaomao coaxing him to "play whatever you feel like" (*Backed* I: 5) contrasts with Ye's deeper utterances contrapuntally and arouses his gambling instincts, thereby underlying the motive for them to set each other up. After Ye discovers he has been the victim of a trap set by Blackface Tiger and Wu Xiaomao and decides to "[try] a trick or two," he is caught red-handed. Blackface Tiger blackmails him with the threat that unless he hands over $15,000 he will lose his only good eye (*Backed* I: 6). In addition, Ye brings into his diatribe the two topics of the financial scam in the Wanli Emporium affair and the money theft in the South China Publishing Company incident. Caught between his fear of Blackface Tiger's threat over his gambling debts and being hauled to jail by police over his court case in the publishing company affair, he decides to flee to Deep Pit Harbor. In the latter incident we hear the stammering Yangzhou accent and reedy voice of the wimpy manager, "you ... you you ... you tell me if you haven't dishonored the venerable Mr. Yao ... You stole money ... tomorrow ..... tomorrow don't show up for work—" (*Backed* I: 7) The feeble stuttering baritone staccato plays off Ye's deep angry tone contrapuntally to create an effect of musical burlesque. It is interesting to note that Wang conveys this staccato effect through the use of ellipses, which are traditionally applied to indicate broken speech and are used liberally throughout the work. The repetitions of the manager's faint stop-start remarks are in fact Ye imitating the baritone staccato of the former in his own rich bass. Dramatic tension is thus achieved as the two melodies appear contrapuntally. Later the manager decides not to bring charges against Ye, saying, "We deal with matters on the principle of compassionate lenience in punishment. In this case we are not expecting you to return the funds, nor will we press charges in court. The issue is finished and done with. We have especially allowed you a way to help yourself to make a new life ..." (*Backed* I: 7). Ye, however, suspects the other's motives and responds, "Could anyone have it this good? Leave me a way to turn over a new leaf and make a new start in life just especially for me? No need to return the money? No criminal suit! And no lawsuit! I began to wonder how and when my luck had taken such a turn for the better" (*Backed* I: 7). His retort is clearly contrapuntal to the manager's remarks: one shows forgiveness, the other rejects the kindness. The counterpoint of these opposing melodies not only builds up the theme of conflict, it also implies that Ye is basically a thorough reprobate and hints at his ultimate pathetic downfall. The insertion of *zhuyin fuhao* (Mandarin Chinese phonetic symbols) representing the pronunciation of the word *ne* (呢/ㄋㄜ) in Ye's denunciation is a brilliant touch. In lending the speech a derisive tone, it effectively brings out his devil-may-care attitude, thus supporting Wang's own statement that sound is not only about euphony; its main purpose is to convey meaning or emotion.

The second movement tells how Ye, having fled to Deep Pit Harbor and unable to find any other means of livelihood, resorts to conning money with his half-baked fortune-telling skills. This passage is like the second movement in a symphony in further developing the theme of flight presented in the first movement. This new part opens with Ye asking himself, "Wherefore depart I not?" (*Backed* I: 10) and replying, "Because there's nowhere to go.—" (*Backed* I: 10). He goes on to conclude: "—So it seems as though Deep Pit Harbor is the only spot in the entire world left to live in" (*Backed* I: 10). With no place to go and no means of making a living, "Consequently, on the third day after I got here that day I started up and set up a stand as a fortune-teller—" (*Backed* I: 10). He gives himself the name Lone Star (because he has only one eye) and begins to predict life and death for the fishermen. This movement involves the inscrutable fate of the fishermen at sea; its tempo is therefore measured and low-key, adagio sereno. Not a single customer shows up on the first day due to the high charges, so on the second day he offers "PRICE-SLASHING BUDGET-GOUGING, INSANE REDUCTIONS" (*Backed* I: 47) of five yuan per person. His offer finally succeeds in attracting four customers. A man wearing white long johns approaches meekly and stammers: "I'd like, ... a, ... I'd like, a reading, please." (*Backed* I: 48) The staccato baritone set against Ye's running bass produces a dissonant harmony[32] that implies the helplessness of man confronting the immense forces of nature, while the fortune-teller, seemingly fate's spokesman, wields power over life and death. One look at the man and Ye reckons to himself: "Wow! Red veins transversing pupils, bluish veins, what's more, below the eyes—this was a person close to **imminent death!**" (*Backed* I: 48). But he exercises restraint and merely says to him, "The best thing, for the next few days, the best thing for you would be to take a little extra care with things, all of them, the important ones and the little ones, whatever it is, treat it with a bit of caution, caution in everything, yes, that's it. ..." (*Backed* I: 48). In the original Chinese version, through the use of several blank spaces and elliptical marks, Wang slows down the tempo of Ye's speech to show his hesitation in breaking the bad news. This is a good example of Wang's control of rhythm. Accompanying the man in white is a teenager in a red jacket, who says fearfully "—Aw, I I couldn't do that" (*Backed* I: 48). The childlike tenor voice expresses alarm against fate as he recoils in fear. Ye sees that the young man is the most fortunate person in the whole harbor area, so he comforts him in his steady bass, "Don't be nervous, there's nothing to worry about—It'll be fine. ... [W]e won't find anything wrong, no, not a thing, nothing here now" (*Backed* I: 48). The contrasting melodies of Ye and the young man form a dramatic counterpoint about the twists of fate. (The young man dies from a disaster at sea the next day.) The third customer is a boat captain wearing a large black baseball cap. He begins hesitantly, "Eh-h-h ... errrh. ..." then in a stronger voice, "I, I wanted to, to ask you about

---

32. Boyden, *An Introduction to Music*, 47.

something ... see if you'd do a trigram for me, check things out. ..."
(*Backed* I: 50). Again the captain's stammering baritone is in dissonant
harmony with and discordant counterpoint to Ye's deeper-voiced proc-
lamations on fate. The captain wants to know whether it would be safe
to catch fish at sea the next day. The fortune-teller's pronouncement, a
definitive "not appropriate" (*Backed* I: 51), hits the captain like a thun-
derclap. "A touch of sadness appeared on his face. But he was a brave
man and he was still going to go out to sea anyway,—" (*Backed* I: 51). Ye
doesn't like the look of the fourth customer, a man with heavy stubble,[33]
so he declares brusquely, "[You'll be] **dead soon**, in three days, within
three days!" (*Backed* I: 53).[34] Hearing this, the man curses loudly, "Fuck
you, you mutha fucka! — ..." (*Backed* I: 53). The loud clear tenor in which
the bearded man swears in defiance of the pronouncement of his death
sentence or in rebellion against fate creates a strong counterpoint to Ye's
bass pronouncement. Undeterred, the fortune-teller retaliates in kind.
He describes the duel of curses between them as "the duet ... taking
turns trading some basic vocabulary singing our ABCs sorta. ... " (*Backed*
I: 53). Wang evidently treats their mutual cursing as a counterpoint of
two voices. The fortune-teller's predictions for the captain and the other
two turn out to be surprisingly accurate: the captain's boat capsizes, and
although the captain survives, the man in white long johns and the man
with the stubble both die. The seer's only miscalculation is the young
man in a red jacket (the captain's eldest son), whom he saw as highly
favored by fate. But the young man also dies in the disaster. However,
owing to his accurate predictions of the two deaths, he becomes in-
stantly famous and is revered as a living god. Some of the sick even
come to him for cures.

The third movement centers on the BOCDO and makes a mockery of
various gods, so the tempo is light and quick, allegro animato. The first

---

33. The Chinese characters "鬃鬃鬃髯髭髭" (covered all over with stubble)
used to describe his face convey a visual effect on top of the audio one. This is
one of the many examples showing that Wang pays attention to musical as well
as visual effects.

34. "**Dead soon**" in Gunn's original translation is not in boldface type, but
it is changed to bold here to conform to Wang's Chinese characters in bold type.

civil servant from the office Ye meets is the tall and hefty Zhang Fawu
(*Backed* I: 61), who during their first encounter is seen juggling a gaso-
line drum single-handedly on the pier. At the second meeting Zhang is
goose-stepping and seeing off the departing "vessel of doom" with a
military salute (*Backed* I: 60). Their meeting sets out one of the two
themes of this movement: that the BOCDO is a rest home for sick civil
servants, where all workers spend their days idling and fooling around.
Bemused by Zhang's antics, Ye asks him the reason, whereby Zhang replies: "It's fun!" (*Backed* I: 61). His answer explains the motive behind the
loafing and clowning on the part of the BOCDO staff. Such idleness and
horseplay call for a light and quick pace, which is a distinct contrast to
the slow and heavy tempo of the earlier movement. Ye asks his second
question: "Then what do you do here for a living—" (*Backed* I: 61), meaning to find out why he has ended up in Deep Pit Harbor just like himself.
Unexpectedly, Zhang cuts him off smugly in the tone of one enjoying a
special privilege: "Oh! Over at the Bureau" (*Backed* I: 61). Their queries
and answers amount to a curious counterpoint: a baritone-bass duet between a servile office worker and a homeless person. Ye learns from
Zhang about a virtual paradise hidden in the hills behind the Mazu Temple, a place called "Bureau of Compilation, Research, Investigation, Editing, Filing, Classification, and Management of Materials on Regional
Speech and Popular Local Customs during the Past Century, Deep Pit
Harbor Branch Office," known by its acronym BOCDO.[35] At Zhang's
suggestion, Ye begins taking his meals at BOCDO, where he sees that all
of the civil servants there—from the director to the clerks to the janitor—fool around all day because they have nothing to do. The correspondence clerk, Tang Lin, a short, monkey-like figure and the butt of everyone's taunts, almost always strikes back with deliberate pranks. He is a
repulsive figure when he "goes around with this sort of self pitying ...
manner ... with his head tilted over to one side talking in this affected
mincing cutie cute cutesy tone" (*Backed* I: 75). One day after work he
puts a tin bucket on his head and, with broom in hand, jumps up onto

---

35. This bureaucratic office with its lengthy pompous name is a satire in itself.

the desk yelling in his falsetto (or alto): "yayayaya"; whereupon the cook, Lao Qiu, bangs on the bucket with fire tongs. At this point Tang's buddy Zhang pleads on his behalf in the baritone voice: "Hey, hey, hey, ... now let's not hold it against him, okay he's a little guy" (*Backed* I: 77). Tang's harmonizing high-pitched yells add to the grotesque atmosphere at BOCDO. The secretary, Fu Shaokang, likes Ye's handwritten sign "Close Door When Entering or Leaving" in the calligraphic style of "the stele of Yan Family Temple" posted on the door of the toilet and promises to get him a job at the office (*Backed* I: 89). This foreshadows the incident in volume 2 in which Ye, having failed to get the job, vents his anger and frustration at the office. Ye later makes the discovery that everyone in this office is an invalid with some disease or other and this out-of-the-way station is actually a sanatorium for ailing civil servants (*Backed* I: 90). Yet these patients talk light-heartedly about their illnesses and are seemingly oblivious to the threat of imminent death. Lao Qiu the cook, when relating his experience with stroke, says: "Fuck it, I'm sick all over — — can't die and I can't get well, either!" (*Backed* I: 91). Another man, named Pi, says of his own illness: "I'll never live to 42," whereupon his audience laughs heartily in merriment (*Backed* I: 91). A tuberculosis patient, Yu Shiliang, is reduced to skin and bones but is gentle and mild-mannered. He has four children. His mentally ill wife becomes pregnant again and the baby dies in the womb. Yu, lacking the money to pay the hospital for disposing of the dead fetus, buries the body himself in a public cemetery where the crowds are admiring the full moon on the night of the Mid-Autumn Festival.[36] He recounts the sad incident with a gentle smile. Ye's response was a hearty "Ha ha ha, ha ha ha" (*Backed* I: 102), a cruel bass harmony (like the harsh tone of a cello) of black humor against Yu's resigned high tenor (like the plaintive sounds of a violin).

In this movement, Ye also aims his mockery at an array of gods, including Mazu, Buddha, Guanyin, the Venerable Guandi, Lü Dongbin, Li Taibo, plus an assortment of other deities. He regards their collective

---

36. The description of crowds converging on a cemetery to admire the moon and that of Yu burying his dead baby constitute a surreal scenario, thus eliciting Ye's guffaws.

presence in the Mazu Temple—some "visiting," others "vacationing"—as "Greek polytheism" (*Backed* I: 64), in effect turning the temple into "The Number 1 Tourist Hotel in Deep Pit Harbor" (*Backed* I: 64). Ye's ridicule of the gods here is entirely a solo performance. Regarding the poem of sudden enlightenment by the Sixth Patriarch (638–713 CE) of Chinese Zen Buddhism—"Bodhi is no tree at all / Neither is the mirror a mirror / Everything by nature is Nothing / How can it gather dust?"[37]—Ye's comments can be considered his dialogue with as well as a counterpoint to the Sixth Patriarch across long-distance space and time. To Ye, a has-been poet known as "The One-Eyed Recluse," the lines quoted above are considered by him "the finest, the very finest, and the most enduring, simple little verse ever written in the history of Chinese literature" (*Backed* I: 66). He even goes so far as to think writing poetry is like "'sexual intercourse' ... —(both exhilarating and fatiguing). ..." (*Backed* I: 69). Despite his appreciation of the Sixth Patriarch's poem, Ye considers him an outstanding poet rather than a religious personage. In fact, by linking the motivation behind the Zen poem to sexual yearnings (*Backed* I: 69), he subverts the teachings of Buddhism and reflects his own lust-fulness and disregard for the essence of Buddhist teaching on abstinence from all sensual pleasures.

The tempo of the fourth movement, which deals with Ye's various sexual encounters, is one of wanton urgency, presto passionato. Lecher-

---

37. The translation is by the author of this essay. This poem by the Sixth Patriarch was a deconstruction of the poem by Shenxiu, the Fifth Patriarch's senior disciple, "The body is a Bodhi tree / And the mind a mirror / Keep cleansing it all the time / And it will not gather dust" (translation is also by the same author). The Fifth Patriarch thought that Shenxiu's poem did not achieve enlightenment as did the one by the Sixth Patriarch, and hence chose the Sixth Patriarch as his successor. Ye, being a great deconstructionist of religions, relishes the poem by the Sixth Patriarch. See Zheng Hengxiong 鄭恆雄, "Cong ji-haoxue de guandian kan *Bei hai de ren* de zongjiao guan" 從記號學的觀點看《背海的人》的宗教觀 (The view of religions in *Backed Against the Sea*: a semiotic interpretation), in *Wenxue yu zongjiao: Di yi jie guoji Wenxue yu zongjiao huiyi lunwen ji* 文學與宗教—第一屆國際文學與宗教會議論文集 (Literature and religion—collected essays of the first international conference on literature and religion) (Taipei: Shibao wenhua chubanshe, 1987), 407.

ous by nature, he hastens to seek sexual gratification on the next night after he begins telling fortunes. He enters a tiny cubbyhole, empty except for a tatami mat, plywood partitions, and a small pile of white toilet paper. In this "economizing" room sits a thin prostitute with a huge head and long hair. As she often rolls her eyes and purses her lips while saying "Yuck,"[38] he gives her the nickname "Yuck." When Ye orders her to "strip − − strip − −" and reaches out to pull off her thin sweater, she reacts angrily and says: "Stop pulling it − − don't pull it − −! You're tearing up my sweater − − yuck!" (*Backed* I: 108). The two strip naked in the cold January air (except for the socks, which the girl refuses to take off), and conclude their business amid much fumbling during which Ye emits a loud sneeze. Afterward the prostitute rolls her eyes at him, muttering "Yuck − −!" (*Backed* I: 108–13). This episode is highly comic, with the girl's impatient mezzo-soprano playing off his fussy bass to produce a satirical counterpoint. On Ye's second visit to the whorehouse, he ends up with a woman resembling the goddess Guanyin, who heaps sexual abuse on him and sends him packing in humiliation. Ye finally learns the truth of the saying: **"Wisdom grows out of experience"** (*Backed* I: 119). This goddess look-alike cries in a shrill soprano voice: "Curse me again!," **"No you can't!** − −" "Now I want you to get out of here! − − Get out − −" (*Backed* I: 117–18). He escapes ignominiously with his tail between his legs. Here the soprano-bass counterpoint serves to point out the just punishment his lechery brings on him. A typical bully, Ye makes his way to a teahouse for a spree of sexual fondling the night after his visit to Yuck and meets a taciturn woman, a "Sleeping Beauty ... sunk way down deep in her dreams" (*Backed* I: 120) who allows him to have his way with her without a single word. Only when she can no longer endure his rough pawing does she say softly: "Wait a moment, hold it, just a moment, ... I'll get you someone else, ... just take it easy a little ..." (*Backed* I: 120). Her timid, broken utterances in mezzo-soprano remind him of a woman he once met in a teahouse in Taipei, who was equally docile. These submissive teahouse women may all be

---

38. The original utterance of this prostitute in Chinese characters is 葉葉葉 (*yeyeye*), which conveys impatience in Taiwanese South Min.

named Meizhu. Whenever he enjoys their favors he feels he learns so much about life and society. He therefore concludes that "the tea room is a classroom," and every customer is a "thoroughgoing humanitarian" (*Backed* I: 122), The counterpoint of Ye's coarse, low voice overwhelming the soft, meek mezzo-soprano tones of the teahouse women shows the sadness and helplessness of the women forced to sell their bodies to make a living. Yet he discovers that not all teahouse women are "crybaby sob-sisters, oh no,— — there are also some that are so happy" in what they are doing (*Backed* I: 124). Two nights before the last (on the night of January 10, to be exact, because Ye's nightlong monologue has lasted until the early hours of January 13), while on his second visit to a teahouse in Deep Pit Harbor, he meets a really happy hooker. Not only is she happy, she is healthy as well, laughing and singing nonstop "authentic, unadulterated '**workers' songs**'!" (*Backed* I: 124). When he asks her the reason for her joyousness, she replies: "It just seems I was born happy the way I am, ... Even if I wanted to be sad, ... I still couldn't be sad" (*Backed* I: 125). Her joy and the workers' songs cause Ye to feel a degree of rapture as never before, and her cheerfulness succeeds in raising his low vocal range by at least an octave, ending in the word "**Daybreak**, — —"[39] (*Backed* I: 128) and concluding his monologue in counterpoint to the woman's gleeful soprano warbling.

Volume 2 as a Variation on Volume 1

"Writing a sequel to a novel is always harder than writing the first—ideas don't come as easily" (*Backed* II: 205). Ye's pronouncement is testimony to Wang Wenxing's own tortuous labor to bring the second volume of *Backed Against the Sea* into being, an effort that took seventeen

---

39. When Wang finished recording the first volume in 2002, he was already sixty-three, so the voice in the recording of the last three paragraphs is not raised one octave higher. But it is comparatively higher than that in reading the preceding paragraphs to express Ye's excitement (see CD of Wang, 2010) However, if this novel is adapted into a musical, raising Ye's voice one octave higher should not be a problem.

years, three times longer than its predecessor. Volume 2 is another over-night monologue by Ye, from February 20, 1962, to the dawn of the 21st prior to his death, and covers the one and a half months of his fugitive life in Deep Pit Harbor (since January 2 in volume 1). The focus is on his experiences after January 13. As in volume 1, he begins by ranting bit-terly against his misfortunes: "Damn! ..." (*Backed* II: 185), and then goes on to reveal the themes of the book: "Yes, so much has happened within the past six weeks. I've had to '**resort to**' fortune-telling; gotten seri-ously ill; fallen in passionate love; stolen; robbed; killed (a dog); and almost got **myself** killed!" (*Backed* II: 186–87). Like the prelude to a mu-sical composition, his invective sets out the themes. However, since vol-ume 2 is a variation on volume 1, it does not follow the structure of four movements in a classical symphony, instead resembling to a greater de-gree Paganini's *24 Caprices for Solo Violin, Opus 1, No. 24*, in presenting Ye's rambling, at times even delirious, ravings. In fact, his babbling is more like a rhapsody,[40] a free-ranging variation on the themes without any set rules. Unless we interpret volume 2 as a variation, it would be difficult to understand the repetitions of the episodes having to do with the prostitutes and BOCDO. Under the influence of two whole bottles of rice wine, Ye's speech here is even more slurred and sluggish than in volume 1, indicated by the larger number of blank spaces and incoherent chatter. In keeping with the saying, "Those whom God wishes to destroy, he first makes mad," his ranting foreshadows his own eventual death. Since Ye is so drunk that he does not give explicit dates of some of the incidents, in Table 8.2 I set out the sequence of events during the six weeks from January 13 to February 21 and try to determine the date of each episode whenever possible. If the exact date cannot be identified, I mark the entry "Date undetermined."

The second volume has ten variations on the five themes presented in the first volume: sex, illnesses, BOCDO, means of livelihood, and food and drink. The theme of Ye's fears of revenge emerges briefly five times

---

40. The rhapsody is a piece of musical composition with no specific form (*Oxford Companion to Music*). An example is Rachmaninov's Rhapsody on a Theme of Paganini mentioned earlier.

Table 8.2 Chronology of Ye's Ordeals in Deep Pit Harbor (Volume 2)

Date	Incident and Livelihood	Food and Drink	Sexual Encounters
From January 13 onward	Continuous rain keeps fortune-telling customers away; Ye fails to find a job; is desperate; has no money and is unable to leave Deep Pit Harbor (pp. 185–86).		
(Date undetermined)			For two weeks he falls rapturously for a red-haired woman, writes her three love letters, which are returned via Zhang Fawu. He bawls in disappointment (pp. 189–234).
(Date undetermined)			Recalls Cai Suzhen's crush on him in Taipei and his rejection of her love (pp. 234–69).
(Date undetermined)	Falls sick (flu and constipation) (pp. 270–85).		
(Date undetermined)	Ping-Pong game and other forms of horseplay at BOCDO (pp. 285–305).		
(Date undetermined)	Borrows $50 from a foreign priest (pp. 305–22).		

Date	Events
February 1 (27th day of 12th lunar month)*	A dog appears in the Cao family's vegetable garden (p. 364).
February 3 (29th day of 12th lunar month)	Helps the Caos kill the dog and eats dog meat (pp. 362–69).
February 6 (2nd day of first lunar month)	Director Wei at BOCDO tells Ye that no job vacancies are available (pp. 323–26).
February 7 (3rd day of first lunar month)	Vents his anger at BOCDO (pp. 327–30). Is banned from taking meals at BOCDO (p. 340).
February 8 (4th day of first lunar month)	Dong Yutang, a rich man, spends a night at Ye's home, but the latter fails to gain any profit (pp. 187–88, 340–57).
February 9 (5th day of first lunar month)	Tries stealing but fails (pp. 357–58).
February 10 (6th day of first lunar month)	Fails at two robbery attempts (pp. 359–60).

(continued)

Table 8.2 Continued

Date	Incident and Livelihood	Food and Drink	Sexual Encounters
February 18	Goes without sleep from midnight until monologue ends in the early morning of February 21 (pp. 188, 361).		Uses services of a prostitute without paying (p. 360).
February 19	Has his head shaved (p. 188).		Goes to another whorehouse and visits three prostitutes without paying (p. 361).
February 20	At midnight he soliloquizes about having only $3 left (p. 185), his illnesses (pp. 270–85), his love and sexual experiences (pp. 189–269, 360–61), his attempts at theft (pp. 357–58) and robbery (pp. 359–60), the dog-killing incident (pp. 362–69), his bleeding hemorrhoids (p. 362), seeing the black eagle circling above his head (p. 362), and his fears of revenge (pp. 187, 234–35, 322, 335, 361).	Has already drunk two bottles of rice wine before beginning his monologue, smoked all his cigarettes, drunk all the water, even burned all his candles. He is truly at the end of his rope (p. 187).	
Dawn/early morning, February 21	Finally ends up being killed (p. 369).		
Noon, February 21	Epilogue: rain stops and the sun appears; Ye's body floats on the sea (p. 371).		

*Conversion between the solar and lunar calendar dates is provided by the present author based on the "perpetual calendar," because Wang Wenxing gives only the dates of the lunar calendar.

like an undercurrent throughout this volume, but does not constitute a variation by itself.

Variation on Sex (1): Rapturous Love

That lecherous Ye falls for a red-haired, thin, bug-eyed, raspy-voiced, flat-bosomed, ugly prostitute is totally unexpected. He himself regards his crush on her as a form of settling some debt incurred between them in three previous lives (*Backed* II: 189). The woman, however, snubs him and takes up with Zhang Fawu instead. Ye writes three passionate love letters to her, even proposing marriage in the third, but she returns the letters to him through Zhang. Deeply disappointed, Ye breaks down in tears and howls: "I'm not as good as you, I know that now, **you win!**" (*Backed* II: 227). This variation is a rich blend of harmony and counterpoint. For example, to win the woman's love, Ye gives her a beaded handbag for which he has pawned an old treasured watch; their dialogue is a duet constructed from the harmony and counterpoint of their respective contralto and bass voices. Since the dialogue itself is presented through Ye's deep voice, a harmony is formed between his imitation of her contralto voice[41] and his own. The exchange between them counterpoints two melodies, as shown by the text quoted below:

"Someone told me to give this to you,— —[42]" I said.
"Who —?[43]"

---

41. The female contralto voice, the lowest of the three principal female voices (the other two being soprano and mezzo-soprano), is close to the male alto (or falsetto, the male voice higher than tenor) in pitch, and hence Ye has to raise his voice to the level of falsetto to imitate the red-haired prostitute's contralto voice as can be heard in Wang's reading of the following dialogue on the CD of Wang 2010. (For definitions of "contralto," "alto," and "falsetto," please see *Oxford Music Online*.)

42. Based on Wang's recording, the dash here indicates a rest (see CD of Wang, 2010).

43. Based on Wang's recording, the dash indicates lengthening of the sound (see CD of Wang, 2010).

"You'll know in a couple of days."
"Is it you?"
"Me?"— Ye asked myself.
"Is it —?"
"As you wish"
"As I wish?" She rushed one step toward me, "this is what I wish," raising the bag high in the air she then hurled it to the ground, saying: "—This is what I wish!—." She again moved forward, **stamping** her FOOT on the handbag.
"Oh —! Ah —!"
"Oh Ah —" she mocks in imitation. (*Backed* II: 222–23)

In this piece of comic dialogue (to him, a truly miserable experience), the woman's mocking contralto voice harmonizes with Ye's deep tone of diffidence, constituting a highly dramatic counterpoint. In writing the dialogue Wang uses a variety of typefaces and punctuation marks to control rhythm. Dashes indicate hesitancy or drawn-out sounds. The dashes in Ye's speech in lines one and five stand for rests, implying his timid hesitation when giving the handbag to her, while the dashes in the woman's questions "**Who**—?" and "Is it—?" stand for prolonged sounds representing the challenging tone of her utterances. When she throws the bag to the ground and tramples on it, Ye's reaction is marked by two dashes indicating the lengthening of exclamations, showing how deeply crushed he is. When she imitates his exclamations, however, there is only one dash, which denotes a less drawn-out sound and therefore her scorn. Moreover, bold typefaces signify loud or strong voices, just like strong syllables in poems and strong notes in music. Blank spaces denote pauses just like dashes; multiple spaces mean longer pauses. Finally, it is worth pointing out that Wang uses the formal character 壹 (one) instead of the more common and simplified 一 when describing the woman putting one foot down heavily on the handbag. His purpose here is to make readers pay attention to her action, emphasizing that her *foot* seems to be so heavy while stepping on it. The analysis of the dialogue between Ye and the red-haired woman demonstrates the meticulous care with which Wang creates his style, to the point of treating each

Chinese character like a musical note. When readers confront a work so rich in the musicality of language, it is imperative that they interpret it in terms of musical concepts and apply the same attention to each note and each pause, as listeners do to a musical composition.[44]

Ye's infatuation with the red-haired woman lasts for about two weeks. She soon moves to Taipei, either due to a lack of customers in the economic depression or to escape his attentions. His one-sided love affair having ended, Ye goes back to the pawnshop to redeem his watch. He receives only $2 in payment, causing him to lament: "Deep Pit Harbor may be the place, in the entire world, where inflation is the highest" (*Backed* II: 222).

Variation on Sex (2): Rejection of Love

Ye sums up the ending of his unrequited love for the red-haired woman thus: "So the whole thing is over, it no longer exists in this world; it has faded—to—nothing" (*Backed* II: 234). He comes up with a formula for love by concluding: "You love her, she loves another, another loves you!" (*Backed* II: 234). He recalls a woman named Cai Shuzhen whom he met while living in Taipei. "She loves me, but her 'passion' doesn't arouse in me any excitement, none at all" (*Backed* II: 234). Ye treats Cai Shuzhen with abominable abuse, to the point of setting up a scheme he dubs "Nanshijiao Secret Military Operation" to lure her to Nanshijiao to satisfy the appetites of his gambling buddy "Old Dog." Fortunately, she sees through the ploy and does not fall into the trap.

Ye's cruel treatment of Cai Shuzhen can be seen in the following dialogue when she visits him at his home:

> "Who is it?"
> "— Suzhen. "
> "— Suzhen?"
> Ye walked over and opened the door.
> "I knew I felt there was someone inside."

---

44. Shan Dexing, "Wang Wenxing on Wang Wenxing," 182.

Ye stared at her, looking.

"Were you sleeping?"

"Sleeping? —no I wasn't." Ye replied.

Her mouth opened wide.

"Then what were you doing?"

"— Nothing!"

She was silent.

"What're you doing here? — Didn't I tell you **NOT** to come here again, didn't I tell you?" (*Backed* II: 237–38)

The frosty tone Ye uses with Suzhen contrasts sharply with his tenderness in wooing the red-haired woman. The soft, warm mezzo-soprano of "—Suzhen" counterpoints the harsh questioning bass of "—Suzhen?" The same name is uttered in directly opposing pitches. When she asks in helpless surprise: "Then what were you doing?" he replies in the same rough voice: "—Nothing!" Finally he rejects Suzhen outright, concluding that love is not charity, not a "product of morality"; therefore his repudiation of her love "does not cause him the least bit of **remorse**" (*Backed* II: 269).

Variation on Sex (3): Whoring for Free

After his failures at attempted theft and robbery on February 9 and 10, respectively, the now penniless Ye visits a brothel on February 19 with no intention of paying. As he puts it: "—I **DON'T CARE** anymore—" (*Backed* II: 360). The next day he visits another whorehouse and demands the services of three hookers for free, because he wants "to enjoy to the full like an **EMPEROR**" the pleasures of debauchery (*Backed* II: 361). His actions incur the hostility of the brothel owners. Ye notes that knife-wielding thugs hired by whorehouse bosses will probably "**come after** me, after dark, come up the hill, and **come after** me" (*Backed* II: 361). He knows by now that he is doomed.[45] Wang uses the largest bold typefaces to show Ye's decision to throw caution to the wind, to expend the last of

---

45. In fact, in his monologue during the night of February 20 until dawn of

his vitality on a final fling, to revel in sexual pleasures "like an EM-
PEROR." Throughout this variation only Ye's solo bass voice is heard. His
overindulgence in sex finally leads to his death. It is quite ironic that he
should die at the hands of the whorehouse thugs instead of his archenemy Blackface Tiger.

Variation on Illnesses: Ye's Taiwanese Version
of the Seven Deadly Sins

In volume 1, Ye mentions that he is plagued by ulcers, asthma, and hemorrhoids (*Backed* I: 9). The theme of the illnesses recurs in volume 2, but
with a difference; he now suffers from the flu, constipation, and after his
lustful ventures, bleeding hemorrhoids (*Backed* II: 361–62). For the flu,
he has an unusual explanation: "—It **was**, an affliction I, brought upon
myself" (*Backed* II: 270). Two days before falling ill, he was thinking
cockily: "—So strange, I for a long time for a long time, I haven't even
been sick at all" (*Backed* II: 271). His present bout with constipation has
been the longest he has suffered so far, lasting for half a month. Since he
is penniless he has not gone to the doctor for either illness and instead
has managed to recover on his own. He does observe, however, that
"even if I had had the money, I would not have gone to see a doctor—
Simply because I have no faith in doctors, whether Chinese or Western"
(*Backed* II: 278). He goes on to name the failings of both Chinese and
Western medicine. As for his recovery from the ailments, Ye's observation is thus: "Rather than treatment, I prefer resigned acceptance"
(*Backed* II: 278). The bleeding hemorrhoids occur after three sleepless
nights and his visits to the whorehouses. As he puts it: "Misfortunes
come in threes" (*Backed* II: 361). In fact, his suffering is brought on by
overindulgence, and he muses to himself: "Do you think, you're nearing
the end?" (*Backed* II: 362). He goes on at this point to recall a black eagle
circling above him after his return from the brothel on February 20,
thinking: "Is it cooking up a scheme to feast on my dead body?" (*Backed*

---

the next day, Ye expresses his fears of retribution. See Table 8.2, the entry for
February 20.

II: 362). The lone dark eagle appears in both volumes and is an important symbol. It first shows up on page 18 in volume 1, in Ye's words: "... diving, darting, wheeling, soaring about as it pleases. ..." Zheng Hengxiong [Hengsyung Jeng] sees the eagle as having a similar meaning as in *Thus Spoke Zarathustra*, symbolizing "Ye's desire to soar freely in the air."[46] Edward Gunn, however, argues that "the narrator's counter-cultural vision succumbs to the environment" because in *Thus Spoke Zarathustra* the eagle is often accompanied by a serpent hanging around its neck, representing wisdom.[47] In his view, since the eagle in Wang's novel does not appear with any serpent and is therefore without wisdom, it signifies submission.[48] At that time (1987) Zheng stated that the true symbolic meaning of the eagle had to await the publication of the second volume to become definitive.[49] From Ye's foreboding in the second volume regarding whether the eagle has come to feast on his corpse and the description of the bird in the epilogue to volume 2 "over the rooftop of this bathroom, it took wing, **whirling** in circle after circle, soaring higher and higher, exuberantly, exaltedly" (*Backed* II: 371), it can be surmised that the eagle has at least two symbolic meanings. It represents Ye himself, his alter ego, a roving nomadic figure; it also signifies his death, as indicated by his remark about the eagle devouring his body, and the description of its flying higher and higher, like his alter ego or his soul leaving the Earth and soaring to the heavens. At this point the two symbolic meanings merge into one: despite the fact that Ye is physically

---

46. Zheng Hengxiong, "The View of Religions in *Backed Against the Sea*," 411.

47. Edward Gunn, "The Process of Wang Wen-hsing's Art," *Modern Chinese Literature* 1.1 (1984): 39.

48. In a later section, Ye does indeed bow to his environment (the Catholic Church) and borrows money from the priest. But the eagle does not appear during this episode; therefore the symbol should be explained according to the text and not entirely from the Western viewpoint contained in *Thus Spoke Zarathustra*.

49. Zheng Hengxiong, "The View of Religions in *Backed Against the Sea*: a Semiotic Interpretation," 411.

mired in his sins of alcohol, lechery, money, anger, pride,[50] tea,[51] and
cigarettes (his seven deadly sins), he still attempts to transcend his limitations and hopes to soar in the sky like the eagle. What is ironic, however, is that he can achieve complete freedom from his sins only after
death.

Ye's seven deadly sins echo Christianity's wrath, greed, sloth, pride,
lust, envy, and gluttony, thereby becoming a modern Taiwanese version
of the allegory in its embodiment of the concept that an unrepentant
sinner is ultimately doomed. Of the sinners in modern-day Taiwan, Ye is
but a symbol, and his plight an allegory. Western literary history abounds
in works dealing with the theme of the seven deadly sins, the most famous of which are Dante's *Divine Comedy*, "The Parson's Tale" in Chau-
cer's *Canterbury Tales*, and the fifteenth-century allegory *The Summon-
ing of Everyman*. If Ye is Everyman, then this novel is a burlesque
variation on the above-mentioned Western classics. Wang's treatment of
the theme is an important milestone in Taiwanese literary history. This
variation deals with the themes of illness and death in connection with
the reappearance of the eagle, intensifying Ye's worries, so his custom-
ary deep voice acquires melancholy overtones. In addition, the reemer-
gence of the black eagle foreshadows the scene in the epilogue in which
the bird soars toward the heavens. The appended section, far from superfluous, serves to highlight the motive of the black eagle and is thus an
essential part of the structure, like a coda at the end of a musical composition. Once again, this variation on his illnesses consists only of Ye's
lone bass voice.

---

50. When Ye mentions Sheng Qizhi at BOCDO, he says: "He's arrogant is
he—**I can be even more snooty!**" (*Backed* I: 107). This shows Ye's prideful nature.

51. Ye regards tea as one of the sins. He says: "People usually couple cigarettes with alcohol. No one ever adds tea to the list." He then goes on to say:
"Why the special leniency towards tea?" (*Backed* I: 25). According to the latest
medical reports, tea drinking may benefit health, but strong tea can be harmful
to the stomach. Since his habit of drinking strong tea has caused his ulcer to
bleed, his naming tea as one of the sins is understandable.

Variation on BOCDO: Buffoonery of the Ping-Pong Game and Other Things

The employees at BOCDO, bored out of their wits, spend their days clowning around and taunting each other. This variation in volume 2 mainly consists of Ping-Pong games between Zhang Fawu and Tang Lin. For example, they hog the Ping-Pong table, declaring their intention "to win a test of endurance," and prevent anyone else from playing (*Backed* II: 285). They hit each stroke deliberately, sending the ball high in the air, as if playing volleyball. Despite their slow movements, however, each is quick in blasting the other: "—I'm going to kill you; to kill you; —You big fat hog, I'll kill you and skin you. ... " and "This'll waste you, crush you to death, —You puny little bedbug, —Give up, why don't you, —down you go, down, scat ... " (*Backed* II: 287–88). Contrasted with their slow movements, their quick repartee makes for a comic scene. Since Tang Lin ends up losing every game and they always quarrel over trifles, the two finally part in acrimony, and the hitherto-coupled proper name "Zhang Fawu–Tang Lin" becomes a thing of the past (*Backed* II: 299). Other characters such as the cook Lao Qiu and the mentally ill janitor Pan Zhongliang also horse around. On one occasion Pan turns the hands of the big clock on the wall back by several hours, an act that results in him being severely beaten by Cui Liqun, Sheng Qizhi, and Lao Qiu. The episodes of tomfoolery at BOCDO in volume 2, as a variation on those in volume 1, are likewise rendered in a light and playful tempo, with the back-and-forth between Zhang's baritone and Tang's alto presenting a rowdy and dramatic counterpoint.

Variation on Means of Livelihood (1): Borrowing Money from the Priest

In desperation and as a last resort, Ye goes to the Catholic church on the hill to borrow money from the priest. In volume 1, Ye reveals himself to be an atheist and dead set against Christianity. His favorite reading consists of *Thus Spoke Zarathustra* by Nietzsche, *The Fruits of the Earth* by Gide, *Resurrection* by Tolstoy, and *Notes from the Underground* by Dos-

toyevsky, all of which share a common anti-Christian view (*Backed* I:
22). He often mistakes the light of the guard house on the hill for sunrise
and dubs it "False light! False Messiah!—" (*Backed* I: 70). Now that he has
to borrow money from the priest, he is forced to greet the latter in an
obsequious manner, saying: "—Ah, —Father, good day to you!" (*Backed*
II: 308). He even "places his two palms together, in front of him, as if
praying to the goddess Guanyin, praying, praying, — and then crosses
himself, making the sign of the cross several times" (*Backed* II: 308). Ye
thinks "all foreigners, have money, —and the church, **being** a charitable
organization, maybe it'd be possible to borrow some money" (*Backed* II:
312). To this end, he even engages the priest in small talk about religion,
such as asking him why he entered the priesthood, and why the om-
nipotent God allows humans to suffer so much. Finally he asks to borrow $100 dollars. The priest hands over $50, but reminds him to return
the cash soon as it is intended to help pay for an operation for Mrs. Zhu.
Ye promises to pay back the money. With cash in hand, he feels it unseemly to leave right away and asks the priest: "Ah, yes, Father, I'm very
interested in learning more about the Catholic faith. Can I, can I, come
to talk to you?" (*Backed* II· 317–18). The priest gives him two pamphlets.
Ye soon spends the $50 and, instead of paying back the loan, wishes to
borrow more (*Backed* II: 318). When he again visits the church, however,
the priest is not in, so he fails to get any money and returns to the town
in dejection (*Backed* II: 321). In contrast to Ye's anti-Christian stand in
volume 1, the variation in this passage shows him currying favor with
the church and feigning an interest in religion to borrow money. Out of
a sense of uneasy guilt, he speaks slowly, in his adagio bass voice, and
his speech here goes beyond a mere variation to become utterly off-key.

Variation on Means of Livelihood (2): The Fracas at BOCDO

Having failed to borrow more money from the priest, Ye takes the opportunity of the New Year's gathering at BOCDO on February 6 to ask
Wei, the director, whether there is a job for him. Upon hearing the latter
reply that the vacancy has already been filled, he becomes infuriated and
immediately decides to go to the office the next day to give vent to his

anger in an episode similar to the famous argument in the Beijing opera "Wreaking Havoc in Wulong Mansion" (*Backed* II: 327). He rushes into the director's office at nine o'clock, screaming and shouting, calling the director by his nickname Stomach Ulcer (a play on his name "Wei," homophonous with "stomach" in Mandarin Chinese), and banging on the desk before finally departing (*Backed* II: 330–31). The incident effectively ends his relationship with BOCDO for good, not only depriving him of an opportunity for a job but terminating his meals there as well, aggravating his already dire situation (*Backed* II: 340). The altercation between Ye and Director Wei creates a vitriolic counterpoint composed of a bitter tongue-lashing delivered in a bass voice against overbearing baritone officialese.

Variation on Means of Livelihood (3): Encounter with Dong Yutang

On the second day after the brouhaha at BOCDO, a wealthy man named Dong Yutang[52] appears at Ye's living quarters. He has been transacting business in Deep Pit Harbor and, because it is too late for him to return to Taipei, he has been advised to spend the night with Ye (*Backed* II: 340). "Dong is a tubby man, wearing a suit and carrying a briefcase under his arm.—This MAN, soon after sitting down, this, rich man, first hands me his name card, then proffers a cigarette and proffers a light. I note his cigarette to be 'State Express 555;' his lighter, gilded through and through, and looks to be, encrusted with diamanté" (*Backed* II: 342). Ye asks his advice on how to make money. Dong replies that he too started

---

52. But on page 187, Ye says: "That rich man Dong Yutang arrived here three days ago" (that is, on February 17), which contradicts the date (February 8) given on p. 340. Whether the discrepancy is due to Ye's confusion in his drunkenness or an error on the part of the novelist cannot be determined. Editor's note: We received a letter from Wang Wenxing on July 15, 2014, in which he explained the scheduling of *Backed Against the Sea* by saying: "Professor Hengsyung Jeng's correction is correct. When I wrote the novel, I did not check the lunar calendar for the year 1962. That caused a difference of nine days in the conversion of dates between the lunar and solar calendars in the novel. The conjecture I made caused the errors in the dates. I am thankful to Professor Jeng for his correction."

out a penniless beggar. Later when he was making a living as a rag picker in an area inhabited by U.S. military men, he managed to pick up discarded toasters, hair dryers, and typewriters, which he exchanged for cash. He then opened up a little eatery selling soybean milk, fried bread sticks, and sesame buns, and later began offering rice rolls. Now he has become "the king of rice rolls" (*Backed* II: 350). Ye finds "his story—very **morale boosting**—and useful" (*Backed* II: 350), and thinks that since his own experience is similar, he also has the chance to become rich. But Dong goes on to say that making a fortune is not only a matter of luck; one needs to set up a method of operation. Since he has to supply 20,000 rice rolls a day, there has to be a very efficient system of production and sales. Besides, strict discipline has to be maintained to guarantee the highest efficiency. He has come to Deep Pit Harbor to promote the sale of his rice rolls during the coming fishing season (*Backed* II: 354). Having talked himself out, Dong soon falls asleep and begins to snore. At first Ye thinks of stealing his money, but heedful of the fact that the chief of police in town is Dong's old friend, he refrains from doing so. Ye soon falls asleep himself, and upon waking, finds that Dong has already departed. Deeply chagrined at his failure to profit from the incident, he berates himself for "**missing** his chance despite spending a whole night —with the **money god**" (*Backed* II: 357). In this variation, even though Ye realizes that Dong's success story is morale-boosting, he thinks only of getting money without making an effort. Dong's high-pitched tenor while recounting his story set against Ye's affirmation of his success in deep bass provides the counterpoint in this passage. The contrast also highlights the disparity between the two: Dong works hard at building his business as top dog, while Ye dreams of becoming rich overnight as underdog.

Variation on Means of Livelihood (4): Failures at Theft and Robbery

With no way out of his desperate situation, Ye decides to try his hand at stealing. On the night of February 9, he hides under a kitchen window in the BOCDO housing compound. Suddenly a large pail of water is thrown out of the window, thoroughly drenching him. The entire night turns out to be a failure, and he gives up the attempt (*Backed* II: 358).

He then makes two attempts at robbery the next night. His first victim, an old lady, shouts, "**No money**, **no money**!" (*Backed* II: 359). Seeing a gold ring on her finger, he tries to take it but ends up being bitten. He yells in pain, and the old lady vanishes. On the same night at midnight, he tries again to rob an old man, who starts to scream loudly enough to wake the entire harbor. In desperation, Ye hits him on the head with the handles of a pair of scissors, whereupon the man faints. The perpetrator, fearing he may have a dead body on his hands, makes his escape.

The entire farcical variation involving theft and robbery highlighting Ye's humiliation is conveyed in a speedy presto rhythm. During the robberies, the high-pitched, loud, shrill screams of the victims in the quiet night form a piercing dissonance, scaring Ye into abandoning his plans.

Variation on Food and Drink: Canicide

Having failed at attempted theft and robbery, the only recourse left to Ye is to "— **kill**; yes, to kill a person even, I can do it" (*Backed* II: 362). But lacking the courage to actually kill a person, he ends up killing a dog. As he tells it: "— That day, I **killed** a **dog**. —" (*Backed* II: 362). Three days before the lunar New Year, a large dog weighing about forty kilos, breaks into the Cao family's vegetable patch. They decide to kill it and enjoy a feast. Two days later, in the evening, the entire family (father, mother, and three sons), with the exception of the youngest daughter, takes up arms to catch the dog. After beating the dog unconscious, the elder Cao hands Ye a knife and asks him to finish the animal off. He summons up his courage and "with one **blow**, kills it" (*Backed* II: 368). Within three hours the Caos and Ye finish off the meat (*Backed* I: 369). By killing and eating the dog, Ye has committed the sin of gluttony[53] in addition to his Taiwanese version of seven deadly sins, resulting in his punishment of

---

53. Gluttony is one of the seven deadly sins in Christianity. In addition to his Taiwanese version of seven deadly sins, Ye has added an eighth sin from the

"having to fart—SIXTY, or SEVENTY times" during the night (*Backed* II: 369).

During the dog-killing incident, Mrs. Cao shows her bravery by confronting the onrushing dog with a sharp bamboo spear. Her seventeen-year-old son hits at the dog with a wooden stick until it loses consciousness and wins high praise. Yet they agree that the "**gutsiest**" of all is the dog (*Backed* II: 369). Ye, too, can be said to show courage in his part of the affair.

In describing the precise movements of everyone in the episode, Ye's account is characterized by short sentences in the presto tempo. The breathless tempo also anticipates Ye's own death, as not long after killing the dog, he meets his own end.

Coda

Many operas and musicals have been adapted from novels with the characters assigned the female voice parts of soprano, mezzo-soprano, and contralto and the male voice parts of alto, tenor, baritone, and bass. The composer writes music according to the personality of each character and the elements of the plot, and provides each role with a corresponding voice part. Given the many common traits between music and language, the characters in a story naturally assume different voices interacting with each other in line with the development of the plot. It is therefore logical, in interpreting the two volumes of *Backed Against the Sea*, to establish the voice of Ye as the root note, against which the soprano of the Guanyin look-alike prostitute, the mezzo-soprano of Cai Shuzhen, the contralto of the red-haired call girl, the alto of Tang Lin, the tenor of Dong Yutang, and the baritone of Zhang Fawu and Director Wei of BOCDO all serve as harmonies and counterpoints in various moments of interplay. It is amazing that the whole gamut of voice parts is covered in this novel, attesting its unexcelled musicality. Furthermore,

---

Western version. Many people nowadays also commit this sin by frequently eating at the all-you-can-eat buffet.

the recording of Wang Wenxing's reading of the two volumes of the novel (edited by Peng Yi) was published in 2010.[54] Based on the recording, it would be possible to produce a musical work such as a *Backed Against the Sea* Concerto with Ye's monologue set to orchestra.[55] Equally conceivable would be a symphonic composition based on the four movements and variations discussed in this essay, or a tone poem similar to Richard Strauss's *Thus Spoke Zarathustra*. The novel could even be made into a musical to highlight the comic interactions between the various voice roles. A union between the novel and music would allow more readers to appreciate the multilevel musicality of language in *Backed Against the Sea*. Wang himself has said that he first established Ye's voice in the novel before matching the character to it using the technique of realism.[56] His statement shows that the sound of the language is the central figure in the narrative. He also stresses that "an ideal reader, like an ideal classical music listener, should not miss a single note, not even a pause."[57] Only through an analysis of the musicality of the novel, based on the concepts of rhythm, motive, melody, theme, movement, harmony, counterpoint, form, variation, and the various female and male voices, can the texture created by the multiple levels of sound be understood and the full extent of the hidden narrative structure together with the themes of the work be appreciated. In this novel, the writer's intricate craftsmanship in presenting the rich and varied musical quality of the Chinese language goes far beyond his achievement in *Family Catastrophe*. The musical quality of this novel is truly unprecedented in twentieth-century Chinese fiction.

---

54. Wang Wenxing, *Collection of Wang Wenxing's Manuscripts*.

55. In a discussion with the author of this essay on the musicality of the novel after the essay was presented, Shu-ning Sciban brought up the form of the concerto. Therefore, the author thinks that if Ye's low-pitched monologue is used as the solo part, it would be conceivable to set the writer's recorded voice to orchestra to produce a *Backed Against the Sea* Concerto to fully express the novel's musical qualities. The cello may also replace the monologue to create a cello concerto.

56. Shan Dexing, "Wang Wenxing on Wang Wenxing," 189.

57. Ibid., 182.

* * *

The author expresses his gratitude to Kang Laixin of National Central University, Taiwan, for inviting him to present the Chinese version of this essay on *Backed Against the Sea* at the International Conference on Wang Wenxing's Works (held on June 4–5, 2010), Chu-yun Chen (Mrs. Wang Wenxing) for her precise and elegant English translation of this essay, Yi Peng for providing the CD of Wang's reading of this novel, Shu-ning Sciban and Ihor Pidhainy for editing this English version, and finally my younger son, Zheng Hong, a conductor of wind bands and graduate student of music at Soochow University, Taiwan, for helping me with the correct use of musical terms.

9   The Stream-of-Consciousness Technique in Wang Wenxing's Fiction

Te-hsing Shan
Academia Sinica

I. Introduction

In 1981, Wang Wenxing published the first volume of his second novel, *Bei hai de ren (shang)* 背海的人 (上) (Backed against the sea, vol. 1), which, to my knowledge, is the longest stream-of-consciousness novel yet produced in Chinese fiction.[1] In comparison with his first novel, *Jia bian* 家變 (Family catastrophe),[2] however, *Backed Against the Sea*—the product of a painstaking, almost six-year effort by a serious writer who writes only about one hundred words per day—seems like a pebble cast into the sea, immense and indifferent. Up to the very present moment, few ripples have been seen.[3] One of the main reasons is that in addition

---

1. Wang Wenxing, *Bei hai de ren* 背海的人 (上) (*Backed against the sea*, vol. 1) (Taipei: Hongfan shudian, 1981). All subsequent references to this novel are cited parenthetically in the text.

2. Such a vehement argument over a single novel is an unprecedented phenomenon in Taiwan literary circles. For the pros, see *Zhongwai wenxue* 中外文學 (Chungwai literary monthly), esp. 1, nos. 11 and 12 (1973), and the cons, *Shuping shumu* 書評書目 (Book review and bibliography), esp. no. 6 (1973). *Backed Against the Sea* was written from January 6, 1974, to October 19, 1979.

3. Wang Xuanyi's 王宣一 "*Bei hai* kuang cao—Wang Wenxing de liangge chang ye (shang) (xia)" 背海狂草—王文興的兩個長夜(上)(下) (Cursive writing

to maintaining the stylistic idiosyncrasy of *Family Catastrophe*,[4] *Backed Against the Sea* has as its organizing principle the seemingly disorganized flow of consciousness of an anonymous, one-eyed narrator. This in itself is enough to constitute an insurmountable obstacle to an impatient or poorly trained audience.

Looking a little bit further into Taiwanese fiction, we will find that stream of consciousness not only has played a significant role in Wang's total creative output but is also a technique familiar to many Taiwanese writers.[5] This essay is a preliminary study of the adoption of a foreign literary technique by a person who is at once a student of foreign literature, a creative writer, and a professor of literature. My discussion focuses on his three short stories and the novel *Backed Against the Sea*.

---

in *Backed Against the Sea*—Wang Wenxing's two long nights (Pt. 1) (Pt. 2) published September 11 to 12, 1980, in the literary supplement of *Zhongguo shibao* 中國時報 (China times) before its eight-day (September 14–21) serial, was based on an interview with the author. The serial is one-sixth of the novel. The *Tamkang Review* editor's notes on the serial publication of this novel in the magazine classified it as an anti-novel, see *Chungwai Literary Monthly* 9, no. 5 (October 1980): 178–79. More than half of the novel appeared in three installments in this monthly from October to December 1980. Lin Xiuling's 林秀玲 book review, the only article of its kind, appeared in *Taida ren yuekan* 台大人月刊 (Taiwan University people monthly), issue of December 1982: 30–34. Chen Ruoxi 陳若曦, Wang's classmate at National Taiwan University, mentioned the novel in passing in her article appearing in the literary supplement of the *Lianhe bao* 聯合報 (United daily news), May 17, 1983. Edward Gunn, "At Play in the Fields of the Word," April 1982; "The Process of Wang Wenxing's Art in *Backed Against the Sea*," October 1982. Both are unpublished papers. Editor's note: Gunn has since published "The Process of Wang Wen-hsing's Art," *Modern Chinese Literature* 1.1 (1984): 29–41.

4. As for Wang's remarks on the stylistic similarities between *Family Catastrophe* and *Backed Against the Sea*, see my interview with Wang, which appeared in the inaugural issue of *Modern Chinese Literature*, published in September 1984, and is included in this volume. Hereafter, this interview will be referred to as "Shan's interview."

5. The case is especially true for those majoring in English and American literature, for instance, Shui Jing, Cong Su, Bai Xianyong, and Ouyang Zi.

Wang's Stream-of-Consciousness Short Stories

"The Marriage of a Civil Servant"

"The Marriage of a Civil Servant" was published in *Wenxue zazhi* 文學 雜誌 (*Literary review*), when the author was a twenty-year-old sopho- more in the Department of Foreign Languages and Literatures at Na- tional Taiwan University.[6] It was among Wang's earliest writings which, having been regarded by the author as works of his apprenticeship, have never been included in his collections of short stories. Like Ring Lard- ner's short story "Haircut," a work Wang probably had read,[7] the whole story is presented from the viewpoint of a gossip. As we read, or rather overhear, this talkative neighbor's one-and-a-half-hour soliloquy, the main action of the story is gradually revealed.[8]

The narrator provides us with necessary information as she describes the event to her neighbor: how a thirty-odd-year-old college graduate, most probably a mainlander serving as a civil servant, came to wed a socially and intellectually inferior native maidservant who handled food arrangements in the rooming house where he lived. From this chatter- box we learn about incidents, large and small, that culminated in the infamous wedding between the "honorable" civil servant and the preg- nant maidservant.

Rather than telling the story directly, the author chooses a narrator through whose mouth exclusively the story is told. In so doing, he not only gives us the narrator's version and criticism of the whole event, but

---

6. Wang, "Yige gungwuyuan de jiehun" 一個公務員的結婚 (The marriage of a civil servant), *Wenxue zazhi* 文學雜誌 (Literary review) 5.6 (1959): 41–47.

7. See Shan's interview.

8. In the second chapter of *Stream of Consciousness in the Modern Novel*, Robert Humphrey divides the techniques of the stream-of-consciousness novel into direct interior monologue, indirect interior monologue, omniscient descrip- tion, and soliloquy. He defines soliloquy as "the technique of representing the psychic content and processes of a character directly from character to reader without the presence of an author, but with an audience tacitly assumed." *Stream of Consciousness in the Modern Novel* (Berkeley: University of California Press, 1954), 23–41, esp. 36.

also tacitly offers an opportunity to judge for ourselves the event and the narrator's value system. A sense of reader participation is thus achieved, adding significantly to the interest of the story.

The author's method of presentation endows what originally was a not unusual story with something rich and new. A very consistent story is told through the narrator's soliloquy, which, in contrast to direct or indirect interior monologue, gains "a great coherence, since the purpose of it is to communicate emotions and ideas which are related to a plot and action."[9] What makes this story more profound and interesting is the discrepancy between the narrator's view and the author's. We observe that the critical narrator is also implicitly criticized by the author's vivid portrayal of her as a typical gossip. The beginning and concluding paragraphs skillfully reveal how this chatterer, who is bored in her own house and comes to her neighbor's for a chat, does not allow the listener to get a word in edgeways. Her criticism of the event reveals her value judgment—"This is truly a scandal! How can a maidservant become a madam? Gege, it's very funny. Yes, it's too bad" (p. 41).

She keeps a very close eye on the affair. Yet her close observation is that of a peeping Tom. She even knows how these two persons came to spend the night together—"You must wonder how I could have known it so clearly. I won't tell" (p. 43). From her knowledge of the details of the event, it is not difficult for us to infer her undue interest in this affair.

While repeating old Mr. Wang's consoling words—"Society today would not allow such old-fashioned misconceptions" (p. 46)—she is herself among those who hold these misconceptions. The observer and criticizer is thus observed and criticized implicitly through her own words and actions. This is the special interest of the story, which greatly benefits from the use of the stream-of-consciousness technique.

"Mother"

One year later, Wang published the short story "Muqin" 母親 (Mother) in *Xiandai wenxue* 現代文學 (Modern literature), of which he was one of

---

9. Ibid., 35–36.

the cofounders and editors.[10] In the preface to his *Fifteen Stories* published in 1979, Wang wrote:

> "Mother" and "Midsummer on the Prairie"—especially the latter—are works that I can mention with a smile. I wrote the way I pleased, despite what others might think. To hell with the story, the characters, the psychology. I am sorry that after these two works, I did not stick to my ideals and thought too much of others' understanding and agreement.[11]

Just as Wang wrote, the reader who is trying to find a story here will be greatly disappointed. What is placed before him is not a story with the traditional structure of beginning-middle-end or exposition-complication-climax-denouement, but the stringing together of scenes—external and internal (the latter in the sense of "psychological"). These scenes are presented via the cinematic technique of "montage."[12] The internal scene depicts the flux of the neurotic mother lying in bed and worrying about her only son. This presentation of the mother's inner movements is flanked by two external passages—the preceding, a description of a hot

10. Wang Wenxing, "Muqin" 母親 (Mother), *Xiandai wenxue* 現代文學 (Modern literature) 2 (1960): 67–70. There are some typographical errors (five spaces are missing) in *Shiwu pian xiaoshuo* 十五篇小說 (*Fifteen Stories*) (Taipei: Hongfan shudian, 1979), 29–33. The reader is advised to read this story collected in Wang Wenxing, *Wanju shouqiang* 玩具手槍 (The toy revolver and other stories) (Taipei: Zhiwen chubanshe, 1970), 33–38, though in that collection one space is still missing. Wang's importance as one of the editors of *Modem Literature* is acknowledged by Bai Xianyong and Ouyang Zi, see Bai Xianyong, 白先勇 *Moran huishou* 驀然回首 (Looking backward suddenly) (Taipei: Erya chubanshe, 1978), 81; Ouyang Zi, 歐陽子 *Xiandai wenxue xiaoshuo xuanji* 現代文學小說選集 (第一冊) (An anthology of the stories from modern literature, vol. 1) (Taipei: Erya chubanshe, 1977), 28. This anthology is edited by Ouyang Zi and prefaced by Bai Xianyong, Wang Wenxing, Chen Ruoxi, and Ouyang Zi—all classmates at National Taiwan University.

11. Wang Wenxing, "Xu" 序 (Preface), *Shiwu pian xiaoshuo* 十五篇小說 (*Fifteen stories*) (Taipei: Hongfan shudian, 1979), 2.

12. For Wang's appreciation of montage, see Shan's interview.

July afternoon; the following, an account of her son's entrance into the house of a young and fashionable divorced woman.

One of the stylistic characteristics of this short story, unique in some of his writing, is the appearance of a space after every sentence. A staccato effect is achieved by this typographical arrangement.

The fifth paragraph, which occupies two-fifths of the whole work, marks a sudden inward turning and is the only stream-of-consciousness passage. Yet its effect is amazing. This longest paragraph, with the exception of the last two sentences describing the heroine's falling asleep, presents the flow of consciousness of the neurotic mother in bed. Let us map the stream of her consciousness from her awakening to falling asleep once again in Table 9.1.

From the outline in Table 9.1, we can see how the movement of the

Table 9.1 Outline of Paragraph 5 of "Mother"

Sentence(s)	Content
1–7	Her worries about her only son who slipped away while she was asleep.
8–14	Her efforts to calm down, as advised by the doctor and her husband.
15–22	Her unfounded worries about her son being mistreated by his schoolmates.
23–42	Her efforts to be a good girl for the doctor by not giving in to fear.
43–61	The game of hide-and-seek between the young mother and her son when he was a small boy.
62–63	His totally different situation now (the estrangement between mother and son).
64	His boyish expression in the hide-and-seek scene (the once close relationship between mother and son).
65–73	The gap between mother and son now.
74–98	Her lapsing into unnecessary worries and picking herself up again.
99–115	Her thinking of something relaxing—Mrs. Zhang's visit and gossip (mainly about the divorced woman)—and falling asleep once again.

mother's stream of consciousness is "controlled by the principle of free association through memory, the senses, and the imagination"[13] and how past and present are immediately juxtaposed.

By using the stream-of-consciousness technique, the author makes us directly experience the unfounded worries of the neurotic mother who tries in vain to tie down her growing son.[14] We are in the stream and achieve a feeling of intimacy and immediacy.

"Strong Wind"

"Da feng" 大風 (Strong wind), published in *Modern Literature* in 1961, describes a middle-aged pedicab driver riding out into a stormy night to carry passengers to earn more money for his sick wife.[15] Instead of a gossip or a neurotic mother, we are confronted with a male narrator of forty-two who, while struggling with an astounding natural phenomenon, narrates things admirable and abominable.

This story can be divided into two parts based on narrative method: the narrator's talking to the other characters (the two passengers and his wife) and his speaking to himself. Through his narration we know that the hero is faced with different natural and human antagonists. What impresses us most is how he fights against the typhoon (one of the most overwhelming natural disasters in Taiwan); how he gets hurt, yet remains undefeated; and how he comes home triumphantly with his gains.

The greatest conflict in this story is that between man and nature. By way of the narrator's live report, we thrillingly experience the horrible and destructive force of the typhoon as well as the petty man's self-reliance and perseverance in the face of such an enormous and hostile natural force. It readily reminds us of Hemingway's *The Old Man and the Sea*, a novel Wang was reading at the time.[16] Encountering this tremen-

---

13. Humphrey, *Stream of Consciousness in the Modern Novel*, 46.

14. See Shan's interview.

15. Wang Wenxing, "Dafeng" 大風 (Strong wind), Xiandai wenxue 現代文學 (Modern literature) 11 (1961): 66–72; later collected in *The Toy Revolver and Other Stories*, 62–74, and *Fifteen Stories*, 57–67.

16. See Shan's interview for Wang's admiration for Hemingway.

dous force, the man can rely on nothing but his own strength, experience, and endurance. The primary motivation of his struggle is survival —his and his wife's survival in the world. He could retreat, yet where there is danger, there is profit; or, as he says, "The more violent the wind, the more difficult the ride, the more money" (p. 60).

It is in his struggle to survive that we perceive different forces at work that suggest the idea of the law of the jungle. As mentioned earlier, he tries to survive the typhoon by keeping a stiff upper lip. Moreover, he is not incapable of violence when his survival is threatened. The threat of the taxi introduced in the first paragraph appears in two forms—the danger of being hit and the competition to get passengers. The cruel beating of the lone taxi driver bespeaks the pedicab driver's capacity for anger and revenge. Also in contrast to the taxi driver, the pedicab driver can resort to little in the way of mechanical assistance. All he can rely on is his own flesh and blood. This greatly adds to his heroic stature.

When confronted with his passengers, he is able to practice deception in order to get more money than he should. He cunningly cheats the first passenger out of two more dollars by saying he has no change. As a matter of fact, he hides small change in another pocket. Cunning as he is, he is honorable in his own way. For besides his violence and deception,[17] he is careful, tender, and responsible, as shown by his saving a girl who contemplated suicide and his thoughtfulness toward his wife. If his account to the second passenger is reliable, he was compassionate enough to carry the girl at an unbelievably low price, careful enough to detect there was something wrong with her, and enthusiastic enough to call the police to prevent her from committing suicide.

By this vivid presentation of the narrator's feelings and thoughts through his flow of words, we intimately experience his various encounters and realize the noble and nasty sides of the hero who, in order to

---

17. These are negative qualities as far as absolute morality is concerned, yet positive qualities in a world where the law of the jungle dominates. Although the appearance of the police in the first paragraph is a slight negation of the law of the jungle, the beating of the imprisoned pedicab driver ironically proves that even for the police, the law of the jungle prevails.

survive all kinds of challenges, must play tough, yet is not without ten-derness.

The First Paragraph of *Backed Against the Sea*: An Explication

The very first paragraph of *Backed Against the Sea*, an example of Wang's stream-of-consciousness work published twenty years after "Strong Wind," poses some serious questions. Being one of the most obscene and offensive passages in contemporary Chinese fiction, few readers will read it without a blush. At first sight, it seems to be nothing more than a long list of dirty words that people would never utter under normal cir-cumstances. Seldom have we been thrown so immediately and blasphe-mously into the flux of a narrator-protagonist's thoughts and feelings. Does this paragraph merely aim to shock the reader? After reading a few pages (if we are patient and tolerant enough), we realize the situation is indeed unique and that the language is necessary as far as sound, sense, and structure are concerned.[18] As we delve into the consciousness of the drinking and gradually intoxicated narrator, the necessity and even the merits of this passage slowly come into sight. In this section I make a somewhat bold attempt at a detailed analysis of this paragraph—in my opinion the epitome of the whole book—by drawing on internal evi-dence to support my argument. It is my conviction that a careful analy-sis of this paragraph will do justice to the author's craftsmanship and reveal to us many of the important aspects of this novel.

In the presence of work by a serious writer who advocates "econ-omy," who believes that "words are everything," who emphasizes the importance of reading closely and gruelingly (oral reading—one thou-

---

18. See Shan's interview for Wang's ideas on sound and sense. As for his concept of structure, see Wang Xuanyi, "Cursive Writing in *Backed Against the Sea*—Wang Wenxing's Two Long Nights (PT. 1) (PT. 2)" *China Times*, September 11 1980," 8; and Li Ang's 李昂 interview Changpao xuanshou de guji" 長跑選手的孤寂 (Loneliness of a long-distance runner), *Zhongguo dangdai yishujia fang-wen* 中國當代藝術家訪問 (Interviews with contemporary Chinese artists) (Tai-pei: Dahan chubanshe, 1978), 81–82.

sand words per hour, two hours per day), who practices the doctrine of writing slowly and surely, who strives to combine sound and sense, and who wants to utilize poetized language in his work, the way for the reader to get the most out of it is to follow his doctrine and advice as far as our patience and ability will allow.[19] However, nowhere in Wang's previous works have we seen such an intensity and complexity of words as in the first paragraph of this novel, a work whose diction in Wang's opinion follows the same direction of *Family Catastrophe* yet with more freedom.[20] To facilitate our discussion, it is necessary for us to chart it in Table 9.2.

It goes without saying that the transliteration loses much of the flavor of the original text, because in it we cannot find the characteristic Chinese *sisheng* (四聲 four tones), which contribute greatly to the acoustic effect. Meanwhile, the visual effect of the Chinese script has also been completely lost. Nevertheless, for readers of the Chinese text, even the most careless ones will notice some striking points, such as its obscenity, its long series of exclamation marks (twenty-six in all), its debasing animal imagery, as well as the repetition of words and sounds.

Generally speaking, this paragraph of condemnation not only sets the tone for the whole book, it also arouses and orients the reader's anticipation. It tells us the narrator's attitude toward his subjects and dictates our attitude toward them. But just as in "The Marriage of a Civil Servant," we are not going to take the narrator's words on trust. First

---

19. These ideas are expressed in almost every preface he writes and interview he gives.

20. See Shan's "Wang Wenxing on Wang Wenxing," an interview conducted in 1983 for the stylistic connection between these two stories. The interview is reprinted and included in this volume, on page 276 where detailed information about its publication is given in footnote 1. The characteristics and merits of the language of *Family Catastrophe* have been explored by Ouyang Zi 歐陽子, "Lun *Jia bian* zhi jiegou xingshi yu wenzi jufa" 論「家變」之結構形式與句法 (A discussion of the form and sentence structure of *Family Catastrophe*), *Zhongwai wenxue* 中外文學 (Chungwai literary monthly) 1:12, 51–67; and by Zhang Hanliang 張漢良, "Qiantan *Jia bian* de wenzu" 淺談「家變」的文字 (A brief discussion of the language of *Family Catastrophe*), *Zhongwai wenxue* 中外文學 (Chungwai literary monthly) 1:12, 122–41.

Table 9.2 Paragraph 1 of *Backed Against the Sea*

Transliteration	Cao!	Wo!	Cao!	Ta	ma	le	ge	bi!	Cao	ta	niang!
Word order	1	2	3	4	5	6	7	8	9	10	11
Phrase order	1	2		3					4		
Sentence order	1	2		3					4		

	Gou!	Gou!	Bi!	Gou	pi!		Dao	zhe	gui	di	fang	lai!
	12	13	14	15	16		17	18	19	20	21	22
	5	6		7			8					
	5	6		7			8					

	Ma	le	ge	wu	gui.	Jiu	shi	wu	gui,	gui	tou,
	23	24	25	26	27	28	29	30	31	32	33
	9			10				11		12	
	9										

	lan	jiao,	chi	Wo	de	lan	jiao!	Chi	ta!	Chi!
	34	35	36	37	38	39	40	41	42	43
	13					14		15		16
								10		11

Gui	*gong!*	*Xiang*	*gong!*	*Tu*	*zi!*	*Bai*	*tu!*
44	45	46	47	48	49	50	51
17		18		19		20	
12		13		14		15	

Gou	*yang*	*de!*	*Gou*	*pi!*	*Gou*	*pi!*	*Gou*	*zhua!*	*Gou*	*tui!*
52	53	54	55	56	57	58	59	60	61	62
21			22		23		24		25	
16			17		18		19		20	

Gou	*lan*	*jiao!*	*Gou*	*tou!*	*Gou*	*shi!*	*Gou*	*ya!*
63	64	65	66	67	68	69	70	71
26			27		28		29	
21			22		23		24	

Gou	*ti*	*gou*	*bian!*
72	73	74	75
30		31	
25		26	

and foremost, what we should do is listen to what he tells us, that is, his account of the events, and then his vantage points and prejudices.

We can infer from this paragraph that the narrator is alone and is in one of the innermost and most private moments of his life. When a person is in the company of others, he may utter some lewd words. But it is highly unlikely that he would utter such a long list of words of damnation. Only when he is absolutely alone, physically and psychologically, would he be able to express freely what has been so long suppressed. On the third page, we are told he is drinking bad wine. As we all know, alcohol makes us garrulous, especially during the early moments of drinking. It is also beyond doubt that the intoxicating effect of alcohol liberates a person from his daily restraints and reveals the deeper level of his mind. What is closely connected is the revelation of his antisocial mentality, his feeling of abusing and being abused, his desire to condemn, to rebuke, and to shout loudly and lewdly against himself as well as the world in which he lives.

This paragraph can be said to be structured on free association or, to be more specific, word association—one of the major techniques of the stream-of-consciousness novel. I will point out just some of the obvious associations in terms of sentences, phrases, words, and sounds in Table 9.3.

As for the discussion of rhythm, the list in Table 9.4 will be helpful.

We can see that this paragraph is characterized by short sentences, mostly in the form of two-word sentences—the commonest form of curse. The seventy-five-word paragraph is divided into twenty-six sentences by twenty-six exclamation marks—with an average of 2.88 words per sentence/exclamation mark. The shortest sentence is composed of one word, the longest, eighteen words (even the longest sentence is composed mainly of two-word phrases). This long sentence, separated by one dash and four commas, is placed there for rhythm's sake. With lower pitches and shorter pauses between phrases than those of other sentences, it creates the effect of variety. Compared with the number of sentences, the proportion of phrases in this paragraph is high (83.87 percent)—a very rare case in terms of syntax. The effect of rapidity and forcefulness is created by the combination of the shortness of the sen-

Table 9.3 Scheme of Word Association in Paragraph 1 of *Backed Against the Sea*

A	Same sentences	7, 18
B	Same phrases	10, 11; 13, 14 (in addition to A)
C	Similar sentences	6, 7, 17, 18, 19, 20, 21, 22, 23, 24, 25, 26
D	Similar phrases	13, 14, 26; 19, 20 (in addition to C)
E	Same words	1, 3, 9; 2, 37; 4, 10; 5, 23;7, 25; 8, 14; 12, 13, 15, 52, 55, 57, 59, 61, 63, 66, 68, 70, 72, 74; 16, 58; 26, 30; 27, 31, 32, 44; 33, 67; 34, 39, 64; 35, 40, 65; 36, 41, 43; 45, 47; 48, 51
F	Same sounds	29, 69 (in addition to E)
G	Alliteration	8, 14, 50, 75; 16, 56, 58; 5, 23; 17, 20, 38, 54; 4, 10, 33, 42, 48, 51, 62, 67, 73; 6, 22, 24, 34, 39, 64; 28, 35, 40, 65; 7, 12, 13, 15, 19, 25, 27, 31, 32, 44, 45, 47, 52, 55, 57, 59, 61, 63, 66, 68, 70, 72, 74; 18, 60; 1, 3, 9
H	Rhyme	4, 5, 10, 23, 42; 2, 6, 7, 18, 24, 25, 37, 38, 54; 22, 50; 1, 3, 9, 17, 35, 40, 65; 34, 39, 64; 12, 13, 15, 33, 52, 55, 57, 59, 61, 63, 66, 67, 68, 70, 72, 74; 8, 14, 16, 20, 56, 58; 73; 26, 30, 48, 51; 11, 46, 53; 45, 47; 19, 27, 31, 32, 44, 62.

Table 9.4 Analysis of the Length of Sentences in *Backed Against the Sea*

Three one-word sentences	1, 5, 11 (11.54%)
Seventeen two-word sentences	2, 6, 7, 10, 12, 13, 14, 15, 17, 18, 19, 20, 22, 23, 24, 25, 26 (65.38%)
Three three-word sentences	4, 16, 21 (11.54%)
One five-word sentence	3 (3.85%)
One six-word sentence	8 (3.85%)
One eighteen-word sentence	9 (3.85%)

tences, the large number of exclamation marks, and the repetition of sentences, phrases, words, and sounds.[21]

This paragraph of word association can be considered the apex of Chinese dirty words, with their characteristic obscenity and offensive-

---

21. See Lin Xiuling's book review, 31.

ness. This use of word association is repeated later in the novel. Here I cite three examples. On page 32, the narrator tells us how the landlord gets water into the reservoir by connecting bamboo pipes overhead to a mountain spring. Then we have a series of seven expressions beginning with an appropriate phrase and ending surprisingly with the name of the American sex symbol Marilyn Monroe—from "flying spring" (a spring coming from above) to "bath water from heaven" to "joy from heaven" (a Chinese idiom meaning an unexpected joy) to "the water of the Yellow River comes from heaven" (a famous line by the Chinese poet Li Bo, which also suggests the narrator's literary background) to "heaven(ly) river" (another name for the galaxy, which hints at a fortune-telling motif), to "flying waterfall and angry tides" (a Chinese idiom describing dangerous waters and the Chinese translation of a movie starring Marilyn Monroe) and finally to Marilyn Monroe. The associative line is constructed on water imagery, the dominant imagery of the novel. Moreover, the Chinese translation of Marilyn Monroe's name is closely connected with water imagery. In China, a woman is said to be made of water and sometimes even disparaged as *huoshui* 禍水 (ominous water; the source of trouble) and the Chinese transliteration of "-roe" in Monroe is *lu* 露 (dew).

Then word association based on the sound "zhong" appears on page 119. There the director of the half-forgotten office says:

Zhong guo cai, zhong qi shi zu, zhong xin geng geng
(Chinese dishes, very strong, most loyal!)
中國菜，中氣十足，忠心耿耿

Here, high-sounding, semantically unrelated words are forced together by the ridiculous director of that superfluous office simply because they have the same sound "zhong," creating an effect of irony and humor. In fact, the behavior of all the members of that office is absurd and laughable.

Word association of great thematic and structural importance appears again on page 99. The narrator goes out to urinate and, seeing the light of the inspection station on the mountain, says that he often mistakes it for sunrise. He continues, "Deceiving light!—Deceiving Messiah!—" At the very beginning of the next paragraph, he exclaims excitedly, "Halleluiah, halleluiah—I remember—Zhang Fawu ..."

The path from "deceiving light" to "deceiving Messiah" and to "Halleluiah, halleluiah" is clearly traceable. But all these utterances have a close connection with the whole book—for instance, the light/darkness imagery, the religious overtones, the ironic stance, and the image of the false prophet.

On first reading, the transition from "halleluiah" to "Zhang Fawu" seems somewhat abrupt. But in Chinese, "Messiah" is pronounced "misaiya" and "halleluiah" as "haliluya." So the transition from "*misaiya*" to "*haliluya*" is both religious and phonetic, while that from "*haliluya*" to "*Zhang Fawu*" is phonetic, though not so obvious.

The association, nevertheless, is not as simple as it appears, for on the narrator's initial acquaintance with Zhang, the latter is playing a trick on the dock. With his gigantic stature and imposing, deceptive behavior, Zhang is virtually a deceiving messiah. Therefore, the narrator's exclamation of "halleluiah" is both sarcasm directed at Zhang and an expression of his excitement at finding his lost thought stream.

This shift is of great structural significance, for ten pages earlier the narrator's flow of thoughts, then concentrating on Zhang Fawu, had been interrupted by a cock crow. His thoughts stray from Zhang to the cock. The runaway flow of thoughts is not recollected until the "deceiving Messiah" reminds him of the subject dropped earlier—to play on words, we may say Zhang is both a deceiving messiah and an abnormal subject to the narrator.

Nevertheless, these three examples, delicate and functional as they are, cannot match the delicacy and function of the first paragraph.

Also obvious in the first paragraph is the abundant use of animal imagery: the dog (fourteen times), the turtle (four times), and the rabbit (twice). All these images are used in a degrading sense. The dog, no longer a faithful animal, is downgraded and becomes one of the dominant images of the novel; the turtle, no longer a symbol of patience and longevity, is used to describe the male sexual organ; the rabbit, no longer a lovely animal and pet, means a homosexual (similarly the once honorific title *xiang gong* for young gentleman came to mean a male prostitute).

Here I turn my discussion to the related dog imagery on the second page. In the fourth paragraph of the book, the narrator says:

> What I cry out is like the barking of the dog, yea, meaningless dog barking, that will disperse in the boundless dark night, without a single trace. ... once a person holds his pen, he will not have the desire to talk crazily as he pleases ... So what I am saying now is purely for my own hearing—no, no, even I myself don't want to hear it, I just want to talk, no, not talk even, I just want to *bark* and *bark*. (p. 2)

When rendered into English, *liushu* (六書), the six principles of formation of Chinese characters—pictograph, form indication, ideograph, sound indication, figurative extension of meaning, and making one form stand for another word—are almost done away with. The following interpretation does not follow these six principles. My purpose is different: to show the effect of montage, a cinematic technique derived by Sergei Eisenstein to a great extent from Chinese characters (see Table 9.5).[22]

These words, except the first one, in themselves create the effect of montage. When put together and seen in light of the whole book, the effect is enormously multiplied and the meaning is marvelously enriched.

---

22. According to Eisenstein, "Two film pieces of any kind, placed together, inevitably combine into a new concept, a new quality, arising out of that juxtaposition" and "Piece A (derived from the elements of the theme being developed) and piece B (derived from the same source) in juxtaposition give birth to the image in which the thematic matter is most clearly embodied." Sergei M. Eisenstein, *The Film Sense*, trans. and ed. Jay Leyda (New York: Harcourt, Brace & World, 1942), 4, 11. Elsewhere, Eisenstein cites some Chinese characters to show that "by the combination of two 'depictables' is achieved the representation of something that is graphically undepictable." Among them are: a dog + a mouth = "to bark" (吠); a mouth + a child = "to scream" (叫); a mouth + a bird = "to sing" (鳴); a knife + a heart = "sorrow" (忍); Eisenstein, *Film Form*, trans. and ed. Jay Leyda (New York: Harcourt, Brace & World, 1949), 30.

Table 9.5 Etymological Analysis of 4 Characters Associated with Dogs in the 4th Paragraph of *Backed Against the Sea*

Quan	犬	*A dog.*
Fei	吠	The barking of a dog, coming from *kou* 口 (mouth) and *quan* 犬 (dog), meaning the sound out of the dog's mouth.
Gou	狗	Originally a dog, coming from *quan* 犬 and the phonetic of 句; here we may run the risk of interpreting it as *quan* (dog) and *ju* 句 (sentence), so what the narrator utters is "dog's sentences"—nonsense, coming from the dog's mouth.
Wang	汪	Originally a pond, now often used as the Chinese onomatopoeia for the sound of the dog; if separated into *shui* (water) and *wang* 王 (king), this character goes with the prevailing water imagery and the narrator's appearance as a living prophet and demigod (esp. p. 20 and p. 80) in this coastal village, deciding the life and death of the villagers like a king.
Kuang	狂	Originally crazy, coming from *quan* 犬 and the phonetic of *wang* 王; of divided into *quan* (dog) and *wang* 王 (king), it can be further interpreted as "dog king"—thus a graphic and onomatopoeic representation of the crazy sentences of the dog king.*

*In this novel, people seem to be the underdogs of fate, while the narrator, himself an underdog and fortune-teller, is also a "prophet" mediating between fate and man.

Therefore, the author's repeated use of dog imagery in the first two pages is more than clear; the effect of ambiguity and richness is striking, and his intention is not to be mistaken.

Food and sex, two major motifs in this novel, are also present in this paragraph. The verb *eat* appears three times, and dog, turtle, and rabbit are all edibles in China. Furthermore, what ties the whole book together is the narrator's drinking and smoking (in Chinese, drinking and smoking are often expressed as "eating wine" and "eating smoke"). On the other hand, words carrying sexual overtones occupy more than half of the exclamations of the first paragraph.

Throughout the book, the narrator seems to be obsessed with these two motifs. In addition to "eating wine" and "eating smoke," which relate to the narrator's present moment, his thoughts center upon, among other things (the most prevalent of which might be fish, fate and fortune-telling), food and sex. The narrator's observations of the place include interesting statistics that seem to be a declaration of mankind's joy and equality in terms of food and sex:

> This place has more sex-selling brothels and teahouses than any-thing else. Next in number is the food-selling stands. Altogether; brothels: 4, teahouses: 3, snack bars: 5. The food-selling and sex-selling shops outnumber everything else, so we can see that "eat-ing" and "whoring" are indeed two of the most significant things of life ... it seems that "eating" and "whoring" include all the hap-piness in the world. Yes, that's correct indeed, ... with "food" and "sex" you will not miss gardens and mansions, gold and US dol-lars, cars and swimming-pools ... So the happiness of "food" and "sex" is indeed the most, most inexpensive among all desires. You may even say that "food" and "sex" are the real, undiluted happi-ness of "THE DOCTRINE OF PEOPLE'S RIGHTS"—rich and poor alike will get them, the extent of the enjoyment of food and sex is the same regardless of their being rich or poor, it may even happen that the happiness of the rich cannot match that of the poor. (pp. 17–18)

Here is the equality of all men in food and sex. The food and sex images can be seen throughout the book, and there are many passages wholly devoted to these two aspects: for example, his going to a food stand (pp. 20–22); his spiritual food and material food (p. 29);[23] his din-ner in the superfluous office (p. 115–25); the longest passage on sex

---

23. His spiritual food includes eleven pornographic photographs, a self-copied collection of modern Chinese poetry, Dostoyevsky's *Notes from the Un-derground*, Nietzsche's *Thus Spake Zarathustra*, Gide's *Fruits of the Earth*, and Tolstoy's *Resurrection*. All these reveal him as he is—a poet, a prophet, an exile, a sex-seeker, and a man in search of hope and rebirth. The fortune-telling book, as a means to keep his body and soul together, is regarded by him as his material food.

and his whoring experience (pp. 152–82), about one-sixth of the whole book.

But sex, the happiest and most democratic object in the world, is also a filthy and fearful thing. On page 162, the narrator tells an allegory of man's dilemma as a sex-seeker: a person who jumps into a filthy pond over and over again in order to catch the moon.[24] The narrator cannot rid himself of sexual desire, nor can he fully enjoy his sexual life. In addition to his impotence and premature ejaculation, his sexual act is also over-shadowed by his fear of catching venereal disease. He will not enjoy his sexual life without a condom. Yet this protective measure either causes temporary impotence (p. 157) or fails him at the crucial moment (pp. 160–61). His being seduced by the Bodhisattva-like female sadist is his most painful and humiliating experience.[25] There he is an underdog, a plaything, a mouse in a cat's paw—a sharp contrast to his role as a gallant (pp. 173–74), an aggressor (p. 170, pp. 171–72, and p. 176), or a happy companion (pp. 176–82).

Food and sex culminate in the last phrase/sentence of the first para-

---

24. Here, like the word association analyzed earlier, the author alludes to Li Bai who, according to a legend, drowned himself because when drunk he wanted to catch the moon in the lake. Obviously, this legend has been burlesqued. Also here is the absurdity of sex-haunted men, or, if I am allowed to burlesque the title of John Synge's famous one-act play, the absurdity of "Jumpers into the Pond" is in sharp contrast to the tragic sense of those who go to sea to catch fish despite the "oracle" of the prophet, the death of his crew, and even the death of his beloved son: "Jumpers into the Pond" versus "Riders to the Sea." Yet these "Riders to the Sea" may also be "Jumpers into the Pond"—another illustration of man's contradiction, see pp. 75–76, pp. 84–86, and p. 1.

25. This is also symbolized by his being led upstairs by this goddess-like lady only to be mortified the more—the ascent to heaven turns out to be a descent into hell. With a knife on his neck, he is forced to sorely and ironically experience the Chinese proverbial wisdom "Sex is a knife at one's head" 色字頭上一把刀 (sezi toushang yi ba dao) (p. 167). Like another proverb, "Patience is a knife at one's heart" 忍字心上一把刀 (renzi xinshang yi ba dao) (see n. 22, the last Chinese character cited by Eisenstein), it is characterized by the fact that "by the combination of two 'depictables' is achieved the representation of something that is graphically undepictable."

graph—dog penis, a Chinese folk aphrodisiac to be eaten for the sake of increasing one's sexual power.

The narrator's denunciation of the fishing village as *gui difang* 鬼地方, a "ghostly place," "place of ghosts," or "hell," carries a much richer meaning than it appears. First, this condemnation fits perfectly with the name of the place (literally, deep pit bay), the phantom-like people, and the prevailing gloomy atmosphere.

In Chinese culture, ghosts and gods (*gui shen*, 鬼神) are often mentioned together and are two indispensable factors of Chinese religious life. Thus this phrase conveys a religious overtone. The traditional Chinese religious attitude as well as the invasion of foreign religion can both be detected in the text that follows.[26]

The phrase "ghostly place" expresses the psychological implications in terms of the contradictions in the narrator's mind. Because some rascal claimed his only eye, he came to "deep pit bay" to save "the window of his mind" (p. 36) and wait for fish, a symbol of life and hope.[27] But many of the expressions of this man "at bay" also unmistakably show his death wish, for instance, his drinking wine is compared to drinking poison (p. 3), the bathtub in which he sleeps is fit for a coffin (p. 25). He is both expecting and forsaking life, maintaining and giving up hope of resurrection, struggling between his psychological death wish and biological instinct to survive.

Closely related to the religious and psychological aspects of the book is its philosophical and mythical orientation. As far as the philosophical level is concerned, man stands between gods and ghosts, heaven and hell, a creature of life carrying the seed of death inside him, or, to go with the fortune-telling motif of this novel, carrying his fate on his palm, his face, and his birth date. In Alexander Pope's philosophical poem "An

---

26. The religious overtone can most easily be found in p. 1, p. 16, pp. 19–20, and pp. 90–92. To a larger extent, the villagers' religious attitude reflects not only the traditional Chinese culture but also the Chinese attitude toward foreign culture.

27. In contradiction to the dog imagery, which serves to downgrade man, the prevailing fish imagery stands for something positive.

Essay on Man," we have one of the best portrayals of man's dilemma and self-contradiction:

> Placed on this isthmus of a middle state,
> A being darkly wise, and rudely great:
> With too much knowledge for the skeptic side,
> With too much weakness for the Stoic's pride,
> He hangs between; in doubt to act, or rest,
> In doubt to deem himself a god, or beast;
> In doubt his mind or body to prefer,
> Born but to die, and reasoning but to err;
> Alike in ignorance, his reason such,
> Whether he thinks too little, or too much:
> Chaos of thought and passion, all confused;
> Still by himself abused, or disabused;
> Created half to rise, and half to fall;
> Great lord of all things, yet a prey to all;
> Sole judge of truth, in endless error hurled:
> The glory, jest, and riddle of the world! (Epistle II, 11.3–18)

The narrator's self-criticism is the same: "Contradiction! Contradiction! I am a big big big big and big contradiction!—I AM 'CONTRADIC-TION'" (p. 31).[28] His allegory of "Jumpers into the Pond" also vividly shows the absurdity and irrationality of man as described by Pope.

On the mythical level, the narrator is greatly honored and worshipped because he delivered an oracle which, to his fortune and to others' misfortune, came true. He is even idolized. Yet his role as a prophet is also satirized. For, unlike the archetypal prophet Teiresias, who loses his sight but gains insight and foresight, the one-eyed narrator with his self-title *Danxingzi* (Master Lonely Star) can only "guess" fortunes, not

---

28. When asked whether he had Pope in mind when he wrote these sentences, Wang replied that he did not pinpoint Pope, though he knew the same idea had been expressed by people before, including Pope. See Shan's interview.

tell them.[29] He is so blind to his own fortune that his "fortunate" rendez-vous with the Bodhisattva-like lady turns out to be "unfortunate," unforgettable, and formidable—another proof of his contradiction? Even he himself is aware of the contradiction and absurdity of fortune-telling and his role as a fortune-teller, though he pretends to be a prophet granting oracles of life and death.

Besides food and sex, word association, animal imagery, montage, and the "ghostly" implications discussed here, we also notice different dialects at work, not only in the first paragraph but also throughout the novel. His most extended use of dialect can be seen on the first day of his fortune-telling. Advertising himself at length in Taiwanese, he is able to attract a big audience (p. 64). The narrator's comment also shows his talent in language acquisition. From his own words, we know that he wonders why most people cannot speak the local dialect after as long a period as fifteen years, while he is able to learn a dialect even if he lives in a place for just one week (p. 63). His functional command of northern and southern dialects reveals his cosmopolitan character and his ability to adapt himself to different circumstances.

In the above analysis, I may have run the risk of overinterpretation, but only in order to demonstrate that the first paragraph of *Backed Against the Sea* is well structured and meaning-laden beneath the deceptive surface of disorder. It flows spontaneously from the consciousness of an outcast who is exiled from and exiling his society, but paradoxically clings to some hope half-heartedly and some "vision" half-wittedly. Hanging between heaven and hell, church and red-light district (p. 1), he displays his personal dilemma and suggests the greater dilemma of human beings. This paragraph is indeed the epitome of the whole book.

From the discussions of the three short stories and the explication of the first paragraph of *Backed Against the Sea*, we can see Wang Wen-xing's application of various stream-of-consciousness techniques, the characteristics of each story, and his artistic achievements. If we follow Humphrey's classification, "The Marriage of a Civil Servant" and "Strong Wind"—with their greater coherence and unity and "with an audience

---

29. Wang models this narrator after Teiresias; see Shan's interview.

tacitly assumed"—are soliloquies, while the stream-of-consciousness passage in "Mother" and *Backed Against the Sea*—with greater "incoherence and fluidity" and with "negligible author interference and with no auditor assumed"—are direct interior monologues.[30]

Reading Wang's writings, especially his later works, is seldom easy, often challenging, and always stimulating. They are painstakingly written and should be read accordingly. By plunging ourselves into the narrator's flow and being swept down the stream marked by many sudden turns and unexpected scenes, we enter the deepest and darkest region of the human mind, marvel at the richness and profundity there, and acquire a new insight into our own mind and life. After finishing the last page of *Backed Against the Sea*, we emerge from the narrator's stream of feelings, thoughts and impressions, which has been our companion throughout the voyage and is thus familiar, and with him we utter, "IT'S DAYBREAK—"

* * *

I acknowledge my special thanks to Wang Wenxing for granting me interviews on two occasions: June 19 and September 4, 1983.

Editor's note: This essay was first published as "The Stream-of-Consciousness Technique in Wang Wen-hsing's Fiction," *Tamkang Review* 15 (1985): 523–45. Transliterations have been changed to pinyin. Bibliographic references have also been updated.

---

30. Humphrey, *Stream of Consciousness in the Modern Novel*, 38, 36, 27, and 25.

REFLECTIONS ON TRANSLATION

10 The Poetics of Rhythm in Wang Wenxing's Novels

Sandrine Marchand
Artois University

WANG WENXING EMPHASIZES the importance of language in his work—language that leaves the narration withdrawn, language that is recognized for its musicality and is close to poetry. The more one reads his novels, the more this becomes evident. Wang himself states that he felt freer using his own style in *Bei hai de ren* 背海的人 (Backed against the sea) and one cannot help but be struck by the graphic evolution that occurs in the second part of the novel. It seems that the second part repeats the first, doubling it, but reducing the story to its structure and accentuating the narrator's anti-narrative and digressive character, like a never-ending image in a mirror. This use of language reveals a conception of literature that emphasizes orality, which must not be confused with spoken language, as we will see.

I consider the poetics of Wang Wenxing's novels, emphasizing language and rhythm—to the detriment of narration. In his work on language, which is as much visual as auditory, Wang makes use of a poetic rhythm through which sense is expressed; rhythm and sense are therefore inseparable. It takes life on the page where the voice seems to become consistent. Rhythm must be defined here as movement in language. As Henri Meschonnic, whose theoretical reflection seems to be the closest to the approach of Wang Wenxing, writes: "The voice that can make the syntax and the rhythm, can make its typography; that is why a poetics of typography and of the visual, far from being separate from orality, can display the relationship between the oral and the visual. And it does."[1]

Initially, I investigate the relationship between language and poetry in reading, and then I examine the poetry and poetics of the two novels *Jia bian* 家變 (Family catastrophe) and *Backed Against the Sea*. Following this, I consider the poetics of space in the second volume of *Backed Against the Sea*, in its relationship with the rough draft and calligraphy. Finally, I make some suggestions for a poetics of translation.

The Music of Words

The link that Wang's language connects with poetry defines itself initially by musicality, which is acquired through the exercise of reading and by the adoption of a clear rhythm.

Wang Wenxing is a great reader of classical Chinese poetry, and the relationship of his work to poetry is a consequence of his daily practice of reading poetry. In some of his published reflections on poetry reading, one becomes aware of the importance he grants to poetic musicality: although Wang is a true music lover, as a consequence of writing making up an essential part of his life, he decided to give up listening to music. He no longer needs to listen to music because reading poetry has completely replaced it. In saying that he "listens to the music of poetry,"[2] he states that the music of poetry has the same value for him as music itself.

The musical richness of poetry is due perhaps to the absence of manifested sound. In François Jullien's concept of blandness, the totality of sound held back in silence (unarticulated sound) contains more flavor

---

1. Henri Meschonnic, *Les états de la poétique* (The state of the poetic) (Paris: Presses Universitaires de France, 1985), 130.

2. Wang once said, "Because I have heard music in poems," 因為我已從詩裏 聽到音樂 (*yinwei wo yi cong shili ting dao yinyue*). Wang Wenxing, "Jinri mei yu" 今日美語 (Contemporary language aesthetics), *Xing yu lou suixiang* 星雨樓 隨想 (Random thoughts from Star-Rain Tower) (Taipei: Hongfan shudian, 2000), 168.

and resonance than sound actualized in music: "They [the tones] are all the better in a position to last and to deepen [in the consciousness of the listeners], that they are not definitively actualized, that they possess what makes them unfold, that they keep something secret and virtual and remain penetrating."[3]

Although the musicality of poetry corresponds to the traditional ideal of Chinese scholars, ideals that Wang Wenxing tries to embody when he reads classical poetry, it is also concerned with another dimension in writing, since musicality is connected to a quest for rhythm. Rhythm is a combination not only of all the elements of sound but also of that which plays in the words and between them, as rhythm is transmitted through language and introduces the author's own voice.

This musicality—this poetic rhythm—runs through the novels of Wang Wenxing, who, though not writing poetry, introduces it into his prose. Wang had attempted to write poetry and gave it up, saying that there is no metric for the vernacular Chinese language (*baihua* 白話) and consequently, "it would be like playing music without a score."[4] However, his daily reading of classical poetry augments his art of novel writing as sunshine permeates a room, which is explained in the postscript to the English translation of *Family Catastrophe*. For him, language is musical. Borrowing Gustave Flaubert's remark, he says, "This novel would make the kind of music the cello makes."[5] Although style may be defined by the relationship between language and music, the fact remains that Wang considers rhythm to be the most important part of music.

Reading, which reveals the musicality of the text, also corresponds to the process of writing. Musicality, reading, and writing represent three aspects of the same action.

---

3. François Jullien, *Eloge de la Fadeur* (Arles: Philippe Picquier, 1991), 41.

4. My interview with Wang Wenxing at Luming Guesthouse, National Taiwan University, in July 2007.

5. Wang Wenxing, *Family Catastrophe*, trans. Susan Wan Dolling (Honolulu: University of Hawai'i Press, 1995), 249. Flaubert's comment is found in his correspondence. For a translation of the relevant passage, see Timothy A. Unwin, ed., *The Cambridge Companion to Flaubert* (Cambridge: Cambridge University Press, 2004), 167.

In his article "Endless War,"[6] we observe that the same process of slowing down and controlling rhythm occurs in reading and writing. Wang explains how at twenty years of age he understood he had to conquer his own language, which he says was "disordered" and had not yet achieved a "stable rhythm." What he heard in the Western works he admired was a kind of music (*shengyin* 聲音 sound) that he was unable to create in his own language. The achievement of musicality in the writing of novels was accomplished first in his reading.

Reading cannot be separated from writing. Before identifying himself as a writer, Wang defines himself as a reader. In a short autobiography, he says: "Normally, outside of my teaching, I only do two things: read and write. I cannot be counted as a professional writer (because I do not make my living by my pen) but I consider myself to be a professional reader."[7] The two activities—reading and writing—are joined, and reading seems even to dominate writing in requiring more time and effort to concentrate and to seek silence in his environment. Reading for Wang is conscious reading. His method derives from reading classical Chinese poetry just as Friedrich Nietzsche found his own in reading ancient Greek. This in turn is applied to all works, modern and Western, poetry and prose. For Wang, it is necessary to read line by line and character by character.

Wang demands this same effort from his readers when they read his novels. In the introduction to *Family Catastrophe*, he warns the reader: "The four movements of a concerto cannot be played in ten minutes. The ideal reader also has to be an ideal music-lover. He omits no single note (word) not even a rest note (punctuation)."[8]

To appreciate the musicality of a text, the reader must feel its rhythm. Its different speeds must be perceptible to the reader, who must then

---

6. Wang Wenxing, "Wu xiuzhi de zhanzheng" 無休止的戰爭 (Endless war), *Shu he ying* 書和影 (Books and films) (2nd ed.) (Taipei: Lianhe wenxue chubanshe, 2006), 195–98.

7. Wang Wenxing, "Zizhuan" 自傳 (Autobiography), *Xiaoshuo moyu* 小說墨餘 (Beyond fiction) (Taipei: Hongfan shudian, 2002) 179.

8. Wang Wenxing, "Xu" 序 (Preface), *Jia bian* 家變 (Family catastrophe) (Taipei: Hongfan shudian, 1978), 2.

conform to it like a musician in front of a score. Being aware of the rhythm of a text necessitates slowing down the reading: "The ideal reading speed is about one thousand characters per hour, and less than two hours per day."[9] In effect, many readers have a tendency to read too fast, being transported by the plot without considering the significance of the words as the most important aspect of prose as they are of poetry.

To slow down reading, one needs to be aware of the rhythm, which is also important in writing. The battle Wang conducts with language consists of taking into consideration the slowness of the work of writing: "... [E]ach day I can write only a few words ... avoiding writing too much, too fast ..."[10] If a word in the manuscript must be changed, he will rewrite the entire sentence, because all the words mutually support one another in their musicality and an unsuitable note can cause the music to drag. From the first draft to the final manuscript, Wang may rewrite a sentence more than ten times before being satisified with it and does not care about the time involved in its production.

Reading also takes place after writing—Wang read his novel out loud several times. This practice revealed the possibility of transmitting a text to a public that would be more receptive to words communicated by the writer's voice rather than the reader's voice. Reading out loud restores the orality of literature. Orality is not meant here to be spoken language. Instead, I refer to a conception of literature in which orality is not opposed to writing, as living is opposed to dead text, but in which orality disseminates itself through the written text. By the exigency of the reader and himself as reader-writer and by his practice of reading, moving from a solitary act to a public act, Wang reconnects to the conception of the poetic: "reading-writing" or *mikra*, a Hebrew term borrowed by Meschonnic from biblical writings: "Thus the text, by its rhythm, by its rhythmic organization, its way of making sense and causing one to be transported, is above all an effect of oral literature and oral literature that signifies collectivity."[11]

---

9. Ibid.
10. Wang, *Books and Films*, 195–98.
11. Meschonnic, *The State of the Poetic*, 50.

Wang Wenxing's novels seem to be turned, before and after writing, toward reading. In his preface to *Backed Against the Sea*, he said he had nothing to add to what he had written and was therefore only able to comment on the period following the writing of his novel, the two years during which he prepared the clean copy of the final version of the manuscript for its formal printing. During this same period he reread old books and realized that rereading is like a new reading. Reading is without end and renews itself each time it takes place. Writing is also manifold, offering a diversity of interpretations. It is an open work, as defined by Umberto Eco, meeting "the multidirectional world of a serial piece of music."[12]

The usage elaborated by Wang reconnects to a definition of literature that exceeds the usual dichotomy of oral/written and does not limit itself to its resonant aspect (musicality/voice). According to Wang, literature is multidirectional (*duofangxiang* 多方向): visual as much as oral. For him, all literature is in the "language" (*wenzi* 文字, the characters, the words), "all the components (*lingjian* 零件) of the literature, the subject (*zhuti* 主題), the characters (*renwu* 人物), the ideas (*sixiang* 思想), the texture (*jili* 肌理), all have to be expressed in words."[13] The word *wenzi* has three aspects: image (*tuhua* 圖畫), sound (*shengyin* 聲音), and a specific form (*xingxiang* 形象). *Xingxiang*, which includes the other two elements (*tuhua* and *shengyin*), constitutes the identity of the word. As image, sound, and form, each word carries within itself the responsibility of the text, a responsibility shared with the entirety of the written text, which must form a whole, harmonious and ordered, in accordance with a certain ideal. Image must complement sound; image and sound must complement meaning. One cannot separate orality from writing, sound from form, rhythm from syntax, musicality from silence. Everything is a question of rhythm; rhythm of the text, rhythm of the voice, rhythm resonant and visual.

Through his conception of language, Wang transports us far from

---

12. Umberto Eco, *L'Œuvre ouverte* (The open work) (Paris: Editions du Seuil, 1965), 38.

13. Wang, "Preface," *Family Catastrophe*, 2.

the semiotic that favors severing the manifested world from the hidden one, spirit from body. The Chinese language, too often considered only ideographic or pictographic, is reestablished in its unitary dimension, simultaneously image and sound, concrete and abstract, form and sense.

The Rhythm in *Family Catastrophe* and *Backed Against the Sea*

The poetry of *Family Catastrophe* is more immediately accessible than that of *Backed Against the Sea*. It appears in descriptive fragments that are as much poetry as prose. We have, for example: "Above the transom in Mother's bedroom was a pane of stained glass";[14] "With the advent of rain came the plaintive cries of wood pigeons, surge upon surge, whirling round in concentric echoes";[15] "Around five or six in the afternoon, bats flew, helter-skelter in front of the house."[16] In these sentences we can easily see what was just theorized: words that possess the quality of images in motion, like a movie. In fact, many readers of these novels have perceived the unique cinematographic atmosphere of Wang's descriptions, an observation confirmed by his description of himself as a real cinema enthusiast.

The poetry of these short chapters is often linked to images of nature, particularly of the river, and in this they echo the classical poetry of Wei Yingwu (韋應物, c. 737–791), one of whose poems appears within the narration. But the poetry also touches the description of objects of modernity: "In the corridor at the back of the house was 'A guide to Morse Code'—he had no idea how that book had got there."[17]

Poetry is also introduced directly into the interior of the narration, where it is more sensitive to rhythm that often relies on the incantatory value of repetition. In the first lines of the novel, one finds the sound *li* three times: "the gate of bamboo fence" (*limen* 籬門), "toward the back

---

14. Wang, *Family Catastrophe*, 18.
15. Ibid., 77.
16. Ibid., 85.
17. Ibid., 42.

of the bamboo fence" (*xiangli* 向籬後), and "to quit" (*liqu* 離去). Then
the character *zhuan* 轉 in "to turn the body" (*zhuanshen* 轉身), "turn the
head" (*zhuantou* 轉頭), and "to turn around" (*zhuanwan* 轉彎).[18]

In these opening lines, which contain the most important event of
the novel, tension is maintained thanks to these repetitions of words,
which cause the old man to disappear within larger and larger circles of
words. This first chapter sets the tone for the rest of the novel and shows
that the event takes place within the language—that "the language is the
event," as Gilles Deleuze has put it.[19] The repetition gives the rhythm its
force and makes the phrase a musical line. The repetitions, present
throughout the novel, penetrate the language and concentrate attention
on it. In the preface to *Family Catastrophe*, Wang affirms what is important to him: the language and nothing else. The second volume of *Backed
Against the Sea* shows language playing an even more prominent role in
Wang's writing process, to the extent of causing the continuity of the
narrative to disappear and make the simple written characters points of
support for the rhythmic development of the phrase.

With *Backed Against the Sea*, the poetics of rhythm is more insistent,
especially in the second part. Although it appears to mirror the first part,
repetition (consistent with Deleuze's explanation) introduces a difference.[20] This divergence causes the novel's narration to swing into a multidirectional, multidimensional text, where time and space, orality and
image, create a kind of theater on the page. The language of *Backed
Against the Sea* is poetic, but there is no reference to poetry as a genre.
Backed Against the Sea is poetic in its link with the voice, the rhythm,
but also in the layout of the words. Repetition, a characteristic of Wang's
language, here attains an extreme form, since it goes as far as stammering and stuttering. The presence of this excessive repetition deliberately
inscribes the text in orality, like a voice wanting to impose itself upon

---

18. Ibid., 1.

19. Gilles Deleuze, *La logique du sens* (The logic of sense) (Paris: Les Editions
de Minuit, 1969), 34.

20. Gilles Deleuze, *Différence et répétition* (Difference and repetition) (Paris:
Presses Universitaires de France, 1969).

the narration. Even though the novel proposes a specific typographic disposition that we will discuss later, the repetition appears as typographic rhythm within the orality itself. Not only can one see the voice, thanks to the typographic process, one can also hear it, thanks to the repetition.

As an "open work," this novel attains maximum extension—as it lacks centrality and a point of convergence. It does so in order to dissolve imposed identity through repetition and to cause the difference— precisely crafted by constant repetition and infinite circumvolution—to leap out: "The identity of the thing read completely dissolves into a defined divergent series through esoteric words, as the identity of the subject reader dissolves into off-centered circles of the possible multireading."[21] We become aware of the rhythm of the text in its resonant and typographic dimensions because a gap has appeared between the form and its usual sense. In effect, this nonlinear novel functions through a disjointed series that transmits a multiplicity of senses. The stammering and slowing down of speech, which becomes intensified, deeply questions the relationship of literature to language.

It is not just a matter of the character of the anti-hero, whose existence is devoid of sense and who embodies the paradigm of a derelict society in a ruined world. It is also a matter of questioning one's own language in order to give it the possibility of inscribing the differences inside its identity—an identity defined by the use of common language. The search for one's own language is a way of taking a step away from the established order of an official language that can represent uniform power over the free individual. Even if Wang is not a politically committed writer, he is committed intellectually in his language.

Backed Against the Sea comes within the scope of "minor literature" as defined by Deleuze,[22] the works of writers in a foreign language who do not hesitate to shake up that language to make it say other things, to make it return to its emergent force, examples being Samuel Beckett,

---

21. Ibid., 95.
22. Gilles Deleuze, *Kafka, pour une littérature mineure* (Kafka, for a minor literature) (Paris: Editions de Minuit, 1975).

Franz Kafka, and Gherasim Luca. It is interesting to note that although Wang writes in Chinese, having left China for Taiwan he could deterritorialize his own language by calling into question both its familiarity and its foreignness. Thus, in this project of minor literature, he achieves a result that is even better than writers of foreign languages: "A style comes to stammer its own language. It is difficult because it is necessary that such a stammering was needed, not to have a stammer of his words, but to have a stammer of the language itself, like a foreigner in his own language."[23]

The character of Ye in *Backed Against the Sea*, physically deformed because he inhabits multiple forms himself (in his different levels of speech), incarnates this "stammer of language itself." The language becomes consistent in the character of Ye to give him life, so that all the senseless adventures that happen to him are only adventures of language, events that happen in language. Those events are, above all, accessible in the organization of the page.

Emergence of the Typographic Space

In the short story "Muqin" 母親 (Mother), one of the first short stories written by Wang Wenxing, one finds blank spaces on the page for the first time. The story is centered on the stream of consciousness of the mother who takes and even absorbs her son's words. This woman is depressive; she cannot stand that her son is growing up. Her language is not the usual language; it is close to delirium. She is in a state of suffering, blind to reason. She confuses reality and desire.

In *Backed Against the Sea*, the layout on the page with blanks and long dashes becomes more insistent when Ye speaks of his physical pain. Even if one notes that the delirium begins in the first part of the novel, it is at the moment when the physical and moral suffering of the character becomes acute that this layout becomes prominent in the narration itself.

---

23. Gilles Deleuze and Claire Parnet, *Dialogues* (Paris: Flammarion, 1977), 10.

On the pages of the novel, the written characters occupy space like traces of a voice, and the layout causes one to hear the rhythm of this voice. Wang's text responds not only to a spatial writing but also to time. This achieves a space-time full of efficiency.[24]

The most remarkable thing on the page is the blank space that can appear between a group of words or between isolated words. The blank spaces are not regular, but are prolonged by long dashes:

當 ， 爺 ， 　 走 上 來 的 時 候 ， ——爺看到 ， 　 一·巜
乙 ， ——洋 神 父 ， 歲 數 蠻 大 　 來 了 ， 立 站 ， ——這 一
個 ， 天 主 教 教 堂 的 ， 邊 邊 　 ， —— 　 ㄋ ㄜˋ 一 扇 ，
邊 門 ， 他 的 手 ， 扶 到 ， ——半 拉 開 着 　 ， —— 站 在 那
一 　 個 　 地 方 ， 看 注 着 爺 。[25]

In quotation, one can see that blank spaces and dashes have the same importance as words; thanks to them, the sentence reveals itself both as resonance (sound) and image. Words, dashes, and blank spaces together make the rhythm visible and audible at the same time.

Poets have theorized about and practiced manipulation of text on a page, Stéphane Mallarmé being a precursor. According to Albert Thibaudet, the space on a page accompanies the affirmation of free verse and tends to "cause to occur in the aspect of the phrase, something of the act that it describes."[26] Blank space in some writers' hands is not mute; it possesses as much significance as the written word. Speaking of the poetry of Mallarmé, Paul Valéry says that his choice "corresponds to the profound and singular experience of making inseparable the written and

---

24. According to Marcel Granet, "Rhythm in Chinese prose possesses the same function as the syntax." *La pensée chinoise* (Chinese thought) (Paris: Albin Michel, 1968), 71. Thus the extreme contemporaneousness of Wang Wenxing's text echoes the most ancient Chinese conceptions.

25. Wang Wenxing, *Bei hai de ren* 背海的人 (Backed against the sea) (Taipei: Hongfan shudian, 1999), 308.

26. Guillaume Appolinaire, *Œuvres complètes* (Paris: Gallimard, La Pléiade, 1965), 1074.

the blank spaces which penetrate it, surround it, following a proposal, an after-thought, gone."[27]

Anne-Marie Christin is interested in the relationship between a text's content and visual image and has emphasized the importance of blank spaces in French poetry,[28] imparting to them an entirely exceptional value and not a void, or lack, as has been done in Structuralist interpretation (by Roland Barthes in particular).[29] Christin also sees in the fullness of blank spaces a recognition of Asian culture, an observation that would be inconceivable in an alphabetic culture. One rests there while reading the text, as at a sign before it is decoded, faced with the juxtaposition of the image and the abstract alphabetic writing. The idea of "mixing supports,"[30] which Christin introduces, corresponds very well to the layout of Wang's text with words, blank spaces, and punctuation marks, not to mention the different typographic processes that reinforce the "sonorization" of the page with written characters that are boldfaced, underlined, or magnified and also accompanied by Mandarin phonetic symbols (*Guoyu zhuyin fuhao* 國語注音符號).

The use of this alphabetic system is ironic in light of the Western fascination with Chinese as a pictographic language. Through his text layout, Wang does not emphasize the visual image of written Chinese. Although we assume Chinese writing contains pictographic elements, what appears by contrast are its inscribed resonant qualities reflected in the spelling itself: how sound is abstractly transcribed by the assembly of lines. The Chinese language is neither only ideographic nor pictographic but rests on different elements: strokes, phonic clues, semantic clues. Whatever the type of writing, Chinese or alphabetic, the process of reading is analogous and is constructed jointly from visual and phonic information.

Through the layout of the text, and contrary to the Western writer

27. "Lettre de Paul Valéry," *Catalogue Mallarmé, 1842–1898* (Paris: Gallimard, RMN, 1998), 113.

28. Anne-Marie Christin, "Ecriture et Iconicité," *Europe*, January–February 2007, 196–209.

29. Ibid., 197–98.

30. Ibid., 205.

who revels in the imaged part of his language, Wang Wenxing favors the phonetic part of his language. The language on the page that is laid out typographically is not only "visual language" but also "audible language." From this, the only connection one is able to make between the work of Wang Wenxing and concrete or spatial poetry is that the typographic disposition favors a multiplicity of meanings and readings. In using space on the page to convey meaning, all writers—Western and Eastern—tend to reveal the living part of literature.

Through this typographic endeavor, Wang's text is linked to the conception of an open work as described by Umberto Eco: "The blank space, the typographic game, the layout of the poetic text, all contribute to create a halo of indetermination around the word, to charge it with various suggestions."[31] What is remarkable, then, is that the layout of the page does not take place in a poem but in a long narration, which multiplies the difficulty and also the interest.

Thanks to Wang's phonetic transcriptions, orality is thrown into relief and redoubles the resonant effect of the text. Sometimes these phonetic transcriptions only represent onomatopoeia or the phonetics of a written word. Blank spaces, dashes, words, and phonetics are all placed within the same scheme, increasing the multiplicity of meanings, emphasizing the text as multidirectional art. The page is transformed into a partition of silent music, which causes a multiplicity of languages to be heard, suggesting to the reader a coming together with the Japanese language (even if unsought by the author), associating Chinese characters with *hiragana* or—more profoundly—suggesting the emergence of a foreign language contained within the mother tongue.

The Calligraphic Space

The typographic space of Wang's novel cannot be appreciated without referring to the rough draft, which does not take place at the origin of the process of writing but almost in the middle. This is not the time or

---

31. Eco, *The Open Work*, 22.

place to analyze it, but it would be very interesting to ask why there is a necessity to return to the origin of writing, to the rough draft, just before making a clear copy. In "Endless War," Wang mentions the importance of the rough draft: "In order to write a book, it is necessary moreover to begin by making a rough draft (it is the easiest thing in the world) and from the rough draft to take word after word in order to make a text, then recopy the definitive manuscript."[32] The facility of the rough draft maybe comes from the spontaneity of gesture. Wang throws his words onto paper without constraint. The handwritten rough drafts, which in their abstraction and movement bring out the stroke and line of Chinese characters, are close to calligraphic art; paradoxically, they seem to be born from an alphabetic language. In calligraphy, even a rough draft with alterations or ink marks can be considered a work of art. Getting to the heart of the matter, what counts is the preservation of movement and a disinterest that touches on the freedom of art.

Whereas the final manuscript presents characters drawn slowly and precisely, according to the disciplined movement of regular writing, the rough drafts present traces rather than words, emphasizing the stroke as the foundation of all writing. According to ethnologist André Leroi-Gourhan: "The first art is abstract. It takes form from signs which express rhythms and not forms."[33] These traces of writing that link back to the origins of humanity are also those of tender childhood, "where the drawing line of movement comes to light from thought" registered in the first design.

Sketching the rough draft must be considered similar to writing. It emphasizes the line that represents the awakening of thought, its movement in full awakening, before it comes to a stand-still in rational language and, thanks to this, retains traces of its initial indeterminacy. The rough draft is halfway between design and writing. It is the impression of thought, when words are only sounds, only rhythm. "In the most perfect design, it (the line) takes on something of the lightness of the lines

---

32. Wang, "Endless War," 196.

33. André Leroi-Gourhan, *Le geste et la parole* (Paris: Albin Michel, 1964–65), 263–66.

of thought ... the less body it has, the better it expresses."[34] Between the rough drafts and the ordered page, there is no qualitative leap, simply a rhythmic continuity that comes within the scope of the blank spaces, in the dashes, in the reading of the characters that read like calligraphy, a reading which is made in the space of time, in a linear manner, but also following the rhythm of drawing. Wang wrote this about calligraphy: "Chinese calligraphy belongs especially to abstraction; it is only the gathering of drawings and of blank spaces."[35] These drawings, which become the elongated dashes and the blank spaces on the typographic page, reestablish the movement and the rhythm of paintbrush calligraphy.

The calligraphic feature of the rough drafts reveals the importance accorded to visual image in his work; they are also as musical and oral as the typographic text.

To Translate the Rhythm

It almost goes without saying that to translate a text of Wang's requires attention and faithfulness to the rhythmic space on the page. Not only is it necessary to reproduce and respect the spaces, the dashes, and the transformations sustained by the words, it is also necessary to find a way to render the resonant space of the page without calling into question the fluidity of the reading to which Wang is particularly attached (a fluidity that does not have to be as smooth and even as editors wish).

Even before translating, translation appears similar to the process of reading. To translate a text, it is first necessary to read consciously, not omitting a single word or punctuation mark. The translator must at least be a faithful reader. He must respect the rhythm of the phrase, which contains all of the orality of the text. The rhythm of the translation also responds to the duration of the reading and writing accorded to the text—to read and translate even as slowly as Wang writes. This means

---

34. Emile Chartier Alain, *Système des Beaux-Arts* (Paris: Gallimard, 1953), 317.

35. Wang, "Contemporary Language Aesthetics," 157.

the ideal translation of *Backed Against the Sea* would take twenty-five years.

The translation must not cause the reader to forget that it is a translation; it must not erase the particulars of the language. Translation of Wang Wenxing's text, according to Meschonnic, must concentrate on orality.[36] In Wang's text, this orality contains the entire text in its multiple directions, auditory, visual, as well as rhythmic. The translation, without opposition between sense and form, must apply itself to follow the movement of the sentences in all their hesitation and stammering. This imposes a slowing down on the reading process and a prolonged plunge into the language.

Wang's novels teach the translator not to limit the translation to being an instrument of communication and information. To translate, therefore, is an act of language that must permit linguistic experimentation in each of the two languages. It is a matter of emphasizing the differences between languages and within the writer's own language, when each word is precisely chosen for its special meaning and particular form. Therefore, the work of translation requires consciousness of the fact that it is not a matter of translating thought to thought, for one thinks and writes in a specific language, one that is forged into the writer's entire person and entire experience.

The translator must be aware of the fact that the novel must be read out loud to be understood. Even if Wang has not created a new language within the Chinese language, he has introduced elements of another language that cannot be regarded as a dialect (or oral language) but which could be the language of exile. The translator, in turn, must create a linguistic system that gives him the possibility of integrating another language, an oral language, into the language of the translation. My own translation of *Backed Against the Sea* is still a work in progress, consequently I cannot yet reveal which method I have decided to use. Nor can I be sure of its efficiency and legitimacy. The main difficulty here is that contrary to experimental writers who do not care whether they are

---

36. Meschonnic, *Poétique du traduire* (Poetic of translation) (Paris: Verdier, 1999), 29.

readable, Wang's ideal is clarity and limpidity. How to make these two ways of writing, which seem to be opposed, consistent with one another? This is the task of the translator of *Backed Against the Sea.*

In conclusion, Wang's text manifests the multidimensional character of literature—the orality, the rhythm, the inherent movement of the language—thanks to its typographic layout. Not only does the text impose itself visually, like chaotic space leaving a large place to the blank spaces, like a breath or a sigh, it also makes the written page a contemporary musical partition introducing the difference, as a break with the habits of usual language. The poetry in Wang's novels and prose writings keeps to the non-opposition between prose and poetry, to the attention on language as a way of dissidence within the language. Because of his work on language, Wang appears as a foreigner in his own language in a Deleuzian sense.

From a more general point of view, these processes of "typographic orality" liberate a reading imprisoned in the narration from the oppositions oral/written, reader/writer, base/form, and reveal another dimension of literature—which should be the case for all literary texts, poetry or prose, original or translation—where orality and rhythm are freed from the dominance of sense.

11 Translating and Editing Wang Wenxing

Fred Edwards

THIS IS HOW Wang Wenxing describes how he reads: "*yi ju yi ting, yi ju yi xiangde zai du*" 一句一停, 一句一想 的再讀 (He reads one sentence and pauses to think about it. Then he reads it again).[1] Only in this way does he feel he can grasp the meaning and appreciate the beauty of a work of literature. The innate complexity of literature, in his view, demands that a reader slow down or risk overlooking "hidden and beautiful meanings"[2] in the text.

That also is the way a translator or editor reads a text. In fact, a translator goes through the process twice, first to understand the original text and then, when reading the resulting translation, to ensure it is faithful to the original in both content and style. In other words, complexity demands slowness. It also means that most of a translator's work occurs on the microlevel, thousands of decisions about individual words and phrases, even punctuation—in Wang's case, particularly punctuation.

Translation is a deceptively simple process. A text in the source language (SL) is converted into a text in the target language (TL). Straddling the linguistic and cultural divide between the texts is the translator, who converts the SL text into an equivalent TL text. But as with Wang Wenxing's fiction, it is more complex than that. Behind the SL text is the

---

1. Wang Wenxing, "Du yu xie" 讀與寫 (*Reading and writing*), address to the "Art of Chinese Narrative Language: International Workshop on Wang Wenxing's Life and Works," University of Calgary, February 20, 2009.
2. Ibid.

writer, a unique human being shaped by unique forces. Behind the writer is the native language itself, and the culture from which it originated. As Mexican author Octavio Paz has noted, the original text is itself a translation, as the writer has had to translate nonverbal thoughts into his or her own language.[3] In the case of Wang Wenxing, we have a writer who was born in mainland China during World War II and immigrated to Taiwan with his family after the communist victory in the Chinese civil war, undoubtedly a tremendous upheaval in the life of a child. Intellectually, he has been shaped by multiple cultural and literary influences, including the classical Chinese tradition; modern—mainly American—popular culture; and Western literature and philosophy. All of this biographical background echoes through Wang's work, meaning that the SL text is a complex cultural artifact. On top of that, it also is a work of art.

The picture on the other side of the equation is equally complex. A translator is not a computer but a human being with his or her own unique cultural background and literary and language skills. In my case, I came to Wang's work as a native English speaker who grew up in a society quite unlike postwar Taiwan. My cotranslator, Jia Li, was born in mainland China during the Cultural Revolution and immigrated to Canada in the mid-1990s. She brought essential linguistic and cultural knowledge to the translation process, although as Wang Wenxing has noted, native Chinese speakers often react negatively to his experimentation and nonstandard usage. The translation process thus involved two people who were forced to adopt Wang's reading style of一句一停, 一句一想的再讀. Nor did the complexity end there. The work was undertaken as part of an anthology of Wang's short works, fiction and nonfiction as well as a one-act play, proposed by Shu-ning Sciban of the University of Calgary, a Taiwan native who acted as overall editor. The anthology, titled *Endless War: Fiction and Essays by Wang Wen-hsing*, was published by Cornell University's East Asia Program in 2011. There were thirteen translators in all, some native English speakers, some na-

---

3. Cited by Susan Bassnett-McGuire in *Translation Studies* (New York: Routledge, 1980), 46.

tive Chinese speakers. Inevitably, there was considerable stylistic variation among the translations, so Sciban and I acted as arbiters; she to
ensure fidelity to the original text and I to make the English as natural
as possible. Nor was that the end of it, as external reviewers at publishing houses also made recommendations to change and "improve" the
translations.

The translation process, like language itself, is complex, requiring
countless decisions at the micro-level by people who, like the writer, are
unique individuals with distinct cultural, psychological, and intellectual
identities. There is one other factor, however, and that is the writer's
status as a creative artist. The text the writer has produced is a work of
art, not an essay or a piece of journalism. This above all makes it very
difficult for a translated text to be in any way equivalent to the original.
The translator must have not only the requisite linguistic skill but also
literary skill. Of those two, the latter likely is more important—witness
Ezra Pound's translations of classical Chinese poetry, still regarded as
the classic of the field.

Wang Wenxing is not a typical Chinese writer but an avant-garde
stylist who draws on China's ancient literary tradition and experiments
with modernist techniques such as nonstandard typography and punctuation, neologisms, and the use of foreign scripts, including the International Phonetic Alphabet. Sciban has argued that Wang is a practitioner of "poetic language," the goal of which is "deautomatization"—the
violation of language norms—for "aesthetic effect."[4]

Wang also admits to being deeply influenced by cinema and has said
he first imagines a scene visually and attempts to re-create it precisely
through the use of detailed description and various sound and visual effects, such as phonetic (non-Chinese) spellings, boldface fonts and blank
spaces, as well as exploiting certain latent visual and acoustic capabilities of Chinese characters. In response to critics who have claimed the
result is much "superfluous language,"[5] Wang has said: "Words have to

4. Shu-ning Sciban, "Wang Wenxing's Poetic Language" (dissertation, University of Toronto, 1995), 14–15.
5. Ouyang Zi, cited by Sciban, Wang Wenxing's Poetic Language," 7.

be like mathematical symbols, each one having its own function. One word too few, and the piece falls apart. One word too many, and the piece buckles under its own weight."[6]

So how to proceed?

First we adopted a rough set of guidelines:

- Fidelity to the meaning of the original text.
- An attempt to convey or approximate the author's unique language usage and literary style.
- Awareness of the target audience, in this case scholars and students.
- Retention of a sense of "foreignness."
- And, in a rare resource for a translator, awareness of Wang's own comments about his writing.

The first point seems obvious, although as Canadian novelist Wayne Johnston described in a hilarious article in *The Walrus* magazine some years ago, many writers have discovered that translators have not hesitated to impose their own will on a text, including adding completely new material thought necessary to satisfy the local audience.[7]

The second point follows naturally from the first but is more difficult given the intensely personal nature of any writer's literary style. One advantage we had, though, was that most of these stories were written before Wang began to employ some of the more adventurous techniques described above, especially the coining of neologisms and nonstandard use of Chinese characters, which strike me as virtually untranslatable. Where his experimentation could be presented easily, as in the use of long spaces between sentences in "Mother" and the use of complicated punctuation and boldfaced fonts in "M and W," we followed the originals

---

6. Wang Wenxing, "*Xin ke de shi xiang* xu"《新刻的石像》序 (Preface to *New Stone Statue*), *Xiandai wenxue* 現代文學 (Modern literature) 35 (1968): 218. The translation is by Martin Sulev.

7. Wayne Johnston, "Gained in Translation," *The Walrus*, June 2004; http://http://thewalrus.ca/gained-in-translation/ (accessed January 23, 2011).

exactly. Elsewhere it was largely a matter of attempting to capture his tone, which tended to combine emotional and psychological intensity with cool external observation, occasionally satirical in nature.

As for the target audience, translation theory generally makes no distinction among potential readers. A reader is a reader, period. Yet even in Chinese, Wang's prose is aimed at a highly literate, educated audience. Likewise, the current anthology of his short works is not directed at a mass audience but a narrower group of scholars and students who presumably want some insight into his unique style. A translation that was too "creative," that tried too hard to find "equivalence," could mislead serious non-Chinese readers concerning the nature of Wang's writing style.

Besides attempting to retain aspects of Wang's style, there is the broader point of retaining a sense of foreignness in the translated text. Theoretically, the language in a perfect translation would be completely familiar to TL readers, yet as language theorists keep insisting, language contains cultural and temporal limitations. "Even apparent synonymy does not yield equivalence," says Susan Bassnett-McGuire.[8] A "perfect" translation would create a false impression that the SL and its culture are in some way congruent with the TL and its culture. Although Matthew Arnold may have been overly dogmatic when he insisted the translator must serve the SL with complete commitment,[9] retention of aspects of the SL does preserve more of the integrity of the original text. Besides, there is an aesthetic consideration. We read foreign texts in part to escape our own culture. As Susan Levine has put it, "We translate in order to be translated."[10] The reader wants and expects a Chinese or Russian story to sound different than an American or British story. Sidney Monas makes this exact point in the preface to his translation of *Crime and Punishment*. Referring to his retention of the Russian naming system, he says, "It seems to me a healthy reminder to the reader that he is, after all,

8. Bassnett-McGuire, *Translation Studies*, 14.

9. Cited in Bassnett-McGuire, *Translation Studies*, 69.

10. Susan Jill Levine, *The Subversive Scribe: Translating Latin American Fiction* (St. Paul, MN: Graywolf Press, 1991), v.

supposed to be in Russia, not America or England."[11] There is another point: even in our native language certain words are used more for flavor and music than to convey meaning. This is especially true concerning vocabulary relating to some specialized area, such as food, clothing, sports, and science. One does not have to understand all of Patrick O'Brian's naval terminology to enjoy his Aubrey-Maturin novels; likewise with Joe Simpson's heavy use of the jargon of mountaineering in his harrowing nonfiction.[12] In a way, the initial lack of understanding can even make the reading more enjoyable as we are translated to another place. This may be a vulgar consideration, a kind of exoticism, but it does provide a way of retaining color in a translated text rather than turning a word with cultural resonance into a less specific TL word. Furthermore, Wang himself uses many foreign words in his writing, and since it is impossible to convey in a translation the visual and semantic impact of an English word in the midst of a Chinese text, the preservation of the occasional Chinese word or turn of phrase approximates this practice.

That, at least, was how we started out. But the first set of translations, including my own, had a certain bilingual quality, the result of our attempt to maintain that sense of foreignness. Many Chinese words were retained; footnotes were plentiful; underlying Chinese grammar was evident in many sentences. As the text went through further editing and reediting—and reediting and reediting—over a period of about three years, many of these bilingual elements were squeezed out, footnotes dwindled, and Chinese words were eliminated. I was not entirely comfortable with the outcome—there had been very valid reasons for our original approach—but given the collaborative nature of the project, compromise was demanded of everyone. Compromise among a group of scholars also fits into the "pragmatic" as opposed to "theoretical" nature of the translation process.

---

11. Fyodor Dostoyevsky, *Crime and Punishment*, trans. Sidney Monas (New York: Signet, 1968), v.

12. For example, O'Brian's *Master and Commander* (Philadelphia: J.B. Lippincott, 1969) and Joe Simpson's *Touching the Void* (London: Johnathan Cape, 1988).

The two works Jia Li and I translated for the anthology were an early short story, "Jian yue" 踐約 (Contract fulfilled), written before Wang's more radical experiments, and a one-act play, "M he W" M 和 W (M and W), which contains features of his mature style.

The plot of "Contract Fulfilled" centers on a young man's sexual initiation. The characters include the young man himself, Lin Shaoquan, his parents, Professor and Mrs. Lin, his sister, Lin Xun, and Lin Xun's friend Liu Juan. Referred to but not present is Lin Shaoquan's older brother, who is studying in the United States. The action takes place in late summer in Taipei in the 1950s or early 1960s. The narrator reveals that the Lin family has been living in the same house for fifteen years, and neighbors remember Lin Xun as a smiling, toothless infant. Wang describes Lin Xun as having grown into a "hao meilide shaonü" (好美麗的少女). Shaonü (少女) usually is defined as "young girl," an ambiguous term in English, but referring specifically in Chinese to an adolescent. Wang writes that even their parents have had to recognize that Lin Xun and Lin Shaoquan already are "zhangda" (長大), grown up.[13] So the initial translation of "hao meilide shaonü" was "beautiful young woman." Later, however, we meet Lin Xun, and the term "beautiful young woman" seems inappropriate. Her behavior is girlish and she is described as "pang-pangde" (胖胖的), which literally means "fat" or "stout." Her brother calls her "ban da bu xiao" (半大不小), literally "half big not small," or half adult but no longer a child. Further inconsistency appears later when she is described as a champion broad-jumper, and at the end of the story it is learned that she has borrowed clothes from her friend Liu Juan—who is so thin that her breastbone is visible at her collar— to attend a dance party. So Lin Xun is a "young girl," "grown-up," "beautiful," "fat," a successful athlete, and able to wear the clothes of a thin friend. In the SL text, all these terms work but the inconsistencies were jarring in the original translation. The first issue was how to deal with the descrip-

---

13. There is some ambiguity here, as *zhangda* can simply indicate that someone is older than before, but since it is applied collectively in this case to both children, and Lin Shaoquan already is a university graduate, the initial impression is that Lin Xun, like her brother, is "grown up."

tion of Lin Xun as a "hao meilide shaonü." Unfortunately, standard English does not have a single word for this type of person, as the terms "youth," "teen," and "adolescent" are gender-neutral and clinical. "Young woman" and "young girl," or simply "girl," are misleading or ambiguous, whereas "shaonü" is quite specific. One solution was to use the word "lass," a suggestion offered by my Chinese cotranslator. Initially, this seemed inappropriate, since "lass" introduces another cultural flavor. In the context of the story, however, "lovely lass" accurately describes Lin Xun, including her precocious, playful nature. Although Chinese–English dictionaries give the definition of shaonü as "young girl," English–Chinese dictionaries include "shaonü" as a definition for "lass." Thus "lass" was used in the initial translation, including the version first submitted to a publisher. Ultimately, though, the cultural reference seemed just too discordant and "hao meilide shaonü" became "lovely young lady." As for "pangpangde," in this context it appeared to mean healthy or robust, so it was translated in verb form as "glows." Elsewhere, Lin Xun's face is described as "xianhong ru zuiyun" (鮮紅如醉暈). *Xianhong* means "bright red" or "scarlet." *Zuiyun* means "tipsy" or "drunk," while *ru* means "like" or "as." To describe the rosy cheeks of a teenaged girl as being like the flushed face of someone who has been drinking is common in Chinese. It is a positive description, regarded as charming. In English, however, the effect is negative and rather odd. Even though the phrase conveys a certain cultural distinctiveness, it was dropped and Lin Xun was described simply as having a "rosy face."

Another example of SL/TL incompatibility comes near the end of the story when Lin Shaoquan receives a letter from his friends telling him to come to a hotel for his long-awaited sexual encounter. In the letter, which is signed in English, "Lost Generation," Lin Shaoquan's friends use the four-character *chengyu* (成語) "linzhen tuotao" (臨陣脫逃). A *chengyu* is an idiomatic saying that contains the essence or moral of a famous story from Chinese history or literature. "Linzhen tuotao" refers specifically to deserting on the eve of battle, or more generally to sneaking away at a critical juncture. What Lin Shaoquan's friends are telling him is that all the arrangements have been made and he should "Come quickly, immediately, as soon as you receive this letter!" Then comes the sentence "Linzhen tuotao dehua, na ni jiu tai meizhong le!" (臨陣脫逃的話, 那你就太沒種了!). *Meizhong* (沒種) means to lack grit or guts. *Dehua* (的話) and *jiu* (就) are an emphatic "if ... then" structure, so the literal translation would be "if you desert on the eve of battle, you really have no guts," although the *chengyu* provides extra cultural/historical depth in Chinese. To provide some color but without wanting to sound anachronistic, and keeping in mind the letter has been written by young men, the current translation says: "If you bug out now, you have no guts!"

These all are examples of microlevel decision making. As you can see, in the case of "linzhen tuotao" and "xianhong ru zuiyun," we actually violated our principle trying to retain a sense of foreignness in favor of words more accessible to English-language readers.

The initial translation had also retained certain Chinese words, again to emphasize the Chineseness of the original text. For example, the members of the Lin family refer to each other not by name but by relationship. Mrs. Lin calls Lin Shaoquan "Xiao Di," literally "Little Brother," and Lin Xun "Xiao Mei," literally "Little Sister." Lin Xun calls her brother "Er Ge," literally "Second Brother." Rather than translate these terms, in the initial translation they were left in Chinese and footnoted. As the editing process proceeded, however, a decision was made to make the text as English as possible. I had also retained the honorifics Lao and Xiao in names, feeling that they lent a certain flavor to the text. Besides, I have never liked the use of "Old" for "Lao" because it takes a word that in Chinese conveys a certain affectionate respect and turns it into something that in English is almost insulting—just think of the connotation of saying "Old Smith" or "Old Jones." Translating "Xiao" as "Little" is just about as bad. Initially at the suggestion of an outside reader and partly because of what appears to be a growing convention in Chinese-to-English translations, the various "Laos" became "Olds." The final decision about the Lin family was a little more complex. To have a mother referring to her children as "Little Brother" and "Little Sister" seemed unnatural in translations that now were straining to be as natural as possible in English (this illustrates a problem with the whole notion of "equivalence"). Was there any alternative? One was to look for words that might be used in English for a younger son and daughter. "Sonny" is not uncommon in that context, and for the girl "Missy." Both words also have a late 1950s feel to them, which fits the time frame of the story. The right decision? Who knows? As for "Er Ge," it was translated literally as "Second Brother."

Other Chinese words fell by the wayside. During Lin Shaoquan's long interior monologue on female anatomy, he uses the word 胸 兜 (xiongdou), a triangular piece of cloth that was worn on the upper body as underwear in traditional society. In the original translation, the Chinese word was maintained and footnoted. Again, the rationale was that this added some cultural resonance—it was a specific Chinese thing, like a samovar is a Russian thing, or a hijab is an Arab thing. Those words tend not to be translated, so why not leave *xiongdou*? As other Chinese words began to be converted into English equivalents, however, and with "Contract Fulfilled" at one point possessing no fewer than fifteen footnotes in a twenty-two-page text, *xiongdou* became "slip."

Other footnotes, though, were retained. At one point in the story, Lin Shaoquan recites a classical Chinese poem. Because of its familiarity to Chinese readers, it is not identified. In the translation, it is footnoted. After the poem is recited, there are another two phrases embedded in an interior monologue that come from a Tang Dynasty poem. Again, to alert the English reader to the "literariness" of Lin Shaoquan, the phrases are footnoted.

Obviously, footnotes need to be used sparingly in literary works, but this anthology is the first to bring together all of Wang Wenxing's short fiction, so it seemed worthwhile to explain all that needed to be explained, including words and phrases that appear in English in the original text. These have a striking visual affect in the Chinese text, much like—to refer to Pound again—the Chinese characters that appear in some the Cantos.[14] One suggestion was to italicize the English words,

---

14. For example, Cantos LI, LIII, and LXII, *Selected Poems of Ezra Pound* (New York: New Directions, 1956), 145–47, 151.

which would have created a visual impression, but that was problematic given Wang's existing use of nonstandard fonts for very specific purposes. So they were footnoted and stayed footnoted.

Readers familiar with Wang or Chinese prose can skip the footnotes, but the notes—now much reduced in number—may be useful to those coming to this material for the first time. Likewise, the translation generally has erred on the side of inclusiveness. Wang Wenxing is less a storyteller than a literary stylist, so it has been incumbent on the translators to try to capture all aspects of his style. Nowhere is this more problematic than in his idiosyncratic use of punctuation.

Classical Chinese had no punctuation,[15] so Western readers often find punctuation in Chinese prose to be unusual. Wang complicates matters by injecting punctuation marks drawn from modern Western literature, such as long dashes and multiple dots. The stories contain some examples but in "M and W," which was written in 1987, the use of distinctive punctuation is rampant. An example: "En,——qishi hai bucuo. Wo wangle wen ni, duile, ni jintian wanshang, zheme wangle, shi wei shenme da zhege dianti xialoude?——Ni zhu zai zhelide loushang ma?——Haishi,——ni shuo,——ni zhu zai Tianmu?" (嗯,——其實還不錯. 我忘了問你，對了，你今天晚上，這麼晚了，是為什麼搭這個電梯下樓去的?——你住在這裏的樓上嗎?——還是,——你說,—— ——你住在天母?).[16] Here we see long dashes following commas and question marks, clearly indicating long pauses between each phrase. The translation kept all the punctuation because it was so distinctive and so much a part of Wang's style: "You, hmmm,—really not bad. I forgot to ask you, yes, tonight, so late, why did you take this elevator down?—You live in this building?—or,—you said,—you live in Tianmu?" The play also contains a similar doubling of ellipses with other punctuation, the ellipses appearing to play the same function as the long dashes. In his attempt to re-create oral speech, Wang also uses doubled exclamation marks, and combina-

---

15. Punctuation rules were promulgated in China in 1919, but usage still has not become standardized.

16. Wang Wenxing, "M he W" M 和 W (M and W), *Xiaoshuo moyu* 小說墨餘 (Beyond fiction) (Taipei: Hongfan shudian, 2002), 215.

tions of exclamation marks and question marks, as well as boldface text. All of these features, distinctive elements of Wang's mature style, were retained in the translation.

A different sort of punctuation problem occurs in "Jian yue." There is a section describing Lin Shaoquan smoking a cigarette. The Chinese is: "Ta penchu liaorao ru si de bai yan, ding tou, zhe de mantiandi, shi na yi zhang yi suo, qing leng, ru ying chong bandi xingzi" (他噴出繚繞如絲 的白煙，頂頭,遮得滿天底，是那一張一縮,清冷，如螢蟲般底星子).[17] The first phrase means: "He exhales white smoke that curls like silk (or thread)." The second part literally means the "top of the head," but here means "over" or "above his head." The third part means "covers the entire sky." The next phrase refers to something "expanding and contracting" or "stretching and shrinking." The next two-character phrase means "cold" or "clear and cold," and the last part means "stars like fireflies." Wang's use of commas makes it unclear whether it is the smoke rising over Lin Shaoquan's head that is expanding and contracting and covering the sky, or whether it is the stars, not expanding and contracting but blinking like fireflies, that cover the sky. He also has isolated the two-character phrase that means "clear and cold" between commas, causing some confusion as to whether cold refers to the night or the light from the stars. The initial translation was: "White smoke he exhaled curled up like thread, over his head, covering the sky, where the cold stars blinked like fireflies." After further consideration, the first phrase was turned into a separate sentence: "The white smoke he exhaled curled up like thread. Over his head, covering the sky, the cold blinking stars were like fireflies." This seemed too choppy and sacrificed the poetic effect of the long sentence, so the version that was submitted for publication reads: "He exhaled silken white threads of smoke. Above his head, the sky was covered with cold stars blinking like fireflies." Another reading could be: "He exhaled curling threads of white smoke. Over his head, covering the entire sky, were the stars, pure and cold, blinking off and on like fireflies." Perhaps that comes closest to the poetic effect Wang was striving

17. Wang Wenxing, "Jianyu" 踐約 (Contract fulfilled), *Shiwu pian xiaoshuo* 十五篇小說 (Fifteen stories) (Taipei: Hongfan shudian, 1979), 87.

for with his busy punctuation. Unfortunately, the book had already been printed, so any revision will have to wait for a second edition.

While these examples involve cases of decision making on the micro-level, Wang Wenxing has provided a couple of precious gifts for translators seeking to emulate the overall tone or flavor of his work. These are his own comments about what he has tried to do in his writing, and that the dominant influence on his prose is, in fact, an English-language author—Ernest Hemingway. The combination of Wang's stated goal of "precision" in the use of language and his desire to follow Hemingway's "shining example"[18] provides a useful clue to translators about how Wang should sound in English: cool and terse. This guided my translations and editing of the other contributions to the anthology. Thus, during the translation and editing process, there was a tendency to simplify, to hack away at the semantic density of the original Chinese, to select short, strong words and to break up long sentences.

Another significant editing intervention was based on Wang's admission of having been influenced by cinema to the extent that he starts with a mental visual image of a scene and then attempts to describe it in words, including the use of visual and acoustic effects. Like Christopher Isherwood, Wang might well say, "I am a camera."[19] With that in mind, several stories were converted during the editing process from traditional past-tense narration to the present tense to convey the unfolding action more "cinematically." Nor was this a particular violation of the original Chinese, given the language's lack of complex verb tensing. It also gave life to the at times static and claustrophobic nature of Wang's stories and highlighted his tendency to use the description of physical

18. Wang Wenxing, "Wu xiuzhi de zhanzheng" 無休止的戰爭 (Endless war), *Wenxing* 文星 (Literary star), 103, 104–5; reprinted in Wang Wenxing, *Shu he ying* 書和影 (Books and films), 195–96.

19. The line comes from the first page of "A Berlin Diary (Autumn 1930)" in *Goodbye to Berlin*: "I am a camera with its shutter open, quite passive, recording, not thinking. Recording the man shaving at the window opposite and the woman in the kimono washing her hair. Some day, all this will have to be developed, carefully printed, fixed." Christopher Isherwood, *Goodbye to Berlin* (London: Hogarth Press, 1939), 1.

action to reveal the psychological state of his characters. To mention just one example, use of the present tense in the story "Afternoon," which recounts a disastrous and tragic few hours of babysitting, injected a visual quality to the mounting horror, just like watching a movie. An excerpt:

> She pushes him around until she is out of breath. Then she lies on the floor panting hard, her face drained white. She smiles weakly. Little Mao is still stuck in the stool unable to move a muscle. He cannot even turn his face and just makes a low whimpering sound. But the sound is weak and Ah Yin is light-headed from her playing. She pays no attention to him.

The translation and editing processes described above conform more with the approach of U.S. translator Douglas Robinson than with any particular theory of literary translation. In his book *The Translator's Turn*, Robinson emphasizes the role of pragmatic decision making at the microlevel and dismisses the reliance on normative rules as "actively pernicious."[20] His list of guidelines for translators includes this sentence that provoked a nod of recognition and approval: "Translators feel their way to the 'right' TL words and phrases in a complex two-way dialogue with the writer of the SL text and the reader of the TL text."[21] Even so, the decision-making process in the Wang translation project was broadly consistent with modern translation theory, particularly regarding the tug-of-war between respect for the SL text and the need for a fluent TL end product. Thus the emphasis was on the meaning of the original text rather than word-for-word translation.[22] In this regard, we were fortunate that many of the problems identified in translation theory simply are not present in Wang's work; we did not have to deal with linguistic

---

20. Douglas Robinson, *The Translator's Turn* (Baltimore: Johns Hopkins University Press, 1991), 259.

21. Ibid.

22. For example, see Bassnett-McGuire's comments on the need for "stylistic equivalence," *Translation Studies*, 34.

archaisms or any imperial/colonial dichotomy. Even the cultural divide was relatively narrow, given that Wang's world is highly Westernized— no bound feet, Daoist sages, or people's communes. To some degree, this made the gradual retreat from preserving the foreignness of the text easier. Even so, our goal was to achieve a linguistic balance that merged English usage with content originating in another society at another time in another place. Sometimes that meant being faithful to original usage; sometimes that meant choosing a reader-friendlier TL alternative. While SL-TL tension is a key concern of modern translation theory, it is actually an age-old problem. To quote George Steiner: "Over two thousand years of argument and precept, the beliefs and disagreements voiced about the nature of translation have been almost the same. Identical theses, familiar moves and refutations in debate recur, nearly without exception, from Cicero and Quintilian to the present day."[23]

A modern example of this ongoing argument, one that has spilled out of the academy into the popular media, involves the translations of Russian classics by Richard Pevear and Larissa Volokhonsky, a.k.a. "the world's only celebrity translation team." Pevear and Volokhonsky lean heavily toward fidelity to the SL in their work, even at the risk of considerable awkwardness in the finished product. Their recent version of *War and Peace* was praised by Orlando Figes, a British scholar of Russian history, as an "extraordinary achievement" for its "absolute fidelity to the language of Tolstoy."[24] Yet the U.S. writer Francine Prose, commenting on the *New York Times*'s online book discussion forum, complained that she "kept stumbling across phrases in the Pevear and Volokhonsky that simply didn't mean anything in English or seemed awkward and stilted." She also found the heavy use of footnotes offputting.[25]

---

23. Cited in Peter France, *The Oxford Guide to Literature in English Translation* (Oxford: Oxford University Press, 2000) ,5.

24. Orlando Figes, "Tolstoy's Real Hero," *New York Review of Books*, November 22, 2007.

25. Francine Prose, "Footnote Fatigue," *The Reading Room: Conversations About Great Books*, http://readingroom.blogs.nytimes.com/2007/10/30/footnote -fatigue/comment-page-1/?_php=true&_type=blogs&_r=0 (accessed February 24, 2014).

Whatever the merits of Pevear and Volokhonsky's work, Prose's experience to some degree echoed mine when I read my own original translation of "Jian yue": this isn't real English but a kind of third language, translatorese. This was the result of adhering to certain theoretical principles rather than sound English usage. So I return to the point made by Douglas Robinson, that translators have to "feel" their way through the linguistic thickets to create a "working TL text."[26] The solution we stumbled on was to combine natural English usage with resonant cultural and stylistic markers from the SL text.

What of the final product? What is Wang like as an English writer?

Ironically, despite his reputation as a modernist, these stories—most of them written at the beginning of his career—seem rooted in time and place, the conservative Taiwanese society of the late 1950s and early 1960s. They are very much the work of a young man, earnest and serious. Indeed, almost half of them—"Paralysis," "The Toy Revolver," "Calendar," "The Happiest Thing," "Song of the Earth," "Conclusion," "Contract Fulfilled," "Line of Fate," "Cold Front," and "Flaw"—make up what I came to think of as the "young man stories." In each, the central character is an edgy young male, ranging in age from boyhood to university student, physically frail, bookish, and sexually obsessed/repressed. Professor Guo in "Withered Chrysanthemums" seems like an older version of these youths, as does, in a negative sense, Mr. Jin in "The Black Gown." With very few exceptions, the social milieu is not particularly Chinese, which made abandoning Chinese names and words in the final translations even easier. The heroes of "The Toy Revolver" and "Song of the Earth" could very well have stepped off the screen from an earnest black-and-white Hollywood film about 1950s youth in the United States. Of course, there are some differences. These Taiwanese youths express rebellion by excelling in school and dreaming of being writers rather than football players and rock and roll stars, but they are very much in the sensitive teen mold of James Dean and seem far removed from the type of society described by Lao She or Lu Xun.

One curious subtheme in these stories regards the portrayal of

---

26. Robinson, *The Translator's Turn*, 259.

women. For the most part, they are distant and rather threatening, so much so that the lovesick boys are afraid to express their feelings, as with Hu Zhaosheng in "The Toy Revolver," who is ritually humiliated over his secret infatuation; Lin Shaoquan in "Contract Fulfilled," who literally runs and hides when his sister's friend comes into the house; and Huang Guohua in "Cold Front," who is terrified of his (never explicitly named) nocturnal emissions. The seamstress in "Flaw" defrauds many people in the neighborhood; Ah Yu in "Two Women" takes possession of her husband's life; even little Qiuqiu in "The Black Gown" gets the best of Mr. Jin. Perhaps most terrifyingly symbolic of all, Ah Yin casually kills Little Mao in "Afternoon." Ironically, given the heightened sexual awareness of many of these characters, the sex act itself seems to stimulate only disgust, as in "The Happiest Thing" and "Contract Fulfilled." So the overall impression is of weak, feckless men and overpowering women.

As for style, the experiments Wang is famous for lie mostly in the future. "M and W" is an exception, and there is the extra spacing after each sentence in "Mother." For the most part though, the most striking features of the writing are the vivid and at times fevered portrayal of adolescent psychology and the tendency to try to describe movement with almost cinematic precision—like the dancing in "Paralysis." This leads to a tricky dichotomy in tone, with intense interior monologue mixed with cool, detached physical description and bursts of lyricism. At one stage in the editing process, overly conscious of the influence of Hemingway, the sentences actually got too short, and the overall effect was rather lifeless, so during the final edit some long sentences were restored to recapture Wang's frequent lyrical forays.

For the young Wang at his lyrical, cinematic best, take this excerpt from "Midsummer on the Prairie:"

> The ant-like line of men, an apricot-colored army flag in the lead announcing their presence, emerges into the abrupt expanse of this vast world. Their route suddenly appears to lack any fixed direction and they fall out of step. Nervousness, a lack of confidence, spreads among the troops. A man wearing a yellow hel-

met, who had been standing apart from the soldiers, accompanying them independently as they forged ahead, now quickens his pace and runs to the head of the column. In a loud voice he reprimands a soldier, and the troops' forward march comes to a complete halt. The soldiers at the head of the column shift direction, resuming the advance. The march is still ambling and awkward because the ground beneath their feet is rugged and rough. The man wearing the yellow helmet stands motionless, both hands on his waist, legs spread wide and firm like two poles, looking sideways at every soldier who passes in front of him. They are all extremely young and dressed identically: a rifle on every man's right shoulder, a small wooden stool hanging from the left wrist, an extremely wide cartridge belt buckled tight around their slender waists, a bayonet on their belts hanging flat against their buttocks, its handle tapping the canteens at their waists. This tapping, the sound of the metal ring on the rifle strap, the footsteps of more than one hundred men, all combine to generate the strange sound of these troops. Nothing else can be heard, not even the voice of one man talking among them.

And for male angst, again with cinematic description, "The Toy Revolver":

Hu Zhaosheng deeply resented other people making fun of his shortcomings. When they mocked his slight physique especially, a hot flush filled his entire body. What Zhong Xueyuan had said not only made him flush, but it was embarrassing to be grabbed and shaken roughly. He felt it was demeaning, an insult. He had wanted to push Zhong Xueyuan away but was afraid the others would notice, so he just slipped out of Zhong Xueyuan's grasp. He did not know if the others had seen him do it or not. He hoped not. He hoped the others had not taken Zhong Xueyuan's remark as an insult, but he recalled he had clearly heard them roar with laughter. So they did know he had been insulted. Feeling anxious, he drew himself up rigidly in his chair.

Literary translation is a vexed business, as is evident from the constant retranslation of classic works. Even during the five or six years of this project, previously fixed principles were abandoned, and during the final edit the only criterion seemed to be "does this sound right?" Of course, some of it doesn't. In part that is because some of the stories are too bound by their time and culture to speak naturally to the modern English reader ("Paralysis" and "Conclusion" come to mind), but there remain shortcomings in the translations largely because the translators tended to be scholars or, in my case—God help us—a journalist, while the writer is an artist working within his own language and culture. Ah, to have had an Ezra Pound among us!

12 *Reflections on Translating* Jia bian

Susan Dolling

SINCE I AM writing as the translator of *Jia bian* 家變
(Family catastrophe), I thought I would talk a little bit about my philosophy of translation and why I think *Family Catastrophe* was such a nice
fit for me.[1]

First, as a translator, I begin on the premise that literary translation
is an impossible task. Since literature is based on how one particular
language is used to create a particular work of art, and language itself is
built from years and years of cultural experience, how can one hope to
reproduce the words of one language arranged in this particular way by
words from a wholly different culture? In other words, literary translation is a quixotic task. For me, the choice of which windmill to tilt is at
least half the battle—in this case, this very fortunate choice was made for
me or at least brought to me by Yvonne Sung-Sheng Chang, who introduced me to Wang Wenxing's work—for me, the process of what or who
to translate is very much like that of choosing a friend: you are first attracted to the work as a reader, begin in sympathy, understanding and
grow in empathy, and eventually, because this "friend" is speaking a
"foreign language," you have to translate him or her for your other
friends. To be as faithful as possible to this friend, however, you must

---

1. Editor's note: This is a slightly edited version of a speech that Susan Dolling gave at the international conference on Wang Wenxing's writing at the Central University in Zhongli, Taiwan, on June 4–5, 2010.

first trust him or her to know what he or she is doing with his or her language—this is where the translator must first be as good a reader as he or she can manage to be (let me neutralize the masculine pronoun in the English language from this point on and use it to indicate all third persons). Now the friendship metaphor can only go so far. Once you begin to take on the task of translation, you must also take on the responsibility of expression, and to give voice to your author, you must be *willing* to borrow the author's voice and speak for him in your own language (i.e., the target language).

I think it is because literary translation demands more than just "moving words from one page to another" (搬字過紙 *ban zi guo zhi*) and requires the translator to put so much of himself into the process both as reader and writer, that translators have sometimes taken on a rather aggressive, testosterone-driven stance, for example, describing the process as a kind of taking over or possession/penetration of the original text. I would agree with the description if, at this point, the translator is solely using the original text as fodder and reproducing it in his own voice. In my own experience, though, the degree of success in a translation depends more on compatibility than conquest, which takes me back again to the friendship metaphor. In other words, even though I agree with these other translators that translation is not merely a readerly activity but a combination of readerly and writerly mentalities and capabilities, I approach the responsibility of giving voice to the original text as a performer and not an author. If anything, to be true to the original, the translator must be willing to sacrifice his own voice; this is what I meant by being "willing to borrow the author's voice." Put another way, the art of translation is really a performance art; one does not impose oneself or one's voice on the given work of art but one renders and, by rendering, necessarily colors the original with one's own reading or interpretation. I happen to know that Wang would be in agreement with this because he talks about it in his own preface, that *Family Catastrophe* would not be *Family Catastrophe* but for what it is made of, in other words, its words, those Chinese words which it is made of, in that certain order, etc. (Even if some of them are made up, or precisely because some of them are made up!) He goes on to make the analogy between this and a piece of classical music, that is, it is there to be performed, indeed, whether in reading or in translation.

In my case, because I came to *Family Catastrophe* as a translator of Chinese classical poetry, mostly from the Tang and Song periods, I feel that has equipped me with the sensibilities of a reader of poetry which *Family Catastrophe* demands of its readers. What I am trying to say is that a poetry reader is a slow reader and not just any slow reader but a slow reader à la Wang Wenxing. A literature professor of mine once told me he read four words an hour and I remember thinking rather smugly that I did that, too. This is because I am a poetry reader and as such I have a physiological relationship with language, and I think this must be why I was fascinated with *Family Catastrophe* at first reading, even before I comprehended the whole of it!

The two things that first attracted me to *Family Catastrophe* were the rhythm of the language and the tone. By rhythm, I mean both the ebb and flow of the sentences themselves as well as the juxtaposition of the very lyrical passages against the very harsh expressions, from ideal to reality. By tone I am referring to the rebellious tone of the subject matter, which I find very moving in itself. For more on this subject, the subject of father and son, country and self, I refer you to the couple of little essays on my approach to the book at the back of *Family Catastrophe*.

Now I am going to say something completely contrary to what I said before about the impossibility of translation, because the best compliment I have been given as a translator is when the reader of the original text comes back to me to say how much the translation reminded them of the original even in terms of tone and texture. In this again, I credit my background as a poetry reader in that because my relationship to language is such a physiological one, I never merely "read" or translate/ write "in my head." That is to say, I pay as much attention to the sound of the text as I do to its substance. I read out loud. Always. To me, the music of the language communicates as much as its pictures and/or ideas. Having said that, let me read you one of my favorite lyrical passages. I have many favorites but only have time for one right now. I am a mother (and at the time when I began translation of *Family Catastrophe* my two children were five and seven), and Fan Ye's youth and his relationships with his parents were particularly touching to me. Sections 85 and 86 beginning on page 99 of the English text. I love the way Wang works these classical poems into the narrative. The section starts up with the poem:

> In South Garden when walks are green
> And half of spring has still to come—
> the sound of horses shrill in the wind,
> green plums like baby beans, willows like brows,
> days long, and butterflies flit about ...

He had forgotten the rest of the song, not just the tune, but the lyrics. He decided to start singing it over again. Maybe this go round the whole thing would come back to him. It didn't. "Days long, and butterflies flit about ..." Then what? What came after that? He repeated the song another time from the beginning:

> In South Garden when walks are green
> and half of spring has still to come—
> the sound of horses shrill in the wind,
> green plums like baby beans, willows like brows,
> days long, and butterflies flit about,
> flowers heavy with dewdrops,
> grass bathed in smoke,
> and every household has left its blinds hung down,
> and the swing is idle, and I have unloosed my dress—
> home to the gallery a pair of swallows come to nest.

I should have translated the word *jie* 解 as "unloosed" as opposed to "unloosened," which is how you will find it in the book because it both sounds better and gives the feel of the fall of the dress—and some would say more grammatical, depending on what dictionary you use. Anyway, going back to *Family Catastrophe*, the passage that follows, Section 86, runs:

He discovered that he liked his mother's face very much; it was a very pretty face. She had a proud-looking nose, tall and straight, and thin eyebrows. In fact she had plucked all the hair on her brows, and a new pair was drawn on with a stiff eyebrow pencil. There were also a few freckles on her face. (She called them "mosquito shit." He had them too, she said, "because you're my son.") And she had little holes in her earlobes, where once she had worn earrings, but they had now closed up. Around the house, she wore an old pair of black woolen slippers and an old dress, loose and soft, made of a red and brown gingham material. The tiny, neatly woven curls of her permed hair made the back of her head look like a round packet of noodles.

In the next section they go to have noodles.

It's such a wonderful association of ideas, one to the other, relating and enriching our understanding of Fan Ye's feelings for his mother; this associative way of thinking really appeals to me, perhaps because this is the way I think as well. Of course, this particular passage also reminds me very much of my own mother.

I hope my enjoyment of such passages as these is apparent. I had so much fun; those four years were not four years of drudgery but four, five years of excitement and discovery; I did not sit down to translate most of this, but was wandering around the house, fooling around with different ways to bring across my discoveries. Besides, four years to translate a whole book is no time at all; it took me fifteen years to translate Bai Juyi's 白居易 "Yan shi" 燕詩 (Swallow song),[2] but that's another story!

Another thing I really enjoyed doing was solving some of the problems Wang presented me with. Solving this kind of problem, unlike getting the feel of a passage just right or keeping pace with the original, and so on, is relatively uncomplicated, yet there are times when one is stuck

---

2. Editor's note: The full title of the poem is "燕詩示劉叟" Yanshi shi Liusou (A swallow poem written for Liu). The translation was published in *Asian American Quarterly* in 1999. Page and issue nos. are unknown.

and cannot move forward without fixing it. So this is a minor challenge if you will. I'll cite one example of this kind of hump.

When Fan Ye got sick when he was a little boy, among other things, one of the things that he talks about is when they took him for the diagnosis the doctor said his tonsils were infected. In Chinese tonsils is *biantaoxian* 扁桃腺, and in it is a word, *tao* 桃 (peach), which was associated in the boy's mind with the bananas he later craved. Now, having understood that, how do I translate that into English? What I did was something of a sleight of hand; I expanded the doctor's explanation a little bit to say that the tonsils were very close to his Adam's apple. In so doing I lost the peach, kept the tonsils, and brought in an apple for the needed associative idea. So that's one example that took me over two weeks to solve, and believe me I patted myself on the back when I finally came up with the apple!

Well, that is one of many such examples. And even the "mosquito shit" from the earlier passage was not mosquito shit in the Chinese ... what was it? It was a fly, not a mosquito in the original, but fly shit just doesn't have the ring that mosquito shit has. ...

On more than one occasion in Part 1, the sound of trains passes through the narrative, and we all know how important train rides and train noises are in *Family Catastrophe*. I believe the first time it occurs is during their move to Taipei, in Section 52. I haven't done a word count, but it seems to me that from here on out the word *kong* 空 (empty) begins to appear with some frequency. The train here is described as making a *kongtong kongtong* 空通空通 noise, which, on the surface, I totally overtranslated as "humpety-dumpety thrum-thrum-thrum." Then in Section 53, the dormitory they were moving into is described as *konghuang* 空荒 and so on, and then in Section 68 right after the episode with his *erge* 二哥 (second older brother) taking him to the theater and the great letdown and fear afterward, we have the desolate and lonely description of the train in the distance (bringing to my mind the magpie after the storm at the very beginning of the novel; in fact, that magpie stayed in my mind throughout my reading as something of a source of strength). Anyway, back to the train. Here, in Section 68, the sound is described as *kongqi kongqi* 空其控奇, which I find I have rendered as "humch-dum humch-dum." Some may dispute the accuracy of my translation here, but I believe that these noises are much more than onomatopoeic, that they not only resonate throughout the novel but each has its own meaning attached. Take *kongqi kongqi* 空其控奇, for example, there is the word "empty" and the words "control" and "strange" (we may even read the phrase as "making empty its strange control"!). This, coming in the context of the aftermath of the theater episode, makes it imperative that the translator try to bring over all these ideas evoked by the sound produced by the train. I imagine you have heard that behind my noises is the figure of Humpty Dumpty and his story of a fall from which it was impossible to recover.

Translators are constitutionally defensive. Let me admit to at least one failure before I bring this to a close. One thing that I feel I had really failed to bring over—I think I do a maybe 80 percent acceptable job in the mostly lyrical passages—but it is the halting, deliberate awkwardness of the language in places that makes one stop and think before reading on that I have not brought across. Perhaps I did not dare to be awkward because I am translating and not inventing my own text. So the translation is less daring, a little too smooth. But I did do my best to bring over what I can of those made-up words even if they were done by every other means than reproduction. Maybe that is literally impossible.

REFLECTIONS ON
WANG WENXING'S LIFE

13   *A Quiet and Simple Life*

Jeannette Chu-yun Chen
National Taiwan University

I WAS BORN at the very beginning of the postwar baby boom, to parents who came from very different areas in China. My father's origins were in Guangdong in the south, while my mother's family came from the central province of Hubei (Hupei). They would never have met were it not for the Sino-Japanese War. Both had left home and ended up in the wartime capital of Chongqing (Chungking) in southwestern China.

They married after the Japanese surrender, and a year later I was born in Nanjing (Nanking), the city to which the Nationalist government had returned and reestablished as its capital.

When Wenxing and I traveled the Yangtze River by boat on our first visit to China in 1989, I was struck by the fact that this was actually my second trip down the river. I had first made the voyage from Chongqing to Nanjing in late 1945 while I was still in my mother's womb.

My father's first overseas assignment with the Foreign Ministry took us to Sydney, Australia, at the end of 1946. We remained there until 1953, when we returned home, not to Nanjing but to Taipei. Subsequently, my father's postings abroad took us to Seoul, Korea, then to Bangkok, Thailand, and finally to Nicosia, Cyprus. In 1963, I returned to Taipei with my family and entered college, first at National Chengchi University and then, beginning from my sophomore year, at National Taiwan University (Taida), where I obtained a master's degree in 1969.

An event took place at this point that enabled me to play a very minor part in Taiwan's recent history. Wenxing had been awarded a one-year visiting fellowship at the State University of New York at Buffalo. At the same time, I won a scholarship from a local foundation for study in the United States. It was very generous, but one of its conditions was that the recipient had to remain single. We had planned to be married that summer and to travel to Buffalo together. So without a second thought, I gave up the money. Much later, I learned that the grant went to the runner-up, a law major, who put the scholarship to good use. This person later built an illustrious career in public service and played a leading role in Taiwan's democratization process.

In contrast to my earlier nomadic experience, the latter half of my life has been remarkably settled. I regard the Taida campus as my true home, physically, mentally, and emotionally. It is where I met Wenxing, where I spent thirty-five years teaching, and where I am now doing volunteer work at the library and the university archives. Except for brief stays in Buffalo from 1969 to 1970 and later in Jacksonville, Florida, from 1976 to 1977, this little corner of Taipei has been the center of my life for over four decades. It is where Wenxing and I have built our life together.

A Plain Vanilla Life

If there is one expression that describes that life, it is the phrase "plain and simple." We started out with an absolutely no-frills wedding: we stood before the justice of the peace at the Alameda courthouse in Berkeley, California, in the summer of 1969, on our way to Buffalo. Two friends served as witnesses. The ceremony took all of ten minutes and was followed by a modest lunch with just the four of us at a local Chinese restaurant. A few days later, we were on our way to the East Coast. The reason for holding the marriage ceremony in the United States rather than at home in Taipei was that Taiwan was still under martial law at the time, and married couples were forbidden from leaving the country together.

We began married life in an unfurnished apartment in Buffalo, with whatever pieces of furniture and household utensils we managed to borrow. That year was memorable for another reason. It was during the height of the antiwar, anti-establishment movement in the United States. Every single window in every campus building was smashed. Students and teachers held endless meetings to discuss and debate social and anti-war issues, when they were not out in the streets throwing stones and shouting derogatory remarks at the police. Nobody went to class. Compared to life in Taiwan under the strictures of martial law, the experience was a real eye-opener for us.

We returned to Taiwan in fall 1970 to settle down at Taida and begin life as a family. During the first few years, both of us were busy with our jobs. Teaching salaries were abysmally low then (I started out at NT$3,000 a month),[1] so we both had to take on extra work to pay the rent. Wenxing taught a class at Tamkang College, while I held a part-time job writing English letters at the Council for Economic Cooperation and Development. It was not until late in 1975, when we were assigned free campus housing, that we felt financially secure enough to drop our second jobs.

During the next thirty years, from 1975 to 2005, when both of us retired from teaching, we gradually settled into a routine that continues today, less by conscious choice, more out of necessity. My classes at Taida were scheduled for the mornings, while Wenxing taught in the afternoons or evenings. My elderly parents-in-law were living with us, and in this way one of us would always be at home.

Besides teaching class, which he really enjoys, the centerpiece in Wenxing's life has always been his writing, something he had been doing since he was in high school. One of the things that impressed me most when we first met was his resolute sense of purpose. I didn't know what I wanted—I still don't—and naturally admired anyone who so clearly did. Teaching is perhaps the only profession that allows one enough free time to do this, and Taida was perhaps the only place.

During those early years, a person's time was pretty much his own,

1. The exchange rate in 1970 was NT$36.68 for US$1, making for a monthly income of US$82. U.S. Department of Agriculture Economic Research Service, http://www.ers.usda.gov/Data/macroeconomics/Data/HistoricalRealExchange RatesValues.xls (accessed December 23, 2010).

as long as he fulfilled the required teaching quota. There were no requisite office hours, no demands for administrative duties, no committees to sit on, and no community services to perform.

Wenxing therefore set up a regular daily schedule for his writing, mainly during the late afternoon, for two hours at the most. He is known for how slowly he writes, even by many who are unfamiliar with his work. People would often ask me in disbelief: Is it true he writes only fifty words a day? I would reply: "No way, what gave you that idea? He writes thirty words per day, and that includes punctuation marks."

Actually, since he writes for only two hours, that translates into about four minutes a word, which sounds much less shocking, especially considering that what is produced is the final version, without any additional revisions. As to why he works for such a short period, the reason is that writing for him has always been a most strenuous task, not only mentally but physically as well. Not for him the quiet scribbling on paper or soundless tapping on a keyboard. He literally pounds out his words in the form of dashes on tiny scraps of used paper, using very short and worn-down pencil nubs to nail down *le mot juste.* These efforts are accompanied by grunts, growls, and other vocal expressions. He is literally fighting a battle at such times. The exhausting physical labor involved makes any other form of exercise or workout unnecessary for him.

Bearing the battle scars of these abuses is a faithful thirty-year-old writing desk that came with the apartment. Countless gashes and gouges mark its surface. When finally satisfied with the output for the day, he transcribes by hand the marks on the scraps onto a clean sheet of paper with an old-fashioned fountain pen filled with black ink. Frequent suggestions from well-meaning friends that his laborious method of setting down words on paper could be made so much easier by the use of a computer have so far fallen on deaf ears. Nor does he need a scenic, out-of-the-way place to work in, as some people also believe. He is happiest writing in a tiny cell of a room—without a view. Measuring four feet by seven feet, it is actually one end of an enclosed balcony, with my exercise bike sharing the limited space. During the two hours of intense concentration, he is oblivious to everything and everyone around him.

In the early days, the manuscript pages were placed in a large metal biscuit box and kept in a wooden cabinet. Fortunately, the box was metal; we discovered later that termites had eaten up almost everything in that same cabinet—documents, diplomas, and even our marriage certificate. Not long afterward, the manuscripts were donated to the Taida library. As for the manuscripts of his work in progress, these are kept in a safe-deposit box at a bank. With the most important task of the day finished, it is time to unwind. What follows is one of the most enjoyable times of the day. We go out to have dinner. This may sound much fancier than it is. We usually go to one of the places catering to students near Taida that serve very simple fare. Since this is the only meal we have together, we use the time to talk over the events of the day or discuss more pressing matters that require attention. After dinner, further relaxation is achieved by carrying out what has become a favorite pastime: browsing through one or two bookstores in the neighborhood. There are at present around ten such locations to choose from, and by alternating among them enough interest can be sustained. Finally, we take a twenty-minute walk through the campus and reach home around ten o'clock each evening.

For most people, retirement means the freedom to take up new activities. They indulge in pleasures and hobbies that have been denied them during their working years. For Wenxing, however, these last four years have meant a further streamlining of his already simple life. Whatever hobbies he used to love in earlier times—movies, photography, exhibitions, performances, concerts, travel—he has all but given up in recent years. I remember during some of the foreign film festivals held in Taipei during the 1980s we would average three different movies in an afternoon and evening. Now it has been so long since we have seen one that I cannot even recall the title of the last movie we saw in a theater. For a time he would listen to music at home or watch a movie on the VCR in an effort to save time, but now has abandoned even these pastimes. Our collection of tapes and CDs, numbering well over 1,000, has been handed over to the Taida library.

His one remaining interest is reading, which he does at odd times throughout the day but mostly at night when the surroundings are quiet.

Besides Western literary works, his favorite subjects include classical Chinese poetry and prose, philosophy, and religion. But he loves Chinese calligraphy and seal carving best. He sees both of these as the topmost art forms that not only are unique to Chinese culture, but constitute its most significant contribution to the world.

He reads as he writes—very slowly. To appreciate the text as fully as possible, he spends large amounts of time consulting the dictionary and other reference works, especially in the case of classical Chinese poetry.

Frugal Habits

Simplicity is the keynote of daily living. He likes ordinary foods, such as plain white rice, bananas, and watermelon, all local products of Taiwan. He prefers fish to red meat, even those varieties with tiny bones. On rare social occasions he likes to drink Taiwan beer, a little brandy, or white wine. He finds putting together an outfit an irksome and time-consuming task, and would much rather wear a daily uniform to save time and bother. Despite his indifference to his own attire, however, he likes to watch other people dressed in stylish clothes. Whenever we come across window displays of the designer brands, whether of clothes or jewelry, he is the one who stops and marvels at the creations. I remember on our first trip to Singapore in 2005 we walked up and down the famed Orchard Road three times in the sweltering heat so he could study the window displays.

Neither of us drives, a car being too much trouble to maintain, so taxis are the preferred mode of travel for longer distances. Because he eats, works, and sleeps at odd hours, I have worked out ways to fit housekeeping chores around his reading and writing schedules. Since we keep different routines we often communicate by leaving each other handwritten notes. I often get up in the morning to find scraps of paper bearing questions and instructions on the kitchen table. Over the decades these writings, if saved, would have made a considerable volume.

As a further means to save time, he has also cut back social activities to a minimum—our neighbors so rarely see him that some of them can be forgiven for believing he lives abroad. He does not use e-mail or the cell phone and very rarely talks on the phone. But he is by no means completely averse to electronic advances; he is pretty skilled in the use of the copy and fax machines.

Needless to say, he does not watch TV, and he barely scans the headlines of the local daily newspapers. However, he maintains a keen interest in world events and keeps up by reading the major newsmagazines such as *Time* and *Newsweek* in detail. As a result, he is deeply concerned about the geopolitical changes around the globe and worries over the political and economic ramifications of the current financial crisis. He is particularly disturbed by the destructive effects of global warming. We may perhaps selfishly console ourselves by thinking that the two of us will be spared the final catastrophes to be brought about by climate change decades down the line. But I happen to be a believer in reincarnation and certainly hope to come back someday. So there is no guarantee that we can ever escape the consequences of ecological meltdown.

While most other people cut down on luxuries, we have gone one step further and often cut down on necessities as well. Since long before the current mantra of saving the planet, we have been practicing the three R's—reduce, reuse, and recycle—in our household. Paper, bags, and containers are saved and reused. Our living room set dates back forty years and has been reupholstered twice. We still use an electric fan that is at least fifty years old. Nothing gets thrown away until it is worn out or threadbare. We simply consume as little as possible. If consumption is the key to the economic well-being of a nation, I am afraid we have contributed very little to the economic boom of Taiwan over the past decades and even less to help its recovery from the present slump.

Personality Contrasts

Temperamentally, Wenxing and I seem to be very different, and we have noticed that as we grow older some of the personality differences have become even more pronounced. I have always been impatient and act on impulse; he's methodical and deliberate. For example, before an appointment, no matter how minor, he sets out a schedule beforehand to prepare for the event—down to the precise time for every single task. I leap before I look; he looks and does not leap. Many a time he has come to my rescue after I have gotten into trouble after rushing headlong into a sticky situation. I remember when we were in the States I once took a call from a telemarketer and ended up committing myself to a lifetime of magazine subscriptions. I was so mortified I was practically ready to commit suicide. Luckily Wenxing was able to put an end to my bondage with a single phone call.

I am apt to take people and things at face value and seldom question anyone's motivations. Wenxing is much more cautious when it comes to judging people and events. In 1981 we were on a trip to south Asia and got stuck in a popular religious and tourist site. Despite my repeated efforts at the travel agent, I was unable to get us plane tickets out of the city. Every single seat, it seemed, had been taken, and it looked as if we were going to miss our connecting flight to return to Taipei. Finally Wenxing went to see the travel agent, asked him to do his best to get us tickets while handing over to him a fee for his troubles. (He placed the money in a travel brochure.) The agent nodded, and we were able to leave the city the next day. As we took off, I noticed there were empty seats on the plane, while several travelers, all Westerners, sat in the airport, waiting for vacancies.

Wenxing's more reflective character has made him a much keener observer than I am, especially when it comes to people's faces and minor details of sight and sound. But he can be quite absent-minded as well. He is no good with dates: he probably will not be able to tell you what day, month, or even year it is. He often forgets his own phone number, not to mention his keys. The latter once led to his being locked out of the apartment in the middle of the night for six hours. During the period he was helping with the household chores by taking out the trash every night. Unfortunately, this one time he left the chore until midnight and by the time he discovered he could not get back in I was fast asleep and oblivious to the ringing of the doorbell. There was nothing for him to do but wait outside for the morning. I, in the meantime, had no idea he was not home. I was awakened around seven o'clock by what I thought were loud and persistent bird calls. It was quite a few minutes before I realized they were frantic peals of the doorbell.

Our views and opinions on certain issues can also be widely divergent, so much so that we are often not even on the same chapter, let alone the same page. On the importance of exercise and diet, for example, he is convinced that each of us is allotted a finite number of heartbeats throughout our lifetime; therefore strenuous exercises such as jogging and aerobics only speed up the pulse and bring on a premature end. Look at the giant sea turtles, he says; they live to 150 years or more, not by any rigorous workouts but by moving so very slowly. He also believes that whatever food the appetite craves at the moment is good for the body. Those cravings often involve sweets and other junk foods. In fact, we cannot even agree on what tastes good and what does not. He likes cooked rice to be soft and sticky, while I prefer it more al dente. Over the years we have generally come to respect the other's views and agree to disagree. As for rice, I now cook two types: one of sticky white grain and the other of the tougher multigrain variety.

One element that has worked in our favor, it seems, is the difference in our ages. The six-and-a-half-year gap has perhaps made us more tolerant with each other. He treats me like a younger sister and is therefore less critical, more indulgent and forgiving. I look up to him as an older, wiser brother, and as a result tend to defer more to his decisions. The fact that he sometimes seems a little patronizing can be a little off-putting, but the flip side is that he tends to be more patient and considerate with my shortcomings. Many a big argument can thus be avoided, and even when a fight does take place it is apt to blow over soon.

People familiar with astrology have described Wenxing as a typical Scorpio, especially in his single-minded commitment to and perseverance in his goals. The Scorpio, I understand, is one of the water signs, and since I am a Pisces, I like to think we get along like fish and water.

Conclusion

A relationship that works, it has been said, is like a good espionage operation in that it is one in which nothing unusual ever happens and is never the basis of a good story. An uneventful life would be an apt expression to characterize our partnership. It is one that has lasted for forty years, and hopefully will go on for four more decades. That, I realize, is highly improbable, but the very uncertainty is a reminder that every moment is to be cherished. "Carpe diem," as the saying goes; it is the present moment that counts. And so every single blessing should be counted as well.

14 Wang Wenxing on Wang Wenxing

Te-hsing Shan
Academia Sinica

S: When did you make up your mind to be a writer?

W: It was quite early. I decided to be a writer when I was in junior high school. I admired those who could write well and thought that I might follow suit.

S: You are an established writer now. Is there any difference between your present situation and what you expected?

W: The main difference is the quantity of my works. In my adolescent days, I thought I could finish a book within three years. I didn't expect my writing to be so slow. This is the greatest difference.

S: When did you finish your first work?

W: I finished my first short story when I was a sophomore in high school.

S: And your first poem?

W: About the same time.

S: Did you imitate any native or foreign poets when you wrote poems?

W: No, I didn't. This annoyed me a great deal. I quit writing poems because I couldn't find a definite form to follow, or a model to imitate. When it came to English poetry, I must admit that the collections of English poetry I could read or understand were very few, and the models for me to follow were even fewer.

S: You profited more from your reading of fiction?

W: That's right, because fiction is easier for me to understand and to learn. That's why I went on with my story-writing.

S: What kind of foreign story writers influenced you the most?

W: Short-story writers.

S: Could you be more specific about the influence certain short-story writers, such as Chekhov and Maupassant, had on you?

W: I think it's easier for me to analyze Maupassant's influence, because he taught me a lot about observing people, things, and landscapes, and he also taught me how to handle a story. As for Chekhov, his influence was more vague, probably in the realm of atmosphere. Of course, besides atmosphere, his analysis of human nature is outstanding, so he taught me much about human psychology.

S: So far as your personality and background are concerned, which of the two writers do you feel closer to?

W: That's hard to say. What I mean is, up to now I like them both, and I can't tell which one I like better.

S: You wrote a short story and won a prize when you were a junior in high school. What was the story about?

W: It was about a civil servant who wrote at night to earn money. He didn't write a single word from evening till daybreak. I described his thoughts and how he lay on the desk and had a dream. There was no story line ... just his feelings, his psychological movements in one night.

S: Did you use the stream-of-consciousness technique? Or not until in "Yige gongwuyuan de jiehun" 一個公務員的結婚 (The wedding of a civil servant)?

W: I think I wrote about the mental activities of the character. I don't know whether it could be regarded as stream-of-consciousness or not. Obviously, I didn't intend to use stream-of-consciousness. Even if it appeared to be so, it was an imitation of nineteenth-century literary technique. The greatest influence was Chekhov. This story was very Chekhovian. I remember now, it was influenced by Chekhov.

S: When did you formally begin your career as a creative writer?

W: After I entered college. I didn't like college education. To me, college was only a temporary resting place. I was always interested in writing.

S: Who were your favorite writers when you were in the Department of Foreign Languages and Literatures at National Taiwan University?

W: I spent a lot of time reading Dostoevsky, Tolstoy, Kafka, Camus, Mann, and Hemingway.

S: What were Tolstoy's and Dostoevsky's attractions for you?

W: Tolstoy attracted me in the same way Maupassant did. Dostoevsky's attraction was in his psychological portrayals. In comparison with that of Maupassant, Dostoevsky's was more fearful, more abstract, more representative. Tolstoy placed his emphasis on universality, or rather, on general psychology, while Dostoevsky tended toward something abstract and representative.

S: And your liking for Hemingway?

W: It was later. That was a great discovery, because not only did his style attract me, but he was also the only story writer who could treat a short story as rigidly as a prose poem. This attracted me—how to make a story highly refined.

S: Mann and Beckett were much later?

W: I began reading Mann when I was a senior at National Taiwan University, and I didn't read Beckett until I began my teaching career.

S: Did your enjoyment of these different writers reflect the growth of your thought? Or did you just come to notice some writers who were unfamiliar to you?

W: I think it had to do with growth. Take Hemingway, for example. I read him very early. But that doesn't mean that as a freshman one can enjoy reading Hemingway. The case is the same with Beckett. If you read him too early you won't understand him. Camus is also the same. When I was a college student, I read his *The Stranger* several times, but I couldn't say that I understood him. Twenty years later— I picked the book up last year and reread it. I began to understand its real meaning for the very first time. And it was in my fifth reading that I truly understood what this book is telling me. All my previous readings were misreadings. That is, you understand the surface meaning of each sentence, but you can't figure out the deep meaning or the merit of each sentence. As a matter of fact, all books are the same. If you understand them correctly, you'll understand the meaning of each sentence, and you'll discover that not a single sentence is wasted. If you don't get this impression when you are reading a book, it means that you don't understand it thoroughly.

S: While writing "The Wedding of a Civil Servant," did you imitate any work? Or did you figure out that method all by yourself?

W: I believe there was a lot of Chekhov in it.

S: In his "Haircut," Ring Lardner chose to tell the whole story by the barber. That's very similar to the method you used in "The Wedding of a Civil Servant."

W: I believe when I wrote that story, I had already read "Haircut."

S: But did not imitate it intentionally?

W: No, I didn't.

S: "The Wedding of a Civil Servant" was published in the February 1959 issue of *Wenxue zazhi* 文學雜誌 (Literary review), when you were a twenty-year-old sophomore; "Muqin" 母親 (Mother) was published in *Xiandai wenxue* 現代文學 (Modern literature) in May 1960; "Da feng" 大風 (Strong wind) was also published in *Modern Literature* in November 1961. Your stream-of-consciousness short stories seem to be concentrated in a short period of time. Is there any special significance to that?

W: I was then interested in interior monologue and intended to imitate it. I didn't know much about stream-of-consciousness then. I'm afraid that I didn't conspicuously or intentionally imitate stream-of-consciousness. Interior monologue as a literary technique could be found in many of the stories of the nineteenth and early twentieth centuries.

S: How and when did you get in touch with stream-of-consciousness. What creative and critical works did you read?

W: I don't think I was using the stream-of-consciousness technique when I was writing stories, for I didn't study it intentionally, and I didn't adopt it intentionally. I read the stream-of-consciousness works very late—after I left college. To be frank with you, I learned very little from the masters of stream-of-consciousness, such as Faulkner, Joyce, and Woolf. If I did understand stream-of-consciousness, it came from the small amount of stream-of-consciousness passages in the works of other writers. I guess it's not so much interior monologue as it is first-person narration. It's not necessarily confined to the nineteenth-century European writers. There might be some traces of American writers, such as Mark Twain and J.D. Salinger—the author of *The Catcher in the Rye*, a novel I enjoyed reading when I was young.

S: In his *The Psychological Novel*, Leon Edel mentioned that one of the characteristics of the twentieth-century novel is the inward turning.

W: That's very correct. Novelists do not necessarily use the stream-of-consciousness technique. But so far as subject matter and content are concerned, the twentieth-century novel does turn in this direction.

S: When people talk about the stream-of-consciousness novel, they often separate physical time from psychological time.

W: Yes, they think that psychological time cannot be measured by the clock.

S: Why did you experiment with this technique?

W: Because this technique was strange to me, and I wanted to practice it, to master it. People are curious about strange things. For instance, in that period I didn't try my hand at satire. Then I slowly felt that I should try it, practice it, so later I turned to satire.

S: When did that occur?

W: Quite late—I suppose it began with *Bei hai de ren* 背海的人 (Backed against the sea).

S: You didn't turn to satire simply for the sake of curiosity or practice, did you?

W: No, I didn't. But those were some of the reasons, and because I never tried it before, I was more enthusiastic. Before I decided to write that novel, I had three or four choices in front of me. It's quite possible that I might have written another, different novel. But I chose *Backed Against the Sea*. One of the strongest reasons was that I wanted to write a comic novel, a satirical novel.

S: The editor's notes in the second issue of *Modern Literature* mentioned that "Mother" symbolized the new generation's revolt against the old. "The neurotic mother stands for the shaky and precarious old traditions, old morality." Who wrote these remarks? Did you agree with him?

W: I wrote them myself. Perhaps they were too acute. The original intention of that story might have been so. When we founded that magazine, we wanted to express our ideas about society and morality, in addition to our views on literature. So the creative section was the place for us to express our views on literature, and the preface or the editor's notes became our views about society and culture. *Modern Literature* followed these two directions. My remarks about "Mother" might have been too socially and culturally oriented. In fact, the story contained this kind of consciousness, but after that exaggeration, it might have become a bit too much.

S: The word *montage* appeared in one of the notes of a poem published in the same issue. What are your views on montage?

W: I was impressed by this technique and appreciated it very much, because it's very free and provides a very wide range of creative writing. So I probably would not reject this technique. Maybe I liked this method.

S: So you used it in "Mother"?

W: You might say that. Then the story must have been influenced by this technique.

S: This technique appears many times in your later works.

W: Yes, I preferred to use some modern cutting techniques in my stories. They were, of course, influenced by the cinema. Perhaps they were also influenced by some new novels.

S: Were you thinking of Browning's dramatic monologue when you wrote "Strong Wind"?

W: I had not read his "My Last Duchess" then. I read it later. I think the greatest influence on "Strong Wind" came from Hemingway. What's more, I wanted to experiment with the vernacular. I was then groping for the right language style for myself among numerous possibilities. I adopted the real vernacular only in "Strong Wind." When someone said that it was my only work that was fluent, I gave up vernacular because I didn't think that only that kind of language was fluent.

S: How did Hemingway influence you?

W: Mostly in tone. Although the style was very much vernacularized, the tone was still an imitation of Hemingway. I believe I was influenced by *The Old Man and the Sea*, the novel I was reading then.

S: Including the conflict between man and nature?

W: So it resembles *The Old Man and the Sea* very much—the struggle with nature, the image of a hero.

S: In your preface to *Fifteen Stories*, you mentioned that "Mother" and "Caoyuan di shengxia" 草原底盛夏 (Midsummer on the prairie) were written as freely as you pleased. Do you think these two stories express you most?

W: I guess that only in these two stories did I not want to adjust to others. When they were published, many said that they didn't know what I was writing about. I doubted myself and began to grope for another way. I still cared then about what others might think. Actually, my purpose now is to write in the style of "Midsummer on the Prairie."

S: Were these two stories influenced by the new novel or anti-novel?

W: Probably, probably. But I had read few new novels, or anti-novels. Of course, you might read just one story and be greatly influenced by it. After all, my personal inclination and interest obviously tend toward this direction.

S: What's your definition of *fluency*? It seems that your definition is somewhat different from that of others.

W: Maybe starting from "Midsummer on the Prairie" or "Mother," my definition of *fluency* is personal. I believe that the language of poetry is different from that of prose and that poetized language can be transplanted to fiction.

S: You have respectively compared language to music and pictures. Would you please elaborate?

W: When I am writing, I consider the picture first. Then I believe that if my music is wrong, the picture will be greatly damaged. I aim at the combination of sound and sense—sense is the picture, sound is the music.

S: Many people think that your language is influenced by Joyce. What do you think?

W: If there is any affinity, it is only because both of us are very free. But I dare say that this is the only similarity between us. So far as other aspects are concerned, we are totally different. Why? Because when I was writing *Jia bian* 家變 (Family catastrophe), I hadn't read his *Ulysses*, and when I began writing *Backed Against the Sea*, I finished reading *Ulysses*, but I learned nothing. And I haven't read even one page of *Finnegan's Wake.*

S: What's the difference between the language of *Family Catastrophe* and that of *Backed Against the Sea?*

W: There is none. The language of these two books is continuous.

S: The latter is freer?

W: Yes.

S: So the difference is only a matter of degree, rather than a matter of kind?

W: You might say that.

S: In the symposium on *Family Catastrophe* on May 19, 1973, you said that the language of this novel was very musical, and even recited some passages to prove it. What about the language of *Backed Against the Sea?*

W: Still the same direction, still the same purpose, still the same ideal.

S: People have gradually come to accept your language in *Family Catastrophe*. What do you think about that?

W: Many people nowadays seem to be used to the language of that novel. But I personally still have one goal, and that is, I also hope to meet my audience halfway without sacrificing my artistic ends. I believe it can be achieved, but it's very difficult. My manipulation of language has to be much, much better than it is now.

S: Who, in your opinion, has achieved this goal?

W: Eh, of course, I'm always thinking of Hemingway, that is, Hemingway at his best. But I don't know French, so it is a castle in the air—I believe Flaubert can do that, but I cannot prove it.

S: To be precise on the one hand, and …

W: To be popular on the other. Neither is sacrificed; both ends meet. I am gradually beginning to feel that Virginia Woolf comes closer to that. Sometimes I wonder whether I demand too little of Hemingway, whether he is precise enough. I mean, if he had sacrificed popularity, would he have been more precise?

S: Do you draw your characters from real life?

W: Ah, fifty percent at least.

S: Is it a combination of the different attributes of different persons?

W: Right. I can't write a character before I have a clear picture of him. He has to be very clear, very clear—his birth, personality, background, education—I have to be pretty sure before I write even a minor character.

S: You have to know the ins and outs of a character.

W: Yes. It was well said by Ibsen. He said that he could tell reporters about a character—his age, his height, his weight, his parents, and so on—even if he just made a brief appearance and said only a few words in the play. In other words, he knew his character thoroughly before he wrote about him.

S: It seems to me very similar to Hemingway's iceberg theory. He once mentioned that he could have included the whole fishing village in his *The Old Man and the Sea*, yet he concentrated on one character instead.

W: Originally *The Old Man and the Sea* was probably longer than 200,000 words, then it was reduced to 30,000 words or so. Much had been deleted. Hemingway's iceberg theory is very correct, very correct. Instead of telling the whole story, we like to imply, to suggest. Naturally, some of the preparations are wasted. For instance, the name of the protagonist of *Backed Against the Sea* is Qi Bizhong 齊必忠. Yet the name never appears in the first volume of the novel and will never appear in the second volume.

S: When you wrote your novella "Longtian lou" 龍天樓 (Dragon inn), did you consciously think of the structure of *The Decameron* or *The Canterbury Tales*?

W: A lot of novels and plays have been written in that way and it has become an independent genre. I knew this kind of structure and I consciously adopted it.

S: You strive for precision. And in your postscript to "Dragon Inn," you described it as a symbolic work. What's your opinion on the relationship between realism and symbolism?

W: I didn't mean which one is better. I lean toward symbolic realism. Although I admire Flaubert and Maupassant, yet to realism I would add some symbolism, which they didn't emphasize. *Backed Against the Sea* is the most symbolic among all my works.

S: Compared with your earlier prefaces and postscripts, your later prefaces had a lot of humor. Why did that come about?

W: I think it was a change. I didn't possess a knowledge of comic literature right from the beginning. It was a gradual absorption.

S: A gradual absorption? When did it start? Was it the result of your reading or of personal experience?

W: I began writing about it in *Backed Against the Sea.* But I think my absorption began long before that. I learned a little about comic literature in my early reading of Russian stories and French stories. But my earnest absorption could be said to have begun with Huxley and Beckett.

S: Which of their works impressed you most?

W: Beckett's *Molloy* and Huxley's *Brave New World.*

S: How did they affect you?

W: Through Beckett, I came to realize that comedy could also be very serious; I came to realize the existence of so-called serious comedy. Huxley's comedy is full of life, full of force. I admire it very much.

S: "Strong Wind" and *Backed Against the Sea* are both based on stream-of-consciousness. There is a lapse of twenty years between them. Have you gained any new insight into this technique?

W: No. I read some real stream-of-consciousness stories, but learned nothing.

S: When *Backed Against the Sea* first appeared in *Zhongwai wenxue* 中外文學 (Chung-wai literary monthly), the editor classified it as an anti-novel. What do you think about this classification?

W: It could be right, that is to say, if you set it against the conventional form, it is. But I guess that according to the Western standard, this form has already become part of the convention.

S: You mentioned that you wrote about crises. What are the crises in *Backed Against the Sea?*

W: *Backed Against the Sea* deals with more crises than *Family Catastrophe.* The latter is an in-depth study of one crisis; the former is the presentation of many crises. Its analysis is not so detailed as that of *Family Catastrophe,* but its scope is broader.

S: So you adopted the stream-of-consciousness technique to flow with the narrator's consciousness in order to touch upon different aspects?

W: They are related. The technique fits the content.

S: In his diary, the protagonist of *Family Catastrophe* criticized the family as the most inhuman and unreasonable institution of all. Some people think that this lengthy criticism is a technical defect.

W: I thought about that when I wrote it. But I decided to choose this incongruity, for I felt that only by inserting such an incongruous passage could the idea of this book be fully expressed. I still hold this opinion today. It's the only essay passage in the novel. This was quite a common method in the eighteenth and nineteenth centuries and has been regarded as immature, but I would rather adopt it. What's more, I made some alterations. In the essay passages of the eighteenth- and nineteenth-century novels, the novelists freely expressed their opinions. In *Family Catastrophe,* this essay passage was fictionalized. It's the expression of the character's idea, not mine. It makes all the difference.

S: What titles would you adopt, if you were asked to give English titles to *Family Catastrophe* and *Backed Against the Sea?*

W: I thought about the first one and didn't come up with any. I figured out a name for the second one, but it's not very good, it's too long, and I have no authorized titles.

S: What is the English title for the second novel?

W: "The Man with His Back to the Sea." Although it's too long, it's the original Chinese meaning.

S: What about the relationship between man and nature in it?

W: Throughout the work, the emphasis is on the placing of a tiny man before an indifferent natural backdrop. The setting is consistently present.

S: What about the title "The Man Against the Sea?"

W: "Against?" That may be ambiguous. Do you mean he is "spiritually against" or something else?

S: Because when I was reading the novel, I noticed that in addition to the opposition between man and nature, "fish" and "fish-catching" were mentioned many times. It seems to me that there is still some hope in this almost despairing situation ...

W: Yes, yes.

S: ... so if we use "against," it might mean both "fight against" and "lean against."

W: Of course the word *against* has its ambiguity. But the Chinese meaning avoids this ambiguity. It speaks to his physical position without emphasizing his spiritual position. It's just like the cover design of the book—a man with his back to the sea.

S: The narrator is a one-eyed fortune-teller. Is there any connection with Tiresias?

W: There's a conspicuous connection.

S: Did you have Pope in mind when the narrator uttered, "Contradiction! Contradiction! I am a big big big big and big contradiction!—I AM 'CONTRADICTION.'"

W: No. I didn't pinpoint Pope, though I knew the same idea had been expressed by people before, including Pope.

S: Did you intend to treat it as a low comedy? In some places, it seems to me to come very close to farce even; for example, the parts dealing with the office and the red-light district.

W: Er, intentionally, intentionally. It is loud farce or bawdy farce. What is important is the comic effect. If you don't read it as a comedy, you'll miss everything. Basically, this is a burlesque. Of course, this technique has never been used in Chinese fiction before, but it is very common in European fiction.

S: And your description of the members of the office reminds me of Mann's *The Magic Mountain*.

W: You are right. I was influenced by *The Magic Mountain.* That section was modeled on it; it was *The Magic Mountain* in miniature.

S: But in the form of low comedy?

W: Possibly. Of course, the constituent members are different. In *The Magic Mountain,* it is the assemblage of the upper class—at least, the middle class and above. Here in this section I want to collect the garbage of the whole of China. It's a garbage can.

S: In an interview, you said that while you were planning this novel, you were influenced by many Western novelists, among them Camus, Conrad, Dostoevsky, Kafka, Bellow, and, especially, Hemingway. Are these influences general or specific?

W: They might be general. Of course, that interview missed some, such as Beckett, and the one you mentioned earlier, Mann.

S: You have only finished the first volume of *Backed Against the Sea.* How about the second one? Still the same narrator? Still after drinking?

W: It's another night—still the same person, still after drinking, so the form is parallel.

S: What about the length?

W: Also parallel.

S: How much have you finished?

W: One-fourth—slow, very slow—slower than the first volume.

S: Then it will probably take six more years.

W: At least. When I finish writing the whole novel, I will be nearly fifty.

S: What do you think about your role as a writer?

W: I just want to emphasize once more that my role as a writer is very insignificant. For the past ten years, I have felt more and more keenly my insignificance when compared with other major writers. I just have to think of Henry James, his rich and excellent production, to know at once how insignificant I am.

S: But his innovation in language can't match yours.

W: How can you say that? I think he is a genius. It's beyond my ability to probe into the profundity of later James. I'm not even qualified to understand him. As for early James, I think he almost reaches the ideal I am trying to achieve—to be both precise and popular. Every

time I open one of his books, any single sentence is enough to fasci-
nate me. I often think that I might spend hours and hours to produce
such a sentence, yet he seems to write it without effort.

S: You mentioned earlier that Hemingway is also precise and popular.

W: Yes. But Hemingway's output is smaller. And you can see that
Hemingway is racking his brains when he is writing, while to James,
it's as easy as breathing.

S: And their styles are very different.

W: They belong to different directions. You can't assert that James's
style is inferior to Hemingway's. No. You can't say that. Graham
Greene has summed it up fairly. He thinks that in the history of
English literature, Thomas Browne's style is the best. But when it
comes to modern English writers, he mentions only two—one is
Henry James, the other is Walter de la Mare. I also admire de la
Mare very, very much, but I know that he still can be matched, because his production is not so high and his carefulness can be
learned. James's naturalness cannot be learned. I mention James
simply because he is far beyond my reach. There are still many,
many good writers I can't catch up with. This has been my growing
conviction over the past ten years.

                                                                (1983)

II Appendices

A. OUTLINES OF THE NOVELS

15 Tentative Outline of Family Catastrophe

Shu-ning Sciban
University of Calgary

FAMILY CATASTROPHE DESCRIBES the protagonist Fan Ye's gradually deteriorating relationship with his parents, particularly with his father.[1] The story, divided into hundreds of sections, starts from the present and then moves on with both present and past plot lines intermingled. The author marks sections of the present plot line with letters of the Latin alphabet and sections of the past plot line with Arabic numerals.

Part One

Section A: The father leaves home. (p. 1)
Section B: Fan Ye and his mother discover the father's disappearance. In the late evening, Fan Ye dreams of his father's return. His

---

1. Wang Wenxing's novels possess rather complicated structures; anachrony and fragmentation are their obvious characteristics. To give brief, accurate summaries of the stories is not an easy task. To preserve their structural characteristics, I adapt Shan Dexing's approach, which is to summarize individual events of the stories and present those events in the original order. In this appendix, I construct the outline of *Family Catastrophe*. The page numbers in this outline refer to Wang Wenxing's *Jia bian* 家變 (Family catastrophe) (Taipei: Hongfan shudian, 2006).

285

father, in the dream, looks as young as when Fan Ye was a boy. Next morning he goes out to look for his father; failing to locate him in the neighborhood, Fan Ye phones his second older brother, Fan Lunyuan, and also reports the missing man to the police. (pp. 2–18)

Section C: Fan Ye puts an advertisement on the newspaper and gets ready to travel to the southern part of the island to look for his father. (pp. 1–20)

Section 1: A father takes a child named Mao Mao (Fan Ye's baby name) for a stroll on the street. (p. 20)

Section 2: Mao Mao observes the scene outside a window on a windy day. (p. 21)

Section 3: Mao Mao notices the stained glass in his mother's bedroom. (p. 21)

Section 4: Mao Mao's parents help him memorize his name, age, address, and the parents' names. (pp. 21–23)

Section 5: Mao Mao sees a monster outside the second-floor window, similar to a cow, moving up to the third floor. (p. 23)

Section 6: Mao Mao carefully examines the designs on a teapot and his mother's make-up box. (pp. 23–24)

Section 7: Mao Mao is ill. (pp. 24–27)

Section 8: Mao Mao's mother prohibits him from playing with other neighborhood children because of her family's bureaucratic background. (p. 27)

Section 9: Mao Mao's parents notice that he has grown taller, and sigh that few sons look after their parents after growing up. (pp. 27–29)

Section 10: Mao Mao notices his father has many black moles and his mother has red moles; he himself has both. (p. 29)

Section 11: A description of the father's habit of washing his face with very hot water after a meal. (p. 29)

Section 12: The father helps Mao Mao cut his nails. (p. 30)

Section 13: Mao Mao notices that the nails on his father's baby fingers are thin and long. (p. 30)

Section 14: Mao Mao discovers that after sitting too long, his lower legs become numb. (p. 30)

Section 15: Mao Mao's sister is born. He changes from sharing a bed with his mother to sharing with his father. (pp. 30–31)

Section 16: Mao Mao feels very safe and comfortable sleeping next to his father. (p. 31)

Section 17: Mao Mao's sister dies of hepatitis. (p. 31)

Section 18: Mao Mao's first day of school. (pp. 31–35)

Section D: This is the fourth day of Fan Ye's journey. He arrives at Taizhong. (p. 36)

Section 19: A day at school. Mao Mao is still not used to school life. He often thinks about his parents and is afraid his home will burn down or disappear while he is away. (pp. 36–38)

Section 20: Mao Mao shows particular interest in some common sayings his mother uses. (pp. 38–39)

Section 21: Mao Mao is amused by a female tofu seller's wares every morning. (p. 39)

Section 22: A typhoon day. (pp. 39–40)

Section 23: Mao Mao's parents are pleased with his schoolwork. (p. 40)

Section 24: Mao Mao receives fourth prize for academic excellence in his class. (p. 41)

Section 25: Mao Mao watches a neighbor's funeral through his window and discusses death with his mother. Mao Mao then begins to worry about his parents' death and what would happen to him afterward. (pp. 41–44)

Section E: Fan Ye is walking under the boiling sun after a visit to a church; his search remains fruitless. (pp. 44–45)

Section 26: Mao Mao's second older brother comes home. The mother tells Mao Mao that he is her only child; the mother of his two older half-brothers is dead. The eldest brother is living at a boarding school far away. (p. 45)

Section 27: Mao Mao has a coughing episode but he enjoys listening to the sound and eating malt sugar. (p. 46)

Section 28: After the winter holidays, Mao Mao does not return to school because of his family's financial difficulties. (pp. 46–47)

Section 29: The mother regrets her limited education and blames the father for the family's poverty. (pp. 47–49)

Section 30: The Fans, except the eldest brother, are on a ship from Xiamen, Fujian, to Taiwan. (p. 49)

Section 31: The family moves into a house by the seashore. Both the father and the second brother have government jobs. (p. 49)

Section 32: The father enjoys reciting classical poetry, the melancholy cadence of which much appeals to Mao Mao. (p. 50)

Section 33: Mao Mao finds that his father's drawer is very tidy. (p. 50)

Section 34: Mao Mao finds an old book titled *Correspondence of Qiushui Study*. (p. 50)

Section 35: Mao Mao finds an index for telegraphic codes. (p. 51)

Section 36: Mao Mao thinks his father is very tall. (p. 51)

Section 37: The father's smile makes Mao Mao feel warm. (p. 51)

Section 38: The mother teaches Mao Mao a mysterious way to stop hiccups, and he superstitiously thinks that putting a white handkerchief on one's head is unlucky. (p. 52)

Section 39: The mother uses ancient numerical signs to do her bookkeeping. (p. 52)

Section 40: Mao Mao has a bath with his father and is amazed at the fairness of his father's complexion and the strength of his muscles. The father tells Mao Mao he had studied in France. (pp. 53–55)

Section 41: Mao Mao notices the knick-knacks his mother collected. (p. 55)

Section 42: Mao Mao notices his father frequently uses one obscene expression. (p. 55)

Section 43: Mao Mao learns some military songs. (pp. 55–56)

Section 44: The father comes home late, which makes Mao Mao terribly worried for him. (pp. 56–57)

Section F: Fan Ye is on a southbound train and is attracted to an old man. (p. 57)

Section 45: The father has returned home late at night on several occasions. After fights with the mother, the father eventually comes home right after work. (p. 58)

Section 46: The mother also swears. (p. 58)

Section 47: The family is facing further financial difficulty. (pp. 58–59)

Section 48: Mao Mao is beaten by his father for mimicking his mother's speech. He feels like killing his father and thinks of several possible ways to get revenge, including sending him away in his old age. (pp. 60–63)

Section 49: Mao Mao hates his own face mainly because he finds he has inherited unattractive features from both his parents. (pp. 63–64)

Section 50: He often asks his father to tell him a story, but his father can never find one. (p. 64)

Section 51: The father goes on a business trip for six days and comes home with presents for everyone. (pp. 64–68)

Section G: Fan Ye is in Tainan. He visits a temple to look for his father. (pp. 68–70)

Section 52: The father finds a job in Taipei, so the family moves to the city. (p. 70)

Section 53: A description of their new residence. (pp. 70–71)

Section 54: A description of the river behind the house. (pp. 71–72)

Section 55: Mao Mao goes to school again. (p. 72)

Section 56: Mao Mao is unhappy with his mother's Ping-Pong skill and is afraid of a corner of the house where his mother has placed a sheet of magic figures. (pp. 72–73)

Section 57: Mao Mao, eight years old now, watches an airplane fly over. (p. 73)

Section 58: The second brother borrows a camera from a friend and is eager to take pictures for the whole family. The mother's indifference disappoints him. (pp. 73–78)

Section 59: Mao Mao measures his height once a week. (p. 78)

Section 60: Mao Mao finds it is comfortable to sleep on a shelf in a closet. (pp. 78–79)

Section 61: Mao Mao often sits idly after he gets up in the morning. (p. 79)

Section 62: There are many bottles in the kitchen. (pp. 79–80)

Section 63: A description of a leisure summer mood Mao Mao sensed. (p. 80)

Section 64: An autumn scene in the yard. (p. 80)

Section 65: Winter comes. Mao Mao wishes the snow would fall. (pp. 80–81)

Section 66: A spring scene in the yard. (p. 81)

Section 67: The second brother takes Mao Mao to a play. (pp. 82–90)

Section 68: A black train goes by. (p. 91)

Section 69: Before the rain comes, Mao Mao often hears bogu birds that sound as if they are crying. (p. 91)

Section 70: The mother leaves out some fruit every day for Mao Mao when he returns from school. (pp. 91–92)

Section 71: Mao Mao blows soap bubbles for more than an hour, and is fascinated by them. (pp. 92–93)

Section 72: A list of Mao Mao's favorite dishes. (p. 93)

Section 73: A scene after rain. (p. 93)

Section 74: Walking in farmland, Mao Mao observes various scenes and finally is scared by a person's cough. (pp. 93–94)

Section 75: The smell of morning. (pp. 94–95)

Section 76: The dusty road outside the back window. (p. 95)

Section 77: The father teaches Mao Mao how to avoid getting sunstroke. (pp. 95–96)

Section 78: Mao Mao develops an interest in classical poetry, the musicality of which brings him great pleasure. (pp. 96–97)

Section 79: A morning scene around the river bank. (pp. 97–98)

Section 80: On an autumn day, Mao Mao sees two girls passing by the dike. (pp. 98–99)

Section 81: Mao Mao is upset when his mother goes to the market, leaving him alone at home. (pp. 99–101)

Section 82: About five o'clock in the afternoon, bats fly in front of the house. (p. 101)

Section 83: On a winter evening, Mao Mao does not go home right away after school. He goes instead to a classmate's house to look at his new piano. His father goes looking for him. (pp. 101–2)

Section 84: Mao Mao is fascinated by his father's leather gloves. (p. 102)

Section 85: Mao Mao tries to remember an old song. (pp. 102–3)

Section 86: Mao Mao thinks his mother is very beautiful. (p. 103)

Section 87: Recently, the whole family, except the second brother, has often gone shopping on the weekend. The mother expresses her envy of a female restaurant owner. (pp. 103–4)

Section H: Fan Ye is at Gaoxiong City. He feels the search for his father is hopeless. (pp. 105–6)

Section 88: The whole family, including the second brother, goes on an excursion to Cao Shan. The father takes the opportunity to persuade the second brother not to date girls before his career has developed. (pp. 106–11)

Section 89: Mao Mao grows taller. (p. 111)

Section 90: The father is fifty-two and the mother forty-nine. Mao Mao worries that they might die soon. He thinks that if he physically tortures himself, his parents might live longer, so he slaps his own cheeks. (pp. 111–12)

Section 91: Mao Mao learns a little wrestling; he seizes a chance to try it on his father. (pp. 112–13)

Section 92: The father tries to kill a swarm of termites with a basin of water. (pp. 113–14)

Section 93: Mao Mao does not want to wear a pair of black running shoes; for this, his parents accuse him of disrespect and say that he will not be good to them in their old age. Mao Mao feels guilty. (p. 114)

Section 94: The sound of a train. (p. 115)

Section 95: Mao Mao enjoys the fragrance of jasmine his mother wears in her hair. (p. 115)

Section 96: The father is frightened by something Mao Mao says. (p. 115)

Section 97: The mother nails a butterfly to the wall. (p. 116)

Section 98: The mother prohibits Mao Mao from staying in the sunlight. (pp. 116–18)

Section 99: Mao Mao is disgusted by his mother's vulgar make-up and dresses. (pp. 118–19)

Section 100: Mao Mao admires his father for compiling his volumes of idioms. (p. 119)

Section 101: Mao Mao likes painting water colors. (p. 119–20)

Section 102: Mao Mao's old fountain pen is broken; the father gives him a new one, but he feels sorry about giving up the old one. (p. 120)

Section 103: Mao Mao learns he should seize the joy of the moment, so should not wait too long to use the new pen his father gave him two weeks ago. He is eleven years old. (pp. 120–21)

Section 104: Mao Mao will not wear patched pants. (p. 122)

Section 105: The father shows Mao Mao a pornographic novel. (pp. 122–23)

Section 106: Mao Mao checks his brother's bookshelf, trying to find another work of pornography. (p. 123)

Section 107: Mao Mao obtains a blank diary book from his second brother. In it, he writes about his special feelings for a female cousin and then locks it in a drawer. (p. 124)

Section 108: Mao Mao is extremely upset with his father when he discovers his father has borrowed money from his aunt and does not intend to return it. The consequence is that his cousin stops visiting them. (pp. 124–25)

Section 109: The mother dismisses their laundry woman, accusing her of stealing a handkerchief. However, Mao Mao discovers this is just a slander his mother made up to cut some expenses, and he feels shame for his parents. (pp. 125–29)

Section 110: It is his father's fifty-third birthday. Mao Mao is forced to bow to the ancestors' sacred tablet and to his father. He remembers a dispute with his mother about her being superstitious and forcing him to follow all the ritual rules. His mother again accuses him of being disrespectful to his parents, but he feels ashamed only of compromising with her. (pp. 129–34)

Part Two

Section I: Fan Ye returns home from his fruitless trip in search for his father. He also decides temporarily to stop searching, as well as to cancel advertisements in the newspaper. (pp. 135–37)

Section 111: A jet airplane flies over. Mao Mao is sixteen now. His mother is raging about the neighbors putting one end of a bamboo pole on their fence. His father helps her scare away the neighbors' children. Mao Mao feels shame and anger toward his parents. (pp. 137–40)

Section 112: The father does not seem to get along with his colleagues, and the family's financial situation is getting worse. (pp. 140–43)

Section 113: The father has a severe dispute with Mao Mao's second brother for two reasons. First, the father rejects his new girlfriend because she has been a prostitute. Second, the second brother is bringing home less money since he began dating this girl. (pp. 143–47)

Section 114: There is a typhoon; Mao Mao feels insecure about the old house and his own life. (pp. 147 48)

Section 115: On a hot summer day, the father walks home from the office for lunch to save a bus ticket for Mao Mao. (pp. 148–49)

Section 116: The most painful experience Mao Mao has during this period of his life is the discord between his parents about the father's supposed relationships with other women, which it seems never existed. (pp. 150–55)

Section 117: Mao Mao feels ashamed about the shabbiness of his home, and disgusted by his family's customs. Mao Mao often seeks refuge in Western classical music and masturbation. (pp. 155–59)

Section 118: The father is ill from worrying over a possible demotion at work, but the problem is finally solved. (pp. 160–62)

Section J: Fan Ye now is getting used to living without his father. Although occasionally he still puts an advertisement in the newspaper, he moves out his father's desk and throws his shoes into a garbage basket. (pp. 162–64)

Section 119: Early one morning in the spring, Mao Mao goes boating as a way of escaping from the pressure of his environment. (pp. 164–65)

Section 120: A spring scene. (pp. 165–66)

Section 121: Whenever Mao Mao cannot stand the atmosphere at home, he rides his bike through the neighborhood streets. (pp. 166–67)

Section 122: On the street, the father meets an old friend, whose fake offer of a high-paying job excites the whole family for ten months until the man dies. (pp. 167–75)

Section 123: The father disapproves of the second brother's marriage, which leads to a severe conflict. The second brother moves out of the house. (pp. 175–77)

Part Three

Section K: Fan Ye again puts an advertisement in the newspaper and sets out on his second trip to the south to look for his father, though he is aware he is doing this only to soothe his conscience. (pp. 179–80)

Section 124: An airplane flies over. Fan Ye (Mao Mao) now is twenty years old and is studying in the Department of History of C University. He has developed the habit of being able to read only in an absolutely quiet place. He often is annoyed by his parents' disturbances, along with their other odd habits. (pp. 180–85)

Section 125: Fan Ye becomes furious one day when he learns that his father has looked all over for him when he is late coming home. (pp. 185–86)

Section 126: Fan Ye becomes aware of many shortcomings in his parents that he had previously overlooked. He also begins to suspect their morality. (pp. 186–90)

Section 127: Fan Ye meets an old man whose two children are in the

United States. He greatly respects him and spends a lot of time at his home until the man moves to live with his children. (pp. 190–91)

Section L: Fan Ye puts an ad on the newspaper, looking for his father. When walking on a street of a city in the south, he sees an old man, with mental problem, trying to conduct the traffic. He suspects the old man to be his father, but finds he is not, after a close look. (pp. 191–92)

Section 128: Fan Ye is angry because his father suspects him of having taken the ten dollars the mother had given to the father to buy soy sauce. (pp. 192–93)

Section 129: The mother is as suspicious as before about the father's relationship with other women. Fan Ye calls his father a coward. (pp. 193–97)

Section 130: A typhoon breaks three window panes; the wind blows in and messes up everything inside. (p. 197)

Section 131: A fire breaks out in the neighborhood at night. Fan Ye moves the family's belongings out; afterward, he notices the family's unbearable poverty, which is reflected in the condition of these objects. (p. 198)

Section 132: Fan Ye graduates from university and begins his two-year military service. (p. 198)

Section 133: Fan Ye finishes his military service. The father is accused of forgery and is incapable of defending himself. When Fan Ye helps him solve the problem, he discovers more of his father's shortcomings. (pp. 199–207)

Section 134: The father retires. Fan Ye is forced to take responsibility for supporting the whole family. At the time, he is working as a teaching assistant in the department from which he graduated. (pp. 207–8)

Section 135: Fan Ye cannot stand his father and fights with him almost every day. (p. 208)

Section 136: More on the father's odd and disgusting habits. (pp. 208–10)

Section 137: The father often interrupts Fan Ye's reading. (p. 210)

Section 138: The father dresses very sloppily. (p. 210)

Section 139: The father's slippers are like toy slippers. (p. 211)

Section 140: When the father fetches water from outside, he spills it all over the floor. (p. 211)

Section 141: Fan Ye feels his father likes to lie. (pp. 212–13)

Section 142: The father likes to eat children's candies. (p. 213)

Section 143: The father also is forgetful. (p. 214)

Section 144: The father's most obvious problem is being overly dramatic. (p. 214)

Section 145: The father eats rotten food but does not notice any difference. (p. 215)

Section 146: Though he feels guilty about his father serving him well at lunch time, Fan Ye cannot help getting angry with him when he sees too much rice in his own bowl. (p. 216)

Section 147: Fan Ye is tightfisted in controlling his family's finances after his father's retirement. (pp. 215–16)

Section 148: The father becomes ugly every night by bed time. He also is speechless whenever he hears that friends his own age have died. (p. 216)

Section 149: Fan Ye dreams he and his father have killed each other. (pp. 217–18)

Section 150: Fan Ye often has conflicts with his father, but has no problems with his mother because she caters to his wishes. (p. 219)

Section 151: Half a year after his father's retirement, Fan Ye paints the wall and puts a new door between his and his parents' rooms. (p. 219)

Section M: Fan Ye sees many middle-aged men working hard on the streets; he believes that they all are working to raise their children. (pp. 220–21)

Section 152: Fan Ye criticizes the Confucian concept of the family in his diary, and thinks "filial piety" is just selfish thinking by parents. He decides not to have any children. (pp. 221–24)

Section 153: At night, Fan Ye often feels guilty about his father, and decides to be nice to him. However, he never carries out this intention for longer than two days. (pp. 224–26)

Section 154: Fan Ye breaks up with his girlfriend, which affects the health of his heart for a long time. (p. 226)

Section 155: The father now touches Fan Ye's shoulder or arm, instead of calling him, when trying to get his attention. It is possible the father's voice has become weak. (p. 226)

Section N: Fan Ye visits his second brother in Xinzhu, thinking that his father might be there or, at least, his brother would give him some support, but the visit is futile. (pp. 226–31)

Section 156: Fan Ye tries to ignore the existence of his father. When speaking to him, Fan Ye usually orders him about fiercely. He prohibits his parents from eating with him except when it is someone's birthday or a festival. He also takes away his father's meal to punish him for various reasons. Once Fan Ye locks his father in the bedroom for three days; when the father is allowed to come out, his hair has turned white. Now his father often calls him "Lao er" (the second child). (pp. 231–36)

Section 157: The father is ill for several days; when he gets better, he disappears from home. (pp. 236–37)

Section O: Two years have passed. Now Fan Ye and his mother are living rather pleasantly. Their health also has much improved. (pp. 237–38)

16   Tentative Outline of Backed Against the Sea, *Vol. 1*

Te-hsing Shan
Academia Sinica

The narrator utters a long series of damnations and condemnations. (p. 1)[1]

1. Recalls his coming here. (p. 1)
2. Describes where he lives. (p. 1)

Hears rain. (p. 1)

1. Condemns the world, the present, the past, the future. (pp. 1–2)
2. Criticizes memoirs. (p. 2)

Observes the darkness inside and outside the room, drinks bad wine. (pp. 2–3)

1. Condemns this place. (pp. 3–6)
2. Remembers cheating and being cheated while gambling in Taipei. (pp. 6–7)
3. Rationalizes cheating his relatives and provincials as well as his ingratitude. (pp. 7–11)
4. Recounts his illnesses. (pp. 11–13)
5. Waits for fish here. (p. 13)

---

1. This outline was originally published as an appendix to Te-hsing Shan, "The Stream-of-Consciousness Technique in Wang Wen-hsing's Fiction," *Tamkang Review* 15 (1985): 542–45. The page numbers in this outline refer to Wang Wenxing's *Bei hai de ren*, vol. 1 背海的人 （上） (Backed against the sea, vol. 1) (Taipei: Hongfan shudian, 1981, also 1999).

6. Says why he tells fortunes and comments on fortune-telling. (pp. 13–14)

Hears rain again. (p. 14)
1. Recalls his trip here. (p. 15)
2. Recounts the small shops here. (pp. 16–17)
3. Comments on food and sex. (pp. 17–18)
4. Sees the garbage all around. (pp. 18–19)
5. Comments on the natives' religious attitudes. (pp. 19–20)
6. Recounts food-selling stands here. (pp. 20–22)

Guesses the time. (p. 22)
1. Recounts the lone black eagle. (pp. 23–24)
2. Describes the joy of being an exile and the bathroom in which he lives. (pp. 24-26).
3. Describes the outside surroundings. (pp. 26–27)
4. Describes the inside setting. (pp. 27–29)
5. Recounts his collection of books and pornographic photographs. (p. 29)
6. Philosophizes about modern men's getting and spending. (pp. 29–30)
7. Describes himself as a big contradiction. (pp. 30–31)
8. Describes the lone rock withstanding the rushing and washing of the sea. (p. 31)
9. Describes the surroundings. (pp. 31–32)

Smokes. (p. 32)
1. Comments on tea. (pp. 32–33)

The cigarette tastes wrong. (p. 33)
1. Comments on smoking and man's absurdity. (pp. 33–34)
2. Comments on drinking and eating. (p. 34)

Drops cigarette ash. (p. 34)
1. Comments on man and ash. (pp. 34–35)
2. Describes his countenance; its relation to smoking and fortune-telling reveals his vanity. (pp. 35–38)
3. Comments on his unsightly appearance and poor clothing. (pp. 38–39)

4. Comments on being rich and, as a result, being free. (pp. 39–42)

Is burned by the cigarette butt. (p. 42)
1. Curses his bad memory. (p. 42)
2. Recounts his daydream and nightmare. (pp. 42–43)
3. Comments on the interpretation of dreams and condemns fortune-telling. (pp. 43–47)
4. Believes in fortune-telling secretly and unreasonably. (pp. 47–51)
5. Recounts his life here and how he made fortune-telling his profession. (pp. 51–56)
6. Watches the sea, the sand, and the people. (pp. 56–61)
7. Relates how he told fortunes in the first two days. (pp. 62–75)
8. Tells how a fortune he told partly came true and he became famous. (pp. 75–81)
9. Tells how the boss deals with the shipwreck and criticizes the capitalist mentality. (pp. 81–82)
10. Comments on Chinese funerals. (pp. 82–84)
11. Reports on the captain, who has just lost his son in the shipwreck, riding to the sea. (pp. 84–86)
12. Recounts meeting Chang Fa-wu at the dock. (pp. 86–89)

Hears the cock crow. (p. 89)
1. Damns the cock that crows at midnight. (p. 89)
2. Recalls Freud. (p. 89)
3. Comments on the poor villagers' worship. (pp. 89–90)

Forgets what he was thinking about. (p. 90)
1. Comments on the temple and its gods and goddesses of various origins. (pp. 90–92)
2. Recalls people's worship. (pp. 92–93)
3. Comments on Buddhism, Zen (Chan) Buddhism in particular. (pp. 93–94)

Drinks all his wine and, wineless and waterless, smokes. (p. 94)
1. Expresses his admiration for a short poem by the great master of Zen (Chan) Buddhism and turns to condemn Chinese poets, ancient and modern. (pp. 94–95)

2. Recalls stopping creative writing—the confession of his career as a writer, especially as a poet (pp. 95–99)

Goes out to urinate and, seeing the light, remembers where he lost the flow of his thoughts. (p. 99)

1. Recalls Chang's visit to his room. (pp. 99–100)
2. Relates his joining meals in the office where Chang works. (pp. 100-101)
3. Comments on the office and its appearance. (pp. 101–2)
4. Describes its garbage-like members, their ridiculous interrelations, and farcical performances. (pp. 104–52)
5. Sees Sheng (Qizhi) in the red-light district. (pp. 152–53)
6. Recounts his first whoring experience on his second night here. (pp. 153–61)
7. Worries about getting venereal disease and comments on the necessity and irrationality of sex. (pp. 161–63)
8. Recounts his seduction by the Bodhisattva-like sadist and his painful experience the night before. (pp. 163–67)

Is without cigarettes, wine, or water. (p. 167)

1. Continues to recount his painful experiences. (pp. 167–68)

His hips hurt. (p. 169)

1. Recounts visiting the sex-selling teahouse on his third night here. (pp. 169–71)
2. Turns to his only true love experience with a girl in a Taipei teahouse and his breaking promises to her years ago. (pp. 171–74)
3. Returns to the seaside teahouse and his abuse of this sad girl. (pp. 174–76)
4. Recalls another girl in the teahouse, a born optimist. (pp. 176–82)

Sees daylight. (p. 182)

17 Tentative Outline of Backed Against the Sea, *Vol. 2*

San-hui Hung
National Central University

The narrator complains about "losing everything" and having "no way to go further." (p. 185)[1]

1. Loses job opportunity. (p. 185)
2. Has only three dollars on him. (p. 185)
3. Bad economic condition in the port area. (p. 186)
4. Rain falls without end. (p. 186)
5. Recalls events from the past month and a half. (pp. 186-87)
6. Current status: "lost everything," "no way to go further," and "a shaven head." (pp. 187–88)

Falls in love. (p. 189)

1. Pursues the prostitute Red Hair (p. 189)
   a. Strategy no. 1 in wooing her: waiting at the brothel door. (p. 190)
   b. Strategy no. 2 in wooing her: trying to gain Red Hair's attention. (pp. 191–93)
   c. Other views: Other people comment about Red Hair. (p. 194)
   d. Zhang Fawu and Red Hair. (pp. 195–97)
   e. Courts Red Hair. (pp. 197–201)
   f. Writes love letters to Red Hair asking her out. (pp. 201–15)

---

1. The page numbers in this outline refer to Wang Wenxing's *Bei hai de ren* (xia) 背海的人（下）(Backed against the sea, vol. 2) (Taipei: Hongfan shudian, 1999).

302

g. Asks others to communicate his love to Red Hair. (pp. 216–21)

h. Pawns his watch to buy a present for Red Hair. (pp. 221–24)

i. Gets the presents and love letters that Red Hair returned. (pp. 225–27)

j. Tells Zhang Fawu about his bitterness at being rejected by Red Hair. (pp. 228–29)

k. Keeps trying to see Red Hair. (pp. 229–32)

l. Red Hair unexpectedly leaves the place. (p. 232)

m. Falls in love with another prostitute, Little Flower Face, for a short period of time. (pp. 233–34)

2. Recalls the time in Taipei when Cai Suzhen fell in love with him. (p. 234)

a. Cai Suzhen visited him. (pp. 235–38)

b. Stayed in a hotel with Cai Suzhen. (pp. 239–42)

c. Secretly planned with a drinking buddy to rape Cai. (pp. 243–45)

d. Dated Cai in elementary school. (pp. 245–48)

e. The first meeting with Cai: a bicycle accident. (pp. 248–50)

f. Cai left her family to live with Ye, but she was refused by him outside the door. (pp. 251–59)

g. Farted. (p. 260)

h. Disliked Cai because she was ugly and poor. (pp. 261–63)

i. A movie date with Cai. (pp. 263–67)

j. After their breakup, Cai returned to her family, depressed and exhausted. (p. 268)

3. Concludes about love: Love is not easy; love is like "creation in Art." (p. 269)

Illness. (p. 270)

1. Catches a cold. (pp. 271–73)

2. Pain of illness. (pp. 274–75)

3. Has a fever. (p. 275)

4. Suffering is the "essence of life." (p. 276)

5. The perception of smell changes after recovering from the cold. (p. 277)

6. Comments on Chinese medicine and Western medicine. (pp. 278–79)

7. Suffering from constipation after recovering from the cold. (pp. 279–82)
8. Taking a piss. (pp. 283–85)

Recalls the people and events of the Bureau of Management of Materials on Regional Speech and Popular Local Customs During the Past Century, Deep Pit Harbor Branch Office (BOCDO). (p. 285)

1. Playing table tennis at the office. (pp. 285–89)
2. Tang Lin bought a lottery ticket, dreaming of becoming rich. (pp. 289–90)
3. Tang and Zhang argued about radio programs. Zhang wanted to have the "English-teaching" program while Tang wanted the "local opera" programs. (pp. 291–92)
4. Tang and Zhang argued continuously about different issues. (pp. 292–99)
5. Tang and Zhang argued and went from being friends to enemies. (p. 299)
6. The cook Qiu. (pp. 300–302)
7. The janitor Pan Zhongliang (a mental patient). (pp. 302–3)
8. A BOCDO staff, Cui Liqun. (p. 304)

The Catholic church and the priests. (p. 305)

1. The location of the church: at the top of hill. (p. 307)
2. Looks down to the port from the stairs of the church and observes the terrain of Shenkeng'ao. (pp. 307–8)
3. Meets Father Bi Ke'an. (p. 308)
4. Talks with Father Bi. (pp. 308–12)
5. Goes to the church again three days later to borrow money. (p. 312)
6. Thinks about religion briefly. (pp. 312–13)
7. Meets another priest from Canada. (pp. 313–14)
8. Talks with the priest and asks why people suffer. (pp. 314–16)
9. Borrows money from the priest. (pp. 316–17)
10. The priest lends him fifty yuan and two books (pp. 316–18)
11. Several days later, goes to the church to borrow money once again. (pp. 318–19)
12. Thinks about religion on the way to the church (this is the second time that he thought about religion). (pp. 319–21)

    a. Asks whether man's destiny is determined by God or by one's free will. (pp. 319–20)

    b. Asks which is more important, the current life or eternity. (p. 320)

    c. Asks whether God or the Devil is the source of disasters. (pp. 320–21)

13. Arrives at the church, but the church is closed. The priest has returned to his home country and won't come back for three months. (p. 321)

Hears a noise outside and suspects some people are coming to hurt him. (p. 322)

Speaks about his recent financially difficulties. (pp. 322–23)

Fails to get a job at BOCDO; causes a ruckus there. (pp. 323–30)

Recalls the whole story of trying to get a job at BOCDO. (pp. 330–34)

Meets the rich man Dong Yutang. (p. 340)

1. Dong Yutang, a businessman from Taipei, comes to Shenkeng'ao on a business trip. As he cannot find accommodation for the night, he sleeps over at Ye's place. (p. 341)

2. Dong and Ye talk about Dong's business, the reason he came to Shenkeng'ao, and the trip itself. (pp. 342–45)

3. Dong takes some medicine. This rich man has many illnesses. (pp. 345–46)

4. Dong takes a shit. (pp. 346–47)

5. Asks Dong about how one becomes rich. (pp. 348–55)

6. Dong sleeps soundly, while Ye spends the whole night thinking of ways to steal his money and so sleeps very poorly. (p. 356)

7. Wakes up at dawn only to find that Dong has already disappeared. (pp. 356–67)

Theft and robbery. (pp. 356–60)

1. Secretly goes to the dormitory of the BOCDO officers to steal, but fails. (pp. 357–58)

2. Tries to rob people twice the next day, but fails again. (pp. 358–60)

Is broke and has no way of getting any money; starts to buy on credit. (p. 361)

Goes to see a hooker without any money. (pp. 360–61)

A black eagle circles in the sky. (p. 362)

Kills a dog for Cao and shares some dog meat. (pp. 362–68)

Cries for help while he is being murdered. (p. 369)

Appendix: The rain stops and the sun appears; Ye's corpse floats upon the sea. A black eagle circles in the sky above the public bath where Ye lived. (p. 371)

B. BIBLIOGRAPHIES

Bibliography I: Interviews with and Biographical References to Wang Wenxing

Compiled by Shu-ning Sciban
University of Calgary

with the assistance of Anita Lin, Emily Wen,
and Roma Ilnyckyj

Chinese Materials

Chen, Wenfen. "Wang Wenxing: Kanjian Zhongguo nanxing de liliang" (Wang Wenxing: seeing the strength of Chinese men). *Chengpin haodu* (Eslite reader) 24 (2002.8): 6.

Chen, Ziyu. "Wang Wenxing—xitan *Jia bian* meixue" (Wang Wenxing—detailed discussion of the esthetics of *Family Catastrophe*). *Tianxia zazhi* (World magazine) 340 (15 Feb. 2006): 208–10.

Cheng, Yingshu. "*Jia bian* de yuyan xingshi—Wang Wenxing zhuanfang" (The language form of *Family Catastrophe*—an interview with Wang Wenxing). *Zhongguo shibao* (China times), 23 Nov. 1999, 37.

———. "Ronghui guantong de mofang (1) (2) (3)" (Imitation achieved through comprehensive study [1] [2] [3]). *Zhongguo shibao* (China times), 20–22 Nov. 1999, 37.

"Gudian caizi Wang Wenxing tan xiandai nüquan" (Classical scholar Wang Wenxing on modern women's rights). *Funü zazhi* (Women) 3 (1976): 72–74.

Hai Nan. "Yibu 'renxiang hualang' zuoping de zai pingjia—fang Wang Wenxing xiansheng tan *Hong lou meng*" (A reappraisal of "portrait gallery"—an interview with Mr. Wang Wenxing on *Dream of the Red Chamber*). *Youshi yuekan* (Youth literary) 34.3 (1971): 44–47.

He, Xin. "Jixu *Bei hai de ren*: Wang Wenxing" (Continuing *Backed Against the Sea*: Wang Wenxing). *Lianhe wenxue* (Unitas) 5.6 (1 Mar. 1990): 46–47.

Huang, Shuning. "Xiandai jiaoxiangyue—Wang Wenxing fangtan lu (1) (2) (3) (4)" (Modern symphony—record of an interview with Wang Wenxing [1] [2] [3] [4]). *Lianhe bao* (United daily), 28 Apr.–1 May 2000, 37.

Kang, Laixin. "Tongbantongxue—yi Wang Wenxing, Bai Xianyong weili de suixiang" (Classmates—a random thought about Wang Wenxing and Bai Xianyong). *Oukai tianyan qu hongchen—Wang Wenxing zhuanji fangtan ji* (Glimpses of the world through the inner eye: collected biographies and interviews of Wang Wenxing). Ed. Huang Shuning. Taipei: National Taiwan University Press, 2013. 3–20.

———. 'Xunren qishilu—yingshi Wang Xue jilupian" (Ad of searching for missing persons—documentaries on Wang Wenxing). *Oukai tianyan qu hongchen—Wang Wenxing zhuanji fangtan ji* (Glimpses of the world through the inner eye: collected biographies and interviews of Wang Wenxing). Ed. Huang Shuning. Taipei: National Taiwan University Press, 2013. 119–30.

———, ed. *Wang Wenxing de xinling shijie* (Wang Wenxing's spiritual world). Taipei: Yage chubanshe, 1990.

———. "Wang Wenxing rushi shuo (shang) (zhong) (xia)" (Wang Wenxing says so [Pt. 1] [Pt. 2] [Pt. 3]). *Zhongyang ribao* (Central daily), 29–31 Dec. 1987, 10.

Ke, Qingmin. "Zai Zhongwen xi, yujian Wang Wenxing laoshi, I, II, III, IV" (Meeting Professor Wang Wenxing at the Department of Chinese Literature, I, II, III, IV). *Yinke wenxue shenghuo zhi* (Ink's journal of literature) 5.7 (2009.3): 96–99; 5.8 (2009.4): 92–94; 5.9 (2009.5): 106–9; 5.10 (2009.6): 110–13.

Lan, Lijuan. "Taida waiwen xi jiaoshou Wang Wenxing: yong shufa, shici yannian" (National Taiwan University's foreign literature professor Wang Wenxing: Extending life by immersing himself in calligraphy and classical poems). *Cheers* 30 (2003.3): 113.

Li Ang. "Changpao xuanshou de guji—Wang Wenxing fangwen lu" (Loneliness of a long-distance runner—record of an interview with Wang Wenxing). *Zhongwai wenxue* (Chungwai literary monthly) 4.5 (1975): 30–42.

Li, Shiyong. "Yuyan jiushi yige liyou—Wang Wenxing fangtanlu (shang), (zhong), (xia)" (Language is a good enough reason—an interview with Wang Wenxing [Pt. 1], [Pt. 2], [Pt. 3]). *Lianhe wenxue* (Unitas) 305 (2010.3): 98–105; 306 (2010.4): 84–89; 307 (2010.5): 96–103.

Li, Xinlun. "Kangju sudu de xiandai yinyue: Wang Wenxing zuotanhui" (Resisting the tempo of modern music: Wang Wenxing forum). *Zhongguo shibao* (China times), 15 Dec. 1999, 37.

Li, Ya'nan. "Wang Wenxing wuchu bushi shu" (Everything Wang Wenxing writes is like a book). *Chengpin yuedu* (Elite book review) 1 (1991): 35–37.

Li, Zhexiu. "Yige xiandai Zhongguo zhishi fenzi xinling zhi lü (shang) (xia)" (The spiritual journey of a modern Chinese intellectual [Pt. 1] [Pt. 2]). *Zhongguo shibao* (China times), 19–20 Oct. 1988, 23.

Liao, Linger. "Wenzi de zhujian shi–Wang Wenxing" (Master wordsmith–Wang Wenxing). *GO-SSS* 10 (2000): 16–19.

Liao, Xianhao. "Siwang de ziwei–Wang Wenxing 'Mingyun de jixian'" (The taste of death–Wang Wenxing "The line of fate"). With Jiao Huilan. *Youshi wenyi* (Youth literary) 81.4 (1995): 55–58.

Lin, Huifeng. "Wang Wenxing, Zheng Chouyu: zoushang wenxue yuyan de bu gui lu (shang) (xia)" (Wang Wenxing, Zheng Chouyu: walking on literary language's road of no return [Pt. 1] [Pt. 2]). *Zhongyang ribao* (Central daily), 12–13 Oct. 1987, 10.

Lin, Jingjie, dir. *Xunzhao bei hai de ren* (The man behind the book) (DVD). Taipei: Fisfisa Media, 2012. A documentary film on Wang Wenxing.

———. *Xiaoshuo shengtu* (A saint-like novelist) (DVD). Taipei: Foundation of National Culture and Arts, 2010. A documentary film on Wang Wenxing.

Lin, Shuifu. "Cong *Chenmo* dao *Jia bian*–Endo Shusaku yu Wang Wenxing de wenxue duihua" (From *Reticent* to *Family Catastrophe*–Endo Shusaku and Wang Wenxing's conversation about literature). *Zhongguo shibao* (China times), 17 Nov. 1986, 8.

Lin, Xiuling, ed. "Jianzhu yu wenxue de duihua–lun chuantong yu xiandai: Li Zuyuan jianzhushi yu Wang Wenxing jiaoshou" (A conversation about architecture and literature–discussion the traditional and the modern: architect Li Zuyuan and Professor Wang Wenxing). *Zhongwai wenxue* (Chungwai literary monthly) 30.6 (2001): 320–56.

———. "Wang Wenxing yu Luo Qing zuotan: shi yu hua" (A face-to-face talk with Wang Wenxing and Luo Qing: poetry and painting). *Zhongwai wenxue* (Chungwai literary monthly) 30.6 (2001): 294–319.

———. "Yu Wang Wenxing jiaoshou tan wenxue chuangzuo" (A discussion with Wang Wenxing about works of literature). *Zhongwai wenxue* (Chungwai literary monthly) 30.6 (2001): 369–95.

Lin, Xiuling. "Wang Wenxing zhuan fang" (Wang Wenxing exclusive interview). *Zhongwai wenxue* (Chungwai literary monthly) 30.6 (2001): 32–50.

Liu, Caiyu. "Xunfang wenzi diaozhuoshi—Wang Wenxing" (An interview with a master of language art—Wang Wenxing). *Taiwan wenxue buluoge* (Taiwan literature blog), 15 Jan. 2007, http://140.119.61.161/blog/forum_detail.php?id =709.

Miao, Xiaoxia. 'Wang Wenxing, Tan Jiaming duitan: *Jia bian* gaibian dianying" (Dialogue between Wang Wenxing and Tan Jiaming: the possible adaptation from *Family Catastrophe* to film). *Mingbao yuekan* (Mingbao monthly) 47.3 (2012.3): 65–69.

Shan, Dexing. *Quegu suolai jing: dangdai mingjia fangtanlu* (Reflection: Interviews of contemporary prominent writers and scholars). Taipei: Yunchen wenhua, 2014.

———. "Xiaoshuo beihou de zuozhe shijie: Wang Wenxing dingtanlu" (The private world of the fiction author: the three-person interview of Wang Wenxing), *Quegu suolai jing: dangdai mingjia fangtanlu* (Reflection: Interviews of contemporary prominent writers and scholars). Taipei: Yunchen wenhua, 2014. 95–128.

Shan, Dexing, and Lin Jingjie. "Zongjiao yu wenxue: Wang Wenxing fangtanlu" (Religion and literature: interview of Wang Wenxing). *Sixiang* (Reflexion) 19 (2011.9): 203–31.

———. "Wenxue yu zongjiao: Shan Dexing zhuanfang Wang Wenxing" (Literature and religion: Shan Dexing's interview of Wang Wenxing). *Yinke* (Ink) 7.6 (2011.2): 120–43.

———. "Zai shiguangzhong chuilian wenzi—suxie Wang Wenxing" (Forging language in time—a sketch of Wang Wenxing). *Chengpin haodu* (Eslite reader) 4 (2000): 26–27.

———. "Ou kai tianyan qu hongchen—zai fang Wang Wenxing" (Heavenly glance at the mundane world—the second interview with Wang Wenxing). *Zhongwai wenxue* (Chungwai literary monthly) 28.12 (2000): 182–99. Rpt. in *Duihua yu jiaoliu* (Dialogues and interchanges). Taipei: Maitian chuban, 2001. 80–104.

———. "Wang Wenxing tan Wang Wenxing" (Wang Wenxing on Wang Wenxing). *Lianhe wenxue* (Unitas) 3.8 (1987): 166–95. Rpt. as "Chuilian wenzi de ren" (The wordsmith) in *Duihua yu jiaoliu* (Dialogues and interchanges). Taipei: Maitian chuban, 2001. 39–83.

Shi, Junzhou, ed. "Si shou ci de taolun: Donghua University chuangzuo yu yingyu wenxue yanjiusuo 'Huaren zuojia xilie' zuotan jilu" (Discussion of four lyrics: the record of a forum in the "Chinese writers series" of the Graduate Institute of Creative Writing and English Literature at the Donghua University). *Zhongwai wenxue* (Chungwai literary monthly) 30.6 (2000): 275–93.

Su, Pei. "Wang Wenxing texie: xin zuo yiran kaoyan duzhe" (A close-up on Wang Wenxing: new work still tests the reader). *Taiwan wenxue jingdian yantaohui lunwenji* (The collected essays of the Taiwan literary classics symposium). Ed. Chen Yizhi. Taipei: Lianjing chubanshe, 1999. 90.

"Tui jushi de ren—Wang Wenxing (1939–) yingpian" (Wang Wenxing—the Chinese Sisyphus who pushes the rock uphill). *Zuojia shen ying xi lie er: Di shisan juan* (Portraits of Chinese writers, series 2, vol. 13). Taipei: Chun hui guoji kaifa gufen youxian gongsi, 2000.

Wang, Wenxing, Liang Xinrong, and Li Xinying. "Jie wenxue moli yi mandu" (Dispelling the magic of literature through slow reading—A forum with Wang Wenxing). *Wode xuesi licheng*, vol. 6 (NTU Lectures on the intellectual and spiritual pilgrimage, vol. 6). Taipei: National Taiwan University Press, 2012. 394–453.

Wang, Wenxing. *Wo ruhe xie xiaoshuo* (How I write fiction) (DVD). Taipei: National Taiwan University Press, 2007.

Wang, Xuanyi. "*Bei hai* kuang cao—Wang Wenxing de liangge chang ye (shang) (xia)" (Cursive writing in *Backed Against the Sea*—Wang Wenxing's two long nights [Pt. 1] [Pt. 2]). *Zhongguo shibao* (China times), 11–12 Sept. 1980, 8.

Wu, Huifen, and Lian Lijuan. "Huaibao yongheng reqing de changbaozhe—fang Wang Wenxing jiaoshou" (The eternally enthusiastic long-distance runner—an interview with Professor Wang Wenxing). *Daxue xinwen* (University news), 5 Nov. 1979, 3.

Wu, Qiancheng. "Zhengzhi de wenxue, wenxue de zhengzhi" (The literature of politics, the politics of literature). *Kao'an hangxing* (Sailing close to shore). Taipei: Guiguan chubanshe, 1991. 91–108.

———. "Fang Wang Wenxing tan wenxue de shehui gongneng yu yishu jiazhi" (An interview with Wang Wenxing on the social function and the artistic value of literature). *Lianhe bao* (United daily), 24 Aug. 1977, 12.

Wu, Wanru. "Wenxue de malasong—fang Wang Wenxing tan *Jia bian* zai ban" (Marathon of literature—a conversation with Wang Wenxing about *Family Catastrophe*, 2nd ed). *Lianhe bao* (United daily), 16 Oct. 2000, 37.

"Wushi niandai de xuwu xiandai zhuyi de kuangbiao: fang Wang Wenxing jiaoshou" (The force of 1950s nihilistic modernism: an interview with Professor Wang Wenxing). *Tai da jianyan xiaoqing tekan* (special issue of the anniversary of the founding of the Taiwan University student speech and debate club), 15 Nov. 1988, 2.

Xia, Zuli. "Mingyun de jixian—Wang Wenxing fangwen ji" (The line of fate—an interview with Wang Wenxing). *Wobi de ren* (Holders of the pen). Taipei: Chunwenxue chubanshe, 1976. 21–35.

Xiao, Man. "Wang Wenxing tan gudu zhi biyao" (Wang Wenxing on the necessity of solitude). *Chengpin yuedu* (Elite book review) 1 (1991): 6–7.

Xingren wenhua shiyanshi bianji bu, ed. *Zuojia xiaozhuan: Wang Wenxing* (Writer's biography: Wang Wenxing). Taipei: Xingren wenhua shiyanshi, 2012.

Xu, Kaichen. "Xilan shougao tihui Wang Wenxing de jianchi" (A detailed look at Wang Wenxing's manuscripts to understand his persistence). *Minsheng bao* (People's life daily), 16 Nov. 2000, A7.

Ya, Xian. "Taiwan xiandai xiaoshuo shi taolunhui wai yi zhang—xiaoshuojia de tiaozhan" (Additional chapter of the Taiwan history of modern literature symposium—the challenge of the writer). *Lianhe bao* (United daily), 19 Jan. 1998, 41.

Yan, Jianfu, ed. "Cong 'Caoyuan de shengxia' dao *Bei hai de ren*: yu Wang Wenxing jiaoshou tan wenxue chuangzuo" (From "Midsummer on the prairie" to *Backed Against the Sea*: discussion with Professor Wang Wenxing on literary works). *Zhongyang ribao* (Central daily), 14 Dec. 2001, 20.

Yang, Yuxin, Wang Wenxing, and Ruan Qingyue. "Jian yiduan wenxue guangying" (Catch the light and shadow from literature). *Shengming xiangdui lun* (Relativity about life), vol. 4. Taipei: Guangqi she, 2012.

Zhang, Dian. "Huanman youli" (Being slow is reasonable). *Lianhe bao* (United daily), 16 Oct. 2000, 37.

Zhang, Guoli. "Wang Wenxing daodu *Jia bian*" (Wang Wenxing's guide to reading *Family Catastrophe*). *Zhonghua ribao* (China news), 31 Dec. 1986, 8.

Zheng, Meiling, He Yaohui, and Fu Licui. "Xiaoshuo xiju, xuwu zhuyi, shuojiao wenxue—fang Wang Wenxing tan *Fu yu zi*" (Drama, nihilism, preaching literature—an interview with Wang Wenxing on *Father and Son*). *Zhongguo shibao* (China times), 11 July 1983, 8.

English Materials

Lin, Jennifer. "Wang Wenxing: A Spectacular Life." *Foreign Exchange* 6.2 (2000.12): 1–3.

Shan, Te-hsing. "Wang Wen-hsing on Wang Wen-hsing." *Modern Chinese Litera-*
    ture 1.1 (1984): 57–65.
"Wang Wenxing." *Modern Chinese Writers: Self-portrayals.* Ed. Helmut Martine
    and Jeffrey Kinkley. New York: M.E. Sharpe, 1992. 193.
Ying, Li-hua. "Wang Wenxing, A.K.A. Wang Wen-hsing (1939–)." *Historical Dic-*
    tionary of Modern Chinese Literature. Historical Dictionaries of Literature
    and Arts 35. Plymouth: Scarecrow Press, 2010), 201–2.

Bibliography II: Critiques of Wang Wenxing's Works

Compiled by Shu-ning Sciban
University of Calgary

with the assistance of Anita Lin, Emily Wen, and Roma Ilnyckyi

Chinese Materials

An, Li. "*Gujue* de rensheng—pingjie *Shiwu pian xiaoshuo*" (A solitary life—a review of *Fifteen Stories*). *Zili wanbao* (Independence evening post), 23 June 1986, 12.

Ba Ren. "'Xiangtu wenxue gong yu guo' yanjiang ceji" (Sidelights of the lecture "Merits and mistakes of Nativist literature"). *Xia chao* (Summer tide) 4.2 (1978): 76–77.

Bai, Shaofan, and Wang Yubin. "Di'ershi zhang diyi jie—Wang Wenxing jiqi *Jia bian*" (chapter 20; section 1—Wang Wenxing and his *Family Catastrophe*). *Xiandai Taiwan wenxue shi* (History of modern Taiwanese literature). Shenyang: Liaoning daxue chubanshe, 1987. 489–95.

Bai, Xianyong. "Liuling niandai Taiwan wenxue: 'xiandai' yu 'xiangtu'" (Taiwan literature in the 1960s: "modern" and "Nativist"). *Shu you ru ci* (Even trees are like this). Taiwan: Lianhe wenxue chubanshe, 2002. 182–93.

Cai, Huiyi. "*Longtian lou* xiaoshuoji li de Wang Wenxing" (The Wang Wenxing of the *Dragon Inn* collection). *Xin chao* (New tide) 28 (1974): 32–34.

Cai, Yingjun. "Shilun Wang Wenxing xiaoshuo zhong de cuobai zhuti" (A discussion on the theme of failure in Wang Wenxing's fiction). *Wenxing* (Literary stars) 102 (1986): 118–24.

Chen, Chuanxing. "Zhuodengzhao li de shuiyi yu tuoxie: *Jia bian*—'shijian'"

(The pyjamas and slippers in the table lampshade: *Family Catastrophe*—"time"). *Xiangtu wenxue lunzhan ershi zhounian huigu yantahui* (symposium of the 20th anniversary of the nativist literature debate), 25 Oct. 1997, 1–10.

Chen, Dianyi. "*Jia bian* zhi rensheng guanzhao yu chaofeng" (View of life and irony in *Family Catastrophe*). *Zhongwai wenxue* (Chungwai literary monthly) 2.2 (1973): 148–60.

Chen, Kehuan. "Qingbian he *Jia bian*" (Change of heart and *Family Catastrophe*). *Zhonghua ribao* (China news), 4 Sept. 1973, 9.

Chen, Qiwen. "*Jia bian* xiaoshi—lun Wang Wenxing *Jian bian*" (Understanding *Family Catastrophe*—on Wang Wenxing's *Family Catastrophe*). *Taiwan wenxue zhengdian yantaohui lunwen* (Collected essays of Taiwan literature canon symposium). Taipei: Lianhe wenxue chubanshe, 1999. 76–90.

Chen, Wanyi. "Niezi de xingxiang—Jia Baoyu, Gao Juehui he Fan Ye de bijiao" (The image of the unfilial son—a comparison of Jia Baoyu, Gao Juehui and Fan Ye). *Wenxing* (Literary stars) 102 (1986): 125–29.

Chen, Wenfen. "Wang Wenxing *Jia bian* zhizuo yousheng shu" (Wang Wenxing's *Family Catastrophe* made into an audio book). *Zhongguo shibao* (China times), 12 Oct. 2000, 11.

———. "Wang Wenxing *Bei hai de ren* xiace" (Wang Wenxing's *Backed Against the Sea* vol. 2). *Zhongguo shibao* (China times), 20 Sept. 1999, 11.

———. "*Bei hai de ren* xiaji, Wang Wenxing wenzi jiaodui gongcheng jingren" (*Backed Against the Sea* vol. 2, Wang Wenxing's amazing proofreading project). *Zhongguo shibao* (China times), 5 Jan. 1999, 11.

———. "Wang Wenxing xin xiaoshuo jiu dengle" (Wang Wenxing's long awaited new novel). *Zhongguo shibao* (China times), 26 Dec. 1997, 23.

Chen, Xiaolin. "Qingzhe zi qing, zhuozhe zi zhuo: *Qi wang* yu *Jia bian* zhi duibi" (Clear is naturally clear, muddy is naturally muddy: the contrast between *Chess king* and *Family Catastrophe*). *Wenyi* (Literature) 77 (1975): 3–11.

Chen, Yaohua. "Wang Wenxing yu Qi Dengsheng de chengzhang xiaoshuo bijiao" (A comparison of the coming of age novels of Wang Wenxing and Qi Dengsheng). Dissertation, Guoli Qinghua University, 1994.

Chen, Yumei. "Shilun Wang Wenxing *Jia bian* zhi wenzhi" (The language of Wang Wenxing's *Family Catastrophe*). *Wenxue qianzhan: Nanhua daxue wenxuesuo yanjiusheng xuekan* (Literature foresight: the journal of graduate students of literary studies in Nanhua University) 3 (2002.6): 77–89.

Cun Fu. "Wang Wenxing de suo (shang) (xia)" (Wang Wenxing's lock [Pt. 1] [Pt. 2] [Pt. 3]). *Zhonghua ribao* (China news), 12–13 Aug. 1973, 9.

Di Yi. "Wang Wenxing *Bei hai de ren*: yijiubaling nian zuiju dianfuxing de xiaoshuo" (Wang Wenxing's *Backed Against the Sea*: 1980's most subversive novel). *Wen xun biece* (Wenhsun magazine supplement) 6 (1997): 34–35.

Ding, Bangxin. "'Wenti de yuyan de jichu—lun Wang Wenxing de *Bei hai de ren*' jianping" (Comments on "The linguistic foundation of literary style—on Wang Wenxing's *Backed Against the Sea*"). *Zhongwai wenxue* (Chungwai literary monthly) 15.1 (1986): 158–60.

Dong, Zhige. "*Hei yi*" (The black gown). *Taiwan xiaoshuo jianshang cidian* (Dictionary for appreciating Taiwan fiction). Beijing: Zhongyang minzu xueyuan, 1994. 436–37.

Fang, Yun. "Huiyi xianchang taolun jishi (si)" (Conference site discussion report [Four]). *Cong siling niandai dao jiuling niandai—liang an san bian Hua wen xiaoshuo yantaohui lunwen ji* (1940–1990—collected papers of the conference on China, Taiwan, Hong Kong Chinese fiction). Ed. Yang Ze. Taipei: Shibao wenhua chuban qiye youxian gongsi, 1994. 261–82.

Feng, Tie (Raoul David Findeisen). "*Jia bian* li de bianxie bu wei wenbian—guanyu weilai *Jia bian* biandingben zhi sikao" (Changes in *Family Catastrophe* are not a "Catastrophe": considerations about a future crtical edition of *Family Catastrophe*). In *Kaishi de kaishi*. (The beginning of a beginning). Ed. Yi Peng. Taipei: National Taiwan University Library, National Taiwan University Publishing Centre, and Xingren wenhua shiyanshi, 2010. 121–51.

Gao, Tiansheng. "Xiandai xiaoshuo de qitu—shilun Wang Wenxing de xiaoshuo" (The wrong path of modern fiction—discussion on Wang Wenxing's fiction). *Wenxue jie* (Literary circle) 1 (1982): 75–85.

Geng, Dehua (Edward Gunn). "*Bei hai de ren* yiji fanyi zhunze" (*Backed Against the Sea* and the standards for translation). Trans. Li Yanhui. *Zhongwai wenxue* (Chungwai literary monthly) 30.6 (2001): 115–34.

Gu, Jitang. "Diyi pian diqi zhang: zhuzhang quanpan xihua de Wang Wenxing" (pt. 1, chap. 7: Wang Wenxing who advocates overall Westernization). *Taiwan xiaoshuo fazhan shi* (A history of the development of Taiwan fiction). Taipei: Wenshizhe chubanshe, 1989. 333–44.

Gu, Yuanqing. "Weirao Wang Wenxing *Jia bian* de taolun" (A discussion around Wang Wenxing's *Family Catastrophe*). *Taiwan dangdai wenxue lilun piping shi*. (The history of contemporary Taiwanese literary theory and criticism). Hubei: Wuhan chubanshe, 1994. 444–48.

Guan, Yun. "Man tan *Jia bian* zhong de qianci zaoju" (An informal talk about wording and phrasing in *Family Catastrophe*). *Shuping shumu* (Book review and bibliography) 6 (1973): 93–103.

He, Huaishuo. "He er bu tong—zai da Wang Wenxing xiansheng" (Being similar but distinct—another reply to Mr. Wang Wenxing). *Lianhe bao* (United daily), 16 June 1984, 8.

———. "Dianying hai gai shi dianying" (Film should still be film). *Lianhe bao* (United daily), 22 May 1984, 8.

He, Xin. "Zai changxiao shu paihang bang wai de Wang Wenxing" (The Wang Wenxing left off the list of best-selling authors). *Zhongyang ribao* (Central daily), 1 Nov. 1989, 16.

Hong, Shanhui, ed. *Xibei dongnan—Wang Wenxing yanjiu ziliao huibian* (All points of the compass: bibliographies of Wang Wenxing research materials). Taipei: National Taiwan University Press, 2013.

Hong, Xingfu. "Cong guanhuai dao fangqi—wo du Wang Wexing xiaoshuo zuopin de jingguo yu ganxiang" (From caring to abandonment—my reading experience and thoughts about the works of Wang Wenxing). *Hong Xingfu yanjiu zhuan ji* (Special collection of Hong Xingfu studies). Zhanghua: Zhanghua xianli wenhua zhongxin, 1994. 130–52. Rpt. in *Hong Xingfu quanji jiu—pinglunjuan* (Complete works of Hong Xingfu vol. 9—chapter on criticism). Zhanghua: Zhang Xian wenhua ju, June 2001. 45–70.

Hu, Qiuyuan. "Lun Wang Wenxing de nonsense zhi sense" (Discussing on the sense of Wang Wenxing's nonsense). *Xia chao* (Summer tide) 4.3 (1978): 61–70.

Huang, Jinzhu. "Wang Wenxing *Bei hai de ren* (xia)" (Wang Wenxing *Backed Against the Sea*, vol. 2). *Wen xun* (Wenhsun magazine) 8 (2000): 30–31.

Huang, Shuning, Kang Laixin, and Hong Shanhui, eds. *Mandu Wang Wenxing taoshu* (qi ce) (Slow reading of Wang Wenxing) (7 vols.). Taipei: National Taiwan University Press, 2013.

Huang, Shuning and Kang Laixin, eds. *Chaofeng yu nibian—Jia bian zhuanlun* (Iron and rebellion: critical essays on *Family Catastrophe*). Taipei: National Taiwan University Press, 2013.

———. *Wuxiuzhi de zhanzheng—Wang Wenxing zuopin zonglun* (Shang、xia) (Endless war: general essays on Wang Wenxing's works) (vols. 1 and 2). Taipei: National Taiwan University Press, 2013.

Huang, Shuning, ed. *Oukai tianyan qu hongchen—Wang Wenxing zhuanji fangtan ji* (Glimpses of the world through the inner eye: collected biographies and interviews of Wang Wenxing). Taipei: National Taiwan University Press, 2013.

———. "Qianlun Wang Wenxing yuyan yishu de xiandai yiyi—zichuang zi xiuci chutan" (The significance of Wang Wenxing's language art: a preliminary investigation of Wang's rhetoric of neologism). *Wuxiuzhi de zhanzheng—Wang Wenxing zuopin zonglun* (Shang) (Endless war: critical essays on works by Wang Wenxing, vol. 1). Ed. Huang Shuning and Kang Laixin. Taipei: National Taiwan University Press, 2013. 75–92.

———. "Yonggan maixiang gudu de shiyan chuangzuo zhi lu" (Courageously stepping on the lonely road of experimental writing—Wang Wenxing). *Dishisan jie guojia wenyijiang* (13th National Culture and Art Awards). Ed. Su Yiru and Qin Yajun. Taipei: National Culture and Arts Foundation, 2009. 32–45.

Ji Ye. "Nanxing zhi huangmiu yu zhuangyan ji yixing zhi qixi—wo kan 'Caoyuan de Shengxia,' 'Muqin'" (Male absurdity and solemnity, and the tarrying of the opposite sex—reading "Midsummer on the prairie," "Mother"). *Taiwan wenyi* (Taiwan literature) 104 (1987): 82–86.

Jian, Wan. "Wo dui *Jia bian* de yidian ganxiang" (My thoughts on *Family Catastrophe*). *Shuping shumu* (Book review and bibliography) 8 (1973): 43–46.

Jiang, Baochai. "Tao jin—*Xing yu lou suixiang*" (Panning for gold—*Random Thoughts from Star-rain Tower*). *Lianhe bao* (United daily), 7 Dec. 2003, B5.

———. "Shi shei zai nali *Bei hai*?" (Who is it *Backed Against the Sea*?). *Zhongyang ribao* (Central daily), 25 Oct. 1999, 22.

Jiang, Zhongming. "Wang Wenxing xiang xie zongjiao xiaoshuo, Wang Tuo jiang chong shi chuangzuo zhi bi" (Wang Wenxing wants to write a religious novel, Wang Tuo will pick up writing again). *Lianhe bao* (United daily), 20 Sept. 2000, 32.

———. "*Bei hai de ren*, Wang Wenxing xiele 18 nian" (*Backed Against the Sea*, the novel that took Wang Wenxing 18 years to write). *Lianhe bao* (United daily), 5 Jan. 1999, 19.

Jin, Hengjie. "Zhongguo wenxue zhong de qinzi guanxi—tan Wang Wenxing de *Jia bian* he Xi Song de *Nuozha* (shang) (xia)" (The relations between parents and siblings in Chinese literature—on Wang Wenxing's *Family Catastrophe* and Xi Song's *Nuozha*, vols. 1 and 2). *Zhongyang ribao* (Central daily), 26–27 June 1996, 18.

Jin, Wenjing. "Wang Wenxing xiaoshuo wenti bianxi" (Analyzing the questions of Wang Wenxing's fiction). *Fangfa lun yu Zhongguo xiaoshuo yanjiu* (Methods of discussion and research on Chinese fiction). Hong Kong: Hong Kong University Centre for Asian Studies, 2000. 361–76.

Jing Xiang. "*Jia bian* yu wen bian" (*Family Catastrophe* and literary change). *Shuping shumu* (Book review and bibliography) 6 (1973): 80–82.

Kang, Laixin and Huang Shuning, eds. *Xuanxiao yu fennu—Bei hai de ren zhuan-lun* (Sound and fury: critical essays on *Backed Against the Sea*). Taipei: National Taiwan University Press, 2013.

Kang, Laixin, ed. *Yuanlai shuxue he shige yiyang youmei—Wang Wenxing xin shiji duben* (Mathematics and poetry are equal elegance: a reader of Wang Wenxing in the new century). Taipei: National Taiwan University Press, 2013.

Ke, Qingming. "Liu shi niandai xiandai zhuyi wenxue?" (Nineteen sixties' modernist literature). *Sishi nian lai Zhongguo xiaoshuo* (Chinese fiction of the last forty years). Ed. Zhang Baoqin et al. Taipei: Lianhe wenxue chubanshe, 1994. 85–146.

———. "Mitu de liang dai qing—tan Wang Wenxing *Jia bian*" (The loss of feelings between two generations—on Wang Wenxing's *Family Catastrophe*). *Wei! Ni shi na yi pai* (Hey! Which group do you belong to?). Taipei: Youshi chubanshe, 1994. 113–26.

Lai, Suling. "Wang Wenxing, Wang Tuo toulu chuangzuo daji" (Wang Wenxing and Wang Tuo disclose their writing plans). *Minsheng bao* (People's life daily), 20 Sept. 2000, A6.

Li, Kuanhong. "Shi lun *Jia bian*" (An attempt to discuss *Family Catastrophe*). *Shuping shumu* (Book review and bibliography) 6 (1973): 82–87.

Li, Liguo. "Shitan *Jia bian*" (Probing *Family Catastrophe*). *Jinri Zhongguo* (China today) 33 (1973): 150–56.

Li, Lingyi. "Wang Wenxing changyan xiezuo xixing" (Wang Wenxing talks freely the habits of his writing). *Lianhe bao* (United daily), 18 Nov. 2000, 14.

———. "Zuojia Wang Wenxing shougao zhanchu" (The exhibition of writer Wang Wenxing's manuscripts). *Lianhe bao* (United daily), 14 Nov. 2000, 14.

Li, Oufan. "Zai Taiwan faxian Kafuka: yiduan geren de huiyi" (Discovering Kafka in Taiwan: one individual's recollection). Trans. Lin Xiuling. *Zhongwai wenxue* (Chungwai literary monthly) 30.6 (2001): 175–86.

———. "Guanyu *Jia bian* de duihua" (Concerning the dialogue in *Family Catastrophe*). *Dangdai wenyi tansuo* (Exploration of modern literary arts) 2 (1987).

Li, Shixue. "Wang Wenxing chushou!" (Wang Wenxing strikes!). *Zhongguo shibao* (China times), 16 Sept. 1999, 41.

Li, Wenbin. "'Longtian lou' zhong de xiangzheng jiqiao" (The skillful use of symbols in "Dragon inn"). *Zhonghua wenyi* (Chinese literature and arts) 12.5 (1977): 75–89.

———. "Tan Wang Wenxing 'Longtian lou' de neiyun ji waihan" (A discussion about "Dragon inn" on the surface and implication). *Tai Da qingnian* (Taiwan University youth) 3 (1970): 56–59.

Li, Youcheng. "Wang Wenxing yu xifang wenlei" (Wang Wenxing and Western literary genres). *Zhongwai wenxue* (Chungwai literary monthly) 10.11 (1982): 176–93.

Liao, Binghui. "Taiwan wenxue zhong de sizhong xiandai xing: yi *Bei hai de ren* xiaji weili" (Four modern characteristics of Taiwanese literature: using *Backed Against the Sea*, vol. 2 as an example). *Zhongwai wenxue* (Chungwai literary monthly) 30.6 (2001): 75–92.

———. "Wang Wenxing de chuantong yu xiandian qingjie" (Wang Wenxing's traditional and modern passions). *Zhongguo shibao* (China times), 7 Jan. 1994, 39.

Liao, Xianhao. "Ping Wang Wenxing *Shu he ying*" (Review of Wang Wenxing's *Books and Films*). *Wen xun* (Wenhsun magazine) 1.41 (1989), 89–92.

Lin, Boyan. "Han Yu, baihuawen, *Jia bian* (shang) (zhong) (xia)" (Han Yu, Chinese vernacular language, *Family Catastrophe* [Pt. 1] [Pt. 2] [Pt. 3]). *Zhonghua ribao* (China news), 5–7 Oct. 1973, 9.

Lin, Guoqing. "Yongheng de youji" (A timeless travel journal). *Xiaoyao* (Les losirs) no. 15 (2007.9): 111–13.

Lin, Haiyin, et al. "*Jia bian* zuotanhui" (*Family Catastrophe* forum). *Zhongwai wenxue* (Chungwai literary monthly) 2.1 (1973): 164–77.

Lin, Xiuling. "Wenxue de jiangjiu" (Literary meticulousness). *Lianhe bao* (United daily), 8 Sept. 2002, 23.

———, ed. *Zhongwai wenxue: Wang Wenxing zhuanhao* (*Chungwai Literary Monthly*: special issue on Wang Wenxing). *Zhongwai wenxue* (Chungwai literary monthly) 30.6 (2001).

———. "*Zhongwai wenxue* tuichu 'Wang Wenxing zhuan hao' fuzahua Wang Wenxing zuopin de shuxie meixue" (*Chungwai Literary Monthly*'s "Wang Wenxing special issue" complicates Wang Wenxing's writing aesthetics). *Lianhe bao* (United daily), 17 Dec. 2000.

———. "Tan *Bei hai de ren*" (A discussion on *Backed Against the Sea*). *Hongfan zazhi* (Hongfan magazine) 14 (1983): 3.

Liu, Denghan, ed. "Wang Wenxing, Ouyang Zi deng xiandai wenxue zuojia qun" (Wang Wenxing, Ouyang Zi et al. and the modern literary writers). *Taiwan wenxue shi (xia)* (The history of Taiwanese literature, vol. 2). Fuzhou: Haixia wenyi chubanshe, 1993. 217–30.

Liu, Huizhu. "Lun Wang Wenxing *Jia bian* de fumian shuxie" (Wang Wenxing's negative writing in *Family Catastrophe*). *Xingda zhongwen xuebao* (Chinese literature journal of Zhongxing University) 15 (2003.6): 289–310.

———. "'Niezi' de ziwo yihua yu zhuti fenlie—you Lakang de 'jingxiang jieduan' shenshi Wang Wenxing de *Jia bian*" (The role of self-alienation and subject-cleft playing in unfiliable son—dissecting Wang Wenxing's novel *Family Catastrophe* from the perspective of Jacques Lacan's 'mirror stage'). *Xiuping renwen shehui xuebao* (Journal of humanities and sociology studies of Hsiu-ping Institute of Technology) 3 (2004.3): 156–76.

Liu, Renjie. "Zhishi fenzi yu nongye—ping *Zheyang de jiaoshou Wang Wenxing*" (Intellectuals and agriculture—review of *This Kind of Professor Wang Wenxing*). *Chuban yu yanjiu* (Publishing and research) 56 (1979): 25–29.

Liu, Shaoming. "Shi nian lai de Taiwan xiaoshuo: yi jiu liu wu-qi wu—jian lun Wang Wenxing de *Jia bian*" (The last ten years of Taiwan fiction: 1965–75—also discussing Wang Wenxing's *Family Catastrophe*). *Zhongwai wenxue* (Chungwai literary monthly) 4.12 (1976): 4–16.

———. "Xiandai Zhongguo xiaoshuo zhi shijian yu xianshi guannian" (The concept of time and reality in modern Chinese fiction). *Zhongwai wenxue* (Chungwai literary monthly) 2.2 (1973): 64–79.

Liu, Shuzhen. "Zhaji Wang Wenxing—yuanli yihuo kaojin?—Yige xiandai zhuyi de guancha" (A note on Wang Wenxing—being distant or close?—A modernist observation). *Wen xun* (Wenhsun magazine) 232 (2005.2): 12–15.

Lu, Jingguang. "Ba Jin de *Jia* he Wang Wenxing de *Jia bian*" (Ba Jin's *Family* and Wang Wenxing's *Family Catastrophe*). *Zhongguo xiandai wenxue zhengti guan yu bijiao lun* (The wholistic view and comparative study of Modern Chinese literature). Guangzhou: Guangdong gaodeng jiaoyu chubanshe, 1992. 167–85.

———. "Hong dong Taiwan wentan de *Jia bian*—tan Wang Wenxing ji qi chuang-zuo" (The sensation caused by *Family Catastrophe* in the Taiwanese literary world—on Wang Wenxing and his work). *Wenxue bao* (Literature magazine), 4 July 1985.

———. "Lun *Jia bian* de shehui neirong yu renshi jiazhi" (On the social content and the value of knowledge of *Family Catastrophe*). *Wenyi xin shiji* (New age of literature) 2 (1985).

Lü, Zhenghui. "Wang Wenxing de beiju—sheng cuole defang, haishi shou cuole jiaoyu" (Wang Wenxing's tragedy—was he born in the wrong place or educated in the wrong way?). *Xiaoshuo yu shehui* (Fiction and society) Taipei: Lianjing chubanshe, 1988. 19–35.

———. "'Zhengzhi xiaoshuo' san lun" (Three discussions on "political fiction"). *Wenxing* (Literary stars) 103 (1987): 87–92.

Luo, Shicheng. "Meitian sanshi zi—Wang Wenxing jingdu zuishen de ziwei" (Thirty characters everyday—the genuine taste of Wang Wenxing close reading). *Tianxia zazhi* (World magazine) 297 (15 Apr. 2004): 182–83.

Marchand, Sandrine. "Fanyi Wang Wenxing xiaoshuo de yuanyin" (The reason to translate Wang Wenxing's fiction). *Zhongwai wenxue* (Chungwai literary monthly) 30.6 (2001): 244–54.

Ouyang Zi. "Lun *Jia bian* zhi xingshi jiegou yu jufa" (A discussion of the form and sentence structure of *Family Catastrophe*). *Zhongwai wenxue* (Chungwai literary monthly) 1.12 (1973): 50–67.

Pan, Rongli. "Mugong gonghui qianze Wang Wenxing" (The Civil engineering union censures Wang Wenxing). *Xia chao* (Summer tide) 4.3 (1978): 25–27.

Pi'ai'er-Make.De.Biyaxi (Pierre-Marc de Biasi) and Sangdelin.Maershang (Sandrine Marchand). "Duitan Wang Wenxing shougao" (A discussion on Wang Wenxing's manuscripts). In *Kaishi de kaishi* (The beginning of a beginning). Ed. Yi Peng. Taipei: National Taiwan University Library, National Taiwan University Publishing Centre, and Xingren wenhua shiyanshi, 2010. 41–71.

Rao, Borong (Steven L. Riep). "'Longtian lou' qing wen jian mou, bu shi bai bi—Wang Wenxing dui guanfang lishi yu fangong wenxue de pipan (jieyi)" (In "Dragon inn" both feelings and language are a success, not a failure—Wang Wenxing's criticism of offical history and anti-Communist literature [abridged]). Trans. Li Yanhui. *Zhongwai wenxue* (Chungwai literary monthly) 30.6 (2001): 93–114.

Ruan, Qingyue, and Li Zuyuan. "Pulusite yu Qi Dengsheng / zai du *Jia bian*" (Proust and Qi Dengsheng / rereading *Family Catastrophe*). *Lianhe bao* (United daily), 5 Jan. 2004, E7.

Sangdelin.Maershang (Sandrine Marchand). "Shougao, yige yizhi kongjian" (Manuscript, a heterotopia). In *Kaishi de kaishi* (The beginning of a beginning). Ed. Yi Peng. Taipei: National Taiwan University Library, National Taiwan University Publishing Centre, and Xingren wenhua shiyanshi, 2010. 73–95.

Shen, Jinglan. "*Taibei ren* Bai Xianyong vs. *Bei hai de ren* Wang Wenxing" (*Taipei people*'s Bai Xianyong vs. *Backed Against the Sea*'s Wang Wenxing). *Dang xi feng zou guo—liuling niandai 'Xiandai wenxue' pai de lunshu yu kaocha*" (Going over to Western influences—observations and discussion of the 1960s "modern" school). Dissertation, Guoli Chenggong University, 1994. 33–41.

Shi, Bidu. "Wo baba bi Fan Ye hai xiong" (My dad is fiercer than Fan Ye). *Wenxing* (Literary stars) 103 (1987): 106–11.

Shi, Gong. "Bian ze tong hu" (Will change bring success?). *Shuping shumu* (Book review and bibliography) 6 (1973): 105–13.

Shi, Qipeng. "'Xiaoshuo' 'xiandai': dui Wang Wenxing de 'xiandai xiaoshuo' mei you xinxin, jue bu biaoshi dui 'xiandai xiaoshuo' mei you xinxin!" ("Fiction" "modern": that we feel not confident in Wang Wenxing's "modern fiction" does not express non-confidence in "modern fiction"!). *Taiwan ribao* (Taiwan daily), 23 Nov. 1981, 8.

Shui Jing. "Huran xiangdao" (Suddenly come to mind). *Lianhe bao* (United daily), 13 Jan. 1977, 12.

Si Jian. "Dui wenxue de taidu" (Approach to literature). *Chun wenxue* (Literature) 6.1 (1969): 3–5.

Si Min. "Wang Wenxing jiaoshou de pianjian yu kuanggao" (Professor Wang Wenxing's prejudiced opinion and crazy defiance). *Xia chao* (Summer tide) 4.4 (1978): 6.

Su, Mengzhi. "'Longtian lou,' 'Wanju shouqiang': tan Wang Wenxing de zaoqi zuopin" ("Dragon inn," "The toy revolver": a discussion of Wang Wenxing's early works). *Dongwu qingnian* (Dongwu youth) 62 (1975): 31–33.

Su, Qing. "Ji Hu Qiuyuan xiansheng lun 'Wang Wenxing de nonsense zhi sense'" (Recording Hu Qiuyuan's discussion on "The sense of Wang Wenxing's non-sense"). *Xia chao* (Summer tide) 4.3 (1978): 61–70. Rpt. in *Zhonghua zazhi* (Chinese magazine) 176 (1978): 41–49.

Tan, Yalun. "Du *Jia bian* de lianxiang" (Associations in mind while reading *Family Catastrophe*). *Shuping shumu* (Book review and bibliography) 15 (1974): 3–8.

Tang, Yu. "Wang Wenxing de meixu xiuyang" (Wang Wenxing's artistic mastery). *Zhongyang ribao* (Central daily), 1 May 1988, 17.

Tuohuangzhe. "Hao dai shi zijide" (Good or bad it belongs to you). *Zhongguo shibao* (China times), 11 Sept. 1973, 12.

Wan, Ronghua. "*Jia bian*" (*Family Catastrophe*). *Zhongguo shibao* (China times), 29 July 1993, 27.

Wang, Anqi. "Yi zi zhi mao gong zi zhi dun: Wang Wenxing *Bei hai de ren* zhong de Manshi fengci" (Attacking one's shield with one's own lance: the use of Menippean satire in Wang Wenxing's *Backed Against the Sea*). *Zhongwai wenxue* (Chungwai literary monthly) 30.6 (2001): 187–212.

Wang, Dewei. "Wang Wenxing xinban *Jia bian* de shidai yiyi: zhe cai shi yige ren

de shengjing" (The timely significance of the new edition of Wang Wenxing's *Family Catastrophe*: only this can be called one man's Bible). *Lianhe
bao* (United daily), 23 Oct. 2000, 48.

Wang, Dingjun. "*Jia bian* zhi bian" (Change in *Family Catastrophe*). *Shuping
shumu* (Book review and bibliography) 6 (1973): 103–5.

Wang, Jinmin. "Wang Wenxing de xiaoshuo" (The fiction of Wang Wenxing).
Taiwan dangdai wenxue shi (The history of contemporary Taiwanese literature). Guilin: Guangxi renmin jiaoyu chubanshe, 1994. 244–67.

———. "Taiwan wenyi jie dui Wang Wenxing chang pian *Jia bian* de zhenglun"
(The Taiwanese literary world's debate over Wang Wenxing's novel *Family
Catastrophe*). *Zhongwai wenxue yanjiu cankao* (Reference to Chinese and for-
eign literary studies) 5 (1985).

Wang, Tuo. "Ping Wang Wenxing jiaoshou de 'Xiangtu wenxue de gong yu guo'"
(Review of Professsor Wang Wenxing's "Merits and mistakes of Nativist literature"). *Xia chao* (Summer tide) 4.3 (1978): 71–73.

Wang, Wenxing. *Wanju wu jiu jiang* (Nine lectures on *The Doll's House*). Taipei:
Maitian chuban, 2011.

———. *Jia bian liu jiagn* (Six lectures on *Family Catastrophe*). Taipei: Maitian
chuban, 2009.

Wang, Zhijiao. "Qinmi nanren de biran kunjing—Wang Molin tan *Jia bian*" (The
inevitable predicaments of male bonds—Wang Molin on *Family Catastrophe*).
Zhongguo shibao (China times), 25 Dec. 1994, 39.

Wei, Ziyun. "Ping *Jia bian* (shang) (zhong) (xia)" (Review of *Family Catastrophe*
[Pt. 1] [Pt. 2] [Pt. 3]). *Zhonghua ribao* (China news), 3–5 Aug. 1973, 9.

Wu, Dayun. "Yige zhishi fenzi bailei zhi si—*Bei hai de ren* yuedu shouji" (The
death of an intellectual degenerate—notes made from reading *Backed Against
the Sea*). *Zhongwai wenxue* (Chungwai literary monthly) 30.6 (2001): 227–43.

———. "Wang Wenxing xiaoshuo zhong de zhuangshi jiqiao" (The craftsmanship
of embellishment in Wang Wenxing's fiction). *Xin chao* (New tide) 19 (1969):
20–28.

Wu, Pinyi. "Shangdi yiqi de yingxiong—lun Wang Wenxing *Shiwu pian xiaoshuo*
de mingyun" (The hero deserted by God—on the belief of fate in Wang
Wenxing's *Fifteen Stories*). *Guowen tiandi* (The world of Chinese literature)
22.5 (Oct. 2006): 61–66.

Wu, Xiangguan. "Taiwan xiandai xiaoshuozhong de daode fudan yu liufang
yishi" (The ethical burden and the banished consciousness in Taiwanese
modern fiction). *Xin chao* (New tide) 32 (1976): 82–86.

Wu, Zaixing. "Lun Wang Wenxing *Shiwu pian xiaoshuo* de rensheng guanzhao" (On reflections of life in Wang Wenxing's *Fifteen Stories*). *Tainan shiyuan xuesheng xuekan* (Journal of Tainan Teachers College) 17 (1996): 72–82.

Xiao, Fuyuan. "Ershisi nian yichang *Bei hai* meng" (The twenty-four year dream *Backed Against the Sea*). *Smart shufang* (Smart study) 1998: 230–33.

Xiao, Shuishun. "Qing bu yao zai qingbo nongmin" (Please don't insult the peasants again). *Xia chao* (Summer tide) 4.3 (1978): 28–31.

Xu, Guolun, and Wang Chunrong. "Wang Wenxing de *Jia bian*" (Wang Wenxing's *Family Catastrophe*). *Er shi shiji Zhongguo liang an wenxue shi* (History of the twentieth-century literature of China and Taiwan). Shenyang: Liaoning Daxue chubanshe, 1994. 230–33.

Xu, Jianqiao. "Bei shijian de ren, ying wenzi de hai—Wang Wenxing de xiezuo xinyang yu shijian" (The person backed against the time, facing the sea of words—Wang Wenxing's belief and practice in writing). *Wen xun* (Wenhsun magazine) 246 (2006.4): 17–22.

Yan, Yuanshu. "Ku du xi pin tan *Jia bian*" (A meticulous discussion of *Family Catastrophe*). *Zhongwai wenxue* (Chungwai literary monthly) 1.11 (1973): 60–85.

Yang, Huinan. "*Jia bian* ji qita" (*Family Catastrophe* and other works). *Shuping shumu* (Book review and bibliography) 7 (1973): 79–87.

Yang, Yingjing. "Xiaoshi de fuqin—tan Wang Wenxingde *Jia bian*" (The vanished father—talking about Wang Wenxing's *Family Catastrophe*). *Jinmen wenyi* (Jinmen literature and arts) 2 (2004.9): 27–29.

Yang, Zhao. "'Hengzheng baolian' de zuozhe—yuedu Wang Wenxing" (The "burdensome" author—reading Wang Wenxing). *Zhongguo shibao* (China times), 19 Nov. 1999, 37.

———. "Jiating nei de qimeng beiju—Wang Wenxing de xiaoshuo *Jia bian*" (An enlightening household tragedy—Wang Wenxing's novel *Family Catastrophe*). *Zhongguo shibao* (China times), 30 June 1998, 37.

Yao, Xinjin. "Lunxi *Jia bian* zhi qingjie anpai yishu" (Analyzing *Family Catastrophe*'s artistic plot arrangement). *Zhongwai wenxue* (Chungwai literary monthly) 4.12 (1976): 218–27.

Ye, Shan. "Tansuo Wang Wenxing xiaoshuo li de beiju qingdiao" (Exploring the tragic sentiment in Wang Wenxing's fiction). *Xiandai wenxue* (Modern literature) 32 (1967): 60–67.

Ye, Weilian. "Shuilü de nianling de mingxiang—lun Wang Wenxing 'Longtian lou' yiqian de zuopin" (Mediation on the light green age—discussing Wang

Wenxing's works prior to "Dragon inn"). *Zhongguo xiandai xiaoshuo de feng-mao* (The style of modern Chinse fiction). Taipei: Chenzhong chubanshe, 1970. 29–50.

———. "Xiandai Zhongguo xiaoshuo de jiegou" (The structure of modern Chinese fiction). *Xiandai wenxue* (Modern literature) 33 (15 Dec. 1967): 189–203. Rpt. in *Zhongguo xiandai xiaoshuo de fengmao* (The style of modern Chinese fiction). Taipei: Chenzhong chubanshe, 1970. 1–28.

Ye, Ziqi. "Xin shu kuai ping—Wang Wenxing *Shu he ying*" (Brief review of new books—Wang Wenxing's *Books and Films*). *Lianhe bao* (United daily), 10 May 1988, 21.

Yi, Peng, ed. *Wang Wenxing* (Wang Wenxing). Tainan: National Museum of Taiwan Literature, 2013.

———. *Wang Wenxing shougao ji: Jia bian, Bei hai de ren* (Wang Wenxing's manuscripts: *Family Catastrophe, Backed Against the Sea*). Taipei: National Taiwan University Library, National Taiwan University Publishing Centre, and Xingren wenhua shiyanshi, 2010.

———. *Kaishi de kaishi* (The beginning of a beginning). Taipei: National Taiwan University Library, National Taiwan University Publishing Centre, and Xingren wenhua shiyanshi, 2010.

———. "Yi yi, shu" (The book, of changes—the first draft of Wang Wenxing's *Jia bian*). In *Kaishi de kaishi* (The beginning of a beginning). Ed. Yi Peng. Taipei: National Taiwan University Library, National Taiwan University Publishing Centre, and Xingren wenhua shiyanshi, 2010. 153-78.

———. "Bei xiang wanmei yuyan: *Bei hai de ren* chu lun" (With one's back to perfect language: initial discussion of *Backed Against the Sea*). *Zhongwai wenxue* (Chungwai literary monthly) 30.6 (2001): 138–60.

———. "Jubian sishi: Wang Wenxing de *Jia bian*" (Huge change personal history: Wang Wenxing's *Family Catastrophe*). *Zhongwai wenxue* (Chungwai literary monthly) 27.10 (1999): 134–73.

Yin Di. "*Jia bian* yu 'Longtian lou'" (*Family Catastrophe* and "Dragon inn"). *Shuping shumu* (Book review and bibliography) 6 (1973): 87–92.

———. "Du Wang Wenxing de 'Longtian lou'" (Reading Wang Wenxing's "Dragon inn"). *Ziyou qingnian* (Youth of freedom magazine) 35.7 (1964): 25–27.

Ying, Fenghuang. "Wang Wenxing de xiaoshuo *Jia bian*" (Wang Wenxing's novel *Family Catastrophe*). *Guoyu ribao* (National language daily), 30 June 2000, 5.

You, Shihe. "Ping *Jia bian*—jian lun xiaoshuo yongyu" (Review of *Family Catastrophe*—also discussing the use of language in fiction). *Zhongguo yuwen* (Chinese language) 33.4 (1973): 82–85.

Yu, Tiancong. "Zhan zai shenme li chang shuo shenme hua" (What position to take, what to say). *Wen ji* (Literature quarterly) 2 (1973): 18–27.

Zeng, Liling. "Xiandaixing de kongbai—*Jia bian, Bei hai de ren* qianhou shangxia zhi jian" (The modern characteristics of blank space—aspects of *Family Catastrophe* and *Backed Against the Sea*). *Zhongwai wenxue* (Chungwai literary monthly) 30.6 (2001): 161–74.

Zeng, Xinyi. "Zhuyi! 'Qiong Yao gong hai'—jian yi 'Qiong Yao wenti' dafu Wang Wenxing jiaoshou" (Take note! "Public nuisance Qiong Yao"—using the "Qiong Yao question" to answer Professor Wang Wenxing). *Xia chao* (Summer tide) 4.3 (1978): 74–75.

Zhan, Ziying. "*Jia bian* du hou" (A post-reading of *Family Catastrophe*). *Guoyu ribao* (National language daily), 16 Mar. 1979, 6.

Zhang, Dian. "Lin Xiuling zheng gao, kuayue Wang Wenxing zhangai" (Lin Xiuling solicits for publication and overcomes Wang Wenxing's obstacles). *Lianhe bao* (United daily), 28 May 2001, 29.

Zhang, Hanliang. Translated by Cai Songfu. "Zixingxue he xiaoshuo quanshi—yi Wang Wenxing weili" (Graphemics and novel interpretation—the case of Wang Wenxing). *Wuxiuzhi de zhanzheng—Wang Wenxing zuopin zonglun* (Endless war: critical essays on works by Wang Wenxing). Ed. Huang Shuning and Kang Laixin. Taipei: National Taiwan University Press, 2013. 22–54.

———. "Wang Wenxing *Bei hai de ren* de yuyan xinyang" (Wang Wenxing's language beliefs expressed through *Backed Against the Sea*). *Wenxue yu zongjiao—Diyi jie guoji wenxue yu zongjiao huiyi lunwen ji* (Literature and religion—collected essays of the first international conference on literature and religion). Taipei: Shibao wenhua chubanshe, 1987. 438–60.

———. "Qian tan *Jia bian* de wenzi" (A brief discussion of the language of *Family Catastrophe*). *Zhongwai wenxue* (Chungwai literary monthly) 1.12 (1973): 122–39.

Zhang, Songsheng. "Chongfang xiandai zhuyi—Wang Wenxing he Lu Xun" (Revisiting modernism—Wang Wenxing and Lu Xun). *Wuxiuzhi de zhanzheng—Wang Wenxing zuopin zonglun* (Shang) (Endless war: critical essays on works by Wang Wenxing, vol. 1). Ed. Huang Shuning and Kang Laixin. Taipei: National Taiwan University Press, 2013. 217–39.

———. *Wenxue changyu de bianqian: dangdai Taiwan xiaoshuo lun* (Changes in the literary fields: contemporary fiction from Taiwan). Taipei: Lianhe wenxue chubanshe, 2001.

———. "Xiandai zhuyi xin zuo yu Taiwan xiandai pai xiaoshuo" (New modernist works and Taiwanese modernist fiction). *Wenyi yanjiu* (Art and literature studies) 7 (1988). Rpt. in *Wenxue changyu de bianqian* (The changes in the field of literature). Taipei: Lianhe wenxue chubanshe, 2001. 7–36.

———. "Jiedu Wang Wenxing xiandai zhuyi xinzuo—*Bei hai de ren* xuji" (Interpreting Wang Wenxing's new modernist work—the sequel *Backed Against the Sea*). *Lianhe wenxue* (United literature) 15.9 (1999): 144–48.

———. "Cong *Jia bian* de xingshi sheji tanqi" (A talk starting from the formal design of *Family Catastrophe*). *Lianhe wenxue* (Unitas) 3.8 (1987): 196–99.

———. "Wang Wenxing xiaoshuo zhong de yishu he zongjiao zhuixun" (The pursuit of art and religion in Wang Wenxing's novels). Trans. Xie Huiying. *Zhongwai wenxue* (Chungwai literary monthly) 15.6 (1986): 108–19. Rpt. In *Wenxue yu zongjiao: Diyi jie guoji wenxue yu zongjiao huiyi lunwen ji* (Literature and religion: collected essays of the first international conference on literature and religion). Tapei: Shibao wenhua chuban gongsi, 1987. 421–37.

Zhang, Xinying. "Xiandai jingshen de chengzhang—dui Wang Wenxing xiaoshuo chuangzuo zhuti de yizhong guantong" (The development of a modern outlook—the continuity of the main themes in Wang Wenxing's literary works). *Wenxue de xiandai jiyi* (A modern memory about literature). Taipei: Sanmin chubanshe, 2003. 50–76.

Zheng, Hengxiong. "Cong jihaoxue de guandian kan Wang Wenxing *Bei hai de ren* de Zongjiao guan" (Looking at the religious perspective in Wang Wenxing's *Backed Against the Sea* from the point of view of semiotics). *Wenxue yu zongjiao—Diyi jie guoji wenxue yu zongjiao huiyi lunwen ji* (Literature and religion—collected essays of the first international conference on literature and religion). Taipei: Shibao wenhua chubanshe, 1987. 393–420.

———. "Wang Wenxing de *Bei hai de ren* de wenti ji zongjiao guan" (Wang Wenxing's *Backed Against the Sea* from the point of literary form and religion). *Lianhe wenxue* (Unitas) 3.8 (1987): 199–206.

———. "Wenti de yuyan de jichu—lun Wang Wenxing de *Bei hai de ren*" (The linguistic foundation of literary style—on Wang Wenxing's *Backed Against the Sea*). *Zhongwai wenxue* (Chungwai literary monthly) 15.1 (1986): 128–57.

Zheng, Yao. "Tan *Zhongwai wenxue* bing ping *Jia bian*" (On *Chungwai Literary Monthly* also reviewing *Family Catastrophe*). *Zhonghua ribao* (China news), 2 Aug. 1973, 10.

Zheng, Yayun. "Tan Wang Wenxing zaoqi de *Shiwu pian xiaoshuo*" (A discussion of Wang Wenxing's early *Fifteen Stories*). *Wen tan* (Literary world) 249 (1981): 61–69.

Zhi Ming. "Nan jie de Wang Wenxing de neixin shijie—*Bei hai de ren* du hou jinghua" (Wang Wenxing's incomprehensible inner world—the essence of a post-reading of *Backed Against the Sea*). *Taiwan ribao* (Taiwan daily), 14 Nov. 1980, 8.

Zhong Han. "Wang Wenxing xiansheng, qing ni zunzhong women de wenzi!: du suowei 'xiandai xiaoshuo'—*Bei hai de ren* yougan" (Mr. Wang Wenxing, please respect our language!: reading so-called "modern fiction"—comment on *Backed Against the Sea*). *Taiwan ribao* (Taiwan daily), 17 Nov. 1980, 8.

Zhou, Guozheng. "Ziyou yu zhiyue—weirao Wang Wenxing *Jia bian* zhong wenzi xinbian de taolun" (Freedom and restriction—centering on a discussion of new changes in language in Wang Wenxing's *Family Catastrophe*). *Xiandai Zhongwen wenxue pinglun* (Modern Chinese literature review) 1 (1994): 53–77.

Zhou, Ning. "Yi zhan liangqi de hong deng—ping Wang Wenxing de xiaoshuo *Jian bian*" (A bright red light—a review of Wang Wenxing's novel *Family Catastrophe*). *Wenyi* (Literature) 58 (1974): 79–86.

Zhu, Lili. *Zhishiren de jingshen sishi: Taiwan xiandaipai xiaoshuo de yizhong jiedu* (A personal history of an intellectual's psychology: a decoding of Taiwan modernist fiction). Shanghai: Sanlian chubanshe, 2004.

———. "Taiwan zhishi fenzi de jingshen sishi—Wang Wenxing xiandai zhuyi lizuo *Bei hai de ren* zhong de 'Ye'" (The personal history of a Taiwanese intellectual—the "Ye" in Wang Wenxing's modernist masterpiece *Backed Against the Sea*). *Zhongwai wenxue* (Chungwai literary monthly) 30.6 (2001): 213–26.

Zi Min. "Du *Jia bian*" (Reading *Family Catastrophe*). *Guoyu ribao* (National language daily) 30 July 1973.

"Zuotan zhuti: yu Wang Wenxing jiaoshou tan wenxue chuangzuo" [Forum: a discussion on creative writing with Professor Wang Wenxing]. *Zhongwai wenxue* [Chungwai literary monthly] 30.6 (2001): 369–95.

English Materials

Chang, Han-liang. "Graphemics and Novel Interpretation: The Case of Wang Wen-hsing." *Modern Chinese Literature* 6 (1992): 133–56.

Chang, Sung-Sheng. "Wang Wenxing's *Backed Against the Sea*, Pts. I and II: The Meaning of Modernist in Taiwan's Literature." *Writing Taiwan: A New Literary History*. Ed. David Der-wei Wang and Carlos Rojas. Durham, NC: Duke University Press, 2007. 156–76.

_____. *Literary Culture in Taiwan: Martial Law to Market Law*. New York: Columbia University Press, 2004.

_____. "Modernist Literature in Taiwan Revisited—With an Analysis of Wang Wenxing's *Backed Against the Sea*, Pt. II." *Tamkang Review* 29.2 (1998): 1–19.

_____. *Modernism and the Nativist Resistance*. Durham, NC: Duke University Press, 1993.

_____. "Language, Narrator, and Stream-of-Consciousness: The Two Novels of Wang Wen-hsing." *Modern Chinese Literature* 1.1 (1984): 43–55.

_____. "A Study of *Chia Pien*, a Contemporary Chinese Novel from Taiwan." Dissertation, University of Texas at Austin, 1981.

Chen, Li-fen. "Fictionality and Reality in Narrative Discourse: A Reading of Four Contemporary Taiwanese Writers." Dissertation, University of Washington, 1990.

Cheung, Sally J.S. Kao. "*Chia-Pien*: A Revolutionary Chinese Novel of Today." *Fu Jen Studies* 11 (1987): 1–12.

Dolling, Susan Wan. "Translator's Postscript." *Family Catastrophe*. By Wang Wen-hsing, trans. Susan Dolling. Honolulu: University of Hawai'i Press, 1995. 255–85.

Fung, Carole Hoyan Hang. "Modernism in Taiwanese Fiction: A Comparative Study of the Works of Wang Wenxing and Bai Xianyong." *B.C. Asian Review* 7 (1993–1994): 36–53.

Gunn, Edward. *Rewriting Chinese: Style and Innovation in Twentieth-Century Chinese Prose*. Stanford, CA: Stanford University Press, 1991.

_____. "The Process of Wang Wen-hsing's Art." *Modern Chinese Literature* 1.1 (1984): 29–41.

Jameson, Fredric. "Literary Innovation and Modes of Production: A Commentary." *Modern Chinese Literature* 1.1 (1984): 67–77.

Kinkley, Jeffrey C. "World Literature in Review: China." *World Literature Today* 68.4 (1994): 881.

Lee, Leo Ou-fan. "Beyond Realism: Thoughts on Mondernist Experiments in Contemporary Chinese Writing." *World Apart: Recent Writing and Its Audiences*. Ed. Howard Goldblatt. New York: M.E. Sharpe, 1990. 64–77.

Lin, Hui-Ling. "Ideology and Poetics in Wang Wen-hsing's *Chia-pien* and James Joyce's *A Portrait of the Artist as a Yong Man*." *Dong Hwa Journal of Humanities Studies* 4 (July 2002): 213–60.

Lupke, Christopher. "The Taiwan Modernists." *The Columbia Companion to Mod-*

ern East Asian Literature. Ed. Joshua S. Mostow. New York: Columbia University Press, 2003. 481–87.

———. "Wang Wenxing and the 'Loss' of China." *boundary 2* 25:3 (1998): 97–128. Rpt. in *Modern Chinese Literary and Cultural Studies in the Age of Theory*. Ed. Rey Chow. Durham, NC: Duke University Press, 2000. 127–58.

Marchand, Sandarine. "Religious Thinking in Wang Wen-hsing's Novels." *Religious Thinking in Asian Literature*. Ed. Muriel Détrie. Paris: Youfeng Editions, 2007. 173–83.

———. "Wang Wenxing 'Back to Back' with the Present." *China Perspectives* 65 (2006): 46–55.

Riep, Steven Le Cain. "Writing the Past: Rereading, Recovering, and Rethinking History in Contemporary Literature from Taiwan." Dissertation, University of California at Los Angles, 2001.

———. "A Case of Successful Failure: 'Dragon Inn' and Wang Wen-hsing's Critique of Official History and Anticommunist Literature." *Selected Papers in Asian Studies*, New Series no. 67 (2001): 1–34.

Sciban, Shu-ning. "Introduction: Wang Wen-hsing's Life and Narrative Art." *Endless War: Fiction and Essays by Wang Wen-hsing*. Ed. Shu-ning Sciban and Fred Edwards. Ithaca, NY: Cornell East Asia Program, Cornell University, 2011. xvii–li.

———. "Wang Wenxing's Poetic Language." Dissertation, University of Toronto, 1995.

———. "The Structure of *Jia bian*: A Reflection on the Studies of Twentieth-Century Chinese Fiction." *East Asia Forum*, vol. 2. Toronto: Department of East Asian Studies, University of Toronto, 1993. 36–49.

Sciban, Shu-ning, and Fred Edwards, eds. *Endless War: Fiction and Essays by Wang Wen-hsing*. Ithaca, NY: Cornell East Asia Program, Cornell University, 2011.

Shan, Te-hsing (Shan Dexing). "The Stream-of-consciousness Technique in Wang Wen-hsing's Fiction." *Tamkang Review* 15 (1985): 523–45.

Shu, James C.T. "Iconoclasm in Wang Wen-hsing's Chia-pien." *Chinese Fiction from Taiwan*. Ed. Jeannette L. Faurot. Bloomington: Indiana University Press, 1980. 179–93.

———. "Iconoclasm in Taiwan Literature: A Change in the 'Family'." *Chinese Literature: Essays, Articles, Reviews* (CLEAR) 2.1 (1980): 73–85.

Williams, Philip F. "Book Review—*Family Catastrophe*." *World Literature Today* 70.2 (1996): 470.

Yang, Chun-hui. "Wang Wen-Hsing's *Chia Pien* (the Metamorphosis of a Family): A Translation and Commentary." Dissertation, Brigham Young University, 1988, 1–23.

Materials in Other Languages

Gamarra, Pierre. "Nouvelles Chinoises: De Lu Xun à Wang Wenxing." *Europe-Revue Littéraire mensuelle* 901 (2004): 310–16.

Lachner, Anton. "Sprachinkonvention und Sprachmanipulation Linguistische und Stilistische Untersuchungen zu Wang Wengxings Roman *Jiabian*." Dissertation, Ruhr Universitat, 1986.

Le Mouel, Pascale. "Wang Wenxing Presentation d'un Auteur et Traduction de Deux Nouvelles Typhon et la Ligne du Destin." Thesis, Institut National des Langues et Civilisations Orientales, 1987.

Loivier, Camille. "Avant-propos." *Processus Familial.* Par Wang Wenxing. Traduit par Camille Loivier. Ales: ACTES SUD, 1999. 7–13.

Marchand, Sandrine. "Réminiscences et instants de mémoire." *La littérature taïwanaise, état des recherches et reception à l'étranger.* Paris: Youfeng, 2011. 267–77.

———. "La possession de la langue dans les romans de Wang Wenxing." *Ecrire au present.* Collectif dirigé par Annie Curien, Edition de la Maison des Sciences de l'Homme, 2004. 189–200.

Bibliography III: Translations of Wang Wenxing's Works

Compiled by Shu-ning Sciban
University of Calgary

with the assistance of Anita Lin, Emily Wen, and Roma Ilnyckyj

"A Brief Discussion of Modern Literature (Abridged)" (Qianlun xiandai wenxue). Trans. Christopher Lupke. *Endless War: Fiction and Essays by Wang Wen-hsing*. Ed. Shu-ning Sciban and Fred Edwards. Ithaca, NY: Cornell East Asia Program, Cornell University, 2011. 371–74.

"A Dying Dog" (Yitiao chuisi de gou). Trans. Steven L. Riep. *Endless War: Fiction and Essays by Wang Wen-hsing*. Ed. Shu-ning Sciban and Fred Edwards. Ithaca, NY: Cornell East Asia Program, Cornell University, 2011. 9–13.

"Afternoon" (Xiawu). Trans. Terrence Russell. *Endless War: Fiction and Essays by Wang Wen-hsing*. Ed. Shu-ning Sciban and Fred Edwards. Ithaca, NY: Cornell East Asia Program, Cornell University. 57–74.

Backed Against the Sea (Bei hai de ren). Trans. Edward Gunn. Ithaca, NY: Cornell East Asia Program, Cornell University, 1993.

"The Black Gown" (Heiyi). Trans. Ch'en Chu-yun. *Endless War: Fiction and Essays by Wang Wen-hsing*. Ed. Shu-ning Sciban and Fred Edwards. Ithaca, NY: Cornell East Asia Program, Cornell University, 2011. 256–66. (Revised from "The Man in Black." Trans. Ch'en Chu-yun. *Anthology of Contemporary Chinese Literature: Taiwan 1949–1970*. Ed. Chi Pang-yuan. Taipei: Institute for Compilation and Translation, 1975. 309–18.

"Calendar" (Rili). Trans. Shu-ning Sciban. *Endless War: Fiction and Essays by Wang Wen-hsing*. Eds. Shu-ning Sciban and Fred Edwards. Ithaca: Cornell East Asia Program, Cornell University, 2011. 107-08.

"Le calendrier" (Rili). Trans. Camille Loivier. *La Fête de la déesse Matsu.* Paris: Zulma, 2004. 57–61.

"The Challenge and Primitiveness of Modernism" (Xiandai zhuyi de zhiyi he yuanshi). Trans. Ihor Pidhainy. *Endless War: Fiction and Essays by Wang Wen-hsing.* Ed. Shu-ning Sciban and Fred Edwards. Ithaca, NY: Cornell East Asia Program, Cornell University, 2011. 375–79.

"Cold Front" (Han liu). Trans. Terrence Russell. *Endless War: Fiction and Essays by Wang Wen-hsing.* Ed. Shu-ning Sciban and Fred Edwards. Ithaca, NY: Cornell East Asia Program, Cornell University, 2011. 219–42.

"Conclusion" (Jieshu). Trans. Lloyd Sciban. *Endless War: Fiction and Essays by Wang Wen-hsing.* Ed. Shu-ning Sciban and Fred Edwards. Ithaca, NY: Cornell East Asia Program, Cornell University, 2011. 133–42.

"Contract Fulfilled" (Jianyue). Trans. Fred Edwards and Jia Li. *Endless War: Fiction and Essays by Wang Wen-hsing.* Ed. Shu-ning Sciban and Fred Edwards. Ithaca, NY: Cornell East Asia Program, Cornell University, 2011. 165–88.

"The Day of the Sea-Goddess" (Haibin shengmu jie). Trans. Ch'en Chu-yun. *The Chinese Pen* (Spring 1986): 70–90. Revision in *Endless War: Fiction and Essays by Wang Wen-hsing.* Ed. Shu-ning Sciban and Fred Edwards. Ithaca, NY: Cornell East Asia Program, Cornell University, 2011. 189–205.

Die familiäre Katastrophe. Trans. Anton Lachner. Frankfurt: Peter Lang, 1988.

"Dragon Inn" (Longtian lou). Trans. Steven L. Riep. *Endless War: Fiction and Essays by Wang Wen-hsing.* Ed. Shu-ning Sciban and Fred Edwards. Ithaca, NY: Cornell East Asia Program, Cornell University, 2011. 279–349.

"Endless War" (Wu xiuzhi de zhanzheng). Trans. Martin Sulev. *Endless War: Fiction and Essays by Wang Wen-hsing.* Ed. Shu-ning Sciban and Fred Edwards. Ithaca, NY: Cornell East Asia Program, Cornell University, 2011. 381–84.

Family Catastrophe (Jia bian). Trans. Susan Wan Dolling. Honolulu: University of Hawai'i Press, 1995.

"Family Dysposition: Excerpts" (Jia bian). Trans. Susan Wan Dolling. *Renditions* 39 (1993): 26–38.

"Flaw" (Qianque). Trans. Ch'en Chu-yun. *Chinese Stories from Taiwan 1960–1970.* Ed. Joseph S.M. Lau and Timothy A. Ross. New York: Columbia University Press, 1976. 15–27. Revision in *Endless War: Fiction and Essays by Wang Wen-hsing.* Ed. Shu-ning Sciban and Fred Edwards. Ithaca, NY: Cornell East Asia Program, Cornell University, 2011. 243–56.

"La fête de la déesse Matsu au bord de la mer" (Haibin shengmu jie). Trans. Camille Loivier. *La Fête de la déesse Matsu.* Paris: Zulma, 2004. 141–65.

"The Happiest Thing" (Zuikuaile de shi). Trans. Shu-ning Sciban. *Endless War:*

Fiction and Essays by Wang Wen-hsing. Ed. Shu-ning Sciban and Fred Edwards. Ithaca, NY: Cornell East Asia Program, Cornell University, 2011. 109.

"The Line of Fate" (Mingyun de jixian). Trans. Ch'en Chu-yun. *Anthology of Contemporary Chinese Literature: Taiwan 1949–1970.* Ed. Chi Pangyuan. Taipei: Institute for Compilation and Translation, 1975. 297–308. Revision in *Endless War: Fiction and Essays by Wang Wen-hsing.* Ed. Shu-ning Sciban and Fred Edwards. Ithaca, NY: Cornell East Asia Program, Cornell University, 2011. 207–18.

"Ligne de vie" (Mingyun de jixian). Trans. Camille Loivier. *La Fête de la déesse Matsu.* Paris: Zulma. 2004. 27–45.

"The Lingering Night" (Shou ye). Trans. Rowan Sciban. *Endless War: Fiction and Essays by Wang Wen-hsing.* Ed. Shu-ning Sciban and Fred Edwards. Ithaca, NY: Cornell East Asia Program, Cornell University, 2011. 3–8.

"M and W" (M he W). Trans. Fred Edwards and Jia Li. *Endless War: Fiction and Essays by Wang Wen-hsing.* Ed. Shu-ning Sciban and Fred Edwards. Ithaca, NY: Cornell East Asia Program, Cornell University, 2011. 351–66.

"The Man in Black" (Hei yi). Trans. Ch'en Chu-yun. *Anthology of Contemporary Chinese Literature: Taiwan 1949–1970.* Ed. Chi Pang-yuan. Taipei: Institute for Compilation and Translation, 1975. 309–18.

"The Marriage of a Civil Servant" (Yige gongwuyuan de jiehun). Trans. Howard Goldblatt. *Endless War: Fiction and Essays by Wang Wen-hsing.* Ed. Shu-ning Sciban and Fred Edwards. Ithaca, NY: Cornell East Asia Program, Cornell University, 2011. 15–25.

"Mère" (Muqin). Trans. Camille Loivier. *La Fête de la déesse Matsu.* Paris: Zulma, 2004. 47–56.

"Midsummer on the Prairie" (Caoyuan di shengxia). Trans. Michael Cody. *Endless War: Fiction and Essays by Wang Wen-hsing.* Ed. Shu-ning Sciban and Fred Edwards. Ithaca, NY: Cornell East Asia Program, Cornell University, 2011. 115–31.

"Mother" (Muqin). Trans. Michael Cody. *Endless War: Fiction and Essays by Wang Wen-hsing.* Ed. Shu-ning Sciban and Fred Edwards. Ithaca, NY: Cornell East Asia Program, Cornell University, 2011. 101–6.

"Nights of the Shining Moon" (Mingyue ye). Trans. Ch'en Chu-yun. *Endless War: Fiction and Essays by Wang Wen-hsing.* Ed. Shu-ning Sciban and Fred Edwards. Ithaca, NY: Cornell East Asia Program, Cornell University, 2011. 267–75.

"Nuit au clair de lune" (Mingyue ye). Trans. Camille Loivier. *Neige d'août,* no. 16/17 (Automne 2008): 38–46.

"Paralysis" (Bi). Trans. Lloyd Sciban. *Endless War: Fiction and Essays by Wang Wen-hsing*. Eds. Shu-ning Sciban and Fred Edwards. Ithaca, NY: Cornell East Asia Program, Cornell University, 2011. 47–56.

"Le pistolet d'enfant" (Wanju shouqiang). Trans. Camille Loivier. *La Fête de la déesse Matsu*. Paris: Zulma, 2004. 63–99.

"Le plus grand bonheur" (Zui kuaile de shi). Trans. Camille Loivier. *La Fête de la déesse Matsu*. Paris: Zulma, 2004. 101–3.

"Preface to *New Stone Statue*" (*Xinke de shixiang* xu). Trans. Martin Sulev. *Endless War: Fiction and Essays by Wang Wen-hsing*. Ed. Shu-ning Sciban and Fred Edwards. Ithaca, NY: Cornell East Asia Program, Cornell University, 2011. 369–70.

"Premier amour" (Qianque). Trans. Camille Loivier. *La Fête de la déesse Matsu*. Paris: Zulma, 2004. 5–25.

Processus familial (*Jia bian*). Trans. Camille Loivier. Paris: ACTES SUD, 1999.

"Le serment" (Jianyue). Trans. Camille Loivier. *La Fête de la déesse Matsu*. Paris: Zulma, 2004. 105–39.

"Song of the Earth" (Dadi zhi ge). Trans. Ihor Pidhainy. *Endless War: Fiction and Essays by Wang Wen-hsing*. Ed. Shu-ning Sciban and Fred Edwards. Ithaca, NY: Cornell East Asia Program, Cornell University, 2011. 111–13.

"Strong Wind" (Da feng). Trans. Howard Goldblatt. *Endless War: Fiction and Essays by Wang Wen-hsing*. Ed. Shu-ning Sciban and Fred Edwards. Ithaca, NY: Cornell East Asia Program, Cornell University, 2011. 153–63.

"The Toy Revolver" (Wanju shouqiang). Trans. Jane Parish Yang. *The Chinese Pen* (Spring 1982): 1–32. Revision in *Endless War: Fiction and Essays by Wang Wen-hsing*. Ed. Shu-ning Sciban and Fred Edwards. Ithaca, NY: Cornell East Asia Program, Cornell University, 2011. 75–99.

"The Two Women" (Liang furen). Trans. Chen Li-fen. *The Chinese Pen* (Summer 1978): 79–90. Revision in *Endless War: Fiction and Essays by Wang Wen-hsing*. Ed. Shu-ning Sciban and Fred Edwards. Ithaca, NY: Cornell East Asia Program, Cornell University, 2011. 143–51.

"Withered Chrysanthemums" (Can ju). Trans. Steven L. Riep. *Endless War: Fiction and Essays by Wang Wen-hsing*. Ed. Shu-ning Sciban and Fred Edwards. Ithaca, NY: Cornell East Asia Program, Cornell University, 2011. 27–45.

"Zhongyuan: An Appreciation" (Huai Zhongyuan). Trans. Shu-ning Sciban. *Endless War: Fiction and Essays by Wang Wen-hsing*. Ed. Shu-ning Sciban and Fred Edwards. Ithaca, NY: Cornell East Asia Program, Cornell University, 2011. 385–90.

About the Contributors

Wei Cai (蔡薇) is an associate professor of Chinese at the University of Calgary. She specializes in second language learning. She received her BA in English Education from Hebei Normal University, MA in Linguistics from Beijing Foreign Studies University, PhD in Second Language Acquisition from the National University of Singapore. Her current research focuses on second language listening, vocabulary acquisition, learner strategies, and materials evaluation and production. Her publications have appeared in *the Canadian Journal of Applied Linguistics, Australian Review of Applied Linguistics, Hong Kong Journal of Applied Linguistics, Journal of the Chinese Language Teachers Association, Research on Chinese as a Second Language, Journal of Chinese Language Teaching,* and so on.

Sung-sheng Yvonne Chang (Zhang Songsheng 張誦聖) is a professor of Chinese and comparative literature at the University of Texas at Austin. She received her BA in English from National Taiwan University, MA in comparative literature from University of Michigan, PhD in comparative literature from the University of Texas at Austin, and PhD in Chinese literature from Stanford University. She is the author of *Literary Culture in Taiwan: Martial Law to Market Law* (Columbia University Press, 2004), *Wenxue changyu de bianqian: Taiwan xiaoshuo lun* (Transformations of a literary field: on contemporary Taiwanese fiction, Lianhe wenxue, 2001), and *Modernism and the Nativist Resistance: Contemporary Chinese Fiction from Taiwan* (Duke University Press, 1993). She has co-edited, with Ann C. Carver, *Bamboo Shoots after the Rain: Contemporary Stories by Women Writers of Taiwan* (The Feminist Press, 1990) and, with Michelle Yeh and Ming-Ju Fan, *The Columbia Sourcebook of Literary Tai-*

wan (Columbia University Press, 2014). She served as President of the Association of Chinese and Comparative Literature in 1999–2000.

Jeannette Chu-yun Chen (Chen Zhuyun 陳竺筠) comes from a family with roots in Guangdong, China. Due to her father's career in the diplomatic service, she spent part of her childhood and adolescence in Sydney, Seoul, Bangkok and Nicosia. She received an MA in English and American literature from National Taiwan University. She taught in the Department of Foreign Languages and Literatures at National Taiwan University from 1970 until her retirement in 2005. She has contributed numerous Chinese-English translations, including several short stories by her husband Wang Wenxing.

Susan Dolling (Wen Shuning 溫淑寧) was born in Hong Kong, studied in Japan and the United States, and graduated from Princeton with an AB in English and creative writing and a PhD in comparative literature. She has taught at various universities, including Fordham and the University of Texas at Austin. She is the translator of Wang Wen-xing's *Jia bian* (*Family Catastrophe*, University of Hawaii Press, 1993).

Fred Edwards is an editor and translator who has a degree in Chinese Studies from the University of Toronto. Until his recent retirement, he edited the opinion page of the *Toronto Star*, where he wrote frequently on China-related issues, and he also served as an editorial advisor on *Beijing Review*, a weekly news magazine published by the Chinese government. With Shu-ning Sciban, he was co-editor of *Dragonflies: Fiction by Chinese Women in the Twentieth Century* (Cornell East Asia Series No. 115) and *Endless War: Fiction and Essays by Wang Wen-hsing* (Cornell East Asia Series No. 158).

San-hui Hung (Hong Shanhui 洪珊慧) was born in Taiwan. She received her BA and MA in Chinese Literature from National Tsing-Hua University (Taiwan) in 1993 and 1998, respectively. She was a teacher in colleges in 1998–2011, and stayed in the University of Texas at Austin as a visiting scholar in 2007–2008. In 2011, she completed her PhD dissertation entitled "Newly Carved Statues: A Study of Wang Wen-hsing and His Contemporary Modernist Writers and Their Works," which focuses on a study of the works of Wang and other writers in an effort to demonstrate their creative contribution to the development of modern literature in Taiwan. After receiving her PhD from National Central University (NCU, Taiwan) in 2011, she joined the Department of Chinese Literature of NCU as an Assistant Professor. Currently, she is an adjunct assistant professor in the Center of General Education at NCU. Her research interests include modern Taiwanese literature, culture, and films; she has served as a project manager for some documentary films of Wang, Wen-hsing in recent years.

Hengsyung Jeng (Zheng Hengxiong 鄭恒雄) is a professor emeritus in Department of Foreign Languages and Literatures, National Taiwan University. He was born in Taipei, Taiwan in 1941. He graduated from Department of Foreign Languages and Literatures at National Taiwan University in 1963, and received his MA in TESOL in 1968 and PhD in linguistics in 1976 from University of Hawaii. He has conducted research on linguistics and literature at Stanford University and Harvard University as a visiting scholar. He taught English linguistics, contrastive analysis of Chinese and English, linguistic approach to literature, Austronesian languages of Taiwan and English language courses. He has published several volumes of books and numerous essays in these fields as well as in English testing.

Sandrine Marchand is an associate professor of Chinese at the University of Artois in Arras, France. Her scholarly interest focuses on the issue of memory in Taiwanese modern literature. She is the author of *Sur le fil de la mémoire: littérature taïwanaise des années 1970–1990* (Lyon: Tigre de papier, 2009), and is the editor of the literary review *Neige d'août,* which deals with contemporary European and Asian poetry. She has translated the fictionnal writings of Wang Wen-hsing as well as some Taiwanese poets. She is now working on manuscripts, genetic criticism and creative process as well as on the practice of translation. She has recently published several articles about Wang Wen-hsing and

Taiwanese contemporary poetry, including "The Impossibility of Rectifi-
cation: Study of Scratching, Correction and Addition in Wang Wen-
hsing's Manuscripts) (*Sun Yat-sen Journal of Humanities*, 37 (special
issue on "Genetic Criticism") [2014.7]: 63–82); "De Hemingway au chi-
nois classique: le travail de la langue de l'écrivain taïwanais Wang Wen-
hsing" (From Hemingway to classical Chinese: Taiwanese writer Wang
Wen-hsing's work on Language) (*Continents manuscrits* [En ligne], 2 |
2014, mis en ligne le 04 mars 2014, consulté le 09 mai 2014. URL: http://
lodel.revues.org/10/coma/307); "Deux récits teintés de rouge, *Naufrages*
de Yoshimura Akira et « Nuit au clair de lune » de Wang Wen-hsing"
(Two Carmine Tales: Yoshimura Akira's "Shipwreck" and Wang Wen-
hsing's "Moonlight's Night") in *Merveilleux et spiritualité* ed. Myriam
White-Le Goff (Presses de l'Université Paris Sorbonne, 2014. 185–198).

Ihor Pidhainy received his BA and PhD from the University of Toronto. His research interests include Chinese biography, Chinese histo-
riography, travel writing on China and Inner Asia and the Chinese novel.
His publications and translations have appeared in journals such as
Ming Studies, Universitas and *Education about Asia*. He has recently completed *A History of Chinese Literature* for the *Key Issues in Asian Studies*
series published by the Association of Asian Studies. He is currently
working on a biography of the Ming dynasty scholar Yang Shen (1488–
1559) and a study of the *Ming History*. He is an Assistant Professor of
Chinese History at University of West Georgia.

Shu-ning Sciban (Huang Shuning 黃恕寧) is a professor of Chinese
and teaches Chinese language and literature at the University of Calgary. She received BA in Chinese from National Taiwan Normal University, MA in comparative literature from the University of Alberta, PhD
in Chinese literature from the University of Toronto. Her research interests include modern and contemporary Chinese and Taiwanese fiction,
Chinese woman writing, Chinese diaspora literature, narratology, rhetoric, stylistics, Chinese language and computer-assisted Chinese language
learning. She has co-authored with X. J. Yang *Fayin: Mandarin Pronunciation* (CD-ROM; University of Calgary Press, 2002), with Catherine Yu

and X. J. Yang *Shizi: Chinese Characters* (CD-ROM; University of Calgary Press, 2003). She has also co-edited with Fred Edwards *Dragonflies: Fiction by Chinese Women in the Twentieth Century* (Cornell East Asian Program, 2003) and *Endless War: Fiction and Essays by Wang Wen-hsing* (Cornell East Asian Program, 2011), and with Lai-hsin Kang and San-hui Hong *Mandu Wang Wen-hsing* (Slow reading Wang Wen-hsing) (7 volumes) (National Taiwan University Press, 2013).

Darryl Sterk is an assistant professor in the Graduate Program in translation and interpretation at National Taiwan University. His literary translations have appeared in *The Taipei Chinese Pen, Taiwan Literature English Translation Series, Pathlight* and *Asymptote*, and his translation of Wu Mingyi's *Fuyan ren* (*The Man with the Compound Eyes*, Harvill Secker, 2013; Vintage Pantheon, 2014). His academic specialty is the representation of Taiwan's indigenous peoples in fiction and film.

Te-hsing Shan (Shan Dexing 單德興) is a distinguished research fellow of the Institute of European and American Studies, Academia Sinica, and a distinguished adjunct professor of Humanities, Lingnan University, Hong Kong. He received his PhD in comparative literature from National Taiwan University in 1986. He had served as the general editor of *EurAmerica: A Journal of European and American Studies*. His Chinese publications include *Inscriptions and Representations: Chinese American Literary and Cultural Criticism* (Maitian chuban, 2000), *Re(-)acting (Hi-) Story: American Literary History and Cultural Criticism* (Shulin shuju, 2001), *Translations and Contexts* (Tsinghua University Press, 2007), *Transgressions and Innovations: Asian American Literary and Cultural Studies* (Yunchen wenhua chubanshe, 2008), and *Edward W. Said in Taiwan* (Yunchen wenhua chubanshe, 2011). He has also published two collections of interviews and has translated nearly twenty books from English into Chinese, including an annotated translation of *Gulliver's Travels* (Lianjing chubanshe, 2004), and *Power, Politics, and Culture: Interviews with Edward W. Said* (Maitian chuban, 2005). His research areas include American literary history, Asian American Literature, Comparative Literature, Cultural Studies, and Translation Studies.

Wang Wenxing (Wang Wen-hsing 王文興) was born in Fuzhou, Fujian in 1939. He moved with his family to Xiamen in 1942 and to Taiwan in 1946. While studying Western languages and literature at the National Taiwan University, he co-founded *Modern Literature*, a literary quarterly magazine with several classmates in 1960. He received his MFA in creative writing from the State University of Iowa in 1965, and returned to Taiwan in the same year to teach in the Department of Foreign Languages and Literatures of the National Taiwan University, where he taught Western fiction for 40 years before retiring in 2005. His published works include an early fiction collection *Shiwu pian xiaoshuo* (Fifteen short stories, Hongfan shudian, 1979), and *Jia bian* (Family catastrophe, Huanyu, 1973 and Hongfan shudian, 1978), *Beihai de ren*, Vols. 1 and 2 (Backed against the sea, Hongfan shudian, 1981 and 1999) as well as several collections of essays. In addition to an honorary doctorate conferred by the National Taiwan University in 2007, he also received the National Award for Arts from the government of Republic of China in 2009, the Chevalier de L'Ordre des Arts et des Lettres from the government of France in 2010, and the Huazong Literature Award, presented to Chinese-language writers, from the *Sin Chew Daily* in Kuala Lumpur in 2011.

Jane Parish Yang received her PhD in Chinese from the University of Wisconsin, Madison and was an associate professor of Chinese in the Department of Chinese and Japanese at Lawrence University, retiring in 2015. She taught beginning and advanced Chinese language, traditional and modern Chinese literature, Chinese cinema, and the East Asian studies senior seminar. She co-directed Lawrence University's Freeman Foundation [2001–2005] and Luce Foundation grants to support student and faculty study tours to East Asia and has contributed many publications, including the translation of Nieh Hualing's post-modern novel *Mulberry and Peach* (The Feminist Press, 1997) which won an American Book Award in 1990.

Wai-lim Yip (Ye Weilian 葉維廉) is a professor emeritus at the University of California, Saint Diego. He was born in Guangdong, China. He received his BA (1959) and MA (1961) in English at National Taiwan University, an MFA from the University of Iowa in 1964, and a PhD in comparative literature at Princeton University in 1967. Called by Jerome Rothenberg "The linking figure between American modernism and Chinese traditions and practices," and by Jonathan Stalling "the central force to the development of transpacific Chinese-English poetry and poetics," Yip has been active as a bicultural poet, translator, critic and theorist between Taiwan and America. He is a leading modernist poet and theorist and has won many literary prizes, including an award from the Ministry of Education in Taiwan, and has been recognized as one of the ten major Chinese poets. In recent years he has been the object of considerable attention in China and Taiwan, with exhibitions of his archives and conferences devoted to his poetry. He has published over fifty volumes of books in Chinese and English, including *Ye Weilian wushi nian shi xuan* (Collected Poems by Ye Weilian in the past fifty years, National Taiwan University Press, 2012), *Zhongguo shixue* (Chinese poetics, expanded version, Renmin wenxue, 2006), *Ye Weilian wenji* (9 volumes) (Ye Weilian's complete works of essays, Hanhui Jiaoyu chubanshe, 2003), *Between Landscapes* (Pennywhistle Press, 1994), *Diffusion of Distances: Dialogues between Chinese and Western Poetics* (University of California Press, 1993), *Zhongguo Shixue* (Chinese poetics) (Beijing Sanlian shuju, 1992), *Lyrics from Shelters: Modern Chinese Poetry 1930–1950* (Garland, 1992), *Reading the Modern and the Postmodern: Meditations on Living Spaces and Cultural Spaces* (Dongda tushugongsi, 1992), *Ezra Pound's Cathay* (Princeton University Press, 1969), and edited *Chinese Poetry: an Anthology of Major Modes and Genre* (Duke University Press, 2000).

CORNELL EAST ASIA SERIES

CORNELL
East Asia Series
eap.einaudi.cornell.edu/publications

CPSIA information can be obtained
at www.ICGtesting.com
Printed in the USA
LVHW090227161119
637499LV00019B/45/P